GAME OF
THORNS

GAME OF
THORNS

THE INSIDE STORY OF HILLARY CLINTON'S
FAILED CAMPAIGN AND DONALD TRUMP'S
WINNING STRATEGY

DOUG WEAD

Biteback Publishing

To my grandchildren,
Christian, Matthew, Abigail, Samuel, Ariel and Sophie.

This edition published in Great Britain in 2017 by
Biteback Publishing Ltd
Westminster Tower
3 Albert Embankment
London SE1 7SP
Copyright © Doug Wead 2017

ISBN 978-1-78590-226-0

10 9 8 7 6 5 4 3 2 1

A CIP catalogue record for this book is available from the British Library.

Printed and bound in Great Britain by
CPI Group (UK) Ltd, Croydon CR0 4YY

CONTENTS

INTRODUCTION: AN ALTERNATE UNIVERSE 1

PART I: ELECTION-NIGHT SURPRISE
  Chapter 1: The Clintons' War with the FBI 11
  Chapter 2: The Lost Voters of Elections Past 35
  Chapter 3: Forgotten No Longer 50

PART II: THE COLLAPSE OF THE HOUSE OF CLINTON
  Chapter 4: Why Another Clinton Presidency? 71
  Chapter 5: An Early Clinton Scandal Primer 82
  Chapter 6: The Fu Lin Chinese Restaurant 104
  Chapter 7: The Other Women 119
  Chapter 8: Monica Lewinsky and Impeachment 140
  Chapter 9: The Selling of the White House 150

PART III: THE RISE OF THE HOUSE OF TRUMP
  Chapter 10: Donald Trump, Out of the Shadows 165
  Chapter 11: Saving New York City 178
  Chapter 12: Trump and the Crowded Field 201
  Chapter 13: An Unlikely Nominee 222
  Chapter 14: It's a Trump World 242

PART IV: CLASH OF THE TITANS
  Chapter 15: The Comeback of Hillary Clinton 261
  Chapter 16: Crooked Hillary 276
  Chapter 17: An October Surprise for Trump 290
  Chapter 18: Hillary the Enabler 308
  Chapter 19: The Next White House? 324
  Chapter 20: Landing the Plane 349
  Chapter 21: I Almost Never Lose .370

  Endnotes 379
  Acknowledgments 405

GAME OF
THORNS

AN ALTERNATE UNIVERSE

Life can only be understood backwards;
but it must be lived forwards.
—*Søren Kierkegaard*

Here was the plan: On January 20, 2017, Hillary Clinton would be inaugurated president of the United States. She would enter a pantheon of history that guaranteed greatness. She would be immortal. She would be compared to Cleopatra, Elizabeth I, Catherine the Great, and yet she would have more power than any of them ever had. She would instantly transcend other modern female leaders, such as Margaret Thatcher and Angela Merkel, because she would be running the world's greatest superpower.

Catherine the Great ruled a backward nation of slaves. Elizabeth I lived in a world of equal rivals: Spain, France, and the Holy Roman Empire. During Cleopatra's time, Egypt was a sideshow to the main event, which was the ongoing Roman Civil War. But Hillary Clinton would be president of the United States at a time when that powerful office was on steroids.

Then a strange thing happened. Suddenly there on the inauguration stage were new faces. It was as if the Clinton entourage had been photoshopped out of the picture. And yes, there he was, in the blustery wind, his hand on the Bible, his blond hair lifting at odd angles. It was the billionaire businessman Donald Trump, coarse, full of confidence. And just as he had fantasized, he was being sworn in as president of the United States.

It was as if time had folded in on itself. Had American history entered an alternate universe? Was this some new historical fiction produced on Amazon Prime? The neo-American version of *The Man in the High Castle*? In this eerily familiar new world, Hillary Clinton had not won the election after all. Donald Trump had.

What did it mean? How had the historic Clinton machine sputtered and failed at the last minute, just before the finish line? What had the pollsters and pundits and corporate television executives gotten wrong?

Nate Silver's brilliant blog *FiveThirtyEight* had placed the odds of a Hillary Clinton win at 71.4 percent to 28.6 percent. *The New York Times* gave her odds of 91 percent to 9 percent. *New York* magazine had already published its cover, a picture with the angry, contorted face of Donald Trump and the word "Loser" stamped across it in bold letters. A final kick in the pants from a corporate media arrayed against the brash businessman, whose golden Trump towers dared to rise amidst their skyline.

A week before the election, the Fox News anchor Megyn Kelly quizzed the pundits Karl Rove and Larry Sabato about an outlier poll showing Trump ahead in the race.

Rove was unimpressed. One odd poll was not enough. "He's got seven days and he's got to cover seven states, which is a very large number of states to be focused on as you come down to the end," Rove explained. He admitted that Trump was up in Iowa, Florida, and Ohio but down in North Carolina. He needed to win all of those states and two others that he was now losing."[1]

"What are the odds of that right now?" Kelly asked.

"That's uphill," Rove said.[2]

Larry Sabato, the director of the Center for Politics at the University of Virginia, was even more direct. Sabato's famous "Crystal Ball," which had been featured on Fox News for months, had Clinton winning 322 electoral votes to 216 for Trump. He also projected that the Democrats would take control of the Senate.[3]

The majority of the pundits on all of the major television networks, with the exception of Fox News, were arguably in the tank for Hillary Clinton, and Fox, as in the case of the Republican Party itself, was clearly divided.

Two hundred and forty newspapers had endorsed her candidacy. Nineteen had endorsed Donald Trump.[4]

Hillary Clinton had spent a staggering $581 million. Her super PAC, Priorities USA, raised and spent more money, $192 million, than any super PAC in all of American history.[5] Donald Trump, meanwhile, had raised and spent a total of $340 million, including $66 million of his own money. His Great American PAC, led by Eric Beach and Ed Rollins raised $32 million.

The former CEO of Google, Eric Schmidt, himself helped organize the Clinton campaign's technology system. The best and brightest of the nation's data experts worked for her. Trump relied on his son-in-law Jared Kushner to come up with something.

Hillary Clinton's staff outnumbered Trump's five to one.[6] And their "ground games" could not be compared. On Election Day she would rely on an army of 960,000 volunteers. Nobody bothered to count what Trump would have in place. The manpower infrastructure that had once held up the mighty Republican National Committee for Ronald Reagan had all but evaporated.

Hillary Clinton's own internal polls and computers, likewise, declared her the winner. That included the top-secret "Ada," the magical Clinton software unique to her extraordinary run for the presidency. It was named after Ada Lovelace, a nineteenth-century

British noblewoman who was a mathematician and had worked on one of the world's first computers, the Analytical Engine.[7] Clinton's senior staff members were planning to reveal Ada to the media the day after the election in a show-and-tell of how they won.[8]

But then, Hillary Clinton did not win. She lost.

The morning after the 2016 presidential election, the Clinton machine seemed to be operating on autopilot, like a big 747 landing itself by computer. On a conference call, Hillary Clinton told major donors that the FBI director James Comey's letter to Congress was to blame for her defeat. "There are a lot of reasons why an election like this is not successful," she said, "Our analysis is that Comey's letter raising doubts that were groundless, baseless, proven to be, stopped our momentum."[9]

She had not made the traditional appearance the night of her election loss. The losing candidate usually shows up to graciously concede, to unite the nation, and then to reassure the weeping children, the volunteers. Some of them had given up a year of college or put off marriage or rented apartments in New York City and Washington, DC, to work for her victory.

Early the morning after, a cacophony of iPhone beeps, rings, and chirps played across Manhattan as the Clinton team sent out one last text message to its top team. Hillary Clinton was giving her concession speech and they were needed. Exhausted, sleepless, brokenhearted, many of them wanted to pull the covers over their heads, but they had come a long way with Hillary, some of them years, too long to opt out of the final act.

They took taxis and buses and walked across Manhattan to gather at the Wyndham New Yorker. The ballroom was packed and the weeping inside was contagious. The trick was not to look at a friend, or as someone suggested, to think of Donald Trump in the Oval Office and the resultant anger would block the emotion.

Awaiting Hillary, the television cameras focused on the campaign's chairman, John Podesta. And then eventually Huma Abedin, Clinton's longtime aide, walked into the room. There was a standing ovation for Huma. Then Hillary appeared close behind.

Her concession speech was short and widely praised in the media. "Last night, I congratulated Donald Trump and offered to work with him on behalf of our country," she said. "I hope that he will be a successful president for all Americans. This is not the outcome we wanted or we worked so hard for, and I'm sorry that we did not win this election for the values we share and the vision we hold for our country."

iPhones buzzed as friends and relatives from across the country sent messages into the New Yorker ballroom. "You are on CNN right now. We can see you on camera. You are on MSNBC. Fix your hair. Don't look so sad."

"You represent the best of America," Hillary told this ballroom of her closest supporters, "and being your candidate has been one of the greatest honors of my life."[10] There were loud cheers. It was the last chance for many of them to applaud for her before scattering across the country to resume their lives.

"So my friends, let us have faith in each other, let us not grow weary, let us not lose heart, for there are more seasons to come. And there is more work to do."[11]

It was elegant, it was thoughtful, and it was well planned in advance. No one may have expected there would be the need to execute the plan, but it had been prepared nonetheless. Hillary Clinton had made that point when Donald Trump had knocked her in a debate for spending so much time in preparation. Yes, she said, she had, indeed, prepared for the debates and so too, was she prepared to be president.

Of course, there was a more comprehensive plan for victory.

As the television pundit Chris Matthews would observe, this was a campaign that was prepared for everything.

Meanwhile, her speech to top donors, blaming Comey, was duplicated in a similar "insider" memo that had been leaked to the *New York Times*, which its editors dutifully published. Her major donors could hang up their phones and read the script.

Other staffers repeated the same story, with the same talking point: "Comey's fault." Everyone was operating with discipline, as if the campaign were still on, as if someone in charge would step forward and retroactively stop this Trump thing from happening. As if they would all wake up and find that their investment in Hillary Clinton had paid off after all. It was like a chicken with its head cut off, still racing around the barnyard, even enthusiastically. And, seeing such a thing for the first time, they had all the same questions: Could it be alive? Is it really dead? Are you sure? How can it do this? Look at it go! Only days later, the Green Party's presidential candidate, Jill Stein, announced she would lead a voter recount movement. Hillary Clinton, it was reported, liked the idea.

For the Clintons, the object now was to salvage what they could of their relationships with the thousands of corporate, banking, and foreign-government donors who had invested in their brand. This list included some of the most important names in the world. Some of them may have believed that they owned Hillary Clinton and through her, they owned the United States. They had given millions of dollars to the presidential campaign and the Clinton Foundation. There were questions about contracts with Bill Clinton. Were some of these one-year consultancy fee? And if so, what would he do for them now? Another speech? A weekend seminar-retreat for executives?

Something had gone wrong. Terribly wrong. What had happened?

Was the Clinton campaign right? Was it really all the fault of FBI Director Comey? No. Everybody knew it wasn't that simple. No one even picked up the refrain.

Hillary Clinton and her team had lost it.

And Donald Trump was not the foil that the media had tried to put forward. He had actually won. And on the cheap. He had shown how to win with less money. He had been the magician who diverted our gaze to one hand while the other hand did the trick, sometimes in full view. We can rewind the tape and see it in the replay if we pay attention. He was the master at branding, and he had driven home the point that he would "make American great again."

As John F. Kennedy once observed about political life, "Things do not happen. They are made to happen."[12] Donald J. Trump had helped make all of this happen.

This was a story of people, too. African Americans had turned out in record numbers for Hillary, surpassed only by the turnout for Barack Obama himself, and yet now pundits were blaming them for not doing better, for not doing more.

Mostly, this was the fault of white, Rust Belt, out-of-work Democrats. They had voted twice for Barack Obama, but now they were being told that they were racists or white supremacists for voting for Trump and giving him an Electoral College edge.

The contrarian liberal genius Michael Moore had been a lonely prophet who had seen it coming, but the Clinton team had ignored him, just as they had ignored their own patriarch, Bill Clinton, who sounded the same warning. In a live performance, Moore had teased voters in Wilmington, Ohio, months before the election, telling them that he knew what they were planning to do. And they laughed with him, like guilty children caught in the act by a bemused cousin. He knew they were going to vote for Trump.

He didn't like it, but at least he was one person who could not be fooled.

People who had been overlooked, despised, stomped on, used, taken for granted. This was their moment to speak. They had been shamed into telling the pollsters what they wanted to hear, but in the privacy of their polling booths, they had struck a blow.

This is the true story of the 2016 election cycle. It is a prickly, sometimes circuitous adventure that is both painful and joyous. It is a journey full of plot twists. A story that comes from back rooms of office buildings, backstage at conventions and events, and the back-seats of limousines and taxis. A story from active and retired FBI agents, from political staff members, sometimes from the gilded halls of the Trump Tower. It comes from the green rooms at NBC, CBS, and Fox News, from historians and White House assistants. In some cases, it comes from the presidential candidates themselves.

Some of it will sound vaguely familiar from the echoes of what you have followed on television and on the Internet. But some of it will be surprising and jarring. At times, it will be sad, it will be funny, and it will be disturbing.

This is a story that will be told for generations to come. Someday, you may tell this story to your very own grandchildren. But first you must know it yourself. This is the story of the Game of Thorns.

PART I

ELECTION- NIGHT SURPRISE

CHAPTER 1

THE CLINTONS' WAR
WITH THE FBI

Victorious warriors win first and then go to war, while
defeated warriors go to war first and then seek to win.
—Sun Tzu

On October 20, 2016, backstage at the Alfred E. Smith Dinner in New York City, Hillary Clinton and Donald Trump stood with Cardinal Timothy Dolan to say a short prayer. The Smith Dinner was a rite of passage for presidential candidates. They each exchanged barbs and roasted the other, all in good humor. Most observers would conclude that Hillary Clinton clearly won the hearts and minds at the dinner that night, while critics would savage Donald Trump, saying that he came off as petty and out of place.

The audience did not know, but just after the prayer, before the trio walked out onstage to introductions, Mr. Trump turned to Hillary Clinton and spoke to her softly. "You know you are one tough and talented woman," he said. For Donald Trump, it was the ultimate compliment. "This has been a good experience," he added, "This whole campaign, as tough as it has been."[1]

Hillary seemed momentarily nonplussed, then said, "Donald, whatever happens, we need to work together afterward."[2]

It was easy for her to say. The next day a Reuters/Ipsos States of the Nation project gave Hillary Clinton a 95 percent chance of winning the presidency. She was the most likely winner in the Electoral College, with a tally of 326 votes to only 212 for Donald Trump.[3]

THE FBI IS BACK ON THE CASE

Only eight days after the Al Smith Dinner in New York City, on October 28, 2016, the FBI director, James Comey, announced that the agency was reopening its investigation into Hillary Clinton's secret emails.[4] The election was only eleven days away. Previously, in July, the FBI chief had summed up the bureau's investigation, calling Clinton's handling of classified materials on her private email server as extremely careless but not criminal.

Only moments after Comey's announcement, Donald Trump reacted. He was on a stage in Manchester, New Hampshire. Trump told a boisterous, cheering audience, "They are reopening the case into her criminal and illegal conduct that threatens the security of the United States of America."[5] Trump was uncharacteristically solemn and he was sticking to his script for a change.

Within two hours of the Comey announcement, Hillary Clinton held a press conference in Des Moines, Iowa. She was wearing a favorite dark blue jacket that an enthusiastic follower once insisted would one day be displayed in the Smithsonian Instutution as the jacket worn on the campaign trail by the first woman elected president of the United States. A battery of American flags were draped behind her onstage.

Hillary boldly called for the FBI to release what they had. She told reporters, "Voting is under way, so the American people deserve to get the full and complete facts immediately." Said Clinton, it was "imperative that the bureau explain this issue in question, whatever it is, without any delay."[6]

Then sounding a tone that was very presidential and dignified, she concluded, "I look forward to moving [on] . . . to focus on the important challenges facing the American people, wining on November 8, and working with all Americans to build a better future for our country."[7]

But there was nothing dignified about the reopening of the FBI investigation. Nor the extenuating circumstances. FBI Director Comey explained that his agents had stumbled on to the new emails during a probe on an unrelated case. Agents had discovered the emails on a computer belonging to Anthony Weiner, a former congressman and the estranged husband of Clinton's top aide Huma Abedin. Weiner was being investigated by the FBI after sending an illicit, sexual text message to a fifteen-year-old girl in North Carolina.[8]

Hillary Clinton considered Weiner's wife, Huma, as another daughter. She was so close that there had been discussion of giving her a bedroom in the family quarters of the White House so she could be accessible to Hillary.[9] Apparently there were tens of thousands of emails on Weiner's computer, and many of them were copies of classified emails to and from Hillary Clinton. Abedin was bewildered, saying she hadn't used the computer for ten years. It appeared that the issue would not be resolved before the election.

The US attorney general, Loretta Lynch, and the deputy attorney general, Sally Yates, disagreed with James Comey's decision to alert Congress about the finding.[10] But Loretta Lynch and the Obama Justice Department had little credibility or sense of public trust left in its tank. During the previous summer, when the FBI probe into Hillary Clinton was supposedly reaching its climactic conclusion, Attorney General Lynch had met with Hillary's husband, former president Bill Clinton, aboard a private plane on the tarmac at an airport in Phoenix, Arizona. Both said that the talks were "primarily social," but a story in *Politico* described even some Democrats as "struggling to stomach the optics."[11] The American justice system appeared to be broken.

As to his new probe, Comey said, "We don't ordinarily tell Congress about ongoing investigations, but here I feel an obligation to do so given that I testified repeatedly in recent months that our investigation was completed." Then Comey added, "I also think it would be misleading to the American people were we not to supplement the record."[12]

Many would argue that Hillary Clinton knew full well that the ugly details related to Anthony Weiner would not be helpful. But it was better to stand fearlessly, with nothing to hide, than to shrink from the exposure as if one were guilty of something.

In answering her last question, at a very choreographed, brief, and scripted news conference, Hillary took her own dig at the FBI, suggesting it was now a tool of Republicans. "If they're going to be sending this kind of letter that is only going, originally, to Republican members of the House, [then] they need to share whatever facts they have with the American people."[13]

It was not true. The FBI was loaded with Democrats and Hillary Clinton supporters. The lead investigator into her emails was an avowed Democrat whose wife had run for the state senate in Virginia as a Democrat. The Virginia Governor, Terry McAuliffe, a close friend of Bill and Hillary Clinton, had helped funnel hundreds of thousands of dollars into her campaign, the campaign of the wife of the FBI agent in charge of investigating Hillary.[14]

What was true was that the FBI, as an institution, had many very good reasons to be skeptical of Hillary Clinton. She and the FBI had experienced a long and sometimes contentious relationship. She was not afraid of it. She saw it as a bureaucracy that could not conclude anything quickly or decisively and certainly would not dare to do so now, only days away from the voting. She was calling its bluff.

The Thursday before the election, Hillary Clinton was asked if she would ask for the resignation of FBI Director Comey, were she elected president.

She refused to answer the question.[15]

Meanwhile, in the aftermath of Comey's announcement, Hillary Clinton's internal, twice-daily surveys, showed that the numbers were holding steady. Even so, the Comey letter was clearly a worrisome event. At the very least, it could suppress voter turnout.

THE CLINTONS' TWENTY-SEVEN-YEAR WAR WITH THE FBI

What the public and most journalists seemed to miss was the long and storied history of the Clintons and the FBI. It started years before the email crisis and the investigation into the Clinton Foundation.

Early in public life, Bill Clinton had been accused of using select officers of the Arkansas State Troopers as his own personal police force. They not only protected the Clintons, they also ran errands, picked up laundry, and, according to their testimony, ran interference for Bill Clinton's extramarital affairs. According to the troopers, Clinton, as attorney general and later as governor of the state, often dispatched officers to procure attractive women, ask for their phone numbers, and try to set them up for private liaisons. The troopers sometimes arranged for motel rooms, drove the governor to the points of rendezvous in state-owned vehicles, and sometimes loaned him their own automobiles to avoid the scrutiny of anyone who had become overly curious.[16]

When the Clintons moved into the White House, it may have been natural for them to try to use the FBI and the Secret Service as an extension of their own personal power. Both proud agencies strongly resisted. Very quickly the relationship devolved into something more negative. One Secret Service agent recalls greeting the first lady as they passed on the West Colonnade, outside the West Wing.

"Good morning, first lady," the officer said.

"Go fuck yourself," the first lady allegedly answered. The story was apparently corroborated by other officers with similar stories.[17]

In my interview with a White House service staff member, I learned that the first lady had a pejorative nickname used by her security detail. "I was on my first road trip and was astonished when the lead officer, a female, said, 'Wait right here until I get the first bitch.' It struck me as incredibly unprofessional and disrespectful, but within a few weeks I would completely understand."[18]

A flight attendant on Air Force One gave a graphic account of Mrs. Clinton's famous temper. While President Ronald Reagan enjoyed jelly beans as snacks, it seemed that President Bill Clinton liked to have supplies of raisins, peanut butter M & M's, and Wrigley's Doublemint chewing gum. The plane had landed and the flight attendant was rushing to the front door to prepare the air stair for the First Lady to disembark. To be late for his task would be sorely noted by supervisors.

As he rushed by what was called "vip one," where Mrs. Clinton was seated, she called out, "Do you have something for my chewing gum?"

"Just a minute, mam," the attendant answered, getting to the door and getting it opened and the stair in position. He thought he could circle back and find something to take her gum. But she brushed past him and descended the stairs, with a beaming smile and a wave of her hand to greeters below. He assumed all was well. When he retreated to clean the cabin, there on her table was her chewing gum flattened down and stretched out, stuck in place to do its maximum damage. The message was clear, "When I ask for something, you better get it."[19]

On another occasion she discovered that she had left her sunglasses behind. The Marine One helicopter was going to lift off and this time the president was on board, so there was no waiting. The first lady broke into a profanity filled tirade, "I want my Goddamn sunglasses NOW!" But no one on staff could find them. During the short flight, the first lady began to violently kick the door of the helicopter. Personnel later worked on trying to clean the black marks from her shoes.

One staff supervisor told me, "It was very clear to us, that the Clintons saw us as working for them personally, not for the country, or the government, or our own agency, or our various commands. We were their personal property."[20]

As the reader will learn in future chapters, when the Clintons tried to remove White House employees in the Travel Office, they sought help from the FBI to get it done. In this case, Hillary Clinton was intent on trying to replace long-serving White House employees with her own campaign workers and Hollywood friends, thus securing for them the lucrative charter flight income. Again and again, White House staff pressured the FBI to find something incriminating to justify the action. There is no doubt that the agency resented being drawn into this personal Clinton drama. But when Clinton staff started leveling criminal complaints against the long-standing White House employees, they had no choice but to get involved.

What resulted was a multimillion-dollar investigation that ruined the lives of the White House workers, some of whom had served successive American presidents since John F. Kennedy. Their personally-signed photos from presidents were thrown in the trash and they were escorted from the building. Their legal fees would run into the hundreds of thousands of dollars.

When a jury eventually found them innocent, the central target of the investigation dropped his head and sobbed with relief. Later, at a restaurant in Virginia, some FBI agents actually cheered the acquittal of the man they had investigated under pressure from the White House and bemoaned what was happening to their beloved FBI.

Filegate was a scandal that involved the Clintons' obtaining thousands of personal FBI files of Republican politicians and former White House officials. It led to a congressional inquiry and embarrassing public testimony from the FBI itself, with outrage that the agency had again become the political tool of the Clintons.

When the Whitewater investigation began, Hillary Clinton's own subpoenaed billing records at the Rose Law Firm went missing. They were eventually found, two years later, in Hillary Clinton's possession. They had been in the private family quarters of the White House. It stunned the public and sparked another FBI investigation. The FBI found Hillary Clinton's fingerprints all over the documents, but the Justice Department took no action in the case. Hillary Clinton went into the history books as the only first lady to ever be fingerprinted by the FBI. She was not happy.

With the FBI and the Secret Service reluctant to become the Clintons' personal palace guards, the Clintons simply created their own. The White House Security Office was led by two former campaign staffers, Craig Livingstone and Anthony Marceca. More about this duo later, but suffice it to mention here that they immediately began to improperly access FBI files belonging to the political targets of the Clintons.[21] Incredibly, in the middle of the Filegate scandal, it was learned that Marceca had allegedly accessed his own FBI files, where he learned that two women had made accusations against him. Armed with this insider FBI information, Marceca apparently confronted the women and sued them for slander.[22]

The Clintons professed complete ignorance about the so-called White House Security Office, as if it had materialized on its own, but according to an FBI report, the two men who ran it had been given their positions by Hillary Clinton.

When Vince Foster took his own life, the FBI was kept out of the investigation by President Clinton for several crucial days. Clinton wanted the park rangers to handle the case. They bungled it, losing, for example, the crime scene photos which lead to endless conspiracy theories.

Vince Foster's suicide note was found six days after his death, in his own briefcase, in his White House office. The note included Foster's negative appraisal of the FBI, saying that it had lied in its report to the attorney general about Travelgate. It showed how toxic and bitter the relationship between the Clintons and the FBI had become in their first year in the White House.

When the Monica Lewinsky scandal broke, it was the FBI that had to have an agent present in the Map Room of the White House when blood was drawn from the president, to determine his DNA. And it was an FBI laboratory that compared the president's DNA with the semen stain on Monica Lewinsky's famous blue dress.

Pursuing the cases of the many women alleging affairs with Bill Clinton was a tour of the dark side of power. While the FBI had no prurient interest in the morality or immorality of Bill Clinton's private sex life, the independent counsel's office, operating at the behest of the Justice Department, was pursuing charges of obstruction of justice and perjury. And that necessarily involved the FBI listening to the women's anguished stories.

As the reader will learn, in every case, the women had been outed by others. They had not wanted to come forward. Yet they were being portrayed as nuts, sluts, gold diggers out for money, or partisans put up to their assignments by Republican troublemakers. Hillary would call it "a vast right-wing conspiracy."[23]

What the FBI found instead was a long string of concerted attacks, orchestrated by the Clintons against the women who had come forward. The evidence was stunning. Jack Palladino, a former law school classmate of Hillary Clinton, was hired to investigate the women. He was paid $100,000. Palladino openly bragged that he would destroy the reputation of one of the women "beyond all recognition."[24]

The women claimed that their car tires were shot out by nail guns. That strangers met them on the jogging path, calling out the names of their children. That the postman and others in their small towns warned of creepy-looking people asking about them around the neighborhood. Car windows were shot out from the inside of one of the cars, with the spent shotgun shells inside, lying on the floor. A beloved cat went missing, and a few weeks later a torched cat's skull was found on a front porch.

More troubling and relevant for the FBI were the stories of strangers who offered the women federal jobs if they would keep quiet. And when they declined to take the bribes and insisted on testifying truthfully under oath against the president, they would subsequently be fired from the jobs they had. When inquiries were made, the bosses of the women who had fired them would admit to outside pressure.

Many of the women, including Gennifer Flowers, Paula Jones, and Juanita Broaddrick, were audited by the IRS for the first time in their lives.[25]

One of the terrified victims contacted the FBI with a corroborating witness. When she was approached by a low-level Democratic Party official who had a message for her, Sally Perdue wisely arranged in advance for a coworker to sit nearby and surreptitiously listen in on the conversation. The Democratic official warned Perdue to keep her mouth shut. If she did, she would get a federal job, he promised. If she didn't, they knew where she jogged each day and they couldn't promise that someone might not "break her pretty little legs."

Both Sally Perdue and her coworker, who was the second witness to this conversation, filed affidavits with the FBI field office, presumably in Saint Louis. When Sally left the office, a car attempted to hit her, but she avoided it in the last few seconds. Surveillance cameras outside the FBI building may have offered further information. Perdue claims that the car had no license plates.

Juanita Broaddrick told her story of being pinned to the bed of her hotel room and raped by Bill Clinton in Little Rock, Arkansas. Her friend Norma Rogers found her afterward, huddled in her room, weeping and trembling. What could they do? Go to the police? Bill Clinton was then the attorney general of Arkansas, the chief law enforcement officer in the state. They grabbed their things, checked out of the hotel and immediately fled Little Rock.

The independent counsel asked the FBI to investigate the Juanita Broaddrick story, knowing that it was twenty years old and the statute of limitations had expired for a charge of rape. The investigators wanted to know only if Bill Clinton had asked her to lie about her testimony. Or had offered her bribes. He had not. The final FBI report on Juanita Broaddrick was stamped "inconclusive," but the testimony was so heartrending that word soon spread and several Republican senators asked to read it. The report was provided to them by FBI agents and the senators were required to read the documents in a sealed room. Several senators chose to read the report the day before the vote on impeachment.

In the 1990s, the FBI broke a story that involved massive amounts of foreign money flooding into the Clinton and Democratic National Committee coffers. Some of it was traced back to the People's Republic of China. Some could be traced to companies owned by the Chinese military and security forces.

The FBI was not monitoring the Clintons and the Democrats; they were listening in on conversations taking place in the Chinese embassy. It was through an investigation of Chinese espionage against the United States that the FBI stumbled onto a plan to influence the American presidential elections. The FBI was simply following the trail of money when it unexpectedly led them back to the Clinton White House.

A congressional hearing produced witnesses and participants who had incredible tales to tell the American people. One of those witnesses, receiving death threats, was reportedly promised protection by the Los Angeles office of the FBI. But, at the last minute, the Los Angeles office was told to cancel all protection. The witness's attorney received a package suggesting that his client could plead the Fifth Amendment. He refused. Out of 120 witnesses, he was the only one willing to talk about what had happened.

"Today, I have mixed feelings about the President and the First Lady but I can't help but think that they used me as much as I used them,"[26] said Johnny Chung, one of the principal figures in the Clinton Chinagate scandal. His testimony was carried live on national television. He spoke with disgust about officials at the Democratic National Committee who had begun to condemn him for funneling money from China, when he said they knew very well about the origin of the money.

Before finishing his testimony, he spoke of a menacing message he had received from an American source: "If you keep your mouth shut, you and your family will be safe." He said that a message from the Chinese government was more polite and indirect, more subtle, but otherwise similar. "It said, me and my family would be safe if I didn't talk."[27]

Such stories sound far-fetched, the creation of fringe conspiracy theorists. But they were sometimes sufficiently believable to the FBI agents themselves, that those agents crossed the line and walked away from government careers in disgust. One agent told a Clinton victim of sexual assault that her public testimony probably saved her life.

Bill Clinton would later be asked by a friend if he had ordered the IRS to audit the women who had accused him of sexual assault or the women who had eventually come forward with stories of infidelity? Women like Paula Jones?

"I didn't have anything to do with it," Clinton replied, referring to their ongoing travails with the government. "And I know nobody around here had to do with her getting audited by the IRS. But, independently, it stands to some reason. She doesn't have any visible means of support and is always traveling around and driving a new car, no job, so forth."[28]

But neither did Bill Clinton order his government to stop any harassment or perceived punishment of the women who were claiming to be victims of his sexual assault. He didn't order the IRS to stand down, for example. In fact, he let it be known that he approved of its action. That it was warranted. Nor did he put Johnny Chung in protective custody after he openly declared that he and his family had been threatened. Someone in government had actually called off the FBI, which had apparently wanted to protect him.

The commissioner of the IRS during the Clinton administration was Margaret Milner Richardson. She had worked on the Clinton campaign and served on the administration's transition team for the Justice Department. She was also a longtime friend of Hillary Clinton.[29] As commissioner, Richardson was accused by conservatives of targeting individuals and organizations for audit whom the Clintons considered political enemies, often with alleged threats of property seizure. The NRA, the *American Spectator*, and the Western Journalism Center were all alleged targets. As were Gennifer Flowers and Paula Jones. Was Hillary Clinton using her influence and friendship with Richardson to threaten detractors into silence?[30] Commissioner Margaret Milner Richardson resigned on January 9, 1997.[31] She denied any political pressure to leave.

While most of the committed professionals at the FBI stuck to their own business or even looked the other way, some were troubled.

Heads of state, kings, presidents, mafia chieftains, corporate bosses, seldom had to direct their subordinates about what to do in complicated ethical matters.

One of history's most famous stories has King Henry II exploding in exasperation at the ignorance of his own entourage, seemingly incompetent in discerning the obvious, that his rival, the Archbishop of Canterbury, should be dispatched. "Who will rid me of this troublesome priest?" the king supposedly shouted in frustration.

Catching his drift, four knights in his entourage galloped off to find the king's antagonist the archbishop Thomas Becket, and butchered him near the altar of Canterbury Cathedral. It happened in 1170. And the story has become a metaphor for many similar instances.

If the FBI was not afraid that the Clintons themselves would order wrongdoing, it understood full well that the government was full of people who wanted to be helpful to persons in power.

Years after the Clinton Chinagate scandal erupted, Johnny Chung, still in hiding, received a friendly visit from a retired government worker who was close to the FBI. He was troubled by how Chung's case had been handled and worried about the danger that he still faced.

It was by talking that Johnny Chung would stay alive, the friend counseled. He helped Chung make a videotaped testimony that was given to multiple sources for insurance. After completing his sentence, Johnny Chung lived in peace for several years in Southern California, but when Hillary Clinton began her inexorable political comeback, he fled to China. Attempts by this author to reach him through sources close to his family were unsuccessful. But one of my researchers was able to view in its entirety a copy of his remarkable videotape. And the author has seen large portions.

Reports of these events and personalities, filed by FBI agents all across the country, conducting interviews and doing research at FBI offices in Arkansas, Virginia, Maryland, Texas, Oklahoma, Missouri, California, Illinois, New York, Florida, and many other locations around the country, worked their way into the bloodstream of the FBI. They eventually had their impact.

GETTING AWAY WITH MURDER

Some of the FBI's most spectacular work in the 1970s and 80s was undone by Bill Clinton a decade later with the stroke of a pen. Bill Clinton's action was referred to in the newspapers as a gift to his wife, first lady Hillary Clinton, who was then running for a seat in the US Senate from New York.[32]

The full story is told in later chapters of this book, but suffice it to say here that after careful investigative work, involving almost seven hundred hours of surveillance, the FBI had discovered six safe houses, a bomb factory, and evidence connecting sixteen terrorists to killing and mayhem that had cut a swath across the country from New York to Chicago.

The FALN was a Marxist cell advocating independence for Puerto Rico. It had virtually no support on the island. Its members had set off 120 bombs in New York City and Chicago, leaving behind sixteen murdered and dozens injured and maimed for life. They had blown up the FBI headquarters in Manhattan and hit the federal courthouse in Brooklyn.

Judge George Layton had praised the FBI, saying, "This case . . . represents one of the finest examples of preventive law enforcement that has ever come to this court's attention in the 20-odd years it has been a judge and in the 20 years before that as a practicing lawyer in criminal cases."[33]

Deborah Devaney, a federal prosecutor, described the "chilling evidence" against the terrorists, saying that "a few dedicated federal agents are the only people who stood in their way."[34]

When the terrorists appeared before their judge for sentencing, they mocked him and sneered that they would kill him on the spot if they were not in chains.

Nevertheless, in 1999, some very talented lobbyists for the FALN apparently convinced Hillary Clinton to plead their case and assured her that the 1.3 million Puerto Rican voters in New York State would be very grateful. A New York City councilman later reported that he had personally given Hillary Clinton a package of information on the FALN, along with a letter urging the president to offer the terrorists clemency.

Two days later, on August 11, 1999, President Bill Clinton granted the pardons to the FALN. There was immediate outrage. The terrorists themselves laughed at the US government and turned down the presidential pardons, which had required that the terrorists renounce violence.

The outcry was thunderous. Victims of the bombings told their stories in the newspapers. Hillary Clinton immediately switched positions, denying that she had ever been involved and condemned her husband's pardons. "When the administration first offered these prisoners clemency," she said, "I made it very clear that I had no involvement in or prior knowledge of the decision, as is entirely appropriate, and that the prisoners should not be released until they renounced violence."[35]

The government now began the unseemly task of trying to convince the prisoners and their lawyers to accept President Bill Clinton's pardons. Two of them adamantly refused. The others were finally released on September 8, 1999.

Eventually, there was rejoicing by some in the New York Puerto

Rican community, whereupon Hillary Clinton changed her position yet again. Addressing a small crowd at the World of Women Leaders Conference in New York City, Hillary told the audience that her decision to oppose clemency had been wrong after all. "The consultation process was not what it should have been and that will never happen again."[36]

She had ultimately taken three different positions on the FALN pardons but finally landed on what she believed to be the winning side.

Once more, the FBI had been burned by the Clintons. The US Senate voted 95 to 2 to condemn the pardons. When Congress held an investigation, the Clinton White House invoked executive privilege and refused to allow FBI agents to testify. Neal Gallagher, the assistant FBI director, was finally called before Congress to answer for the pardons. Because President Clinton had invoked executive privilege, Gallagher could not describe the bureau's recommendation on the matter, but he left little doubt where the agency stood about the FALN. "I think they are criminals and terrorists and represent a threat to the United States."[37]

In the last days of the Clinton White House, the president pardoned the billionaire Marc Rich. It is considered by many, to this day, to have been the most corrupt act of a very controversial lifetime career of Bill and Hillary Clinton.

Marc Rich had been on the FBI's famous and feared top-ten most-wanted list. And no wonder: He had been indicted on sixty-five criminal counts. It was the largest tax-evasion case in US history. He had traded illegally with the most despotic and evil regimes in the world. He bought oil from Ayatollah Khomeini, even while Iran held US hostages at the American embassy in Tehran. He worked with the apartheid regime in South Africa and with Gaddafi's Libya, Kim Il-sung's North Korea, and the Soviet Union in the middle of the Cold War.[38]

Even so, his ex-wife had donated heavily to the Democratic National Committee and had given $450,000 to the Clinton Presidential Library.

Congressman Barney Frank said of the pardon, "It was a real betrayal by Bill Clinton of all who had been strongly supportive of him, to do something this unjustified. It was contemptuous."[39]

The *New York Times* called it "an indefensible pardon."[40]

Ironically, Jim Comey, serving in the US Attorney's office in New York, was the prosecutor in charge of the Marc Rich case from 1987 to 1993. And when charges were made against Bill Clinton, James Comey, then US attorney, led the criminal investigation against the former president. But the wife of Marc Rich pleaded the Fifth Amendment, and Comey concluded that without her testimony there was insufficient evidence to prove guilt.[41]

Later, a counsel in the Obama White House said that at the time, then Senator Barack Obama had been "very, very dismayed by the Marc Rich pardon and the basis on which it appears to have been granted."[42] In 2016, as Hillary Clinton's campaign for the White House appeared on the verge of victory, an article in the *New York Post* showed that the Clintons were still making money from the Marc Rich pardon. The headline read, "Bill Clinton's Pardon of Fugitive Marc Rich Continues to Pay Big."[43]

With that pardon, the FBI saw millions of dollars in investigative effort go down the drain. So much for the FBI's once famous top-ten most-wanted list. And Marc Rich was not the only controversial pardon that undid the work of the once proud agency. There was a long list of Colombian drug dealers and politicians. Henry Cisneros, a former secretary of Housing and Urban Development, had lied to the FBI about payments to his mistress. Clinton pardoned them both.

There was a sad feeling among many former agents and even among some active agents. The FBI was now a tool of the politically powerful. The weak were on their own.

WHAT WILL COMEY DO?

As the 2016 presidential election approached, the FBI was faced with the stark reality that Bill and Hillary Clinton would now be moving back into the White House.

Hillary Clinton was about to become their boss.

This was what the corporate media had decided. It was what the big banks wanted. It was what the foreign governments, who had bloated the Clinton Foundation with over $2 billion in contributions, wanted. It was what Wall Street wanted. In fact, while Hillary Clinton's speeches to Wall Street commanded great curiosity and were valuable currency, not a single speech, or line from a single speech, leaked from the thousands of witnesses who had been in her audience. It took hackers, from Russia to give us brief glimpses. The Wall Street insiders were so invested in the Clintons that they had maintained perfect discipline to protect their champions.

It was not the place of the FBI to decide who should or should not be president. Many of the agents, perhaps even a majority of the agents, preferred Hillary Clinton to Donald Trump, who they saw as unpolished and erratic.

While FBI Director Comey was famously a Republican, he was so professional, so fastidiously ethical, that Barack Obama had been comfortable confirming him in the newly created ten-year term. Comey's FBI had long ago made its accommodation to liberalism and to the sociocultural revolution of the left. The American intelligence community had been shaken to its core by 9/11. The change toward diversity had begun in a Republican administration. And most in the FBI, including Comey, agreed that it was needed.

It was more than a cultural issue, it was first and foremost an issue of performance and effectiveness. The CIA had been criticized for its inbreeding, being famously run by a small community of Catholics. Walter Bedell Smith, John McCone, William Colby, William Casey, Michael Hayden, Leon Panetta, and John Brennan had all been powerful directors of the CIA. All were Catholic. James Comey at the FBI was Catholic.

The feeling was that if they were to be effective in understanding and gathering information, they needed youth, Hispanics, blacks, women, Muslims, lesbians, and gays.

There were sometimes complaints from the Obama White House. The pace of promotion and advancement for minorities was still agonizingly slow. Though within the agencies themselves, where performance sometimes took a back seat, it seemed to be moving at stellar speed.

At times, the Pentagon and CIA seemed to have a jump on the FBI. Their walls were plastered with LGBT banners and posters, while the FBI was criticized for being more traditional and stodgy. Still, strides were being made. Bible studies, for example, were now out at all government places, including the FBI, or they had at least gone underground, befitting for intelligence officers. Islamic hijabs, on the other hand, were now out in the open. Meanwhile, at the Pentagon, there was a sense that the entire chaplaincy program would be scrapped within the decade. Chaplains would be counselors, but stripped of any religious doctrine.

So the FBI had made its peace with the idea of a Clinton return to power. It now seemed inevitable. Even if the public knew what the FBI knew, there was not much chance that they would change their minds. In 1990, Washington, DC, mayor Marion Barry had been arrested by the FBI after being captured by video surveillance smoking crack cocaine. The whole nation saw the video. He was reelected mayor of Washington, DC, a few years later anyway. Some people were not influenced by ethics.

This did not mean that the new culturally pure, politically correct FBI was accepted by all without complaint. There were dinosaurs at the FBI. Old agents who griped about two sets of rules. One for the little people and one for the powerful people. Some posted anonymously online, warning that the Clinton Foundation scandal amounted to the selling of America to foreign governments. There were warnings about George Soros, the billionaire who some said had funded many of the programs and social changes in American society.

When Hillary Clinton complained of memory loss and couldn't answer questions posed by the FBI because of her concussion, they asked for her medical records. The Clintons complained to the Justice Department, and the FBI request was denied.[44]

Most older, disgruntled FBI agents just counted the days till retirement, shaking their heads at the preoccupation with political correctness. Meanwhile, the accommodation to the new realities was accepted by anyone who still cherished a future career.

This is not to say that there was not sometimes open rebellion. The old FBI was not dying without spasms. Questions of integrity were harder to stomach.

It was unfortunate that Andrew McCabe was the particular FBI agent who led the investigation into Secretary Clinton's emails. Terry McAuliffe, the former governor of Virginia and one of Bill and Hillary Clinton's oldest and closest political allies, had directed $500,000 in campaign money into the coffers of Jill McCabe, the FBI agent's wife, in her failed bid for state senate. Couldn't someone less conflicted have been chosen to do the work on Hillary? Instead of someone whose wife had been given $500,000?

And it was unfortunate that after the McCabe email investigation, which ended in a recommendation not to pursue criminal charges against Mrs. Clinton, that Andrew McCabe was promptly promoted to deputy director of the FBI.

What was most unfortunate of all, for those more traditional FBI agents who loved their bureau, was to read about it in the *Wall Street Journal* for the first time, only one month before the election. Why hadn't the public been told when it happened? Why did they have to discover these truths so late? If these were truly not shameful admissions, then why had they been hidden? Why was so much important information coming from the pages of supermarket tabloids? It was a dark and demoralizing moment for many FBI agents and their families.[45]

Sometimes an agency office would revolt. Investigations into the Clinton Foundation made in the New York office were troubling. Some agents there were convinced there was some measure of quid pro quo for the donations received. On October 30, 2016, the infighting spilled out onto the front pages. Agents at the bureau in New York were calling for further investigations. Agents in Washington, DC, closer to the heart of the Obama Justice Department, were saying no.[46]

Eventually, agents had to back down. There was a widespread unanimity about the political issues involved. The Clinton email and foundation scandals would have been serious for any other mere mortal, but were not enough to halt the presidential ambitions of one as powerful as Hillary Clinton. Not with an Obama Justice Department willing to back her up.

There was no future in pursuing the Clintons. By the time the investigations over the foundation had reached its end, the Justice Department would be run, once again, by the Clintons themselves, and the Supreme Court, flush with new Clinton appointees, would likely be supportive if the investigation got that far. And even more telling, the corporate media would provide all the cover that the

Clintons needed. If they supported them now, after all they already knew about their many scandals, then certainly nothing the FBI uncovered, legal or illegal, would make any difference. Too many people were invested in the Clintons to let them fail. Too much money was to be made. If the Clintons failed, the whole system would come tumbling down with them. The world would fail. The stars would fall from the heavens.

Still, the inevitability of the Clinton presidency did not mean it would be easy for the FBI to survive with its character intact. It would be an ethical nightmare. Everyone had given the Clintons money, and even by chance the Clintons would do some things that would sometimes benefit those donors. And for those who invested much but were denied what they wanted? Some of them would probably go public, making angry claims against the president and first husband, leaking to the public whatever evidence or leverage they thought they had. What would the Clinton Justice Department expect? What would the Congress expect? What was going to happen to the FBI? To the United States? Would this now be Brazil? Would it be India? Would it be the Congo?

As he approached the final days of the 2016 presidential campaign, James Comey could no longer juggle so many balls in the air at the same time. He surely must have loved the agency that he ran, and he felt the sting of rebuke from its chorus of graying elders. He felt the cynicism of a corporate world that had grown immensely fat on the last two presidencies, a Republican and a Democrat. Yet, he understood the law, and how fragile society really was.

James Comey knew, as did President Barack Obama, that the US Constitution was, itself, the law. It was not a piece of abstract art. When politicians talked about the Constitution being flexible or bending, they were talking about the law being flexible and of the law bending.

Sometime during the late evening of October 27, 2016, James Comey decided that he would do what he thought was the right thing to do and let the pieces fall where they may. It would be controversial. It would provoke howls of anger and outrage. It wouldn't satisfy his critics inside or out of the FBI, and it would surely inflame some of the most powerful people in the world. He would dutifully send his letter updating the Congressional committee that provided the oversight to the FBI. It was what he had promised he would do if the issues warranted. And by anyone's standard, the issues now warranted.

Crucially, it would not change the outcome of the 2016 election. He would only be angering the Clintons, who would soon be his new bosses. And perhaps worse, he would be angering the corporate media giants, who some now believed had as much power as the three official branches of government and who held Comey's legacy and reputation in their hands.

At one time, James Comey may have cared about that. He was six feet eight inches tall. When he walked into a room, he commanded attention. People compared him to George Washington, as a man whose combination of integrity and physical stature won instant respect. But Comey knew that what he was about to do would be seen as beyond the pale. He had earned a lifetime of political and personal equity, but he would spend it all the next day.

"I believe the job of the FBI Director," Comey once said, "is to be as transparent as possible with the American people because we work for them."[47]

Comey was going to do what he believed was the right thing to do, the legal thing, the ethical thing to do. He would be transparent. He was not going to sit on the information he had. He would pass it on to the American people. He was a doomed man. But tonight, he would sleep.

CHAPTER 2

THE LOST VOTERS OF ELECTIONS PAST

The worst feeling isn't being lonely,
it is being forgotten.
—Rousseau

A s the calendar wound down to Election Day and a Hillary Clinton victory, not everybody in her world was happy. Days before the election, Bill Clinton reportedly flew into a rage over what he suspected were flagging numbers. The former president was in Little Rock, at his notorious private pad at the Clinton Presidential Library and Museum. Hillary was on the road.

Bill Clinton got into a shouting match with Hillary on the phone. She was fuming about FBI Director Comey's decision to revive his investigation. She was convinced that it had reversed her momentum.

Bill would have none of it. At least according to the eyewitness. That wasn't the problem. The problem was Robby Mook, Hillary's cocky campaign manager, and John Podesta, Hillary's know-it-all campaign chairman, and yes, the problem was Hillary, herself.

They were all deaf to the needs of the blue-collar workers who had lost their jobs all across America. It was one thing to say in public, out of loyalty, that things were great, but Obama wasn't running, she was running, and people didn't believe that things were great.

Whatever happened to "It's the economy, stupid"?

An aide who was standing nearby described Bill Clinton as "so red in the face during his conversation with Hillary that I worried he was going to have a heart attack."[1]

At the end of the discussion, Bill Clinton took his phone and tossed it off the penthouse roof and watched it sail toward the Arkansas River.

In the twilight of the Hillary Clinton campaign, they were losing rural Americans in key battleground states, Catholics in the Rust Belt states, and evangelicals in suburban small cities in Michigan, Pennsylvania, Wisconsin, and all across the Florida panhandle.

Bill Clinton was reportedly still furious over the campaign's refusal to speak at a Saint Patrick's Day event months earlier at Notre Dame. Catholics wanted to vote for them, if the campaign would just give them a chance. It was as if Hillary's campaign didn't want them.

In fact, a leaked John Podesta email from inside Hillary's machine showed how deeply cynical the staff had been about people of faith, any faith.

In October, *The Catholic World Report* headlined a story entitled "Fake Catholic Groups and the 'Catholic Spring' Emails."[2] When activists set up their own organization promoting the Iran nuclear deal, Podesta praised their work.[3] "We created Catholics in Alliance for the Common Good," he wrote, "to organize for a moment like this."[4]

In October, with the national media focused on an *Access Hollywood* audiotape of Donald Trump making crude and demeaning remarks about women as sex objects, WikiLeaks quietly revealed a batch of internal Clinton campaign memos showing a very clear anti-Catholic, anti-evangelical bias.

Clinton's communications director, Jennifer Palmieri, her chairman, John Podesta, and John Halpin of the Center for American Progress, a Podesta creation, were exchanging emails about Catholics.[5]

Halpin wrote to Podesta and Palmieri in April 2011 ridiculing the media giant Rupert Murdoch for raising his kids as Catholics. Murdoch, an Australian-American, owned News Corporation and a variety of news vehicles, including Fox News, and seemed to walk to a different drummer than all the other media heads who backed Hillary Clinton.

"Ken Auletta's latest piece on Murdoch in the *New Yorker* starts off with the aside that both Murdoch and Robert Thompson, managing editor of the WSJ, are raising their kids Catholic," Halpin wrote.

"Friggin' Murdoch baptized his kids in Jordan where John the Baptist baptized Jesus."

"Many of the most powerful elements of the conservative movement are all Catholic (many converts) from the SC [Supreme Court] and think tanks to the media and social groups. It's an amazing bastardization of the faith."

"They must be attracted to the systematic thought and severely backwards gender relations and must be totally unaware of Christian democracy."

Halpin's email amused Jennifer Palmieri, a Clinton staffer, who answered back:

"I imagine they think it is the most socially acceptable politically conservative religion. Their rich friends wouldn't understand if they became evangelicals."

John Halpin summed it up:

"Excellent point. They can throw around 'Thomistic' thought and 'subsidiarity' and sound sophisticated because no one knows what the hell they're talking about."[6]

It wasn't very often that leaders in the American faith community got such frank confirmation of what they could see being lived out in public life. Catholic and evangelical leaders were not amused by this exchange, and it began to show up in their publications and on their blogs.

The so-called Reagan Democrats were mostly union workers from cities like Milwaukee, Detroit, Columbus, Youngstown, Pittsburgh, and Harrisburg. They were predominantly Catholics. But they were out of work and liked the Trump rhetoric about bringing back jobs. The Obama years had been devastating for them.

Meanwhile, evangelicals were deeply troubled by Donald Trump's *Access Hollywood* audiotape. Some of them, especially their youth, were openly supportive of the Clintons. The Obama campaign had aggressively courted them, launching what he had dubbed "The Joshua Project." A former student body leader at Evangel University in Springfield, Missouri was openly suggesting that students could vote for candidates "downballot" and ignore the presidential race.

Only late in the campaign, when the emails leaked, did evangelical leaders begin to conclude that they were not even wanted by Clinton. They had been born into the wrong faith. Their upbringing had apparently precluded admission to the Democratic Party.

Katy Perry, the pop-rock star, who was the most popular of a long list of Clinton celebrities who sang at her rallies, was raised as an evangelical Christian and had parents who were preachers. Would Palmieri and Halpin consider her a half evangelical? Did her work for Clinton erase some of the stain? Was she now less deplorable?

After the election, Michael Wear, President Barack Obama's key man for outreach to the evangelical world, wrote a piece for the *Washington Post*: "Why Did Obama Win More White Evangelical Votes than Clinton? He Asked for Them."[7]

It was not just that there was no outreach to Catholics and evangelicals—nixing, for example, Bill Clinton's idea of speaking at Notre Dame—and that there was personal hostility, the leaked emails also exposed a plan underway to coopt the Catholic Church itself. There was apparently a long-range plan to effect what Clinton staffers referred to as a "Catholic Spring" sometime after the election, when the Clinton presidency was well under way.

Liberal politicians had long lamented the activism of the religious conservatives. But this plan amounted to liberal politicians infiltrating religion to dictate doctrine. Some Catholic bishops were stunned by just how brazen this idea was.

If, as Bill Clinton worried, his wife's campaign was forfeiting the Catholic and evangelical vote, it was, indeed, an extravagant gift to the Republicans. Twenty-two percent of the nation was Catholic. Twenty-six percent of all voters identified themselves as evangelical, and even more significant, fully forty percent of the nation claimed to be born-again Christians.[8] By comparison, the Clinton campaign was completely invested and predictably winning the African American vote, but that represented only twelve percent of the general population—and would they turn out to vote as they had for Obama? That seemed to be unlikely, even though the president, himself, was making that goal his mission. The Catholics could be the key to seven swing states in the Midwest, and the evangelicals could hold the Republican base in the plains states and the South and be a powerful force in the Florida panhandle.

The national media ignored the WikiLeaks memos and focused on the narrative dictated by the Clinton campaign. It explained that the real story was that the Democratic emails had likely been hacked by the Russians. Should the Russians be allowed to influence an American election? The patriotic thing to do would be to ignore the emails.

There was a great irony in seeing Democrats now raise the alarm over Russia. At one time the Russians were the advocates of Godless atheism, outlawing Bibles and religious symbols, maintaining gulags of hundreds of thousands of "enemies of the state." They were an automatic target for any politician and sure to arouse conservative Catholics and evangelicals. But now Christians were building super-churches within blocks of the Kremlin. Visitors insisted that there was more religious freedom of expression in Russia than in America. The Russians now incarcerated fewer prisoners than Americans did. The highest tax rate in Russia was 15 percent. The Russian boogey-man had lost its visceral power to frighten Americans.

A few days after the Catholic-evangelical email exchange, WikiLeaks revealed a 2015 email to John Podesta from his brother, Tony. John Podesta, the chairman of the Hillary Clinton presidential campaign, was being invited to a "Spirit Cooking" dinner with Marina Abramovic.

Online sites went wild with the information. Referred to as a Satanist, Abramovic was a performance artist, one of whose exotic art concoctions gave the instructions to "mix fresh breast milk with fresh sperm milk."[9]

The national corporate media ignored the whole tawdry subject except to keep beating the drum that Russia was trying to influence an American election. Don't listen to them. Don't fall for it. It was un-American to read the outed emails from the Clinton campaign. That was what the Russians wanted you to do.

Finally, a November 4, 2016, *Washington Post* story tried to mitigate the damage for the Clinton campaign, attacking the *Drudge Report* website for covering the issue. The *Post* story created a straw man out of right-wing rage, pointing out that John Podesta did not actually go to the dinner in question. It was all a fuss about nothing.

Admitting that Abramovic was "known for her often controversial and dangerous performances" the writer for the *Washington Post* detailed a Spirit Cooking installation "where the recipes were written on walls in blood, accompanied by a video projection and a participatory piece where viewers could press their heads against a stone installed on a wall." The *Washington Post* writer conceded, "It might not be everyone's taste in art, and the footage documenting that 1997 installation is potentially disturbing, but it's still art."[10]

Whether or not Podesta drank milk at dinner with a Satanist was not the issue. The Clinton campaign chairman, whose team had ridiculed Rupert Murdoch for his ignorance in raising his children as Catholics, seemed to feel no need to raise any sociointellectual alarm over Tony Podesta's association with Satanists.

"Don't worry," Tony Podesta wrote his brother later, "Marina missed you."[11]

The *Washington Post* must have felt that it had sufficiently laid to rest the whole silly controversy. But Clinton's sympathetic media, in its attempt to be helpful, was sometimes clumsy, only making matters worse. Born-again Christians were not impressed with the *Washington Post*'s description of art with semen and blood. And they were not amused that aficionados of such art believed them to be socially acceptable. Forty percent of the American public? Are you sure?

At a very minimum, infiltrating the Catholic Church for purposes of subverting doctrine and dinners with Satanists was certainly off message.

THE LOST VOTERS OF RURAL AMERICA

For the Clinton machine, there was something even more serious afoot than any social issue. It too was ignored, even denied, by the corporate media but it was real nonetheless. A large swath of Americana still languished in the Great Recession. It was fine for President Obama and the national media to declare that the economic downturn was over, but that did little to reassure people who were actually out of work.

Victoria Sanders, a thoughtful blogger, took a tour through rural Pennsylvania, surveying the blight. "Scrap metal was thrown across front lawns. White, plastic lawn chairs were out on the drooping front porches. There were no malls. No outlets. Most of these small towns did not have a Walmart, only a dollar store and a few run down thrift stores. In almost every town, there was an abandoned factory."[12]

And, she added, everywhere there were Trump signs planted in the front yards.

These were the voters who had slipped past the pollsters unnoticed but who had been tracked down and identified by the intrepid Trump team, led by Steve Bannon, Kellyanne Conway, and Jared Kushner.

These were the poor people of rural America who had lost their jobs.[13] The evangelicals who lived in small towns, where grass and weeds sprung up through the cracks in the asphalt parking lots of abandoned K-Marts. Where the poverty rate now actually outranked the poverty rate of the inner cities.[14] Where drinking water was as hazardous as in Flint, Michigan, and there were no television journalists interested in doing the story. Where the percentage of young people attending college was now less than in the inner city.[15] When was the last time you saw a heartwarming network television show about a billionaire helping underprivileged kids in rural America get a college education?

Many of the evangelicals were missed by the pollsters because they were unlikely voters. Some had not voted in three elections. They were not on anybody's lists. Except Trump's. As a businessman, he knew and understood the depth of the evangelical market. He had gotten there years before, teaming up with a television evangelist named Paula White. And recently, since the Democrats had forfeited the vote, he had made many new friends. When the *Access Hollywood* tape surfaced, so personally damaging to Donald Trump's character, the Democrats sighed deeply, feeling sure that it would sink the cocky evangelical vote. But Tony Perkins, the respected voice of at least thirty million evangelicals, dismissed the whole controversy, casually telling reporters that Christians hadn't chosen Trump because of his personal spirituality. It was all about the Supreme Court. Thirty million evangelicals nodded in agreement and sat back down in their pews. Meanwhile, David Lane, referred to by journalists as the evangelicals' secret weapon, was busy building a Christian organization on the ground. The Clinton's offered no challenge.[16]

Then there were the Democratic Catholic union workers, who lived in the decaying small cities. They voted last time for Barack Obama, thrilled that they were putting a nail in the coffin of racism and proud to see an African American president. They would be dismissed by television pundits as racists themselves, because they had voted for Trump. But they had really voted for Trump because he was the only one who had addressed their fear and their need.

They weren't really workers any longer. These poor people of the Rust Belt had lost their jobs. These were the people who Bill Clinton, in frustration, had watched being passed over by his wife's campaign. They were fat from fast food, the only food they could afford. The companies they had once worked for had not even bothered to tear down the big, empty plants and factories in their small towns, so they had to pass by them and see them as ugly, bombed-out, steel-and-concrete tombstones to a life they had once lived.

The former GOP House Speaker Newt Gingrich, New Jersey governor Chris Christie, former Senator Rick Santorum, and the former New York mayor Rudolph Giuliani were all Catholic supporters of Donald Trump who offered reassurance to these voters, looking to jump one way or the other at the last minute. Joseph Cella, founder of the National Catholic Prayer Breakfast was brought in to help. And George Martin, a talented political operative, was tapped to help find Catholic activitsts and organize them for the Republican campaign.[17]

Just days before the election, Donald Trump visited Minnesota and Wisconsin. A Republican had not won Minnesota since 1972. Even Ronald Reagan's landslide in 1984, which took every other state in the union, could not budge Democratic-held Minnesota, which was home to Democratic legends like Walter Mondale and Hubert Humphrey. Professional politicians were chuckling, some openly mocking Trump. Amateur hour. One pundit called the Trump campaign guilty of political malpractice.

While Trump was busy chasing what the Clinton campaign saw as a lost cause in Wisconsin and Michigan, the interim chairwoman of the Democratic National Committee, Donna Brazile, was spending millions of dollars finding new voters in Chicago and New Orleans.[18] The money was being siphoned off the Clinton campaign, which was outspending Trump in these last weeks almost two to one. Donna Brazile's bizarre plan was based on the fear that Hillary Clinton would easily win the vote in the Electoral College but lose the popular vote to Trump. Even though Louisiana would go for the Republicans with or without millions of new Clinton dollars poured in, it was rich hunting ground for additional African American voters who would help spike her grand total.

Likewise, Clinton had a lock on Illinois—Trump wasn't even trying there—but additional African American voters in Chicagoland were easy to find and might help stave off the embarrassment of losing the popular vote. One had to think of everything. So while the national media and political observers chuckled about Trump's outreach to Wisconsin, their heads were positively spinning at the thoroughness and genius of Hillary Clinton's team and the last-minute money it was pouring into Chicago and New Orleans.

This author of this book met with Donald Trump only days before the election, and he was positive, surprisingly humble, genuinely upbeat, and completely exhausted. His team at Trump Tower in Manhattan was sanguine.

Jared Kushner, Trump's son-in-law, was as calm as an inland lake on a moonlit night. He was the genius behind the social media voter identification process, and the man who was targeting the states that would make the difference in the Electoral College. Kellyanne Conway, Trump's campaign manager, was openly predicting victory, claiming that the Trump team's polling data showed them winning in Michigan, Ohio, and Pennsylvania. Journalists scoffed. Her cheerful predictions were ignored. Most news outlets would not even report her numbers.

THE LAST DAY

On November 7, 2016, the day before the election, Hillary Clinton arrived at the Westchester County airport in White Plains, New York. It had been home base for her since renting her Boeing 737 jet, with "Stronger Together" painted across its spine. Boeing had been good to the Clintons, and it had paid off. The company had gotten special treatment in sponsoring the World's Fair, with Hillary running interference as secretary of state. It had given $1 million to the Clinton Foundation, and Boeing executives had contributed heavily to her presidential campaign. When she became president, they expected a multibillion dollar contract for a new state-of-the-art Air Force One. It was how politics worked in America these days.

Clinton walked to the plane, wearing a red pantsuit, facetiming with her granddaughter, Charlotte, holding up her phone. "Do you see the big plane?" Hillary asked.[19]

That day, she and the plane full of staff and media visited Pittsburgh and Grand Rapids. Sometime on the ground in Michigan, she began to get poll numbers that told her the vote was going to be very close. Much closer than anyone had thought. Perhaps, heeding the warnings given her by her husband, she talked about the Bible in her speech in Grand Rapids. "A lot of people say we've got to heal our country, or as the Bible says, 'Repair the breach.' Because we have so much divisiveness right now."[20]

The Clinton campaign had a fireworks display set to launch over New York harbor, for 9:30 p.m., on election night. It was already paid for and the permits were in hand. But it might be too early to call the election at that point. It would be arrogant to celebrate before it was over. At 3:00 p.m., the Clinton camp called the Coast Guard to say they had canceled the fireworks.

That night, the plane flew on to Philadelphia, where in the evening Hillary held a rally with the president and Mrs. Barack Obama. Bruce Springsteen was there to sing. Most of the nation's celebrities supported Hillary Clinton. Hollywood was gaga over Hillary.

At midnight, the plane landed in Raleigh, North Carolina. It was now officially November 8, 2016, Election Day. Jon Bon Jovi was preforming. And yes, Lady Gaga had joined him onstage. They were singing "Livin' On a Prayer." It turned out that even Lady Gaga was gaga over Hillary. The crowd had been waiting all night for the candidate. She gave her last speech of the campaign. Knowing a little bit better what the rest of the country didn't yet know, she joked with Bon Jovi that she would be living on a prayer tonight as they waited election results.

On the flight back to White Plains, New York, Clinton staff were so euphoric that they were popping open champagne bottles.[21] Someone accessed an image of the upcoming *New York* magazine cover, the one featuring that ugly face of Trump and the bold stamp "Loser" emblazoned across it. The celebrating had already begun.

There was a huge crowd at the Westchester County airport in White Plains. Even though it was 3:30 a.m. and they were exhausted, Bill and Hillary Clinton worked the rope line while music blared: "This is our fight song, take-back-our-life song, prove-we-were-right song . . ."

They had done all they could do. The Clinton motorcade snaked home to Chappaqua.

On his last day of the campaign, Donald Trump had no celebrities to cheer him on, just some old rivals. Governor Chris Christie, Ben Carson, and the former Texas governor Rick Perry came along. It was the last marathon day of the 2016 presidential campaign. They were going to hit several key, normally Democratic-leaning states. A fool's errand, the experts said. But Trump insisted to a reporter, "I think we'll win Pennsylvania."[22] Nobody believed him.

In Reno, Nevada, the Secret Service thought they spotted a gun in the crowd, and Trump was rushed off the stage, returning to later announce, good-naturedly, to the crowd, "No one said it would be easy for us. But we will never be stopped."[23]

Early returns in Nevada showed Clinton doing better than expected, and this in a state that *Time* magazine insisted Trump had to win and Clinton could do without. Like other prognosticators, *Time* had declared "a structural advantage for Democrats in the Electoral College."[24]

Early signs showed the black vote was less than the previous cycle, which might help Trump in South Carolina and Ohio, but the Hispanic vote was way above expectations, which boded well for Clinton in Florida. It was a bad sign for Trump, but he would have none of it.

Trump's strategy of hitting normally Democratic states on this last trip did not alarm the Clinton campaign. In addition to Nevada, he would visit New Mexico, Virginia, Minnesota, Wisconsin, and Michigan. Those last two states, Wisconsin and Michigan, hadn't voted for a Republican since the 1980s.

On board the Clinton jet, Hillary's campaign manager, Robby Mook, mocked Trump's plans for the final day. "Looking at Trump's schedule versus our schedule is pretty emblematic of how we're approaching this strategically," he explained to journalists. "Trump is basically going everywhere. As far as I'm concerned, the more time he spends in Minnesota and Nevada the better."[25]

In Scranton, Pennsylvania, Trump was upbeat, "They say we're tied in Pennsylvania. I don't think so. I think we're going to blow them out tomorrow. Blow them out."[26]

CNN covered the quote, but then added its own commentary; it couldn't trust the viewers to hear Trump without a filter. It showed the latest CNN Poll of Polls that actually had Clinton over Trump 46 percent to 42 percent. "If Clinton can hang on to most states that have voted Democratic in recent elections," CNN said, "and add at most a couple of swing states, she will likely win the election."[27]

In its last poll, CNN not only had Clinton wining in Pennsylvania, she was also winning in the hotly contested states of North Carolina, Michigan, Florida, and New Hampshire.

Trump wowed the live audiences who would wait for him for hours, and he fought back through the television coverage, but sometimes it looked like he was boxing the wind. Everything he said was refashioned by the media filter. He kept insisting he would win.

"The miners are going to come out. The steelworkers who lost their jobs are going to come out. The women are going to come out big. It is all a phony deal. They are telling you a lot of phony stuff."[28]

When Trump publicly stated what early voting was showing and what would, in fact, later be shown to be true, that he was doing better than expected among Africa American voters, the *Chicago Tribune* felt the need to correct his conclusion for its readers, saying that Trump hadn't produced "any evidence," and then telling its readers that "black and Hispanic voters overwhelmingly favor Clinton"[29]—just in case anyone still didn't know that.

Meanwhile, the former Pennsylvania governor Ed Rendell, who was a Democrat, was trying to raise the warning to anyone who would listen. "Democrats in Michigan, Wisconsin, and Pennsylvania, if you heard it was over, if you thought those states were in the bag, don't believe it."[30]

In the United States, only Fox News and the ubiquitous Associated Press even bothered to cover Rendell's warning. It was also carried by the *China Daily* and the *Japan Times*. But the major American media had already picked the winner and they weren't interested in narratives that might confuse their audience.

According to one source inside Donald Trump's own inner circle, who wasn't expecting his man to win, the candidate himself was in total denial. "I think I'm going to win," Trump said on the flight home to New York City. He was exhausted but too excited to sleep.

CHAPTER 3

FORGOTTEN NO LONGER

The wise man does at once what the fool does finally.
—NICCOLÒ MACHIAVELLI

For the Clintons and the Trumps, a strange, eerie silence descended on the campaign. The curtain had come down. The television shows seemed to go blank with boredom. There was nothing to report. The pundits were out of gas. All across America, millions of people were now voting. In schoolhouses and fire stations. In libraries and churches. In the inner cities, in suburban neighborhoods, in small farm towns. People lined up and waited patiently. One by one. They would now have their say. Lady Gaga wouldn't decide for them. Karl Rove would not decide. Michael Moore could needle them, Barack Obama could lecture them, Sean Hannity could harangue them, but this was their vote, one by one, and they would speak now.

In the evening, the Clinton masses gathered at the Jacob Javits Center, with its thousands of panes of glass, symbolic of Hillary Clinton smashing through the glass ceiling that kept women from rising any higher.

The Clinton family and entourage were motorcaded into Manhattan and over to the Peninsula Hotel. On the ground, back at the Javits Center, some old feuds had resurfaced. It was natural to be nervous, and the need for discipline had finally relaxed. For many, there was nothing left to do. It was like a jet hitting a mountain;

they were used to work; how could they just suddenly come to a dead stop?

Throughout the campaign, competing factions had developed, and the closer the US inched toward Election Day, the more anxious some of the campaigners were becoming. People had been worried about who in the Clinton crowd would be going to the White House with Hillary. Who would be going to the transition team? Who would be dumped at the inaugural committee?

In the heat of battle, most of these folks had been shamed back into their workstations. "We'll talk later. Not now. We have to win first."

But now, with victory imminent, there were rumors about staffers getting placed, and there was a sense that the train was leaving the station. If not now, when? You said we would talk later. Well, now it's later.

Little Clinton groups at the Javits Center could be seen breathlessly engaged in conversations that they didn't want overheard. Spies within the various factions were in corners whispering into their cell phones to their masters back at the Peninsula hotel. But those pockets of tension represented only minor moments in the larger political theater. Victory was imminent. There would be plenty of room for everybody. They could feel the power, like a cloak, gently falling on their shoulders. No one doubted. It was coming. Hillary was going to win. She would be the first American woman president. They were all going to win. The world was going to win.

Further away from these clusters of insiders, the masses of less reverent and deferential Clinton supporters were also less uptight. They weren't going to the White House or the inaugural committee. There was a feeling among rank-and-file Hillary supporters that they had been very lucky, indeed, that Joe Biden or Elizabeth Warren had not gotten into the race. And very lucky that Donald Trump had won the draw of straws on the other side. Almost any other opponent might have beaten them.

Initial exit polls looked good for Hillary Clinton. MSNBC's Joe Scarborough called over to Trump Towers to track down Donald Trump's brilliant numbers man, his son-in-law Jared Kushner. "I know what the exit polls say," said Kushner, "I'm looking at our numbers. We're going to win Michigan. We're going to be competitive in Wisconsin. We're looking good in Minnesota. And we're going to win Florida."[1]

Nobody believed it. And nobody reported it either. Nobody wanted to look dumb. And nobody wanted to anger the Clintons.

Most people followed the unfolding election drama on television, with Fox News winning the ratings derby. But the constantly evolving website of the *New York Times* offered moments of tragedy or comedy, depending on your political preference.

At 4:00 p.m., November 8, 2016, the *Times'* website ran a headline, "In Final Hours of a Bitter Race, Voters Get Their Say." It featured a piece by Ross Douthat suggesting, "My prediction: A decisive win for the candidate who actually has a campaign." Douthat had predicted a Trump loss so often and so condescendingly that a *Gawker* page had been created to list the numbered occasions.[2]

At 5:26 p.m., an alleged Clinton spy inside the Trump campaign headquarters leaked some of the first data. Clinton was beating Trump in Florida by three. She was beating him in Colorado by three. She was winning in Wisconsin by five, Nevada by one, and Ohio by one. The only toss-up state looking good for Trump was Iowa, where he was up by one. And this news was allegedly coming from data inside Trump's own war room.[3]

At 6:30 p.m. the *Times'* website had morphed into a new headline, "First Polls Close in a Divided Race, Marked by Doubts." Indiana and Kentucky were called for Trump. Vermont for Clinton. No surprises there. The Ross Douthat prediction was still on the front page.

Clinton leaders, who were scattered across Manhattan, began to get messages about a meeting at the headquarters hotel at 9:30 p.m. Some were at the Javits Center, but most were at dinner in restaurants all over the city. Some were at rooftop parties, celebrating a moment in history.

At 7:22 p.m., CNN reported that Clinton was leading in Florida, 49 to 47 percent.[4] That was big. There were several ways that Clinton could win in the Electoral College without Florida, but Trump had to win the Sunshine State or he would be out.

At 8:45 p.m. the *New York Times* site reported, "Clinton Does Well in Northeast, Trump in South and Midwest." Its polls showed the battleground state of Florida now leaning to Trump, but Ohio, Pennsylvania, and Michigan were all leaning to Clinton. For some reason the Ross Douthat column was pulled. Florida must have spooked the *Times'* editors.

At 9:18 p.m., "Razor-Thin Margins for Candidates in Battleground States." Florida, Ohio, North Carolina, Michigan, and Wisconsin were all now leaning to Trump. The *New York Times* still had Pennsylvania in Hillary Clinton's column. But Wisconsin was a surprise. Many pundits agreed that North Carolina was the state where Hillary could stop Trump and retain her path to victory.

At 9:30 p.m., the Clinton leaders met at the Peninsula hotel on Fifth Avenue. It was only a block from Trump Tower. A source to the *New York Post* claimed that the Clinton team had picked the hotel because "she wants to stick it up his nose when she wins."[5] But one Clinton participant at the meeting that night described the atmosphere like a funeral. Some left early. Some wandered back to the Javits Center on the West Side.

At that exact moment, Donald Trump and his family entered

the campaign war room at Trump Towers. They had just returned from voting, where a crowd of New Yorkers had roundly booed and jeered them. The crowd of workers in Trump Tower gave them a standing ovation. Eric Trump, the thirty-two-year-old son of the candidate, tweeted a picture of the Trump family, along with his running mate, Indiana governor Mike Pence, and his family. They were watching the returns. Donald Trump, with a big smile on his face, was tenderly hugging one of his grandchildren from behind.

The war room was large and spartan, with white walls covered by big screens. There was a Trump poster, an American flag, and another wall of glass looking out on New York City. It was crowded with volunteers and paid workers. They were sitting at tables, busy on laptops, where they were tracking social media. One floor below was the Trump campaign data center, where they tracked precinct-by-precinct the election returns from across the country. A few minutes later, Trump himself tweeted a picture. His wife, Melania, joined them, and there was ten-year-old Barron, in a suit and tie, standing next to his father.

At 10:30 p.m., the *New York Times* website reported, "Trump Showing Unexpected Strength in Battleground States."

Then, at 10:50 p.m., the unthinkable. The headline said, "Trump Takes Ohio, Building Nationwide Momentum." Ohio was the state that always picked the presidential winner. It was one of the battle-ground states that Trump had to win.

After the first positive reports, there was some troubling data for Hillary Clinton. She was not doing as well with black voters as Obama did. Understood. It would have been arrogant to have thought that she would. Evangelicals who had stayed home for Romney, a Mormon, were returning en masse. Okay. No surprise. Late deciders were edging toward Trump, 47 percent to 42 percent.

Not catastrophic. Blame it on Comey. But then, the rural vote was much bigger than the Clinton camp's computer models had anticipated. Hmmm. Who lived in rural America these days?

The music from the Javits Center blared. "This is our fight song, take-back-our-life song, prove-we-were-right song . . ." Some Clinton loyalists were getting irritated by the repetition of the song.

And then, the first signs of concern. Clinton was losing to college-educated whites. Huh? She had always led with this group. What did that mean? And why did Trump get Ohio so quickly? And then the shattering reality began to dawn. It was not certain that Hillary Clinton would win this. She may lose. It would be close. It would be a long night.

Anatoly Lazarev, the Washington, DC bureau chief for Channel One Russian TV, had made the trek to Manhattan, hoping to get credentials into the Trump campaign headquarters at the massive Hilton Hotel. The Russian people were transfixed by the election. Clinton was blaming Russia for leaking emails from inside her campaign. Trump had complemented Russian president Vladimir Putin, saying he was a leader.

At Trump headquarters, in spite of their press credentials, the TV crew from Russia's largest network was turned away. This was no time to be giving the Russians favors. So Anatoly and his team watched Fox News on a giant television screen on the street outside the Trump election-night headquarters at the Hilton.

Later they moved with crowds down the street to Times Square, where the ever-present Fox News still dominated the streets on big screens and picked up the seamless coverage. On their cell phones and back at their New York City offices, they kept checking with CNN, but soon decided that the network was withholding information. Sometimes they delayed a minute or two before calling a state for Trump or Clinton, sometimes up to ten minutes. Both CNN and Fox were getting their raw data information from the same source, the Associated Press.

"There was a feeling that things were not going as expected," said Lazarev. "That history was being made."[6]

11:10 p.m., the *New York Times'* website headline announced, "Trump Takes North Carolina, Building Nationwide Momentum."

The newsroom at CBS turned sullen and quiet. Pundits who had been alive with theory and explanations seemed worn down, as if coming off of a caffeine high.

11:40 p.m. the *New York Times* announced "Trump Takes Florida, Closing In on a Stunning Upset."

A story later appeared online, claiming that by midnight, candidate Hillary Clinton was drunk and had launched into a profanity filled tirade at her staff. The source for the story was Todd Kincannon, a radio host, who appeared on *InfoWars* with Alex Jones. Kincannon claimed that the story came from a source at CNN.[7] But the story was immediately shot down by critics and labeled as "fake news."[8]

Still, the story persisted. Shortly after the Kincannon report a similar account appeared in the *American Spectator*, claiming that Hillary "began yelling, screaming obscenities, and pounding the furniture. She picked up objects and threw them at attendants and staff. She was in an uncontrollable rage."[9]

The author of this book and his own research team were eventually able to speak to an insider who worked for the Clintons for years and a Secret Service agent present at the Peninsula Hotel on election night. The Clinton insider confirmed that while acting outwardly calm and gracious, with a friendly smile in public, Hillary Clinton could be easily triggered into uncontrollable rages when in private. They claimed that Bill Clinton seemed to go into a shell at such moments and was completely quiet, not speaking or touching her in any way.[10]

The Secret Service agent, present for hours at the hotel, confirmed that there was smashing of glass and long periods of heated shouting inside the Clinton rooms but that he, personally, had not seen Mrs. Clinton throw anything. He said that, at times, prominent guests were coming and going and that the brief glimpses inside the rooms confirmed that there were heated discussions underway and that Mrs. Clinton was upset.[11]

At 12:25 a.m., the Fox News reporter Shannon Bream talked to Jason Miller inside the war room at Trump Tower. Boxes of gourmet donuts were out on the tables, but the results were just as gratifying. "We're seeing good things in North Carolina," Miller said, "in Michigan, and in Florida this morning."[12]

As each critical state was announced, the Trump children, and campaign workers, shouted with delight and slapped each other's hands in high-five salutes. The place was going wild. Melania was smiling. Donald Trump was silent, even sullen.

Then, according to a source, he and Melania went alone, upstairs, to their private apartments. They wanted to share a quiet time of reflection alone, to savor the moment as a husband and wife.[13] At 2:15 a.m., Donald Trump and his family left the tower and headed out to the celebration at the Hilton Hotel.

The crowds at the Jacob Javits Center were waiting for Hillary Clinton. At 2:29 a.m., Clinton's campaign chairman, John Podesta, showed up to tell them to go home. "It's been a long night and it's been a long campaign. But I can say, we can wait a little longer can't we?"[14] The crowd roared its assent, even while tears were streaming down faces.

"They're still counting votes and some states are too close to call, so we're not going to have anything more to say tonight. So listen.

Listen to me," Podesta implored, "everybody should head home. Get some sleep. We'll have more to say tomorrow."

They knew. They were going to lose. They wanted to get everybody out before the announcement. They didn't want to produce Hillary. She wasn't going to make an appearance. But the crowd was slow to move. Hillary's fans stood outside and watched big screens wherever they could find them on the streets.

At 2:40 a.m., Bret Baier of Fox News announced that "Donald Trump will be the forty-fifth president of the United States, winning the most unreal, surreal election we have ever seen."[15]

Bret Baier's words were tight but infinitely descriptive. Some said they would be forever remembered in history, as in "Where were you when Brett Baier called the election?" His words would be like Russ Hodges's description of the Bobby Thompson home run that won the pennant for the Giants in 1951 and was later pronounced "The shot heard 'round the world." Or Neil Armstrong's landing on the moon in 1969: "One small step for [a] man, one giant leap for mankind."

According to news sources, CNN's workhorse anchor Wolf Blitzer was "visibly stunned" as a fellow anchorwoman, Dana Bash, passed word to him that Hillary Clinton had just conceded to Donald Trump by phone.

"If Hillary Clinton has conceded, that is dramatic," said Blitzer to his television audience. "That is a dramatic development, Dana, and to hear the words 'president elect,' we haven't yet projected that—but you're saying Clinton made a formal call to Donald Trump to concede?"[16]

Not until 2:48 a.m., with Donald Trump and his family walking onstage at the Hilton Hotel ballroom, did CNN let its viewers know that he had won the election.

At 2:50 a.m., the evolving *New York Times* website was head-lined simply, "Trump Triumphs."

Little knots of Clinton supporters were still holding vigil at the Javits Center as attendants tried to sweep them out of the corners and toward the doors. Some were openly sobbing. Others were hold-ing each other.

Inside the Hilton Hotel, waiting for the president elect, trium-phant Trump supporters, hoarse from cheering, grew suddenly quiet as they waited. A soft, barely audible, chorus broke out on one side of the ballroom. "God bless America, land that I love . . ." And the singing voices swept across the giant room where eventually everyone was singing softly. "Stand beside her and guide her . . ."[17] And now there were some tears in this room too. Tears of joy. "God bless America, my home sweet home."

It was over.

THE MAINSTREAM MEDIA REACTS

Donald Trump as president? The corporate media was incredulous. Some of their experienced journalists who had remained cool under live gunfire in the Middle East, who had stoically reported the trag-edy of 9/11, now came apart. They had remained professional with the twin towers collapsing behind them, tragically taking thousands of lives in their wake, just over their shoulders. But they couldn't remain detached from this story.

For years, they had denied political bias and ridiculed critics who suggested the idea. Hard facts showed it clearly. In 2008, for example, the Democratic Party received donations of $1,020,816, given by more than 1,160 employees representing the major tele-vision networks: NBC, CBS, and ABC. The Republican Party was the recipient of $142,863, which came from 193 donors employed at those networks.[18] In October, 2016, a leaked email would show open collaboration between the Clinton campaign and journalists representing many of the most prominent American media outlets.[19]

Now the network journalists embraced this bias, openly, on air, clearly revealing the political agenda of their corporate ownership. It was out on full display. There was no longer the need for pretense. It was almost a status symbol. We are hurt by this more than you.

At 12:54 a.m., Rachel Maddow of MSNBC told her audience, "You're awake, by the way. You're not having a terrible, terrible dream. Also, you're not dead and you haven't gone to hell. This is your life now. This is our election now. This is us. This is our country. It's real."[20] But she looked like she wasn't sure.

At 1:40 a.m., Richard Engel of NBC said, "Let's just cut to the chase. Assuming that he does win, the people I am speaking to think that it is absolutely catastrophic. That is, catastrophic for the United States. Catastrophic for our position in the world. It emboldens our enemies and adversaries. It makes our allies terrified that we aren't going to be their allies anymore."[21]

Engel described a dysfunctional government, with Trump fighting with the Supreme Court and eventually tied up with an impeachment trial. But that was, as Engel himself put it, "assuming he does win." It was already over, even his own network had called it, but Engel, one of the world's premier investigative reporters, still couldn't accept it.

Chuck Todd appeared on MSNBC a few minutes later and was among the few respected, on-air journalists to report the story straight. Todd instantly saw the reality of what it meant. "He is going to feel like he got a mandate," said Todd. "We are going to treat him like he got a mandate, and for one reason, he blew all of our predictions and models, and you name it, out of [the] water. He is going to feel unshackled."[22]

CNN offered the harshest assessment. Some of its team had already been caught favoring Hillary Clinton earlier in the campaign by sending her debate questions in advance.[23] During the night of reporting, they had delayed passing negative Clinton data to their viewers. The suspicion was that executives were fearful the numbers would depress voter turnout in later states.

Van Jones told his CNN audience, "I have enough class to say that when you outdo expectations, good for you, but there's another side of this. People have talked about a miracle, I'm hearing about a nightmare. It's hard to be a parent tonight for a lot of us. You tell your kids, 'Don't be a bully,' 'Don't be a bigot,' but then you have this outcome. You have people putting their children to bed and they're afraid of breakfast. They're afraid of 'How do I explain this to my children?'"[24]

He went on to describe it as a "whitelash": "It was a whitelash against a changing country. It was a whitelash against a black president, in part. . . . And that's the part where the pain comes."[25]

Jena Friedman, appearing on the Stephen Colbert show, looked into the camera teary eyed and said, "Get your abortions now. Because we're going to be fucked."[26]

Martha Raddatz of ABC, who incredibly enough had been a moderator for one of the debates, almost broke down and cried as she read a quote from Clinton's vice presidential running mate, Senator Tim Kaine.[27] When video copies of the moment went viral online, the network and Ms. Raddatz both denied what everyone thought they actually saw with their own eyes.

Chris Matthews of MSNBC said, "You know, she won every debate by all standards. Best ad campaign, best ground game. This is a shot against meritocracy, I think. Because she merited everything and the normal way you standardize these things, she did what you're supposed to do to win and Trump came in around the corner."[28]

Matthews was interrupted by another reporter, Kasie Hunt, who seemed to be in deep grief and was obviously rattled. "I don't think we should overlook the human element here either. If Hillary should win this thing? I mean it's a devastating end." She clearly meant, "If Hillary should lose this thing."[29]

Fox News, which had, at times during the last two years, been both Donald Trump's friend and enemy, was remarkably phlegmatic. Its anchors and commentators seemed to be the only adults in the room. Criticized in the past for offering too much opinion, Fox News and its little sister, Fox Business Network, were now offering viewers the most compelling, comprehensive, and detached election-night coverage available. Everyone else had emotionally shut down. They were no longer reporting; they were themselves the story.

At one point Tucker Carlson on Fox News said simply, "This is a reaction against the people in charge."[30] It was a crisp summation, and it was as close as Fox got to an opinion that night.

Before signing off in the morning, Lawrence O'Donnell of MSNBC concluded that "America is crying tonight; I'm not sure how much of America, but a very, very significant portion, and I mean literally crying."[31]

Brian Williams offered a gentle reminder that Donald Trump had, in fact, been a creation of sorts of his own parent company, NBC, which had hosted Trump's popular television program *The Apprentice*. It was an intriguing argument. And only the tip of the iceberg. Should the media itself share some of the blame? Had they given Trump a free ride through the Republican primaries? Betting that given the choice between Hillary and Donald, the American people would be forced to choose Hillary? In spite of the scandals?

The next day it got only worse. Jonathan Alter of MSNBC told his television audience that "decency lost last night." He then added some reassurance: "From slavery to Nazism, we have faced challenges before."[32]

The *New York Post*, which during the campaign had featured revealing pictures of Melania Trump from her earlier modeling days, now tripped all over itself, declaring this was "a win for the little guy over the elite."[33] It was as if it was part of the revolution, in the streets with a pitchfork.

"I DON'T LOSE VERY OFTEN"[34]

Soon after the television networks had declared him the winner, Donald Trump's motorcade wound its way to the campaign's election-night headquarters at the Hilton. Notwithstanding CNN's bewilderment, Hillary Clinton had, indeed, called him and conceded.

At 3:00 a.m., Wednesday morning, November 9, 2016, Donald Trump spoke for the first time to the nation as its president elect.

"First, I want to thank my parents, who are looking down on me right now," he said. "Great people. I've learned so much from them. They were wonderful in every regard. I had truly great parents."[35]

His father, Fred, had been a perfectionist. A man who drove his sons. A man who never backed down and taught his sons to stand up for themselves. To fight back if it was necessary, and it was always, eventually, necessary. He had taught them to embrace competition.

Freddy, the eldest son, had failed to live up to those exacting standards, or so the family legend went. But Donald had responded. He had succeeded where his older sibling had not. He got the message. He wouldn't back down. And in time, the father, Fred, recognized that he had succeeded, he had passed the torch.

The old man, Fred Trump, had always wanted the family name to mean something. He fussed about his reputation with customers, with subcontractors, with the banks. He wanted to be remembered. He had once proudly lifted signs that proclaimed "Trump Market" at the grocery store on Jamaica Avenue and Seventy-Eighth Street in Queens. And for a moment, some thought they had seen tears of pride in his eyes. But within a year the store was sold and the sign was taken down.

Yet the father eventually lived to see the rise of the son and to see the name of the family established. Philip Weiss wrote a piece for the *New York Times Magazine* about Donald Trump driving Fred around properties in Manhattan, the father listening to the son's dreams of what would be bought and sold and what would be built. But Fred was slipping into Alzheimer's.[36]

One day in the 1990s Donald had driven Fred down Fifth Avenue and announced he had bought the Empire State Building, or at least the land underneath it—a proud moment for the family.

"That's a tall building, isn't it?" Fred Trump asked. "How many apartments are in that building?"[37] He was already gone, and it was a sad realization for the son.

Carefully, tenderly, Donald Trump cared for the tough old man who had taught him how to survive in the mean streets of New York City. One night in June 1999, Donald visited his father in the hospital. They were alone together, just the two of them. And then later, when Donald was ensconced back in the Trump Tower, in the clouds above Manhattan in his luxury suite, the message came through that Fred had just died. The old man, ninety-three years old, had passed shortly after Donald had left the hospital.

No one was nearby. No wife. No children. All alone, in the clouds above Manhattan, Donald Trump wept. He would describe it as the saddest moment of his life.

So, in the early hours of November 9, 2016, in the New York Hilton ballroom, with thousands of people cheering him, surrounded by his family and the world watching on television, scrambling to find its equilibrium, the president-elect, Donald J. Trump, was understandably thinking about his father. The name that the father had once raised to the top of a grocery store in Queens was now emblazoned in gold on Manhattan skyscrapers, the sun reflecting its golden glory at every New York City sunrise and sunset.

Look at it now, Dad. Would you look at it now?

Donald Trump was uncharacteristically soft and understated in his victory speech. He was generous to the Clintons. He called for America to unite. And he paid homage to those vast numbers of poor in rural and small-town America who had come back to the polls in record numbers and so upset the expectations of the nation's corporate and media elite. They were even now being vilified and disparaged by television pundits.

They had voted twice for Barack Obama but now were called a "whitelash" because they had not voted for a Democrat again.[38]

Trump leaned into the microphone and spoke in a soft baritone. "The forgotten men and women of our country," he said, "will be forgotten no longer."[39]

The New York City audience cheered wildly. But they also cheered in Appelton, Wisconsin, in Kalamazoo, Michigan, in Bethlehem, Pennsylvania, and in Marianna, Florida, on the panhandle.

The experts were wrong. For most voters in those crucial battleground states, the election was not about black and white. It was not about how we should treat our daughters and sisters and mothers. It was about survival.

The American dream was dead. Eighty to ninety percent of everything Americans now bought was purchased from only ten giant companies.[40] And all those hundreds of television channels?

They were owned by only six companies. The poor were getting poorer and the rich were getting richer at an alarming rate.[41] Not only was the middle class disappearing, even many of the rich were disappearing. There was now only room for the superrich. The publicly proclaimed 1 percent.

Protest movements had sprung up on the left and the right. In 2012, Ron Paul supporters in the Republican Party had decried the increasing power of the banks, including the Federal Reserve. In 2016, Bernie Sanders supporters agitated against the "oligarchy" and Wall Street tycoons.

It was no longer an argument about left and right. That was becoming increasingly irrelevant. Now it was about insiders and outsiders. Donald Trump, the billionaire, one of the richest men in America, was ironically seen as an outsider. And now he was threatening to open the door to all kinds of new people to come in. Hillary Clinton, with almost unanimous support of the mainstream media, the newspapers, the major corporations, the Hollywood celebrities, the Wall Street banks, the multinational corporations, was considered by many to be the insider.

This election was about making American great again. One candidate claimed he could do that. The others said it had never stopped being great. It you liked where you were now, you had your candidate. If you didn't, you had no choice but the flamboyant businessman with the outsize promises.

A year before, in the middle of the campaign, when he still hadn't won the nomination, Donald Trump was told that some of his rivals were predicting he would soon fade away. They were planning to pick up the pieces after he left the stage. They only had to wait it out. He would lose.

Trump seemed fascinated by this, and then a little puzzled. "I've been winning all my life," he said. "Like this property. I bought it six, seven years ago. I bought it for a steal. . . . I could sell it for any-thing. I'm not selling, but I could sell it for anything. I always win. My whole life is about winning. I don't lose often. I almost never lose."[42]

PART II
_____

THE COLLAPSE
OF THE HOUSE
OF CLINTON

CHAPTER 4

WHY ANOTHER CLINTON PRESIDENCY?

It's not what happens to you, but how
you react to it that matters.

—Epictetus

Bill Clinton tells a story about how he proposed to Hillary two times before she finally said yes. And then he told her "she was the most talented politician of her generation and should go run for office instead of getting hitched to [me]."

"Oh my God," Hillary responded. "I'll never run for office. I'm too aggressive, and nobody will ever vote for me."[1]

Bill Clinton's first appearance on the national stage was a disaster. In 1988, as the young governor of Arkansas, he was allotted fifteen minutes to speak at the Democratic National Convention in Atlanta. His assignment? Place in nomination the name of Governor Michael Dukakis of Massachusetts as his party's choice for president. It was a great opportunity. Four years earlier, New York's governor, Mario Cuomo, had electrified the delegates and established himself as a national figure when he made the nominating speech.

Clinton's monotonous speech droned on for what seemed like hours. Television cameras began to show members of the audience sleeping. Some delegates on the floor began to defiantly boo him.

More than one pundit intoned that the little-known governor of Arkansas had just ended his political career. But young Governor Clinton was thick skinned. He kept smiling. When he uttered the words, "In closing," the audience erupted into sarcastic cheers. He finished his marathon speech and ignored the catcalls. Four years later, Bill Clinton was president of the United States.

There's a story behind that Bill Clinton speech. It was long because the Dukakis campaign had kept giving him new things to say. Some decided that the Dukakis campaign was purposely trying to sink a rival.

The life of Bill Clinton is one of perpetual cycle. Defeat followed by victory, followed yet again by defeat. Each time the loss seems ever more fatal and career ending, making the successive triumph even more transcendent and breathtaking. If one were to make a dark comparison, it would be to the life of a drug addict, knowing highs and lows that the rest of us will never know. A more positive comparison would be that of the artist, whose work is sometimes genius and applauded while at other times panned. Only, in this case, we are not talking about art, and the drug we are talking about is power.

Not surprisingly, the Clinton cycle is perfectly mirrored in his private life as well. It explains his unspeakable, presumably ongoing relationships with various members of the opposite sex, a subject that journalists don't like to touch publicly but can't get enough of privately.

During the time that President Clinton's White House scandal over Monica Lewinsky was reaching its nadir, I received a call from the then governor, and future president, George W. Bush of Texas. He told me about a lady friend from Richardson who had stopped by to visit him and had recommended that he meet with a prominent Protestant preacher.

"Hibulls," Bush said to me, naming the preacher. "Hibulls. You ever heard of this guy?"

"Bill Hybels?" I asked.

"Yeah, that's it, Hybels," Bush said.

"Yes," I answered. "He's a great contact for you. Had dinner with him once. He's a very popular pastor from Illinois."

"Yeah, that's him. Seems like a nice guy.

"Anyway, he says, 'Governor, before we get started, you need to know something. Shortly after his inauguration, William Jefferson Clinton called me and asked me to fly into Washington to counsel him.

"And I told him, 'I can't do that, Mr. President.'

"And he asked, 'Why not?'

"And I said, 'Because I have to have several hours a month with anyone I counsel.'

"And the president said, 'No problem. Let's do it.'

"'So every month I have been flying into the White House to counsel Bill Clinton."

Bush chuckled at his own story. "I told Hybels, 'I'll bet he was the most conflicted person you ever counseled!'

"He said, 'Well, yes, he is very compartmentalized.' That's how he put it. 'Compartmentalized.'"

We were both fascinated by the story. What was going on? It was publicly known that Bill Clinton was being counseled by three prominent clergymen. The White House had acknowledged as much. There was the Reverend Gordon MacDonald of Grace Chapel in Lexington, Massachusetts; Tony Campolo, the popular Baptist writer, speaker, and Christian sociologist; and the Reverend J. Philip Wogaman, pastor of the Foundry United Methodist Church, which was close to the White House and the church the Clintons often attended. The White House had announced this arrangement. Had there been counseling sessions even before Lewinsky? From the beginning? Was Bill Hybels the fourth man?

A few days later, Governor Bush gave me the green light to send him other prominent religious leaders. He was focused on his reelection as governor of Texas, but there was no harm in meeting leaders of influence who were willing to make the trek down to Austin, Texas, to meet the man who might be the next president—as long as we kept it under the radar.

I called Don Argue, a past president of the National Association of Evangelicals and a man who could be an important ally for the governor.

Argue was evasive, which surprised me. When I persisted, he opened up: "Look, I have been counseling President Clinton now for a long time. From the very beginning, before Lewinsky, I have been going in for regular meetings. I'm not so sure if it is a good idea to meet with Bush too."

I laughed out loud. Another one?

This experience left me genuinely puzzled. On the one hand, I had worked as a political consultant for years and knew how sophisticated and convincing a politician could be when reaching out to an important constituency. Both the president and the target want the seduction to work. The target wants to believe that he is important and that his input is real, and the president, who needs and cares for the person in question, has no reasons to disabuse him of this notion.

But I also knew that there were easier ways to accomplish the same thing. Time was the one commodity that a president had in short supply. As special assistant to the president in the George H. W. Bush White House, I had helped build relationships with leaders of influence by creating events and opportunities for correspondence. This had included religious leaders as well. Sometimes a cardinal would call and ask for my help to write a letter to the president. And when the letter came in, the president would ask me to draft a response. Thus the president's relationship with the cardinal of New York or Boston or a televangelist like Robert Schuller from California was ratcheted up higher and higher, while I was basically writing letters back and forth to myself. There was some sense of satisfaction in knowing that when the two leaders met face to face they would be much closer because of what had been written. And, of course, both busy and important leaders would have appreciated having the process helped along.

The same formula applied to public figures in law enforcement and education, and among leaders of veterans' organizations. But such meetings, when they did happen individually, seldom lasted more than five minutes in the Oval Office. The real work was done by staff.

In contrast, it appeared that Bill Clinton was meeting with these spiritual counselors for hours at a time. Alone. Separately. And monthly. If it were solely a political device, it could have been accomplished more efficiently.

Even before the Monica Lewinsky scandal, even before the White House had announced that the president would be tapping three prominent clergymen to provide him with personal counsel, here was a list of prominent religious leaders, each thinking that he was the anointed one, coming into the White House monthly? Taking up hours of the president's time, alone? With no one there to witness what was said? Was it wise?

Let us assume that these sessions were very real, that they were not political devices but at least partially motivated by the president's need for help. Then they were even more dangerous, even more unwise. Bill Clinton was not only taking great risks in his promiscuous sexual activities, he was taking great risks in his treatment. Unknown to the public, these sessions had been ongoing from the beginning of his presidency and throughout the unfolding scandals.

In his study *Sexual Addiction: Diagnosis and Treatment*, Dr. Aviel Goodman identifies sexual addiction by two telltale manifestations.[2] One, the subject experiences a recurrent failure to control his behavior. And two, he continues the behavior even when it is harmful and self-destructive.

Gennifer Flowers, the object of one of Bill Clinton's earlier extramarital affairs, described a moment after sex when Clinton stood against the wall crying. She said that she had the sense that he was feeling guilty. If so, it would not last long. The Clintons would at first deny Flowers' story and then hire a detective, who said his assignment was to impugn Ms. Flowers' "character and veracity until she is destroyed beyond all recognition."[3]

Flowers, who as far as we know, had the longest love relationship with Clinton outside of his own wife, had her own theory about what drove Bill Clinton. "I think that Bill was addicted to the chase, not the sex act itself but the actual conquering of all those women."[4]

Given the length of these White House counseling sessions, and the fact that some of them preceded the Lewinsky affair, there is every reason to believe that Bill Clinton's inner conflict over his infidelities was genuine. Keep in mind that while a long list of these women are now public figures, their stories well known, many more were watching from the sidelines, and still are not willing to come forward. They watched Bill and Hillary Clinton and their White House, with allies in the mainstream media, successfully savage the reputations of any woman who would dare to claim abuse or misconduct.

How do we know that these women are still out there? In 1994, the independent counsel Robert B. Fiske Jr. called on Arkansas state trooper L. D. Brown to testify in the Whitewater investigation. Brown was not one of the original state troopers who had come forward with information about the Clinton sex scandals in Arkansas. He could not be classified as a "Clinton hater" or a partisan. He had been subpoenaed to testify and had no choice. Under the threat of perjury, the trooper started answering questions, offering a fascinating insight into the dark, underground, otherwise hidden world of Bill Clinton on the prowl. Brown admitted to helping the governor procure more than one hundred women. "Certainly not all of those were successful," said Brown, "but in terms of making approaches, yeah, sure, at least one hundred." Brown said that most of these were "just having a good time." But he admitted that some bordered on sexual harassment.[5] And Brown was with the Clintons for only a few years.

According to such testimony, the victims of Bill Clinton were not a healthy ballroom full, who could appear together on a television news show, like those accusing the comedian Bill Cosby. These women could fill the pages of a university yearbook. There is no question that given the great opportunity to do good, Bill Clinton took extraordinary risks in pursuing his sex addiction, even after he entered the White House and the whole nation was on to him. Hillary took risks too, using her power and influence to silence or frighten off any woman who might dare to speak up.

Notice that Trooper Brown insisted that many of the sexual encounters were unsuccessful. This dangerous cycle of rejection and conquest, spurring more of the same, gives us a psychological template that is predictable and can run parallel from Bill Clinton's private sex life to his public career. Each new conquest represents such a euphoric moment, such a great reward, that it guarantees an attempt to duplicate the feat again, eventually, someday, somehow. And yet for every attempted conquest there are rejections and failures and public humiliation, which cause such remorse and pain that only another conquest can provide the remedy.

"Humiliation" is the exact word that Hillary Clinton used to describe her feeling over her husband's speech at the Democratic National Convention in 1988.[6] Thus Bill Clinton was openly ridiculed on the floor of the convention that year, only to win the presidency four years later, against all odds. Remember that, ironically, in 1987 Senator Gary Hart, the brilliant Democratic front-runner, was taken out of the contest by a sex scandal; four years later, Bill Clinton crossed the finish line with dozens of stories of sexual misconduct carried on his back.

Which brings us to the presidency of Hillary Clinton.

It had to be.

It was an idea born in the midst of the Clintons' greatest defeat: impeachment.

It is all well and good for Bill and Hillary to act confident and to blame the impeachment on "a vast right-wing conspiracy." To say that it was the work of Republicans. Was not the vote strictly partisan? But none of that justifies impeachment.

Defenders of Richard Nixon point out that Lyndon Johnson did the same things. Victor Lasky wrote a bestseller, *It Didn't Start with Watergate*.[7] Nixon apologists say that the Democrats spied on the Republicans too. That Nixon did not order the Watergate break-in. That the cover-up was not about power but about compassion for the families of the burglars involved.

They say that Nixon opened China. That he was brilliant. That he got us out of the Vietnam War. That he was one of the world's preeminent geopolitical giants. A man of history.

Much of that is true, but the stark fact remains that Richard Nixon resigned. He lost the presidency. How can he be called a great president when he couldn't even hold his office?

Well, it was the fault of the media, his defenders persist. They treated him differently than they treated others. But a president cannot blame his failure on changing rules and changing circumstances. He must anticipate those changing rules. He must anticipate those changing circumstances.

Bill and Hillary Clinton knew that they could never erase the impeachment. The argument that it was only political, the deed of cruel Republican partisans, was an argument that would convince friends and supporters. It would work with some in the corporate media who would benefit by their return to power. It would work with those in contemporary academia who shared their ideological persuasion. But it would not work with history. Their legacy was in shreds.

If the impeachment was indeed partisan, how could they explain why it hadn't happened to other Democratic presidents? Why not Jimmy Carter, whose unpopular administration had seen double-digit inflation and had lost the confidence of his own party? And had the Boston–New York–Washington social corridor contemptuous of his quaint devotion to his religion?[8] Or Lyndon Johnson, who served when riots erupted across America with entire neighborhoods in 120 cities burned to the ground, and tanks patrolling the streets of the nation's capital?[9] Or John F. Kennedy, who, at the time, was a despised Catholic politician in a White Anglo-Saxon Protestant world. He had his own sexual improprieties. His campaign had allegedly taken money from the Mafia. Or Harry Truman, who had the lowest approval rating in history? Why wasn't Reagan impeached over lying about Nicaragua? Or George H. W. Bush over Iran-Contra? Only one other president in all of American history had ever been impeached: Andrew Johnson. Nothing would wipe out the stain against Bill Clinton.

Except?

Another presidency.

Having tasted the bitter defeat of impeachment, the Clintons had a need for 2016 that transcended any ambition that Jeb Bush, Joe Biden, Elizabeth Warren, Donald Trump, or any other public figure could bring to the table. They needed the presidency more than any of the others did. Knowing its power, and its unique value for them personally, for their legacy, they could suffer through any pain, any humiliation, endure any privation, to get it.

Were the odds high? Sure—which explains the great risks taken by the Clinton Foundation, eventually accepting donations from almost anyone, representing any nation or corporation. It would be criticized if it took $10,000 so it might as well take $10 million. Looking back, it is possible that almost any credible Democrat who had entered the 2016 presidential race could have beaten Hillary Clinton and won the party's nomination.

Joe Biden? Elizabeth Warren? Every effort was made to keep them out. Every favor extended. Every powerful ally brought to bear, to warn them away. In the end no one needed the presidency as badly as Bill and Hillary Clinton did—and no one was willing to do what they would do to get it.

A hundred years from now, a ten-year-old schoolboy would memorize the names of the presidents. And when he got to those repetitive names—Bush, Clinton, Bush, Obama, Clinton—he would ask the question: If Bill Clinton was so bad that he was impeached, why did the American people elect his wife only a few years later?

Exactly.

Because the impeachment was just what the Clintons had claimed all along. It was political. It wasn't deserved. It wasn't real. Someday, a ten-year-old would be able to see it.

Thus the words and deeds of the Clintons take on new meaning as we explore how and why the idea of a second presidency became critical to the legacy of the first. How each rejection leading up to impeachment spurred the need for a new conquest until a second presidency itself became the only solution.

In the coming pages, we will see how the presidential campaign of Hillary Clinton emerged from the primordial swamp of Arkansas politics and how the seeds of her ultimate defeat were planted in those years. How she would reach spectacular heights. And how it would all slip away.

And Bill Clinton? Only hours before the election, Hillary was laughing with the press about what he should be called. "First dude?"

There have been married women heads of state whose male spouses walked a step behind. There was even once a president-dictator in Argentina whose wife was more popular than he. India saw a daughter of a prime minister rise to power. But there has never been anything quite like Bill Clinton as "first dude." There has never been a man who ran the most powerful nation on earth whose wife, only a few years later, would do the same thing, with him standing at her side.

The rejection by a potential lover, Paula Jones, repulsed by Bill Clinton's allegedly crude, unwanted advances taking place in a hotel room in Arkansas, with no witness present, eventually led to perjury and the impeachment of Bill Clinton. And impeachment was now leading to the very public political return to power for the Clintons.

It was a vicious, terrible, fascinating sequence of events that attracted as much as it repelled. It was a repetitive cycle of darkness and sunshine, private and public. As America approached the election in 2016 there was a feeling by many that maybe something good would now come out of it. And a feeling by others that the election was an ongoing progression of inevitable events that would be played over again in the second coming of a Clinton White House.

CHAPTER 5

AN EARLY CLINTON SCANDAL PRIMER

Occasionally words must serve to veil the facts.
——NICCOLÒ MACHIAVELLI

W hile most voters in 2016 would not take the long view of history, there were many nagging doubts about the idea of a second Clinton presidency. By July, as the Democratic National Convention met in Philadelphia, Hillary Clinton was faced with some curious polling data. While she still led Donald Trump in the presidential preference numbers, she trailed him on a key question of character. According to CNN, fully 68 percent of registered voters said that Clinton wasn't honest and trustworthy.[1]

The email scandal was confusing. Yes, it had compromised national security, but even the FBI director agreed it hadn't been intentional. Anyway, the electronic media was evolving. And Clinton had her own explanations. Who didn't make mistakes with emails and computers? Who didn't have crashes and lost files? The amounts of money taken in by the Clinton Foundation from foreign governments and corporations looked troubling, but then, it was a foundation that was doing a lot of good in the world. Right?

Hillary's poor numbers on character were not alarming for the campaign. She was leading even after Donald Trump experienced his bump from his own Republican National Convention. That was telling. If she could retain the lead even before her own, well-oiled, professionally run convention began, she would be in a very powerful position for the final stretch of the campaign. She would win, even with the net drag of those "untrustworthy" numbers. But they did, nonetheless, offer a slim opening for her Republican opponent, who was calling her "crooked Hillary." And they were a nagging curiosity to her own campaign team and her allies in the corporate media.

The problem for Hillary Clinton was that her email scandal and the questions surrounding her foundation did not just appear in a vacuum. There was a long history of Clinton scandals that preceded them. And if most voters didn't exactly remember the details of those scandals and younger voters didn't even know them at all, there was still a vague, foreboding sense of corruption that shadowed the Clintons. Many voters were uneasy.

What were those early scandals? What had the Clintons done wrong? Or what was perceived as wrong? And what had the Clintons themselves learned from their earlier mistakes? How did they do things differently now? How had they come back to the very brink of power?

Keep in mind as we take this abbreviated journey that the roles of Bill and Hillary were now reversed. As you will see, Hillary took the risks in these famous early controversies, since Bill was the attorney general and then the governor and later the president. He had to be protected at all costs.

With the Clintons planning their return to power in 2016, the pattern would be repeated in the years leading up to the election. But this time, Bill would be assuming the active role, taking some breathtaking chances by his own actions, but protecting Hillary. And once they moved into the White House, what could anyone do? They would not be able to impeach the first gentleman, Bill Clinton, any more than Hillary Clinton could have been impeached as first lady. They could howl and they could complain like they did last time, but there would always be the haters.

The following litany does not represent all the scandals, but rather just enough to help us see the pattern and understand the evolution that produced the Clinton moneymaking machine. It is easy to get lost in the forest of details. And there are so many that one can quickly become inured and lose any sense of indignation.

It is important to note that there are people still serving time in prison for doing some of the things described here—so as they say, "Don't try this at home."

There is another reason to take this quick review course. Some of these scandals are what we could call "Elvis Presleys." They just don't die. In the middle of the Clinton-Trump presidential campaign, some new witnesses and new documents emerged giving these buried events unexpected currency.

The scandals of the first Clinton presidency reached a point of fatigue for the media and for the nation. As you will learn, some of the most damaging evidence emerged after the impeachment trial was over. And no one had taken the time to collect all the new drippings from the table. There was no need. The Clintons were gone. They had suffered enough embarrassment for their sins. Let it be. But now they were coming back. Some voters and even some journalists wanted an updated review of those events. What was the thinking now? What had been proven true? What had been proven as irrelevant and meddlesome? Did any of those old scandals still matter?

Here are what I call the big five, listed conveniently in the chronological order in which they became public issues. These do not include the sexual-harassment complaints (which thanks to the Donald Trump campaign would soon become another discussion altogether); rather, these represent the first round of fiduciary problems.

THE HILLARY CLINTON CATTLE FUTURES CONTROVERSY

This one is all Hillary's, and it is pretty simple. Beginning in 1978, the Arkansas first lady Hillary Rodham Clinton made a series of complicated trades in the cattle futures markets. Some of them occurred multiple times on the same day. And this went on day after day, for ten months. Her initial investment was $1,000. When the ten months were over, that single investment had been parlayed into $100,000.

In today's money, adjusted for inflation, that would be $331,000. A better perspective might be this: in ten months, Hillary's commodities transactions earned twice as much as she and her husband's combined salaries. At the time, she was a lawyer at the Rose Law Firm and he was the governor of the state of Arkansas.

Hillary Clinton, who claimed to be a novice at futures trading, said she made these multiple daily trades herself by "studying the financial news,"[2] but when the scandal later gained wide exposure she admitted that she had received guidance from experts. When it was learned that the experts were associated with Tyson food company, it prompted charges of conflict of interest and bribery, the evidence expertly obscured by the complex maze of transactions.

No one went to prison, although one of those helping Mrs. Clinton make the investments was issued a three-year suspension from the Chicago Mercantile Exchange and another was given a $250,000 fine. At the time, it was the largest fine ever imposed by the exchange.[3]

This was one scandal that the Clintons didn't fight, even during the 2016 election cycle, perhaps preferring to take the hit and move on. A study on the probability of the Clinton investments laced the odds of Hillary's success rate at one in approximately 31 trillion.[4] She was much more likely to win the lottery back to back to back.

As to Hillary Clinton's original claim that she had made the investments herself? In 1996, William Safire, a Pulitzer Prize winner who had publicly supported the Clintons in earlier days, wrote, "We now know that it was a lie told to turn aside accusations that as the governor's wife she profited corruptly, her account being run by a lawyer for state poultry interests through a disreputable broker."[5]

Safire added, "To admit otherwise would be to confess taking, and paying taxes on, what some think amounted to a $100,000 bribe."[6]

Lesson learned? As the Clintons planned to go back into the White House, their roles were going to be reversed. Bill would be tasked with making the money and Hillary would play the role of the hardworking president, removed from the fray and above suspicion. If Bill's new business deals turned out to be shady, he would deny and stall until enough time passed that no one cared about the truth anyway and Hillary would roll her eyes, "What's a lady to do?"

The hope of many who admired the Clintons and shared their political philosophy was that the return to power would be reward enough, that the Clintons would be satisfied and not mess up their second White House experience. Their lifestyle for the next few years would be royal, and their multibillion-dollar cushion at the foundation would afford them a comfortable and meaningful existence after they left office. The danger was that Bill would be offered business deals far more complicated and subtle than Hillary's cattle futures trades and he would revert to form.

There was another lesson that some more benign Clinton critics concluded from the cattle futures scandal; namely, that Hillary Clinton was a high stakes gambler.

Hardly.

She was a person who wouldn't bet unless she knew in advance she could win. In spite of her spectacular performance in cattle futures, she would play at it a little more and then decide not to repeat the showing. Knowing in advance what will happen is not a bad quality for a president to have. But the critics would warn, that in this early controversy, as in many of the others that would follow, Hillary Clinton seemed to have a hard time telling the truth.

THE WHITEWATER SCANDAL

Fifteen people were convicted of forty crimes, but not Bill or Hillary Clinton. In fact, as president of the United States, Bill Clinton would pardon four of those convicted in the final hours of his presidency, prompting yet another scandal.

Whitewater was named for a 1979 Arkansas real estate development owned by Bill and Hillary Clinton and their good friends Jim and Susan McDougal. It represented a complex web of financial deals that defy a simple explanation. The bottom line was that the Clintons and the McDougals were supposed to make easy money, but that didn't happen. High interest rates and the collapse of the savings-and-loan industry ruined what critics suggest may have been a perfect scam.

One of the more egregious pieces of Whitewater included what one observer has described as a predatory mortgage scheme: A buyer would purchase a home, the fine print warning that if he or she missed a single monthly payment, the home would be repossessed.[7] Thus, unqualified buyers could be used to get a down payment and a mortgage loan. The odds were high that they would eventually miss a payment, in which case the property could be flipped to yet another buyer.

The crisis reached a crescendo following a *New York Times* article in 1992 that laid out the maze of financial transactions and questioned the involvement of then-president Clinton.[8] The Whitewater project was so complicated that just when it seemed to be resolved, new loose ends would emerge. Two years later, the Clinton White House was pressured into naming a special prosecutor, Robert B. Fiske Jr., to finally look into the matter.

The Clintons sought to distance themselves from the controversy, claiming to be passive investors and blind partners to the complicated transactions that soon became enmeshed in the savings-and-loan crisis. The problem was that the project was dependent on Jim McDougal's Madison Guaranty Savings and Loan Association, and Hillary Clinton worked as a lawyer at the Rose Law Firm, which represented it. Government regulators would call Madison Guaranty a sham.

The government subpoenaed billing records from the Rose Law Firm to determine how extensive Hillary Clinton's role had been in the operation. But the documents in Arkansas had mysteriously disappeared. When the firm insisted that it had sent boxes of the records to the White House, officials there vehemently denied it. The investigation hit a dead end. Newspaper stories began to refer to "the mysterious missing files."

Hillary Clinton became the first wife of a president ever required to testify before a grand jury. The Clintons would not be charged with a crime relating to Whitewater and, James Carville, a political adviser to the Clintons, would declare that the whole exercise was a waste of government money and time, the Clintons themselves being the true victims.

One of the early causalities of Whitewater was Webster Hubbell, a former attorney at the Rose Law Firm in Little Rock, Arkansas, and a close personal friend of Bill and Hillary Clinton. As governor, Clinton appointed him as the chief justice of the Arkansas Supreme Court. When the Clintons moved to Washington, Webster Hubbell was expected to be a major player. He served on the president elect's transition team and became the White House liaison to the Department of Justice before being approved by the Senate as associate attorney general.

If investigators had run into a brick wall trying to find files relating to Hillary Clinton, they were more successful at uncovering other problems at the Rose Law Firm. Webster Hubbell was indicted for allegedly overbilling clients. He would eventually be sentenced to prison. The scandal was just beginning, but it was already taking down some powerful people.

According to an associate of Jim McDougal, Bill Clinton promised he would pardon McDougal and his wife, Susan, if they would just be patient and stay silent.[9] But the pardon didn't come fast enough. Jim McDougal cut a deal with prosecutors and began talking. McDougal told authorities that Hillary Clinton had indeed worked on issues relating to Madison Guaranty. He claimed that during their time in Arkansas, Bill Clinton had jogged by the offices one day and stopped to talk. Complaining that he and Hillary were short on money, Bill asked if McDougal would let Hillary work on the case to get some billing hours. Both Clintons later denied this story.

Meanwhile, McDougal's wife, Susan, was accused of misusing a $300,000 government-backed loan. And there were allegations that Bill Clinton, acting as governor of Arkansas, had used his influence to help arrange it.

During a grand jury investigation, Susan refused to answer any questions about Bill Clinton. The grand jury specifically wanted to know if Bill Clinton had lied in his testimony at her Whitewater trial. She wouldn't say. This led to a contempt-of-court conviction and an eighteen-month prison sentence.

Prosecutors and journalists moved onto other issues, convinced that Susan McDougal, rotting away in prison, would soon come to her senses and speak up. But she never talked. And Bill Clinton, who hadn't acted fast enough for her husband, Jim McDougal, finally came through with his promise for Susan. After she spent months in prison, almost forgotten, he gave her a presidential pardon. It happened in the last hours of the last day, just before Bill Clinton left the White House, while the whole nation was transfixed on the new president, George W. Bush.

The husband, Jim McDougal, who agreed to tell the truth and cooperated with the grand jury, died of a heart attack in solitary confinement at the federal correctional facility in Fort Worth, Texas, in 1998. He was fifty-seven years old. The wife, Susan McDougal, who kept quiet and served her time in prison, finally walked free. That lesson would not be lost on future associates of the Clintons.

During this investigation, Special Prosecutor Fiske would issue wide-ranging subpoenas for documents from the Rose Law Firm that would lead to another scandal, but before we leave the shores of Whitewater behind, the reader should note that many involved in this controversy, including Susan McDougal, have never completely told their story, preferring prison to talking to a special prosecutor. For Whitewater to stay in the grave throughout the 2016 Hillary Clinton presidential campaign, these individuals would have to continue to keep their thoughts and words to themselves. At least until after the election.

Lesson learned? Many of the people around the Clintons would go to prison. It was a mistake for one to conclude that just because the Clintons were immune to prosecution they would be as well. Yes, the president and his soon-to-be-president wife were survivors, and they would do what they could to protect their own, but they could not always save the other folks riding on the Clinton bus.

TRAVELGATE

This tidy little scandal involved using the FBI to clean out an office full of White House employees to make room for Clinton supporters. The White House Travel Office handled lucrative charter airline contracts. Why not give those to some Friends of Bill (hereafter FOBs)? Some hardworking campaign staffers from Arkansas, a campaign travel coordinator from Hollywood, and a twenty-four-year-old young lady, a distant Clinton cousin, who all openly lobbied for a chance to help run the office.

They all had ideas. Some of them had contracted with airline charter companies during the campaign and knew how to make some money out of the arrangement. Hillary Clinton took the lead, assigning the task to a close friend from the old Rose Law Firm in Little Rock, Arkansas, the new deputy White House counsel, Vince Foster.

Pay close attention to this scandal. Its tentacles spread into dozens of other controversies, and it offers many insights into what some feared might happen in a second Clinton White House, when the roles were reversed, and Bill was playing the part of first spouse.

There is another point about Travelgate that the reader should not miss. This story shows the willingness of the Clintons, from the very beginning, to use the FBI to get things done. The Arkansas state troopers had been an extension of their power from the governor's mansion in Little Rock. So now, in the White House, why shouldn't the FBI be their personal police force as well? As you will see, the Clintons would work the FBI right up to the edge of their second presidency. In October 2016, just days before the election, the *Wall Street Journal* would report that Terry McAuliffe, the Clintons' close friend and the governor of Virginia, would arrange for $500,000 in campaign donations to the wife of the FBI agent in charge of investigating Hillary Clinton's erased emails.[10]

Other presidents remained removed, almost in awe of the FBI, without interference, and never really challenging it, not wanting to tempt fate and see if its fabled powers were still there. For years, presidents had come and gone, while the famous FBI director J. Edgar Hoover with his secret files endured. But past presidents not only feared the FBI, they also valued it. For this respectful relationship had survived the passing of Hoover. Even Richard Nixon, with Watergate in full bloom, finally backed down from the FBI.

The Clintons must have concluded early on that much of the legend of this agency was pure bluff. The institution was made up of men and women with feet of clay. Like all bureaucracies, it was riddled with jealousy and division; incompetents got promoted and legitimate investigations got spiked when it was in the interest of the agency. The FBI's first concern, like the Clintons', was for itself. This they could understand.

In any case, in 1993, Hillary had a problem. Some members of the White House Travel Office had been around since John F. Kennedy. They knew their jobs well, and they did them well too. How was she going to get rid of them?

On January 20, 1993, Bill Clinton was inaugurated as the forty-second president of the United States. On the same day, while watching the ceremony on his White House television, Billy Dale, the director of the Travel Office got a call from an unknown woman who told him that Catherine Cornelius of Arkansas, a twenty-four-year-old third cousin of the president, would soon be working on travel at the White House.

It would later be learned that Catherine was, even then, reporting directly to Harry Thomason, a Hollywood producer who helped with travel during the Clinton campaign, and Harry was reporting directly to the first lady.

Dale also received a call from a man in Ohio who asked how he could get into the White House charter business. "We can make some money here."[11] Dale was encouraged to cooperate. He was stunned.

Billy Dale had worked in the office for thirty-two years. He had served under seven presidents. Only a few months before, he had actually voted for Bill Clinton. The White House Travel Office staff took comfort in the fact that they worked only for the pleasure of the president anyway, and if the Clintons wanted some changes, they would be glad to accommodate them. They knew that they could be fired and replaced with a team of the president's own choosing, in which case they would likely be transferred to other jobs.

Meanwhile, Hillary Clinton and her team apparently decided that it wouldn't look good to pass the travel charter contracts to their old friends; they needed a hook. There had to be a bit of a sting to the dismissals. The Clinton White House ordered an FBI investigation of Dale and all the other staff members in the Travel Office. The process was hampered by a lack of evidence justifying such a decision. The agency was reluctant to be dragged unnecessarily into what it astutely discerned to be some contrived Clinton drama.

As Peggy Noonan remembered the story in a piece for the *Wall Street Journal*, "On May 19, 1993, less than four months into the administration, the seven men who had long worked in the White House travel office were suddenly and brutally fired."[12]

The workers were escorted off the premises, their offices were locked. Their personal pictures and memorabilia from a lifetime of work with past presidents was apparently thrown into the trash, and a new travel team took control.

At this point, the fired employees of the White House Travel Office were in a panic. The dismissals were heartrending—the sudden fall from grace, the loss of personally-signed photos from presidents, memorabilia they had imagined sharing with grandchildren, it was all beyond belief—but now they had to get lawyers to protect themselves from prison. The cost of the investigations soon grew to millions of dollars. The FBI investigation was joined by separate probes from the Justice Department, the Government Accountability Office (GAO), the House Government Reform and Oversight Committee, the Whitewater independent counsel, and a newly animated White House internal inquiry of its own. Having taken such decisive action, the Clinton White House wanted to make sure no stone was left unturned, and the Clintons wanted the reluctant FBI to know that it had better not miss a scrap of information, because they were investigating the investigators.

With such heft, covering every personal and public transaction over a thirty-year period, the investigations eventually found some things that appeared to satisfy the Clintons and potentially work for government prosecutors. On international jaunts Dale had sometimes been lax in dealing with customs and tax issues for the traveling press corps. In hurried moments there had been sloppy bookkeeping and a couple instances of comingling of public and private funds. It would work.

Dale and the fired employees were encouraged to seek immunity deals by agreeing to testify against each other, which led to some confusing moments as the various lawyers involved learned, to their consternation, that there wasn't anything incriminating with which to barter.

Ultimately charged with embezzlement, Billy Dale faced twenty years in prison. His legal bills mounted, reaching $750,000. He and his wife made plans to sell their home and cash in every available asset. His son and daughter were subpoenaed. He was hit with an IRS audit. As the reader will learn, this is almost a rite of passage for persons targeted by the Clintons. Some advised Dale to take a plea deal from the government. Better to serve three years in prison and end the relentless attacks than end up losing everything and dying in prison.

There was one big problem for the Clintons and their investigators. The White House press corps knew the Travel Office employees well, and they knew them to be persons of professionalism and integrity. Sam Donaldson of ABC testified as a character witness at the trial. So did Brit Hume and others.

Billy Dale's case went to a jury on November 16, 1995. After two hours of deliberation, he was found not guilty. When he heard the news, Dale slumped his shoulders, bowed his head, and openly sobbed.

Several months later, in a poignant moment, Mack McLarty, the White House Chief of Staff, apologized to the fired Travel Office workers and helped some of them get other jobs in the administration. Some of them, including Dale, had no interest in trying their luck by working further for the Clintons and took early retirement.

If Travelgate was one of the early Clinton scandals, it has also become one of their most enduring. Interviewed by the Government Accountability Office in the initial investigation, Hillary Clinton insisted that she had no role in the firing of the Travel Office staff members and had had no advance knowledge that it was coming. She denied that she had involved the FBI. She also denied prior consultations with Harry Thomason and his team about taking on the lucrative air charter business.

On January 5, 1996, after the trial of Billy Dale, a memo surfaced from a Clinton White House staffer, David Watkins, to Mack McClarty making it very clear that the first lady was herself directing the attacks on the Travel Office employees and coordinating their replacement with the Clinton donors from Arkansas. The memo included the words, "We both know that there would be hell to pay if we failed to take swift and decisive action in conformity with the First Lady's wishes."[13]

Watkins, a White House aide, loyal to the Clintons and brought into the White House from Arkansas, was clearly under pressure. He described an atmosphere of fear surrounding the first lady. And he clearly contradicted the claim that the first lady was not colluding with Harry Thomason. The Watkins memos described a triad consisting of Clinton, Thomason, and White House Deputy Counsel Vince Foster pressuring Watkins almost hourly to take action and fire the Travel Office staff.

Events reached a climax when Watkins got a call from the White House deputy counsel. "On Friday I was in Memphis, Foster told me that it was important that I speak directly with the First Lady that day."[14]

He called Hillary and she demanded "swift and clear action to resolve the situation."[15]

The memos were damning. They not only seemed to show that the first lady had lied about her role, they showed that the White House had covered up evidence, having withheld the relevant memo from the FBI, the Justice Department, the GAO, Congress, and multiple special prosecutors. William Safire of the *New York Times* wrote about the "sad realization that our First Lady—a woman of undoubted talents who was a role model for many in her generation—is a congenital liar."[16]

In the end, as in scandals that would follow, this early Clinton controversy barely avoided prosecution. The independent counsel Robert Ray decided that Hillary had indeed been involved in the firings of the Travel Office employees, but he nevertheless decided that "insufficient proof exists to convince a jury beyond a reasonable doubt that Clinton knowingly gave false material testimony."[17]

His words would find an uncanny echo in the conclusions of FBI director James Comey years later. It is a common complaint of law enforcement tasked with investigating the Clintons: they are guilty, it just can't be proven.

There is one more, sad footnote to this scandal. Given the emerging truth of what happened in Travelgate, the House of Representatives, in 1996, voted 350 to 43 to reimburse the legal fees for the exonerated Travel Office employees who had been fired by Hillary Clinton. Given talking points from the White House, Democratic senator Harry Reid attempted to block the measure. When the White House was asked if President Clinton would sign such a bill if the measure came out of the Senate and reached the president's desk, a spokesman at the White House was quick to say yes, he would happily do so. But the president's staff was speaking too soon.

Clinton was in fact furious. In what a *Los Angeles Times* writer described as a "rare display of temper" the president contradicted his aides, saying, "Are we going to pay the legal expenses of every person in America who is ever acquitted of an offense?"[18]

Lesson learned? The Clintons appeared to be quite willing to use the FBI, the IRS, and other weapons of government, such as hiring and firing, to get what they wanted. And they would do so without apology. Innocence was irrelevant.

If the public felt that the FBI was acting erratically in the weeks leading up to the 2016 election, sometimes taking actions that favored the Clintons and at other times putting Hillary's campaign in jeopardy, well, the reader can begin to understand the agency's dilemma. If the FBI and the IRS could be bullied into sham investigations by the Clintons during their first White House experience, what could be expected upon their return to power? The FBI, a proud agency with a carefully manicured reputation, was understandably conflicted about how to handle its investigations of Hillary Clinton. Like everyone else in Washington, its staff expected that she would soon be their boss.

A second lesson learned? If you've got something the Clintons want, or you even think that they might want, you better give it to them quickly and get out of their way. Don't quibble. Don't hesitate. Don't bargain. Just drop it and run.

THE DEATH OF VINCE FOSTER

He died on July 20, 1993, an apparent suicide, but the conspiracy theories are legion. Foster's body was found in Fort Marcy Park in McLean, Virginia, not far from the Potomac River. A gun was found in his hand.

Vince Foster was the deputy White House counsel and an old friend of the Clintons from their Arkansas days. He was a partner at the now-infamous Rose Law Firm, where he worked with his fellow attorney Hillary Rodham Clinton.

Questions surrounding his death began immediately. According to White House colleagues, he was the point man for juggling the incoming Clinton scandals, from Whitewater to Travelgate. And there were new ones popping up all the time, simmering at the White House but not yet breaking into the national media.

A member of the White House West Wing staff remembers, "Hillary oversaw everything that followed in the aftermath of Vince Foster's death. Hardly mourning, she sprang into action like a field commander. The very night he dies, her aides were packing up and moving boxes of files to the residence. Some never surfaced for years."[19]

By the next morning there was still no determination regarding the cause of death, and yet Vince Foster's White House office was unsecured. Staffers came and went, retrieving documents and files. Linda Tripp, a White House aide who would earn fame in another Clinton scandal, finally tipped off the Secret Service, who secured the office.[20]

A suicide note was found in Foster's briefcase, in his office, six days later but with no signature. Among other things, Foster wrote that "I made mistakes from ignorance, inexperience and overwork."

He also expressed frustration that "the FBI lied in their report to the AG." Foster was likely referring to the FBI report on Travelgate, which he felt was too forgiving of the seven White House employees whom Hillary had replaced with her own friends from Arkansas.

Loyal to the end, Foster also wrote, "The public will never believe the innocence of the Clintons and their loyal staff."[21] The note had been torn into twenty-seven pieces. One was missing.

Almost all the crib notes on the Vince Foster death repeat the point that five (some say six) official investigations concluded that he had committed suicide. Even the special prosecutor Kenneth Starr, who would prove himself to be a formidable opponent of the Clintons, would conclude the same. Vince Foster's sister and family knew of his depression and have never doubted the story that he took his own life.[22]

The Clintons were irate over media and political organizations that raised questions suggesting that Foster's death was the result of foul play. But if so, their own decisions and actions surrounding the investigations into the death and the follow-up gave their enemies all the ammunition they needed.

The president insisted that the Park Police handle the initial investigation and only critical hours and days later allowed the FBI to help. Incredibly, photographs of the crime scene were lost. Then there were the boxes of files crated off from Vince Foster's office to the private quarters of the White House for review. And the suicide note was only found six days after his death. Yet it was there, in his briefcase, in his office.

Lesson learned?

No one could say it better than Vince Foster himself, who wrote on one of the torn pieces of his suicide note, "I was not meant for the job or the spotlight of public life in Washington. Here ruining people is considered a sport."

And in case you haven't learned by now, the Clintons are tough. They can endure stress and pressure that will break others. As Donald Trump would say, when asked to name something nice about his Democratic opponent, "I will say this about Hillary: she doesn't quit and she doesn't give up. I respect that. She's a fighter. I disagree with much of what she's fighting for. . . . But she does fight hard, and doesn't quit, and I consider that to be a very good trait."[23]

FILEGATE AND HILLARY'S FINGERPRINTS

Filegate involved a Clinton-created new White House Security Office headed by two former campaign people, Craig Livingstone and Anthony Marceca. The allegations were that the duo improperly accessed FBI files. And worse, the files selected belonged to political targets of the Clintons. A Congressional investigating committee challenged their qualifications to run such an office.[24]

Hillary Clinton denied the whole thing, calling it a "pseudo-scandal."[25]

The controversy began on June 5, 1996, when the Congressional committee, headed by Representative William Clinger, announced that they had discovered a White House request to access Billy Dale's FBI background check seven months after he had been fired and after the termination of all the other Travel Office employees.

At first it appeared that Hillary Clinton was using her newly created White House Security Office to fish for information to retroactively justify the hostile action the Clintons had taken against the White House Travel Office employees. But when investigators started pulling on that single thread, the whole sweater started coming unraveled. It turned out that the new White House Security Office was accessing hundreds of FBI files of all kinds of people, including leading Republicans from the prior administration such as Brent Scowcroft and Marlin Fitzwater. The files revealed personal information on each of their targets, including sexual orientation, relationships outside of marriage, alcoholism, health problems, and personal financial matters.

How many files were accessed? Estimates range from four hundred to eight hundred. Since the author of this book had served on the senior staff of the George H. W. Bush White House, it is probable that his files were in the batch.

Only the day after the Watkins memo surfaced, the nation was hit with another startling find. It turned out that those missing files from the Rose Law Firm, the files that had been subpoenaed for the investigation into Whitewater two years earlier, had been found by a White House staffer and close Clinton friend named Carolyn Huber. It turned out that Ms. Huber had also worked at the Rose Law Firm. The 115 pages of billing, which showed Mrs. Clinton's lead role in work with Jim McDougal's Madison Guaranty, had been found in the third floor private residence of the White House.[26] When the FBI checked, Hillary Clinton's fingerprints were, literally, found all over the pages.

One theory postulated by the White House was that they had been carted away by Hillary Clinton by mistake, shortly after the death of Vincent Foster. No one was reassured by this idea.

A report from the Congressional committee declared, "Whether or not these events are shown to be a blunder, the result of colossal incompetence, or whether they are established to be more serious or even criminal, the casualness with which this White House has approached many areas of security and access provided a climate for either of these troubling alternatives."[27]

When the scandal broke into the open, Craig Livingstone became the whipping boy. Republicans portrayed him as a former barroom bouncer, and the Clinton White House cut him loose with no one assuming responsibility for his hire. It was as if he had walked into the White House on his own authority and announced himself as the new "head of personnel security." White House staff members leaked unflattering stories about him and denied his assertions that he had been hired by the first lady. The *Washington Post* described him as "swaggering around the West Wing in dark glasses and attending film premieres with beautiful women."[28]

But according to an FBI report, Livingstone had been given his position because of a friendship between the first lady and Livingstone's mother. Hillary Clinton admitted that she had once been photographed with the woman but insisted that she did not know her.[29]

Meanwhile, Carolyn Huber, the lady who had found the missing Rose Law Firm billing records, wisely secured her own attorney and faded from sight.

On June 10, 1996, the White House issued an apology to the prominent Republicans whose files had been improperly obtained. Leon Panetta, the White House chief of staff, said that the incident was "completely inexcusable."[30]

Try as it may, the White House couldn't seem to keep Filegate in the grave. Two weeks later, when Anthony Marceca appeared before the Senate Judiciary Committee, he refused to answer questions, he said, "on the grounds that it may incriminate me." As mentioned in an earlier chapter, the story was already out that Marceca had apparently accessed his own FBI files and had taken action against two women who had slandered him to the FBI.[31]

The image persisted of Hillary Clinton, sitting up in bed at night in the private quarters of the White House, reading the salacious FBI files of her enemies. Such files had kept J. Edgar Hoover in power for decades. What could the Clintons do with them?

Ironically, Hillary Clinton may have been saved by the young female intern who had an affair with her husband. On January 13, 1998, the independent counsel, hoping to end the matter of Filegate, finally deposed the first lady at the White House. That same day, across town, members of the counsel's staff were listening for the first time to taped conversations of Linda Tripp and Monica Lewinsky. Filegate was left to swim away, there were bigger fish in the ocean.

Lessons learned?

If the Clintons or their team sought information on their enemies during their White House experience of the 1990s, and actually created a department to get it done, one could only imagine what would have been available to them had they returned to the White House for the second time. In the 90s, information still came from the slow process of shoe leather and tedious transcripts of FBI tape-recorded interviews with disgruntled friends and neighbors. Today the information comes electronically from the touch of a button. And for the president, it would come directly from the phone calls and emails of the selected targets.

CHAPTER 6

THE FU LIN CHINESE RESTAURANT

Behind every great fortune lies a great crime.
—BALZAC

I n their storybook rise to power, Bill Clinton was the public figure and Hillary Clinton was the workhorse, devoted to building their net worth. Bill was a superb politician, rising to the
presidency. Hillary was a gutsy but unsuccessful wage earner, taking risks that almost got her indicted.

When Bill Clinton left the White House, those roles reversed.
She became the public figure, the senator, then the secretary of state.
He became the wage earner; and true to form, he succeeded wildly,
although with dangerous issues trailing behind, issues that were
damaging to Hillary Clinton's presidential campaign and threatened to spoil a second Clinton presidency.

By the beginning of the 2016 presidential campaign, Bill and
Hillary Clinton had an estimated net worth of $111 million.[1] Their
foundation had raised more than $2 billion.[2] Of course, they were
both older and wiser than they had been in earlier years, and as a
former president, Bill Clinton was earning money while being married to a woman who was expected to be president herself. So the
circumstances were very different. Still, Hillary gives much credit
to what Bill achieved.

"You have no reason to remember," Hillary told ABC's Diane Sawyer in 2014, "but we came out of the White House not only dead broke, but in debt. We had no money when we got there, and we struggled to piece together the resources for mortgages for houses, for Chelsea's education. It was not easy. Bill has worked really hard. And it's been amazing to me. He's worked very hard."[3]

With their roles now reversed, the question was now what kind of president Hillary would be? And what would be Bill's role? Would he continue to find a way to raise money even as he served as first gentleman? Would that still be necessary? Or would they now rest on their laurels and leave well enough alone? Would it be enough to commit themselves to serving the public? Would Bill Clinton stay away from all that money in his foundation? Would he sit back and enjoy the role of the man in the shadows? Reading memos on the weekends at Camp David? Whispering advice to the president in secret? Would the new President Hillary Clinton be able to separate herself from all that money and the people associated with it?

THE WOMAN BEHIND THE THRONE

The journey began in humble circumstances. Both Bill and Hillary knew that success in public life was dependent on money, and lots of it. The crafty old California Democratic politician Jesse Unruh, would say, "Money is the mother's milk of politics."[4] It is one of those rare quotes that instantly became an accepted axiom in the English language—and with good reason.

Even so, Hillary may have underestimated how overwhelming the process would become. Day after day, month after month, the idea of being the power behind the man, directing public policy, faded, as the overwhelming task of financing the process became all consuming. Again and again, the Clintons were amazed at how much money it took to win a campaign. First for Arkansas attorney general, then for governor, then for president. Eventually, one had to raise millions of dollars to land a job that paid only thousands.

It soon became apparent to Hillary that her role was even more modest than financier of campaigns. She was primarily absorbed with advancing the Clintons' own personal net worth. Others stepped forward to raise the money for the election contests and they could share in the power as their reward. But only Hillary could replenish the personal coffers of the Clintons themselves. Both Bill and Hillary began to see their own lack of private resources as precarious. Yes, it would take lots of money to win public office. They had seen politicians fail for lack of money. They had experienced it themselves. But they had also seen politicians lose their independence and freedom of action and be swept from the public stage because their personal financial base was unstable. They had experienced that themselves, too. They needed to build their own net worth.

It was this mind-set that led to Hillary Clinton's dangerous, and probably illegal, cattle futures scheme, which rewarded the Clintons handsomely. It was also this mind-set that led just afterward to the Whitewater project, which failed miserably as an investment and came back to haunt them as a scandal in the White House.

When the investigations into Whitewater began, the Clintons appealed publicly for money to help finance their defense. It had never been done before, and observers worried that the process was ripe for misuse. Given by the right person in the right situation, how could a donation for the Clintons' legal defense be any different from a bribe? Nevertheless, in June 1994, the Presidential Legal Expense Trust Fund was established. It was designated as a grantor trust to "protect" the president and first lady from taxes.[5]

By 1999, Bill and Hillary Clinton would raise $4.5 million for their defense. One solicitation letter read, "If you are disturbed by the way politics is conducted today, then what better response than to offer the First Family your own gesture of support."[6] Robert De Niro and a host of Hollywood stars agreed and gleefully donated.

It would all lead to yet another Clinton scandal. It would turn out that the money was coming from sources outside Hollywood as well. Foreign money was flowing into the president's legal defense fund. The subsequent investigation would uncover much worse. It would reveal that foreign money, specifically money from the People's Republic of China, was not only flowing into the legal defense fund but had been poured into the 1992 presidential campaign of Bill Clinton and into the coffers of the Democratic National Committee.

Before the Clintons left office, twenty-one people would be convicted for making illegal contributions. When Hillary Clinton started planning for a presidential run in 2008 and her staff sat down to review the positives and negatives, this scandal emerged as the greatest fear, trumping Bill's affairs with women and charges of misuse of the Clinton Foundation. The concern of senior staffers was that the Clintons would come off as "greedy or ethically challenged."[7]

THE CHINESE RESTAURANT IN LITTLE ROCK

The story began in Little Rock, Arkansas. The Clintons frequently visited the Fu Lin Chinese Restaurant where they became friends with Charles Yah Lin Trie, a fry cook in the kitchen and eventually a co-owner. As the Clintons' stature rose in national politics, Charlie Trie's stature rose as well. Within time, the fry cook morphed into an important corporate figure and a prominent Clinton financial backer.

In October 1991, Bill Clinton announced his candidacy for president. That same year, in anticipation of a win, Trie opened a new business called Daihatsu International Trading Company. When Clinton won the election, Trie opened an office of his new business in Washington, DC. The FBI would later learn that there was only one source of income for the company. A $1 million wire transfer from a man named Ng Lap Seng from bank accounts in Hong Kong and Macau. According to one source, Ng Lap Seng ran a prostitution ring in Macau.[8] Pay attention to this name; he will come roaring back in 2016, when the Hillary Clinton campaign would suggest that Donald Trump was colluding with the Russians.

In 1993, after the Clintons moved into the White House, the high-wire act continued. Their sense of urgency and their willingness to take risks infected fund-raising at the Democratic National Committee. Charlie Trie helped organize a $220,000 donation for the Democratic Party. He paid $100,000 for a seat at a presidential gala, with Ng Lap Seng as his guest. A grateful President Clinton made Charlie Trie a frequent White House visitor.[9]

Privately, questions were whispered by some prominent Democrats. How had a fry cook at a Little Rock, Arkansas Chinese restaurant become such a big corporate player? Were the president and the party receiving illegal foreign donations? Who were all the Chinese visitors in the Oval Office?

Charlie's methods of payment lacked subtlety. One wonders if he wanted the president to know that the donations were illegal. When he donated to the Presidential Legal Expense Trust Fund, he delivered envelopes containing numerous checks and money orders. The money orders used different names to meet filing requirements, but had the same handwriting and were numbered in sequence. After making the donations, reported variously at $400,000 to $640,000, Charlie wrote the president a stern letter urging a different Chinese policy and warning that "it is highly possible for China to launch real war."[10]

It was the talking points of the Communist Chinese government, and it used their stilted language. Clinton politely and dutifully responded.

In early 1996, the year of Clinton's reelection, Charlie Trie brought a special guest with him to a White House coffee with the president. The guest was Wang Jun, and he was the head of a People's Republic of China state-owned investment conglomerate. Among other companies, Wang headed up a weapons trading company owned by the Chinese military.

In September of that year, Alan Miller, a *Los Angeles Times* reporter, ran a brief story about a $250,000 contribution to the Democratic National Committee given in April that had now been refunded.[11] It had apparently come from a Korean electronics firm. The head of the firm had appeared at a Democratic fund-raiser where he pledged a sizable contribution. He soon found himself ushered into the presence of President Clinton.

Right on the heels of the Alan Miller story, Bob Woodward and Brian Duffy published breaking news in the *Washington Post*.[12] By then President Clinton had publicly admitted that the meeting with the head of the weapons company owned by the Chinese government was a mistake. There was now a full-blown investigation into where Charlie Trie's donation money had originated, with some alleging that it had come from the communist Chinese government itself. According to Woodward and Duffy's report, the FBI was tracking the evidence. Incredibly, the plot had originated in the Chinese embassy and had been picked up by the FBI's eavesdropping surveillance. The Chinese were trying to influence the presidential election.

Before the year was over a congressional investigation was zeroing in on Charlie Trie. He promptly fled the country. So too did Ng Lap Seng, the man behind the million dollars sent to Trie, the man suspected of funneling money from the People's Republic of China into the Clinton reelection campaign. And so ended all chance for investigators to get answers.

In 2016, the Hillary Clinton presidential campaign alleged that her Republican opponent, Donald Trump, was being helped by the Russians. The allegations were based on the suspicion that emails from the Clinton campaign had been hacked by Russians.

As if on cue, right in the middle of the discussion, Ng Lap Seng suddenly showed up in New York City. He had been out of the country, hiding from US authorities for years. The FBI has a long memory. Ng Lap Seng was picked up and charged with bringing in suitcases full of cash to bribe United Nations officials.[13] The whole investigation was now back on the rails.

Committed to the election of Hillary Clinton, the national media panned the story. To this day, most Americans know nothing about it.

And what happened to Charlie Trie? In 1998, with the country riveted to the Bill Clinton–Monica Lewinsky scandal, and prosecutors busy, he quietly returned to the United States, where he faced trial. The turning point in the proceedings occurred when his long-time office manager, Maria Mapili, testified that Trie had ordered her to destroy business records that had been subpoenaed.

Charlie Trie promptly agreed to cooperate. He was convicted and sentenced to three years, four months of probation. So ended the saga of the humble fry cook at the Fu Lin Chinese Restaurant in Little Rock, Arkansas. Maybe.

JOHNNY CHUNG AND THE STORY FROM THE INSIDE

It turns out that Charlie Trie was not alone. In fact, he was not even the first. There was a veritable flood of foreign money looking for a way to flow to the Clintons. One of the more controversial and maligned of the Clinton donors was a California businessman and a Chinese American named Johnny Chung.

Starting in 1994, Chung began making sizable donations to the Democratic National Committee. They would total $366,000.

The Clintons responded. Within a two-year span, Chung visited the White House forty-nine times and was promoted as a friend of both Bill and Hillary Clinton. On one occasion he was allowed to bring in a group of Chinese friends to a Clinton presidential radio address. A national security official was aghast, characterizing Chung as a "hustler."[14]

By the time investigators zeroed in on Johnny Chung, a number of Chinese donors were in their sights. Almost all of them fled the United States. But Chung, who had converted to Christianity, decided to come clean. He pleaded guilty to election law violations and agreed to cooperate with the Justice Department's ongoing investigation.

Yes, he admitted, there had been a connection to the People's Republic of China. A lieutenant colonel in the Chinese army had given him $300,000 to donate to the 1996 Democratic campaign. Chung had even arranged for the officer to fly to the United States to get his picture taken with Bill Clinton at a Los Angeles gala fund-raiser. But, Chung insisted he had never been an agent of the Chinese government. He seemed to miss the salient point. Regardless of Chung's intentions, this was a direct link from the Chinese government to the Clinton campaign. The Chinese government denied Chung's story.

Johnny Chung offered a remarkable insider account of how casually Clinton staffers regarded campaign finance law and the whole process of outside money. On one of Chung's many White House visits, he met with Hillary Clinton's chief of staff, Margaret A. Williams. In the White House, on government grounds, Chung said he had turned over to Williams a check for $50,000. Unperturbed, and apparently indifferent to federal law, Williams accepted the check and passed it on to the Democratic National Committee.

Chung once said, "I see the White House is like a subway. You have to put in coins to open the gates."[15]

Now that Chung was cooperating with the Justice Department, his testimony before the investigating congressional committee drew a rapt audience and offered a compelling look inside the corrupt flow of money and, more important, the frightening aftermath.

The hearing was telecast live to the nation, with Chung speaking openly about his relationship with Bill and Hillary Clinton. He spoke about the threats on his life and the lives of his family members, threats that were made by both American and Chinese government officials.

"Today, I have mixed feelings about the President and the First Lady but I can't help but think that they used me as much as I used them,"[16]

Johnny Chung was convicted of bank fraud, tax evasion, and two counts of conspiring to violate election law. He received a minor sentence in 1998.

Years later, still in hiding, Johnny Chung received a friendly visit from a retired government official, friendly with the FBI, who perhaps felt guilty about the treatment Chung had been given after agreeing to come forward and tell the truth. The former government worker explained that Chung's odds of survival actually increased by going public. And so, with assistance from the former government official, Johnny Chung produced an elaborate videotaped testimony that was secreted to friends and family to be forwarded to the media in the case of his death. One of my researchers has a copy of this tape in his possession.

THE ARKANSAS BANKER

In 1984, John Huang, an immigrant from Taiwan, became the vice president of the Worthen Bank in Little Rock, Arkansas. Like others in the Clinton orbit, he rode the wave to power, moving to Washington, DC, in 1994 and becoming the deputy assistant secretary of commerce in the Clinton administration.

In 1996, with Bill Clinton up for reelection and foreign money flowing into the Democratic coffers, Huang was in a perfect position to serve as a conduit. He was moved to the Democratic National Committee, where he was made vice chairman of finance. He raised a staggering $1.6 million in contributions.

The FBI struggled to find sufficient evidence proving any nefarious connections to the Huang money, and the Justice Department made unsuccessful offers of a reduced sentence if he would open the door to complicity of higher-ups. Huang refused.

Meanwhile, news of financial irregularities and a fund-raising scheme surrounding a Taiwan-based Buddhist temple were the focus of journalists and television media. The Justice Department found a solution for Huang. He need not incriminate himself or the Clintons, but if he would help them solve the puzzle surrounding the Buddhist temple scandal, they would talk about an immunity deal.

John Huang agreed.

After the election, with investigations into foreign influence in the Clinton campaign growing red hot, the DNC returned all of the $1.6 million that Huang had delivered. In some cases, the money raised by Huang had come illegally from corporations in Indonesia and elsewhere. Republicans in Congress were alarmed when they learned that Huang had been given top secret clearance at the Commerce Department even though his background investigation had covered only his years living in the United States and had not touched on the years he lived overseas. Huang had attended thirty-seven intelligence briefings during his time at the Commerce Department and, incredibly, due to a bureaucratic error, his top-secret clearance was not pulled when he left. Even so, the focus of the Justice Department had moved on to another target.

On August 12, 1999, John Huang pleaded guilty to conspiring to violate campaign finance law. He received only one year of probation. It was his reward for delivering the woman behind the Buddhist temple controversy.

THE BUDDHIST NUNS

If John Huang had raised $1.6 million, Maria Hsia, the woman some say he helped deliver to prosecutors, raised only $100,000. But Maria was the bigger story. She had helped monks and nuns at the Hsi Lai Temple in Hacienda Heights, California, find a way to circumvent US election laws and donate to the reelection of Bill Clinton.

Campaign finance laws limited the amount of money that an individual could donate to a presidential campaign. They ruled out corporate donations, foreign money, and donations from a church or a religious nonprofit. Maria apparently arranged for money from a Taiwanese company to be donated to the temple, which would pass the money on to the monks and nuns, who would write the checks to the Democratic National Committee. Although illegal, such maneuvering is not an uncommon practice in both political parties. Such supporters are called "straw donors."

The murky, complicated maze of the international wire transactions of Charlie Trie, Johnny Chung, and John Huang caused the public's eyes to glaze over. But the Buddhist temple scandal, with monks and nuns running money through their own personal bank accounts, was riveting.

To add to the drama, video emerged showing Vice President Al Gore on a visit to the temple. And it was learned that some of the temple's leaders had met with Bill Clinton. The vice president's office quickly issued a statement saying that Mr. Gore understood that the meeting was community outreach to Asian Americans, but after a howl of ridicule his office admitted that it knew the event was related to fund-raising.

Her trial lasted three weeks. In March, 2000, Maria Hsia was convicted on five felony counts, including making false statements to the government.[17] It could have meant twenty-five years in prison, but the judge delayed sentencing and the national media, perhaps feeling that Maria was a small fish offered up as a sacrifice, moved onto richer stories. Maria Hsia was forgotten.

What happened afterward is instructive for our understanding of what might have happened in a second Clinton White House. Maria's judge was Paul Friedman, a Bill Clinton appointee. Judge Friedman was assigned the Maria Hsia case by Judge Norma Holloway Johnson, also a Clinton appointee, serving as chief judge of the US District Court in Washington, DC. In fact, Johnson would assign Clinton judges to six criminal cases of Democratic fund-raising, including the trial of Webster Hubbell, a Clinton buddy and deputy attorney general. Such assignments were normally rotated by computer. Johnson reportedly made sure that this process was bypassed and Clinton people were in charge.[18]

Two years after the conviction, Judge Paul Friedman handed down his sentence. Maria Hsia would serve ninety days of home detention, three years of probation, and a fine of $5,300.[19] A slap on the wrist.

In the years following Maria's trial, a number of troubling details about the case have raised questions: Why have the Buddhist temple's employees, including the nuns, refused to talk about the case?

Judgment has been passed; why not help clear up the details? It was understandable that they had pleaded the Fifth Amendment when subpoenaed to appear before a congressional inquiry, but now, for the historical record, can't they offer more information? Investigators seeking evidence were told that the nuns had destroyed the lists of donors and all other related documents. An attorney for one of the nuns said that the videotape of the fund-raiser with Vice President Al Gore had disappeared and might have possibly been shipped off to Taiwan. And finally, rumors have now surfaced that Maria Tsia was indeed an agent of the People's Republic of China, an accusation both she and the government of China deny.

RON BROWN AND LESSONS LEARNED FROM CHINAGATE

There is an intriguing footnote to the Chinagate scandal. Ron Brown was serving as the secretary of commerce when the Clinton fund-raising machine began in earnest. Well-educated, soft-spoken, and urbane, Brown was the first African American to hold the position. On Brown's watch, the Commerce Department was asked to sell seats on its international trade missions to big donors to President Clinton's reelection campaign. Brown resisted the idea as crass and probably illegal, but the Clinton fund-raising machine persisted.

It was well known that Secretary Brown's son was in legal trouble. When the investigations into Chinagate began in earnest, a story circulated suggesting that Brown was flirting with the idea of talking to prosecutors in exchange for leniency toward his son.[20]

In April, 1996, on one of the Commerce Department trade missions, Ron Brown died in an airplane crash in Croatia. The circumstance surrounding the crash was a mystery and led to further conspiracy theories. The investigators talking with Brown were forced to drop their inquiry.

There were many other similar stories in Chinagate, all with analogous events and with comparable questions left unanswered. The prosecutors soon moved on to the sensational details of the president's sex scandal and possible perjury over the Paula Jones case and Monica Lewinsky. Some historians believe that the distraction of Bill Clinton's personal life at this crucial time diverted energy and personnel away from Chinagate, saving the president from a more grievous fate, an impeachment trial that he may have lost.

As it was, Bill Clinton escaped any censure from the scandals surrounding Chinagate, although it left its stain.

The American people sensed that something was wrong. And they watched on television as the videos were shown of Chinese donors swarming around the president in the Oval Office. They suspected that there had been some sort of quid pro quo. Republicans said it amounted to treason, that Clinton had changed American foreign policy to suit the interests of the People's Republic of China, and he had done so for money.

A CNN-*Time* magazine poll in May 1998 showed that the American people wanted an independent counsel to investigate. The numbers were 58 percent to 33 percent. And remarkably, just based on the flow of money and their own common sense, even before the evidence had been gathered, the polled Americans believed, 47 percent to 34 percent, that there had been some sort of arrangement in return for the money. Only 19 percent were not sure.[21]

The Clintons may have come away from the experience with a different lesson learned. There was money, big money, available from foreign governments. Most of those governments had no qualms at all about using it to advance their causes. Such money was not enough to move nations to act against their own best interests, but it was surely enough to make an individual wealthy beyond his or her imagination—if there were only an ethical and legal way to tap into it.

In any case, still struggling with their own personal finances, having to plead for money to defend themselves against their own Justice Department investigation, the Clintons must have found it galling to see millions of dollars flowing to the Democratic Party from foreign governments and foreign corporations when it was a photo with them, Bill and Hillary, that was driving the whole process. Why was everyone else getting rich and not the Clintons?

CHAPTER 7

THE OTHER WOMEN

Avoid what is strong and strike at what is weak.
—SUN TZU

Sigmund Freud would have loved the 2016 American presidential election. Havelock Ellis would have been positively riveted, taking copious notes during the debates and public interviews with the candidates. Sex was a frequent subject. First in the Republican primary battles, which we will visit in later chapters, and then again in the general election.

In November 2015, the subject of Bill Clinton's past history with women surfaced on the campaign trail when Hillary Clinton issued a tweet insisting that assault victims deserved to be heard and to be believed. The next month, a participant in a public forum asked the candidate if the same applied to her husband's accusers. "I would say that everybody should be believed at first," she answered, "until they are disbelieved based on evidence."[1]

The national news media made what appeared to be a concerted decision not to rehash the controversial events from Bill Clinton's past. Perhaps it was decided that they were irrelevant. Leaked emails from the Clinton campaign suggests that there might have even been some complicity with the Clintons, that the subject may have been avoided as a political calculation or at least out of respect for the frontrunner. In any case, a new generation was completely unaware of the events, and the older voters had forgotten the details. And then, much about the allegations was unknown at the time.

In October 2016, a revealing *Access Hollywood* audiotape emerged in which the GOP nominee, Donald Trump, spoke off camera about women as sex objects. By anyone's standards it was outrageous. Trump's words were denounced even by his own wife. This appeared to be the so-called October surprise; that is, the last-minute scandal targeting an opponent the month before the election. And it was a good one. The idea was to break a bad story so late in the campaign season that the opponent would not be able to recover.

The Democrats piled on. Many Republicans did as well. It appeared that the Trump campaign for the White House was over.

Donald Trump threatened to retaliate by bringing out Gennifer Flowers, Paula Jones, Kathleen Willey, and Juanita Broaddrick, all claiming to be victims of Bill Clinton and who all agreed with Trump that Hillary Clinton had "enabled" her husband's predatory sexual behavior. He claimed they might be his guests at the next presidential debate.

Some in the Clinton campaign were amused by Trump's bluster. They were ready. They said that Bill Clinton was not running for president, Hillary Clinton was the candidate. And the Clintons had long maintained that what President Clinton did in his own personal life had not been relevant to his work.

In fact, the sex scandals in the life of Bill Clinton had arguably had a major impact on his presidency and the world. According to members of his own administration, "almost nothing of real substance happened after the Lewinsky affair."[2] And the intimate details of Clinton's liaison with a young White House intern, recounted on the front pages of newspapers from Baghdad to Amman, didn't do much to help America's image in the Islamic Middle East.

The United States was the world's greatest exporter of pornography.[3] It was referred to in Iran and many other parts of the Islamic world as "the Great Satan." Now people of the world were reading in detail what the president was doing with his mistress. The fact that Miss Lewinsky was Jewish was heavily promoted in Islamic news outlets in the Middle East. To say that all of this had no impact on world events, including the terrorist activities that were to come, activities that would target America as a corrupting influence in the world, is disingenuous.

In the end, it was not Whitewater, or Travelgate, or Filegate, or Chinagate that would lead to the impeachment of Bill Clinton, and it was probably none of those scandals that was a primary factor in the loss of the 2016 election for Hillary Clinton. As you will see, they eventually led to tough questions surrounding the Clinton Foundation and the selling of the State Department, but if any scandal dragged down the Clinton machine, even in 2016, it was probably the enduring sex scandals of Bill Clinton and the suggestion that his wife, Hillary, participated in the cover-up and persecution of the victims.

Drowning in the negative coverage of his comments on the *Access Hollywood* tapes and recognizing that the national media was not going to discuss Bill Clinton's treatment of women and Hillary's role as an enabler, Donald Trump made good on his threat at the second presidential debate, bringing in Bill Clinton's women victims as his personal guests.

He was forcing the issue.

Even then, only Fox News among the media chose to cover any details of the stories. But that self-censorship by other media organizations may have backfired, forcing a new generation of viewers to search out the stories for themselves, which meant perusing the Internet, where the accounts were even more vivid and salacious than if the media had covered them straight.

Here's what they found:

Hillary Clinton was apparently aware of her husband's emotional and sexual needs from the very beginning of their relationship. He had participated in counseling sessions in the 1980s. Hillary once told a reporter, "I thought he understood it, but he didn't go deep enough or work hard enough."[4] And over the years she would endure multiple stories of infidelities, as well as accusations of sexual assault and harassment. Eventually there would be grand jury investigations, lawsuits, and finally impeachment, all related to Bill Clinton's problem.

Hillary Clinton would lash out at his accusers, sometimes calling them liars, even when it was later learned from members of her own staff that she knew very well that they were telling the truth. As you will see, some of her own staff believed that she leveraged the national media to ridicule and impoverish some of the women who had been her husband's targets.

For many years, additional questions remained. Was Hillary also aware of the detectives who were hired to harass these women? To follow them, to threaten them, to kill their pet animals? Was she aware of creepy-looking men who were hired to approach them suddenly on jogging trails and yell out the names of their children? Was she aware of or involved in the use of governmental power to go after these women? The IRS audits, the threats made to "break your pretty legs"? The damaging of their careers, the rewarding of their silence?

By 2016, some of the answers were known, but there had been no media update, no fresh examination. For example, it was now known that Hillary Clinton not only knew about the private detective who had been hired to harass the women, she had gone to law school with him and had recommended that the campaign hire him. And the method of inquiring about the spouse and children of a witness or victim was an intimidation practice used by both Bill and Hillary on other occasions that followed. When a White House

Secret Service officer was called to give his deposition in the Monica Lewinsky investigation, he returned to work only to be singled out by the president. He was surprised that the president even knew his name. And then the president asked about his wife, whom he named, and the agent's children, whom he also named.[5]

The argument from the Trump campaign was that, yes, Trump had used bad language. But the Clintons had done bad deeds. It was a story that begged telling to a new generation of voters.

BIMBO ERUPTIONS

In 1987, Bill Clinton, the governor of Arkansas, looked on in horror as Senator Gary Hart of Colorado failed spectacularly in his run for president. Hart was intelligent, with great ideas, and an ardent base of idealistic young people had embraced his candidacy. He was considered the likely nominee at the 1988 Democratic National Convention and the likely winner against any Republican opponent. But Hart had gotten himself into trouble. Irritated by gossip about his alleged infidelities, he poked the media bear, inviting it to investigate. "Follow me and see," he challenged. They complied, and Gary Hart was promptly caught spending the night with a young lady he had met on a boating excursion off the coast of Florida. The boat was appropriately named *Monkey Business*. The resultant scandal took him out of the race for president.

With Gary Hart gone, and with the fact that New York governor Mario Cuomo was not going to run, many suspected that Bill Clinton would enter the presidential race. But as his staff knew full well, Clinton had women problems of his own. Betsey Wright, Governor Clinton's chief of staff in Little Rock, felt well within her rights to confront her boss before proceeding any further. She would later tell the story to the author Carl Bernstein. "Let's walk through all the women," Betsey said to Governor Clinton. She was then "hor-rified because I thought I knew everybody. And he came up with these people I didn't know about."[6] Still, something had to be done about the list of names.

Hillary Clinton, meanwhile, took action. According to a story in the *Weekly Standard*, the first lady of Arkansas "deputized two of her law partners, Webb Hubbell and Vincent Foster, to invite the women one by one into the imposing Little Rock offices of their law firm, the largest in the state. There, the two lawyers confronted the women and generously offered to give them free legal counsel if the list was made public. Hillary attended at least one of the meetings."[7] The idea was to let these women know that if they tried to speak up, they'd better have significant legal representation, because the Clin-tons would be coming after them. And if they stayed quiet, their reputations and livelihood would be protected.

Betsey Wright warned Bill Clinton that after the Gary Hart scandal, Bill's participating in a national campaign in 1988, with its intense media scrutiny, might be devastating for his daughter Chelsea. He agreed, using his announcement to lay the ground for a future decision. "I need some family time," he said. "I need some personal time. Politicians are people too."[8]

Within months of the 1988 presidential election of George H. W. Bush, the Clinton machine began formulating its plans for the next presidential election cycle. At one point, an exasperated Bill Clinton, seeing no way to avoid scandal, suggested that Hillary run, but she would have none of it.

Instead, Hillary Clinton would team up with Betsey Wright to form what they called "the Defense Department." They gathered two thousand boxes of personal papers and correspondence, preparing to defend the governor from any charge. It was the precursor of the

Clinton rapid response team that would counter any negative story immediately. The method of transmission in the pre-Internet era was the fax machine. A negative story would hit, featuring charges or allegations, and the Clinton team would hit back immediately, to all news outlets, with an overwhelming paper counterpunch. The operation would be made famous in movies, but few knew that it started out as a wall of defense around Bill Clinton's personal sex life.

All that preparation would soon be tested. In 1990, two years before the presidential election, a disgruntled former Arkansas state employee filed a lawsuit claiming that Governor Bill Clinton had been using state funds to maintain relations with five different women. The related stories were mostly neutralized and prevented from publication, but once Bill Clinton officially announced his campaign for president, one of the stories broke into the open.

An attractive Arkansas television reporter named Gennifer Flowers had been mentioned in the lawsuit and was trying to correct some of the details. She finally had agreed to sit down with a reporter. Before it was over, Gennifer Flowers had ended up telling her story to a supermarket tabloid. According to Flowers, she had been governor Bill Clinton's mistress for more than twelve years.

The Clintons mounted a stout defense. Bill Clinton denied the story. Hillary Clinton called her a liar. It couldn't have come at a worse time. Bill Clinton was the acknowledged front-runner for the Democratic nomination. He had just appeared on the cover of *Time* magazine.[9] The New Hampshire primary, the first in the nation, was imminent.

The crisis reached a fever pitch when the Clintons agreed to appear together on the CBS television show *60 Minutes*. Most pundits agreed that the issue would be settled in the appearance, one way or the other.

On Sunday night, January 26, 1992, after a record audience had just watched Super Bowl XXVI, a demure Hillary Clinton sat next to her husband before CBS television cameras and demanded fairness in media coverage. "You know, I'm not sitting here, some little woman standing by my man like Tammy Wynette," she said. "I'm sitting here because I love him, and respect him, and I honor what he's been through and what we've been through together. And you know, if that's not enough for people, then heck—don't vote for him."[10]

It worked. The American people believed the Clintons. It was the word of a supermarket tabloid against the governor of the state of Arkansas and a contender for president. His wife believed him, so why shouldn't the rest of us? Perhaps more important, the national media, uncomfortable with the demise of Gary Hart, and the random unfairness that allows one politician to get caught and another to live a charmed life, was relieved to see the issue put the rest.

It was not to be. Gennifer Flowers, clumsy and gauche, had an irresistible advantage, which we now can appreciate in hindsight: She was telling the truth. The Clintons were lying. Flowers held a press conference the next day and produced tape recordings of Bill Clinton urging her to just lie about the relationship. "If they ever hit you with it just say no and go on. There's nothing they can do," Clinton said.

But the national media had felt so good about putting the issue to rest they couldn't bring themselves to confront this new reality. CNN, which carried the Gennifer Flowers news conference live, refused to broadcast the tapes on its regular news show, saying that they had not been "authenticated." CBS, which had interviewed the Clintons in good faith on *60 Minutes* the night before, was less squeamish and ran pertinent excerpts.

Flowers said, "Yes, I was Bill Clinton's lover for twelve years, and for the past two years I have lied to the press about our relationship to protect him. The truth is, I loved him. Now he asks me to deny it."[11]

She also had watched the *60 Minutes* show. "I felt disgusted, and I saw a side of Bill that I have never seen before. He is absolutely lying," she said at her press conference. "The man on *60 Minutes* was not the man I fell in love with."[12]

Flowers said she had come forward because she was afraid.

Two of the Clintons' aides, George Stephanopoulos and James Carville, insisted that the Flowers' tapes were doctored and made an effort to intimidate any news outlet that proposed to use them. Flowers was occasionally booked on a television or radio show only to have her appearance canceled at the last minute.

The author of this book had a friendship with the editor of a major magazine at the time, who concluded to me privately that, yes, the Clintons had lied, but they had lied to protect their marriage. Was that a bad thing? Should that be a disqualifier?

Eleanor Clift of *Newsweek* said, "Truth is, the press is willing to cut Clinton some slack because they like him and what he has to say."[13]

On February 18, 1992, Bill Clinton came in second in the New Hampshire primary but went on to win the Democratic nomination for president. During the general-election campaign against George H. W. Bush several more stories of Clinton extramarital affairs surfaced, but the Clinton team managed to keep them out of the news.

Betsey Wright complained to a *Washington Post* reporter that she had spent much of her time trying to stop such stories. She called them "bimbo eruptions." According to Wright, the campaign had hired a private investigator "to obtain information damaging to the credibility of the women involved, which was then used, presumably to persuade them to stay quiet."[14]

Gwen Ifill wrote in the *New York Times* about numerous reports that never saw the light of day because an alert Clinton campaign kept them out of print.[15] George Stephanopoulos would later say that this process worked "more often than you think."[16]

Finally in 1998, forced to testify in a deposition, Bill Clinton admitted under oath that he had indeed had a sexual encounter with Gennifer Flowers.[17] And he said that he had been careful not to lie about it, as everyone was now claiming. He had denied having a twelve-year affair with Gennifer Flowers, which was true. It had been eleven and a half years. But hardly anyone cared. It was a story in the past.

Tending her orchids at her home in Beaver Lake, Arkansas, Betsey Wright, the loyal Clinton aide who had coined the phrase "bimbo eruptions," couldn't resist talking to a reporter from the *Washington Post*. "How many times I asked him about Gennifer Flowers," she recalled. "And how many times he told me that they never had any kind of affair. And then I read in the newspaper that there was.

"I think it has to do with this inexplicable inferiority complex the guy had carried his whole life. It's a sickness and I can't wait till he gets out of the White House and is free to get help for it."[18]

Several reporters who had written defamatory stories about Gennifer Flowers, portraying her as a gold digger, selling a false story to make money, now called her to apologize. They had believed Bill Clinton. They were sorry.

A WARNING TO SALLY PERDUE

In the summer of 1992, a former Miss Arkansas, Sally Perdue, appeared on television to announce that she too had conducted an illicit affair with Bill Clinton in the 1980s. Eventually, over the years, there would be three more Miss Arkansas winners who would emerge to make the same accusation. The beauty contest was apparently good fishing grounds for Bill Clinton the sportsman.

The timing of the announcement was not good. Not for Clinton. Not for the national media. Not for Sally Perdue. Only the day before, Bill Clinton had received the nomination for president of the United States at the Democratic National Convention in New York City.

The Perdue event was a bombshell. The American corporate media was like a deer caught in the headlights. It couldn't move. Most of its producers and editors had covered the Gennifer Flowers story, then had sided with the Clintons when they fiercely denied the allegations of a "twelve-year affair." They were then caught with mud on their faces when Flowers produced her tapes, then told, relentlessly, by Clinton "experts," that the Flowers tapes had been doctored.

Most of the media's corporate executives now accepted that Clinton and his team had lied to them about Gennifer Flowers, but why were such personal matters relevant anyway? The media and the public hadn't exacted such demands from John F. Kennedy. Which of the media board chairmen themselves would want their own personal life open to such examination? Was there no decency left? Was not a lie to preserve a marriage actually an honorable thing? The media had already sacrificed Gary Hart on the altar of propriety; wasn't that sufficient? How many more?

There was also a political calculation. Almost to a man, they favored a Clinton win over the reelection of George H. W. Bush. If a news outlet covered the Sally Perdue story, it had surely better be accurate, or it would pay the price in credibility with its sister television networks and fellow publishers ever after. Bill Clinton was boldly telling reporters that he had never even met the woman.

Sally Perdue's television appearance occurred on the Sally Jessy Raphael show, which had likewise struggled with the idea of an interview so close to the Democratic National Convention. The show would pay a heavy price.

The Sally Perdue story would be even more colorful than that of Gennifer Flowers. Perdue, seven years older than Bill Clinton, said that the governor would call and warn her when he was coming by and she would leave her back door open. It was an arrangement she made because a prominent member of the community lived nearby and might have otherwise noticed the governor coming and going.

Privately, to select friends and sources, Sally depicted a playful Bill Clinton, who once put on her lacy black nightgown and paraded around her house playing the saxophone, with her accompanying him on the piano. She said they laughed as much as they had sex.

Sally told sources that when she asked about Hillary Clinton, he had been circumspect and then said that she preferred sex with women. According to Sally, Bill told her that this preference had started as a fashionable thing in her college years.

This was private-information overload. It was not what journalists were prepared to hear. Nor were the American people. The stories proliferated on the Internet and popped up in tabloid journals in Great Britain during the 2016 election. But the American media, which would not hesitate to air Donald Trump's lewd comments to a reporter from *Access Hollywood* only a month before the election, refused to give Sally Perdue a platform. Ever.

Later, Arkansas State Troopers would be forced to testify under oath and would confirm that they had, indeed, facilitated the governor's extramarital liaisons. This included driving the governor to Sally Perdue's house, among other things. Perdue told a British newspaper that the troopers would "pull up in a wooded area about 30 feet from the house and wait there. When Bill was ready to come out he would signal using my patio light, flicking it on and off."[19]

Except for the stunned, probably disbelieving viewers of the Sally Jessy Raphael show, the American people would not hear or see anything about Sally Perdue. Her story was ignored by the mainstream media. It was as if it didn't exist. With one exception: The next day, the *Los Angeles Times* ran a scathing critique, mocking Perdue and ripping into Sally Jessy Raphael for allowing her guest to besmirch the character of Bill Clinton, the Democratic nominee for president.[20]

But if the national media ignored the Sally Perdue story, the Clintons and their "defense department" were watching and listening to every line. Sally had done her worst, and it had flubbed. Now it was the Clintons' turn.

Prior to the Democratic National Convention, Betsey Wright and Hillary Clinton had tracked seven women who had claimed to have had intimate relations with Bill Clinton. After the convention and Sally Perdue's public appearance, the numbers exploded. Within a week, the Clinton "defense department" was tracking nineteen more women who were making allegations.

The Clinton campaign responded on multiple fronts. First came Bill Clinton's denial. Then the Clinton response team flooded news agencies and television producers' offices with threats of lawsuits, followed by good cop, bad cop telephone tag teams.

Then the campaign went after the women themselves, beginning with Gennifer Flowers but especially targeting the now isolated and vulnerable Sally Perdue. At Hillary's suggestion, it hired Jack Palladino, a San Francisco attorney, to help manage the crisis.[21] Hillary knew him from law school. He ran "one of America's most successful investigative agencies," Palladino and Sutherland. It employed ten detectives and charged as much as $2,000 a day for its work. The Clinton campaign would pay Palladino's firm $100,000.[22]

In a private memo written to the campaign, Palladino defined his goal with Gennifer Flowers, the first of Bill Clinton's women to open her mouth. He declared he would "impeach her character and veracity until she is destroyed beyond all recognition."[23] The phrase was a play on the military acronym FUBAR ("fucked-up beyond all recognition").[24]

"I am somebody you call in when the house is on fire, not when there's smoke in the kitchen," he told Gail Sheehy, the author of *Hillary's Choice*. "You ask me to deal with that fire, to save you, to do whatever has to be done."[25]

Palladino tracked down a long list of Sally Perdue's friends, neighbors, and relatives, looking for what he could find. Sally began getting anonymous phone calls. But Palladino was not the only Clinton attack dog.

On August, 19, 1992, only a month after Perdue's television appearance, she agreed to meet with an alleged official of the Democratic party named Ron Tucker. They met at the Cheshire Inn in Clayton, Missouri.

According to Perdue, "he said that there were people in high places who were anxious about me and they wanted me to know that keeping my mouth shut would be worthwhile. . . . If I was a good little girl, and didn't kill the messenger, I'd be set for life: a federal job, nothing fancy but a regular paycheck, level 11 or 12 (about $60,000 a year). I'd never have to worry again.

"But if I didn't take the offer, then they knew that I went jogging by myself and he couldn't guarantee what would happen to my pretty little legs. Things just wouldn't be so much fun for me anymore. Life would get hard."[26]

There is a little-known twist to this story that gets scant attention, but in light of the 2016 presidential campaign, and the role of FBI director James Comey, it deserves to be revisited. Sally had been worried about the meeting in Clayton and had asked a coworker, Denison Diel, to join her and sit nearby. As it turned out, he was able to get a seat at a bar near their table and overheard the conversation. Diel subsequently wrote a report of the threats, which was submitted to the FBI. A copy was given to the journalist Ambrose Evans-Pritchard and the UK *Sunday Telegraph*.

Ron Tucker's prophesy soon came true. Sally Perdue was fired from her job in the admissions office of Lindenwood University in Missouri. A local lawyer, Paul Ground, told the *Sunday Telegraph* that "a college official had admitted to him that she had been fired because of outside pressure."[27]

Sally began to receive hate mail. She showed reporters a handwritten letter that said, "I'll pray you have a head-on collision and end up in a coma. . . . Marilyn Monroe got snuffed. It could happen."[28] Her car was damaged. She found "an unspent shotgun cartridge on the driver's seat of her Jeep. Later the back window of the vehicle was shattered, possibly by gunfire."[29]

An attempt to go silent was short lived. In 1994, the story of the Arkansas State Troopers surfaced and then the Paula Jones story. Sally Perdue's name was dragged back into public testimony, this time without her participation.

Isolated, living in fear, unable to trust the American government or the American media, Sally Perdue fled the country. She lived in China, taking a job in radio, broadcasting for the blind. And then, in 1998, President Bill Clinton and First Lady Hillary Clinton made a state visit to the country. During their time in Beijing, Sally Perdue's room was raided by Chinese and American agents. The Americans told the manager that she was a drug dealer "who had fled the United States to avoid prosecution."[30]

By the time of the 2016 presidential election, Sally Miller, the former Sally Perdue, was living back in the United States. The anonymous phone calls had started back up. Cars parked on her street and followed her when she jogged. When she would approach such a car, it would speed off. She began to post messages on social media, telling friends that if they were to ever hear that she had committed suicide, they should not believe it.

During the 2016 presidential campaign, Sally "Perdue" Miller once again went public with her story. The British tabloids covered it extensively. The American media ignored it. Sally decided that living in the open offered her more safety than fading from view. Throughout the campaign she slept with a revolver under her pillow.

PAULA JONES, THE DEFIANT

The Paula Jones story led to the impeachment and downfall of Bill Clinton. On May 8, 1991, Paula and a coworker, Pamela Blackard, were Arkansas State employees working the tables for an industrial conference at the Excelsior Hotel in downtown Little Rock, Arkansas. Paula and Pamela were running the registration table outside a ballroom on the second floor. Governor Bill Clinton was expected to be a featured speaker.

According to Jones, at two o'clock in the afternoon a Clinton bodyguard, State Trooper Danny Ferguson, approached their table. He passed Paula Jones a slip of paper and said that the governor would like to meet her in his room.

Jones said, "Well, why does he want to meet with me?"

According to Jones, Trooper Ferguson said, "It's okay, we do this all the time."

Jones and Pamela talked about what it might mean. Jones was then earning $6.35 an hour. Both ladies agreed there was a chance they could get a better state job. Ferguson escorted her up the elevator to a higher floor and down the hall to a room where the door had been left slightly open. Governor Clinton was there and invited her into the room.

According to Jones, they exchanged pleasantries and then abruptly Clinton pulled her toward him and put his hand up her leg. He said he liked her curves and he liked the way her hair flowed down her back. He kissed her on her neck. Jones said, "Don't do this!" She said she clearly rejected him.

Sam Donaldson of ABC television interviewed Paula Jones on *Primetime Live* in 1994. "At that point, Mrs. Jones, a lot of people wonder why you didn't just run out of the room? Leave," he said.[31]

"I was scared," she answered. She assumed that the trooper was sitting outside the door. How could she go to the police? The police had brought her up to the room. And Clinton was the governor and had told her that he knew her boss.

According to Jones, Bill Clinton exposed himself to her and asked her to perform a sex act. She said she was shocked. "No, I'm not that kind of girl. I'm not that kind of girl."

And Clinton apparently responded saying, "Well, I don't want to make you do something you don't want to do."

Clinton then brought up her boss again, suggesting that he could talk to him if she got in trouble for leaving her post. "You're a smart girl. Let's keep this between ourselves."[32]

There was one other observation that Paula Jones would offer as an intriguing side note. She said that Bill Clinton was "beet red." Other Clinton victims, telling their stories separately to prosecutors, would say the same thing.

Jones went back down to her post and told her coworker, Pamela Blackard. Before the day was over she told two others, including her sister.

Ferguson ran into Jones a few weeks later, saying that the governor wanted her phone number. Jones refused to give it. And then, the Paula Jones story went dark.

Paula Jones got married, had a son, and moved to California. As far as Jones was concerned it had been a shocking, surreal moment, but it was over.

Then in December 1993, the *American Spectator* ran a story about Bill Clinton and the Arkansas State Troopers who allegedly kept the governor supplied with women. There was a "Paula" mentioned in the story, with Ferguson apparently referring to her as the governor's girlfriend. There was even a description of a sexual encounter with Clinton and "Paula" at the Excelsior Hotel that day in May.

Paula Jones was outraged and then humiliated. She imagined that her family and friends would hear about the story and see her in a different light. They might now believe that she had not rejected his advances. That something had happened between them. Jones cast about for someone to help her restore her reputation.

Conservative organizations picked up her cause and set up a press conference in Washington, DC. Paula Jones was going public. Many in the mainstream media were disgusted. This was a political witch hunt.

The Clinton team, well practiced in handling "bimbo eruptions," hit back hard. The White House staff called her "a liar" and "pathetic."[33] Said Clinton loyalist James Carville, "If you drag a hundred dollar bill through a trailer park, you never know what you'll find."[34]

The mainstream media fell into line, openly ridiculing and attacking Paula Jones. Evan Thomas, a writer for *Newsweek*, told a television audience that Jones was "some sleazy woman with big hair coming out of the trailer parks."[35] Picking up on the White House version of Clinton's accusers as either "nuts or sluts," *US*

News and World Report described Jones as taking "to wearing short, tight skirts to school, and more makeup than other girls in Lonoke [Arkansas], eyeliner, shadow rouge, red lipstick and lip gloss."[36]

Paula Jones retained attorneys, and they filed a lawsuit against the president of the United States and against Trooper Ferguson. Questions were raised if it were even legally possible to file a lawsuit against a sitting president.

The president's attorney, Robert Bennett, said, "The president adamantly denies the vicious and mean-spirited allegations in this complaint. Quite simply, the incident did not occur." Clinton, himself, refused to respond. "I'm not going to dignify this with a comment."

Uniformly, the national media, on a short leash from their corporate owners, dependent on the government to succeed big, fell into line, decrying the absurdity of the actions of Paula Jones. Women's rights organizations remained unsupportive. "This is just one more political assault on the president," wrote Susan Estrich in *Slate*, "politically motivated and politically pursued. You can't tell me this woman didn't know whom she was hiring as a lawyer, whom she was allying herself with, whom she was using, and who being used by."[37]

Years later, in the midst of the 2016 race, Estrich would attack Donald Trump as "rude, offensive, racist, bombastic, [and] insensitive," and the denunciations continue on. But when Roger Ailes, the president and creator of Fox News, became the target of a sexual-harassment lawsuit, Estrich would rush to become the lawyer in his defense.[38]

Some journalists privately began to have their doubts. It wasn't good for their political career to question the White House, and this "bimbo eruption" business had already been put to rest, but the story of Paula Jones had the ring of truth to it. Why had the president retained Robert Bennett, one of Washington's finest? Why was the president afraid? Jones was making it clear: while her attorneys wanted money, she simply wanted an apology. Jones told reporters that she didn't even know what a conservative was.

When Paula Jones' own sister challenged her story, the media heaved a sigh of relief and begin to put the story on a shelf. And then another bombshell landed. A year into the lawsuit, *Penthouse* magazine published lewd, topless photos of Jones. They were taken by her boyfriend when she was nineteen years old. Jones' lawyers moved to stop the publication but were too late; the photos were splashed all over television, the sensitive parts blurred to meet the standards of the television censors.

Eventually, mostly out of the news, the wheels of justice began their slow, inexorable grind. In the discovery phase of the legal proceedings Paula Jones' attorneys asked the president about his sexual history. By then Washington was abuzz with new stories about the president's girlfriends. The Jones attorneys zeroed in on the items of gossip. Had the president had a sexual affair with a White House intern named Monica Lewinsky?

No, he had not, Bill Clinton replied indignantly. He was under oath, and when the affair with Lewinsky later became public and, eventually, a proven fact, Bill Clinton's denial would become the basis of a charge of perjury and obstruction of justice. It would lead to his impeachment.

Bill Clinton would settle the Paula Jones lawsuit in 1998, out of court, paying Jones and her lawyers $850,000. Clinton never apologized or admitted to any wrongdoing.

Paula Jones, meanwhile, would find herself under constant IRS audit. In October 2000, she would break the hearts of her supporters by appearing again in *Penthouse* magazine, this time with permission and fully cooperative. "I am an adult woman and made the choice to do so," she said. She was now a single mother, constantly under an enormous IRS burden of taxes and under the pressure of mounting bills, she added. "I thought it was the best thing to do for me and my children."[39]

In 2016, in the middle of his presidential run for office, defending himself against attacks from the media and the Clinton machine, Donald Trump would bring Paula Jones back to the national stage. Now a real estate agent, Paula Jones, along with other women who had been the alleged targets of sexual harassment by Bill Clinton, would be in the audience at the final national debate.

Wiser and more mature, Paula Jones returned to public life as a mother and a citizen who had taken a strong stand against one of the most powerful persons on earth. She had refused to be a victim. She was an example and an advocate, urging young ladies to stand up for themselves against powerful men who harassed them.

The national media kept a respectful distance. In the end, many would conclude that it was not Paula Jones who had been "pathetic" and a "liar." Nor was it only Paula Jones who had acted like "trailer park trash." Bill Clinton had called her a "floozy" and a "nobody."[40] But in the end, she brought him down.

CHAPTER 8

MONICA LEWINSKY AND IMPEACHMENT

The measure of a man is what he does with power.
—*PLATO*

On January 21, 1998, the *Washington Post* broke a story announcing that independent counsel Kenneth Starr was investigating charges that Bill Clinton and his close friend Vernon Jordan had tried to get a White House intern to lie to the lawyers representing Paula Jones. According to the allegations, Clinton and Jordan had tried to get a White House intern to deny, under oath, that she had had a sexual relationship with the president of the United States. Paula Jones' lawyers were trying to show that Clinton had a serial, predatory problem with women. And Clinton, they contended, was using his power and influence to obstruct justice.

It was a bombshell. Another "bimbo eruption." This time, inside the White House. Who was she? What would Clinton say about it?

She was Monica Lewinsky, and she would become the most famous presidential mistress in American history.

In some remarkable but destructive ways, Bill Clinton and Monica Lewinsky were a match for each other. Both underestimated critical characteristics of the other.

Sally Perdue said that as a man and as a lover, Bill Clinton had an uncanny way of making a woman feel good about herself, by complementing the shape of her body or describing some aspect of her that took thought and showed sweet devotion. Paula Jones said that he had told her he liked the way her hair flowed down her back. Perdue felt that Bill's ability to understand and say what a woman wanted to hear was almost a gift. For Monica, sensitive to a weight problem, the affirming words of Bill Clinton, the president of the United States, must have been a tonic. In fact, she told Barbara Walters that they often had "phone sex." The words may have aroused and satisfied the sexual needs of the president, but they may have also fed the cravings of a love-starved young girl who needed to be told that she was desirable.

In her interview with Barbara Walters, Monica Lewinsky admitted that she had been in love with Bill Clinton and had told him so. She said that the two had imagined a possible life together, after all the White House business was over. The president had protested about their age difference, saying, "What are you going to do when I am 70 and I have to pee 25 times a day?"[1] That made Monica laugh.

What Monica Lewinsky could not have known was how experienced Bill Clinton was with women. Reportedly she was furious when she suspected he had betrayed her by having sex with Eleanor Mondale.[2] What she didn't know, until deep into the summer, was that according to the Arkansas State Troopers, he had had sex with hundreds of women.

There was no way that summer she could have understood how suddenly, like a tropical thunderstorm, and with such cruel dispatch, Bill Clinton could cut off a relationship when circumstances demanded it. And eventually, the circumstances always demanded it. Always.

In such moments, Clinton, the thoughtful lover, could turn viciously on the very person who had been his sex partner and the recipient of his tender affirmation. He could use his power to isolate and terrorize her.

One could argue that it wasn't personal, that it was only about protecting his position, all for a greater cause, to be able to do good things for people, even good things for women. And one could argue that there may have been a darker need. That Bill's religious convictions made him turn angry at his temptresses and feel justified in blaming them, even punishing them. Regardless, it left the women devastated, and whether real or not, even fearful for their lives. And if Monica was oblivious to this coming train wreck, with the resultant pain, Bill Clinton knew it was coming, every time he took her in his arms, and he knew that she would be hurt badly and he would move on.

But if Monica had set herself up for heartbreak and betrayal, she too was more than met the eye. On the surface, she was a twenty-two-year-old White House intern who had grown up in Beverly Hills. Bubbly and positive, with a playful personality and an infectious smile. She was smitten by the president. What could go wrong? What possible threat could she pose? Even so, as young as she was, she was a far more accomplished seductress than the president might have guessed. She had already experienced a five-year affair with a married man, beginning in her teenage years. Bill Clinton would underestimate her. And it would cost him.

At first glance, the January 2, 1998, *Washington Post* story was made to order for the Clinton machine. It was technically not true. Clinton had not asked Monica to lie about the relationship. And as Clinton had learned, accuracy was everything. If the media would ask the wrong questions in the wrong way, which it almost always did, he could deny them and thus appear to deny the whole context of the story as well.

But there was beginning to be an aggregate effect of all of these scandals. Clinton would deny them, and his team would find flaws in the details of a story or in the character of an alleged victim. By the time the media caught up with the loose ends, the story was old and Clinton would admit to it while pointing out that he had not actually lied, but rather the media had not asked the right question.

At some point, he was going to make a misstep on this high wire. And at some point, the corporate media leaders of influence were going to withdraw their protection and he would come tumbling down. In this metaphor, there was not a net.

The very evening of the *Washington Post* story, President Clinton appeared on the Public Broadcasting System's popular show *The NewsHour with Jim Lehrer*. At the president's invitation, the interview took place in the Roosevelt Room of the White House.

"Mr. President, the news of this day," Lehrer said, "is that Kenneth Starr, the independent counsel, is investigating allegations that you suborned perjury by encouraging a twenty-four-year-old woman, a former White House intern, to lie under oath in a civil deposition about her having had an affair with you. Mr. President, is that true?"[3]

Clinton answered emphatically, looking straight at Lehrer. "That is not true. That is not true." And Clinton said, "I did not ask anyone to tell anything other than the truth. There is no improper relationship, and I intend to cooperate with this inquiry. But that is not true."[4] He sounded very sincere.

Then Jim Lehrer fell into the trap that had ensnared many journalists before him by asking Clinton to define what he meant by "no improper relationship."

Clinton was always happy to be the one to define the terms. It was a long-acquired skill that had led him through many a minefield of interviews and depositions. "Well, I think you know what it means," Clinton said. "It means that there is not a sexual relationship, an improper sexual relationship, or any other kind of improper relationship."[5]

Just to make sure he had it right, Jim Lehrer repeated what he thought he had heard. "You had no sexual relationship with this young woman?"

"There is not a sexual relationship," Clinton reiterated. "That is accurate."

But what was accurate? What Lehrer had said or what Clinton had said? And the answer was, of course, that Clinton was referring to what *he* had said. There was not a sexual relationship. Period. That meant now. At this moment. And that was accurate. He and Monica Lewinsky no longer had a sexual relationship. Thus his answer "There is not a sexual relationship."

For Bill Clinton, it was another easy interview, but he had to know that he was in real danger. Years before, he had revealed a basic rule of Clinton infidelity when he told Gennifer Flowers not to say anything, that there was nothing anyone could do if the persons involved were silent.

He must have thought that he had been careful to be alone with Monica Lewinsky when anything intimate happened. If one was alone, it was simply her word against his, and he had always been the attorney general or the governor or the president. Who would they believe? But that was the point. They—the public, the media, and his own staff—were beginning to doubt him. There were too many accusations. If, as the Clintons argued, this was all driven by money from tabloids or by Republican dirty tricks, then why didn't the attacks target Al Gore or anybody else?

And Monica Lewinsky was not a Republican. She had not sold her story to a tabloid. She was not filing a lawsuit. She admired Bill

Clinton, worshipped him even, and she had been his friend. She had also been an intern, and he had been her boss. What would that mean? Legally? Ethically?

The White House was such a public place, with its stewards coming and going and Secret Service officers everywhere, including the officer who stood outside the door to Clinton's Oval Office suite, a cluster of rooms that included another office, a small toilet, and dining room. In fact, that officer, Gary Byrne, would later write the book *Crisis of Character*, an account of his experiences. There would be some awkward pages that included stories of staff members finding towels in the Oval Office suite with semen and lipstick stains on them. Byrne also described witnessing awkward moments with Clinton and women, including Monica Lewinsky and Eleanor Mondale.[6]

The word coming from sources inside the investigation was that Monica Lewinsky had held firm. On January 7, 1998, she had stated emphatically, "No, she did not have an affair with the president."[7]

At that point, Bill Clinton's biggest concern may have been the corporate media leaders of influence. There was nothing he could do about Fox News. It was a rogue elephant that was out of control. But what if the other prominent news companies grew tired of protecting him? What if they turned their media properties loose to follow the stories where they led? What if they decided that Al Gore would be better for business than Bill Clinton, with all of his personal distractions? The answer was that they were mostly influenced by the public, the viewers and the revenue they represented. Bill Clinton had to rally the public.

On January 12, 1998, Linda Tripp, a former White House staffer and a confidante to Monica Lewinsky, turned over tape-recorded conversations with Lewinsky to the independent counselor Kenneth

Starr. The hours of tape recordings led to days and weeks of further investigations.

On January 26, 1998, Bill Clinton went before the public. In clear and stern tones, as if addressing naughty children, he looked into the camera and lectured, "I want you to listen to me. I'm going to say this again. I did not have sexual relations with that woman, Miss Lewinsky. These allegations are false and I need to go back to work for the American people."[8]

Monica Lewinsky, as in the case of other women before her, was stunned by this stern rebuke. This different face. She was even risking prison to lie for him, to protect him. Now she was "that woman." Deeply hurt and humiliated, Monica retreated into the shadows, hiding from the media at her mother's Watergate condominium. The storm outside raged on, as journalists poured over every detail of her life. Republican and Democratic pundits, each with their own motivations, took to the air to denounce or ridicule her.

But Monica was not as isolated as some of the other women had been. At least she had her mother as her fragile support system, terrified and small as the two may have felt. With giant news organizations and the government aligned against them and an independent counsel already holding her freedom in his hands, Monica slowly began to assess her frightening options. With her mother beside her, she would do what she had to do to survive.

Guided by the tapes from Linda Tripp, Kenneth Starr's investigators zeroed in on one particular conversation with Monica Lewinsky. The young intern was talking about "a blue Gap dress that still bore the semen stain that resulted from her administering oral sex to President Clinton."[9] Tripp urged Monica to keep it as evidence in case there should be some legal ramifications and the White House turned on her. Later, the media mercilessly attacked Linda Tripp for this advice, but given the aggressive actions from the Clinton machine, it turned out to be, in fact, a reasonable suggestion.

Each month, further evidence and testimony from Secret Service agents and White House staff members was making it increasingly clear that Monica Lewinsky's denial of a sexual relationship with the president was a lie. In the end, the blue dress, with its semen stain, saved her. In late July 1998, she made a deal. She would give the dress to the special prosecutor's investigators and agree to hereafter answer all questions truthfully. In return, she was given immunity from prosecution.

On August 3, in the Map Room of the White House, with the president's attorney, a witness from the independent counsel's team, and an agent from the FBI all looking on, the president's doctor took blood samples from Bill Clinton. The president's DNA would be compared with the semen stain on Monica Lewinsky's blue dress. The analysis would be done at the FBI laboratory. The pressure on Bill Clinton during these days of waiting must have been intense. He knew the outcome.

On Saturday, August 15, 1998, according to Hillary Clinton, Bill woke her up and began pacing by her bed. He told her for the first time "that the situation was much more serious than he had previously acknowledged," according to Hillary.

"He now realized he would have to testify that there had been an inappropriate intimacy. He told me that what happened between them had been brief and sporadic." [10]

Hillary wrote in her book *Living History* that he was shamed by the experience and he understood that she would be furious.

"I could hardly breathe," she wrote. "Gulping for air, I started crying and yelling at him, 'What do you mean? What are you saying? Why did you lie to me?' I was furious and getting more so by the second. He just stood there saying over and over again, 'I'm sorry. I'm so sorry. I was trying to protect you and Chelsea.'"[11]

On August 17, 1998, the independent counsel's investigators interviewed President Clinton. They were back in the Map Room. He was being interviewed before a grand jury that was watching on a big-screen television. It was a criminal investigation of the president of the United States. Of special concern was the possibility that the president had helped arrange a job for Monica Lewinsky, and that had he tried to get her to return gifts he had given her, which might have uncovered the truth.

That same day, the FBI had the answer on the DNA from the blood test and the blue dress. It was a match.[12]

Later in the evening of that eventful day, after seven months of denying his affair with Monica Lewinsky, "that woman," Bill Clinton admitted to the nation, "I did have a relationship with Miss Lewinsky that was not appropriate."[13] Many White House staffers were stunned.

"I know that my public comments and my silence about this matter gave a false impression," he said. "I misled people, including even my wife. I deeply regret that."[14]

The next day, Bill and Hillary Clinton, with their daughter Chelsea between them, walked across the South Lawn of the White House grounds to Marine One, the president's helicopter. It was a long walk, and it was watched on television around the world. The Clintons were off to Massachusetts for a family summer vacation. Close friends later said that Hillary had not slept well and she had been crying.

A month later, Hillary Clinton poured her heart out to a close friend. The conversation was with Diane Blair, a political science professor who later died in 2000. Ms. Blair's private notes and correspondence were made public in 2010, long after Hillary Clinton's first run for president.

"It was a lapse," Mrs. Clinton reportedly told Ms. Blair, on September 9, 1998, explaining her husband's affair with Monica Lewinsky. "To his credit he tried to break it off, tried to pull away, tried to manage someone who was clearly a 'narcissistic loony toon' but it was beyond control."[15]

According to Blair, Hillary suggested that her husband had been vulnerable after the sorrowful loss of his mother, and then there was their mutual friend Vince Foster, who had committed suicide. Meanwhile, "the ugly forces started making up hateful things about them, pounding on them."[16]

Hillary Clinton would later write about this time in her book *Living History*. "The most difficult decisions I have made in my life were to stay married to Bill and to run for the Senate from New York."

On December 19, 1998, President Bill Clinton was impeached by the US House of Representatives. They brought two charges, one of perjury and one of obstruction of justice. On February 12, 1999, he was acquitted on all charges.

In May 2015, with Hillary Clinton the favorite to win election as the next US president, Monica Lewinsky was offered $1 million for her blue dress. Lewinsky declined saying, "I, myself, deeply regret what happened between me and President Clinton."[17]

As the 2016 presidential election hit the home stretch, media observers concluded that Bill Clinton's past sins were not a factor. The Associated Press ran a story entitled "Millennial Voters Don't Seem to Care about Bill Clinton's Affairs." One young female voter told the reporter, "The only people I know who support Trump are men, mostly older men."[18] The story was all anecdotal; it contained no polling data.

CHAPTER 9

THE SELLING OF THE WHITE HOUSE

The world has enough for everyone's need
but not enough for everyone's greed.
—*GANDHI*

On February 25, 1997, the *NBC Nightly News* opened with Tom Brokaw breaking yet another Clinton scandal. "Good evening," he said. "It's a great honor to spend a night at the White House, but for hundreds of people in the last four years, 1600 Pennsylvania Avenue turned out to be the most expensive bed and breakfast in North America. They stayed and they paid."[1]

Thus began what became known as the Lincoln Bedroom scandal. It is a story that is still instructive for us today. We are even now still learning how the Clintons made good use of the presidency to raise money. For example, long after the Lincoln Bedroom scandal, we learned that in addition to the 800 individuals who donated and stayed with the Clintons there, another 404 big-donor guests stayed at Camp David, courtesy of the American taxpayers.

Twenty-four years later, many of those Lincoln Bedroom and Camp David guests were still giving money to the Clintons. By January 2016, more than half of the Lincoln Bedroom donors had already given to Hillary Clinton's presidential campaign or supported one of her PACs. Donations from that small universe totaled $1.15 million. The Lincoln Bedroom was a gift that kept on giving.

Scribbled at the bottom of one of the 1996 White House memos eventually obtained by Charles G. Labella, the federal prosecutor investigating the scandal, was a note in the president's own handwriting. It was this simple message: "Ready to start overnights right away."[2]

Would Bill Clinton be writing those words again? Or signaling them? What would be Hillary Clinton's policy for White House visitors? Here is a brief refresher course on what happened last time and how it took the Clintons another step closer to the Clinton Foundation, and how it informed the unprecedented, massive fund-raising effort of the 2016 presidential campaign.

THE LINCOLN BEDROOM SCANDAL

According to White House records, the list of 800 people who spent the night in the Lincoln Bedroom consists only of the numbers compiled during the two years of Bill Clinton's drive for reelection as president. And even beyond that number, others stayed across the hallway in the Queen Mum's bedroom suite, the rooms where Winston Churchill stayed during his 1941 wartime visit with Franklin D. Roosevelt. These rooms were located on the second floor of the White House, in the private family quarters, where the president and first lady are carefully locked in each night.

The sleepovers in the Clinton White House were apparently sold to top donors. At least $5.4 million was raked in just for President Clinton's 1996 reelection bid alone. These sales took place at the same time that all that money was pouring into the Democratic National Committee from foreign governments.

Bill Clinton's guests included a long list of distinguished Holly-wood celebrities like Barbra Streisand, who gave $60,000, and Steven Spielberg, who plunked down $336,000. Lew Wasserman gave $225,000. Some were businessmen, such as Dirk Ziff, who gave $411,000, and William Rollnick, who gave $235,000. Steve Jobs gave $150,000.

The story began to leak out even while a special prosecutor was deep into investigations on Whitewater, the death of Vince Foster, and Chinagate. Most informed observers, including the sophisticated White House press corps, were skeptical. Having participated in White House meetings in both Democratic and Republican administrations and having served on senior staff as a special assistant to the president in the George H. W. Bush White House, the author of this book had experienced the very careful and tedious attention to law and ethics that ruled previous administrations. This applied to Democratic administrations as well as Republican.

I remember a meeting in the Roosevelt Room of the White House with Anne Wexler, an assistant to President Carter. When the conversation became political, she suspended the proceedings abruptly, and everyone moved across the street to another building. The White House could not be used for political activity, and there should not be the slightest misunderstanding about it.

I remember carefully assisting an overnight guest staying in the Lincoln Bedroom in the Bush Sr. White House. He was nervous and wanted some reassurance from an old friend, so I was helping him unpack his things. But he was hardly a big donor. He was the Catholic archbishop of Boston. It was one of a very few times I was in the private quarters. That floor was reserved for family.

After Christmas 1996, the rumors of the pay-to-play Lincoln Bedroom scheme begin to pick up steam. The White House was embarrassed by the stories and initially shifted the blame to an aggressive Terry McAuliffe, then serving as Clinton's 1996 reelection campaign cochairman. McAuliffe, who would later serve as the governor of Virginia, was perfectly willing to fall on his sword for the Clintons and made no protest. But prosecutors, congressional committees, and an aroused media demanded answers. Why was the Clinton White House stalling? Documents had been subpoenaed. Where were they? There were too many people involved. How did they expect to keep it all under wraps? Remember Watergate? The cover-up is worse than the crime.

By February 1997, under pressure, the president released hundreds of pages of related documents, many with the president's own handwriting. The story these papers told was quite different from what the White House's spin doctors had been alleging. The numbers of guests and the amounts they had donated were staggering. For those familiar with the laws and ethics governing the White House, including some very pro-Clinton members of the White House press corps, the news was especially disappointing.

When the president hosted a press conference with Chilean president Eduardo Frei, journalists asked repeatedly about the Lincoln Bedroom story.

A perturbed president dismissed the issue as ridiculous. "We got strict advice about, legal advice, about what the rules were," the president said. "And everyone involved knew what the rules were. Did we hope that the people that came there would support me, particularly after we got into a political season? Of course we did."[3]

When asked about the coffees and special events for big donors, including many who were ushered into the Oval Office, Clinton insisted that "there was no solicitation during the events and the guidelines, which I believe were made available to you also yesterday in the documents, made it clear that there was to be no price tags on these events."

Journalists pointed out that staff members had written dollar amounts next to many of the coffee events.

"That's how much they hoped would come out of their endeavors after their coffees were over," Clinton replied. "And I think if you will ask them, you'll find out that sometimes they did, and sometimes they didn't."[4]

When the Terry McAuliffe memo surfaced it was clear that while he was encouraging an aggressive fund-raising campaign, with coffees, golf games, and events involving the president, he had not, after all, suggested using the Lincoln Bedroom for sleepovers. The memo had not even been written to the president at all, which was wise on McAuliffe's part. It had been written to Nancy Hernreich, the director of Oval Office operations.

There was a curious scribble on the document that caught the eye of investigators and journalists alike. Someone had added a handwritten scrawl suggesting the addition of sleepovers at the White House.

Turning what might have seemed like Clinton White House disinformation into a simple misunderstanding, Nancy Hernreich told the Senate Governmental Affairs Committee that she had written the word "overnights" next to the list of top-ten supporters. It was her fault, she insisted. Or maybe it was the president's idea. "Honestly, I just don't know, really," she said.[5]

When the president, himself, was finally deposed on the issue, he settled the mystery.

"Terry McAuliffe sent a memo suggesting things we ought to do to reestablish contact, which I thought was a good memo. And I told him to proceed," Clinton said. "And I told Nancy Hernreich in addition to that that I wanted to ask some of my friends who had helped me when I got elected president, that I hadn't been in touch with, to come to the White House and spend the night with me." Added Clinton, "The Lincoln Bedroom was never sold."

ALLEGATIONS OF PARDONS FOR MONEY

There have been several high-profile scandals over the years involving governors being bribed to use their power to pardon convicted felons, but Bill Clinton is the first American president to be accused of selling "get out of jail" cards. Pardongate, as it came to be known, was apparently one last-minute attempt to cash in on the White House. It was obviously planned for months, maybe even years. But it was executed with lightning speed in the last hours of the administration. The idea behind the timing was obvious: the Clintons hoped to garner the least amount of attention. The whole national focus would be on the newly elected president and his family and his agenda. What could anyone do? A president had been given the Constitutional power to pardon or commute sentences. He couldn't be impeached now. He was leaving.

Clinton granted pardons to his own associates accused of crimes, including the president's own brother, pardons for political purposes, including to benefit Hillary Clinton's senatorial election campaign in New York, and pardons to bring in money to the wider Clinton family.

It was soon learned that Hugh Rodham, the brother of Hillary Rodham Clinton, "received nearly $400,000 for helping to secure a presidential pardon and a commutation of sentence."[6] Hillary's younger brother, Anthony "Tony" Rodham, joined the queue. He helped his friends Edgar and Vonna Jo Gregory, the owners of United States International, a carnival company, get a pardon for a

1982 conviction of bank fraud. In return, Tony got a $107,000 loan from the Gregorys that was never repaid.

The motives and stories behind these pardons was not immediately known. For example, the loan to Tony Rodham was discovered only in October 2006, when the Clinton watchdog organization Judicial Watch exposed the arrangement. Clinton defenders are now quick to point out that Hugh Rodham eventually returned his $400,000, but not until it was exposed.

Hillary Clinton, meanwhile, denied any knowledge of her brothers' arrangements.

Some of the pardons were so outrageous they provoked censure from Bill Clinton's most ardent defenders. James Carville, the Clintons' most famous and prolific advocate, was amazed and momentarily speechless. "I can't say these are illegitimate questions being brought up because they are legitimate."[7]

Terry McAuliffe, when quizzed by the *New York Times*, wouldn't defend the more outrageous pardons.[8] "I've publicly said the Rich pardon was a mistake," McAuliffe told reporters. "If I were president I wouldn't have done it. All these incidents are unfortunate, frustrating and distracting, but ultimately they will run their course."[9]

The former Democratic president Jimmy Carter was less sanguine, referring to one of the pardon episodes as disgusting. And as to the whole episode, Carter said, "In my opinion, it was disgraceful."[10]

All presidents use their power to pardon. While Clinton pardoned 450 individuals, President Jimmy Carter pardoned even more, 566. President Ronald Reagan pardoned 406. Clinton's predecessor, George H. W. Bush, pardoned only 75. But none had the taint of scandal. And no president had pardoned so many on the last day. More than 177 of Clinton's pardons and many more commutations came on January 20, 2001, his last day in office, when he was trying to slip them by a diverted American public.

Vice President Al Gore was especially stunned. Friends described him as "unnerved by Mr. Clinton's conduct in his final days in office."[11]

THE TALE OF MARC RICH

The pardon of Marc Rich was appalling to federal prosecutors. With it, years of work and millions of dollars were flushed down the drain. The idea of the investigation had been to catch some of the elusive big guys who profited off the Iran hostage crisis and years later the Iraqi food-for-oil schemes that had allowed Saddam Hussein to circumvent the American boycott. People had died in the Gulf War, and the profiteers—or in this case, the alleged middleman—had apparently grown fat with illegal commissions and kickbacks.

Rich had been charged with fifty-one counts of tax fraud, racketeering, and trading with Iran during the hostage crisis. He owed the government $48 million in taxes.[12] At the time of the pardon, Rich was living in Switzerland, untouched by US law.

The story that emerged was that Denise Eisenberg Rich, the former wife of Marc Rich, had made a hefty donations to the Clinton Presidential Library. ABC News reported that she had given as much as $450,000 to the library, and put her contributions to various Democratic causes at $1 million.[13] Those causes evidently included Hillary Clinton's New York senate campaign.

Had the Marc Rich pardon been the result of a bribe to the president of the United States? The first federal prosecutor tapped to investigate the president was Mary Jo White. She would be followed in the job by James Comey, a respected Republican. Comey would eventually determine that there had been no crime on the part of the president.[14]

Marc Rich died in June 2013.

AN INVITATION TO TERROR

Even before the unprecedented pardons on Inauguration Day 2001, President Bill Clinton had given the nation and prosecutors a trial balloon for what was to come. On August 11, 1999, Clinton commuted the sentences of more than sixteen terrorist members of the Fuerza Armadas de Liberacion Nacional (Armed Forces of National Liberation, or FALN), a terrorist organization that had set off 120 bombs, mostly in New York City and Chicago. The FALN was held responsible for sixteen dead and lifetime injuries to dozens of others. Critics said that the president's commutations were a ploy to help his wife, Hillary, get elected to the US Senate in New York. Some Puerto Rican leaders in New York were lobbying for the FALN.

The FALN was a terrorist organization committed to the independence of Puerto Rico. It had virtually no support from the people of the island. Its agenda was not really liberation but terrorism.

The group's bombs had exploded on New Year's Eve 1982 at One Police Plaza in New York. There had been gruesome casualties. One police officer lost a leg, another was blinded and lost fingers on one of his hands. Another was blinded in one eye. Four bombs would be exploded at the same time across the city. The FBI headquarters in Manhattan would be hit, as would the federal courthouse in Brooklyn.

In a heartrending 2008 piece for the *Wall Street Journal*, Debra Burlingame, a director of the World Trade Center Memorial Foundation, would quote Detective Anthony Senft describing one of the victims. "He was ripped up like someone took a box cutter and shredded his face," said the detective. "We really didn't even know that he was a uniformed man until we found his weapon, that's how badly he was injured."[15]

The FALN had been at work for decades. On January 24, 1975, it blew up the Fraunces Tavern in Lower Manhattan. The tavern is a historic landmark where George Washington said farewell to the officers of his army. The FALN, a pro-Castro Marxist organization whose leaders were trained by Cuban intelligence, specifically targeted the tavern, which had been a watering hole for Wall Street executives for years. The explosion blew the place apart. Four people were killed and sixty people were injured. One of the dead bodies was decapitated in the explosion.

That same day, Joseph Connor waited for his father to come home to celebrate his ninth birthday and his brother's eleventh birthday. It was going to be quite a celebration. But the father was killed in the Fraunces Tavern explosion. Joe Connor told the *Daily Wire*, "I remember my dad always being there for us, taking us to Met games, playing with us, playing basketball with us, playing, kicking around a soccer ball. . . . He was a young guy, he was only 33. And he loved us, and he gave us a great childhood until that day."[16]

In 1980, eleven FALN members were caught with a van full of weapons and explosives. They were planning a robbery.

When they appeared before Judge Thomas McMillen in 1981 they seized the platform to promote their cause. FALN leader Carmen Valentine told the judge, "You are lucky that we cannot take you right now."[17] She sneered that the judge himself was the terrorist, and that only her shackles kept her from killing him on the spot.

FALN member Dylcia Pagan threatened the court: "All of you, I would advise you to watch your backs."[18]

FALN member Ricardo Jimenez announced to the judge, "You can give me the death penalty, you can kill me now."[19]

Ida Rodriquez said, "You say we have no remorse. You're right. Your jails and your long sentences will not frighten us."[20]

Judge McMillen replied, "I'm convinced you're going to continue as long as you live. If there was a death penalty, I'd impose the penalty on you without hesitation."[21]

On August 11, 1999, President Bill Clinton granted pardons to the FALN. Two days earlier, a New York City councilman said that he had personally given Hillary Clinton a package of information about the FALN and a letter to the president to urge him to consider clemency. Eight of the terrorists who had threatened the court that day in 1981 would receive pardons from Bill Clinton. One FALN terrorist would reject the offer.

The public outrage over the whole process was intense. Families of the victims were furious. In the uproar Hillary Clinton would eventually change her position on the pardons three times.

The prisoners were released on September 8, 1999. A *New York Times* editorial ran the headline "Bill's Little Gift."[22]

Eventually, with 1.3 million Puerto Ricans living in New York State, and Hillary in the middle of her campaign for the US Senate, she decided it was the right political decision and accepted some of the credit.

The outrage in congress was bipartisan. The Senate voted 95 to 2 to condemn the pardons.

The long list of unjustified pardons is almost numbing to read. It includes everyone from drug dealers who were part of the murderous Cali Cartel to corrupt politicians who had taken bribes. The amount of work that went into investigating and prosecuting and trying these criminals was incalculable. It was all undone in a few moments.

A few years later, in 2007, President George W. Bush would commute the sentence of Lewis Libby Jr. He had been the White House assistant to Vice President Dick Cheney and had been accused of outing a CIA agent who had criticized Bush's handling of the Iraq War.

Shortly thereafter, Bill and Hillary Clinton were campaigning in Iowa. Hillary was making her move to run for president the first time. "It was wrong to out that CIA agent and wrong to try to cover it up," former president Clinton lectured. "And no one was ever fired from the White House for doing it."[23] His audience was duly indignant. No one remembered. No one cared.

WALKING OUT WITH THE FURNITURE

When the Clintons left the White House, they had to file financial disclosure forms. It turned out that they were taking $190,027 in "gifts."[24] The Hillary Clinton political machine co-opted this story online much as it did other negative stories, by creating a straw man and then reducing it to shreds. The fact is, the amount of gifts was unprecedented, and at the time it sparked outrage.

By the time of their departure from the White House, the Clintons owned two homes, one in Washington, DC, and one in Chappaqua, New York. They needed to furnish them. Most of the gifts came from Hollywood friends and Democratic donors. The gifts included art, furniture, china, and rugs. Some of the gifts were touching remembrances. Ted Danson and Mary Steenburgen gave china worth $4,787. Steven Spielberg and his wife, Kate Capshaw, spent $4,920 for another set of china, donated to the Clintons.

The controversy stemmed from a *Washington Post* story.[25] The newspaper learned that some of the gifts had not been given to the Clintons at all. They were donations to the White House that had been crated up and hauled off. The story broke on February 5, 2001. The Clintons eventually returned the $28,000 worth of gifts in question. Other media reports were quick to make comparisons. George H. W. Bush, the Clintons' predecessor, had left the White House with $52,853 of gifts in 1992.

The controversy only increased when it was learned that among the Clintons' gifts were $7,375 for tables and chairs from Denise

Rich, the ex-wife of the FBI's top-ten most-wanted fugitive Marc Rich, whom Bill Clinton had pardoned.

As with many Clinton stories, this one disappeared from the front pages before the most damaging facts come to light. In 2002, the *New York Times* learned that the actual value of the items taken by the Clintons from the White House was $360,000,[26] almost twice what had been reported as outrageous, and almost seven times what their predecessor had taken.

In retrospect, some believed that the scandal had been exaggerated. There was a congressional investigation that found no provable, intentional criminality involved. Clinton supporters saw it as persecution. Still others, including fellow Democrats, were relieved to see the Clintons finally leave the White House. There were always explanations for the charges leveled against them, but the fact was that there were never the same scandals ensnaring Al Gore or Barack Obama or George Bush.

For some, the image of the Clintons stealing art and furniture from the White House on their way out the door was the perfect, final reprise for a presidency that had been beset by controversy from its very beginning. There was a sense that the Clintons were finished. Former White House staffers began to take jobs, and some openly separated from the Clintons and spoke out against the pardons or the deceptions surrounding the sex scandals or the revictimization of the women involved. But quietly, almost unseen, as the house of Clinton seemed to come crashing down around them, the seeds of yet another recovery were sewn. In the 2000 election year cycle, as the Clintons moved out of the White House, Hillary Rodham Clinton was elected as a senator from the state of New York.

PART III

THE RISE OF THE HOUSE OF TRUMP

CHAPTER 10

DONALD TRUMP, OUT OF THE SHADOWS

To succeed in life, you need two things:
ignorance and confidence.
—*MARK TWAIN*

There is an eerie familiarity to the Donald Trump family story. We have heard it before. It is reminiscent of the story of other presidential families. There is an ambitious parent, in this case, the father, Fred Trump Sr., and there is a chosen, anointed son, the heir apparent; in this case, Fred Jr., or "Freddy." The chosen son fails or dies young or, as in the case of Freddy, does both. But there is another son standing in the shadows, overlooked, who is watching this process with a measure of envy, rehearsing for his own chance without any pressure or expectation. It is this son, the man in the shadows, who fulfills the father's dreams. And it is this son who becomes the president of the United States.

In the spring of 1743, Augustine "Gus" Washington lay dying at his home in Virginia. His family had gathered at his bedside. Gus was looking to his firstborn son, Lawrence Washington, to pick up the ambitious plans he was leaving behind. All his hopes and dreams had passed to Lawrence. This son was given a superb education at schools in England. Now he would get the family business, the ironworks. He would get almost all of the land, including the place on the Potomac where he would one day build Mount Vernon. A second son would also be prepared as a backup. He too had been given an education in England.

And finally, there was another boy, eleven years old, standing unseen at the foot of the bed. He would be given no education and no land. After the death of Gus, he would find some of his father's old surveying tools left behind, and this would be his inheritance, his link to the proud man he adored and whose approval he so desperately sought.

Gus Washington had no way of knowing that in a few short years, his son Lawrence would follow him to the grave and that the little eleven-year-old boy at the foot of the bed, George Washington, was in fact a man of destiny, who would found a new form of government and a giant empire that would span two oceans. Nearby, where Gus lay dying, there would one day rise the capital city of that empire, and it would be named after his family. There would be a marble monument, reaching to the skies, that would survive for hundreds of years, in honor of the little boy who was only a few feet away, in the shadows.

The choice of an heir is not rigidly linked to birth order. Rather, it is based on expectations. Sometimes, as in the case of the Eisenhowers and later the Bushes, a younger son becomes the anointed one, the one expected to inherit the ambitions of the father. In those cases the firstborn was able to shed the burden only to later return from the shadows as president.

There is a scene in my book *The Raising of a President* in which the father, Joseph Kennedy Sr., is sitting in an automobile with a friend outside a factory. It is bitterly cold, and Joe and his friend are keeping warm with the car heater, while outside a young Jack Kennedy is shaking hands with workers entering the factory. Jack is running for Congress.

Joseph Kennedy Sr. is telling his friend that he never expected to see this moment. Not in a thousand years. He had always thought that the firstborn, namesake, Joe Kennedy, would run for office. Jack had always been sickly. But Joe had died young in World War II and another son, John F. Kennedy, or "Jack," had picked up the dream.

Now, once again, as so often in history, Freddy Trump, an anointed son with all the expectations and hopes of his father on his shoulders, died young at the age of forty-three, an alcoholic, while the younger brother, the one who had been sent away to military school to shape up, Donald J. Trump, had stepped from the shadows to become the forty-fifth president of the United States.

BORN CONFIDENT

Donald John Trump was born on June 14, 1946, to Fred and Mary Trump in Queens, New York. He was one of the middle children in a family of two brothers and two sisters. In his bestselling autobiography, *The Art of the Deal*, Trump describes his family as close knit, with his father being the greatest influence in his life. In the book, Trump spends page after page describing the values instilled in him.

Fred Trump, the president's father, was a tough negotiator and a fierce fighter. He would never back down. He would hold tight in any negotiation, not wanting to lose even a small portion of his profits. Still a teenager, Fred Trump took on his first construction project building a two car garage for a neighbor. It was the beginning of a modest business. In a few short months and years Fred grew his business to cater to the newly emerging middle class. They were now earning enough to buy their own automobiles, and Fred would build the needed garages.

Fred's first business venture, Elizabeth Trump and Son, soon began building modest working-class single-family homes. Many of them are still carefully maintained all across Brooklyn, sturdy monuments to the businessman whose son became president.

After the Great Depression the supermarket trend began to sweep the country. That's when Fred built Trump Market on the corner of Jamaica Avenue and seventy-eighth Street. He later sold it to the massive King Kullen chain, so the sign that proudly broadcast the family name to the neighborhood soon passed.

During World War II, business boomed. Fred Trump built apartments and barracks along the East Coast. Within time, Trump began developing real estate in Queens and Brooklyn. By the time he was finished, he had built an empire of more than twenty-seven thousand apartments.

According to friends who grew up with him in Queens, Donald Trump was a miniature version of the 2016 presidential candidate. At the Kew-Forest School in Forest Hills, Queens, he was described as a tough guy who was stubborn about his views. Sometimes he would adamantly hold to a contrarian version of the facts, long after he was proven wrong by his classmates, and then keep insisting he was right even years later. He was given so many detentions at school that other classmates referred to them as "DTs."

Trump himself admits, "When I look at myself in the first grade and I look at myself now, I'm basically the same. The temperament is not that different."[1] By his own account he punched a music teacher in the face because the teacher didn't know anything about music. Although Trump now says the story had been exaggerated.

He was taller than everybody else his age and intimidating on the playground. He loved baseball and played the position of catcher. When at bat, he always hit for a home run. When opposing teams would shift to cover his long ball to left field, he didn't adjust and hit the ball to right, to get an easy base hit. He still went for the home run. According to an old friend, when they played dodge ball, "The Trumpet was always the last man standing."[2]

It might be easy to speculate that Donald Trump's big size fed his confidence, but there is an intriguing story from an old babysitter. He was a teenager, asked to watch little five-year-old Donny Trump during one of his dad's visits to a construction site. The bored babysitter descended into the sewer beneath the city of New York, and the five-year-old future president of the United States dropped down into the darkness to follow close behind. The babysitter marveled years later that he could still see the little five-year-old boy, following behind deeper into the darkness beneath New York City, exhibiting not the slightest fear.

By all accounts, Donald Trump loved his childhood. Fred Trump lived in a big house with white columns on the front porch and two Cadillacs parked in the driveway. There was a cook and a chauffeur, a color television and a fancy intercom system. In Queens, New York, in Donald Trump's small world, he and his family were kings.

Throughout these years, Donald and his siblings were always active participants in the family business. When Fred would visit a building under construction, the Trump children were brought along to clean the site or collect bottles for recycling. Donald was an apt pupil, observing his father's hard-line stance toward contractors who wanted more time or money, and his unyielding attitude for tenants who refused to pay their rent.

It was some of Donald Trump's own adolescent adventures into Manhattan that finally aroused the wrath of his father. He'd received too many reports of misbehavior at school and around the neighborhood. Donald had two strikes against him and didn't know it. When Fred learned about Donald's secret trips into the city and then finally found his hidden switchblade knife, he took decisive action.

Fred announced to his son that he was going to be sent to the New York Military Academy. It was a crushing blow to a boy who loved his idyllic lifestyle and worshipped his successful father. Trump didn't drink. He didn't smoke. He had never been arrested. But now his childhood that had promised to stretch into many years ahead had suddenly and abruptly ended. His father was sending him away. He couldn't bear to tell his friends. That fall, when they all returned to the eighth grade at Kew-Forest School, Donald Trump had just disappeared.

FREDDY WAS A GREAT GUY

Donald Trump got a rude awakening at the academy. Retired colonel Theodore Tobias remembers the big kid who arrived from Queens. "I put [him] down at the end of the hall," Tobias told Ailsa Chang on the NPR series *Journey Home*. "He didn't know how to make a bed. He didn't know how to shine his shoes. He had a problem, you know, with being a cadet. You know, being a cadet, you gotta take care of yourself."[3]

Tobias, a tough World War II veteran, was intimidating to the students. He didn't care who their parents were or how much money they had, and that included Donny Trump. Tobias ran the dorm by his rules, and the cadets had to fall into line quickly. Even so, he remembers Donald fondly as "aggressive but so coachable."[4]

Perhaps, the crusty retired colonel reminded Donald of his demanding father. Whatever the reasons, Trump had met his lion tamer, and he flourished. Many of the students were preppies from socially prominent families who saw Trump as emerging from a blue-collar milieu. But he soon pushed his way in. Trump was outstanding academically, socially, and in almost any kind of competition. He was captain of the soccer team, the football team, and the baseball team. He played tight end on the football team and was the star pitcher on the baseball team.

Like the other students, Donald Trump was drilled daily. You don't cheat, or lie, or steal, or tolerate those weaknesses in others. You speak honestly and forthrightly. Let the chips fall where they may.

The academy was in Cornwall, New York, only seventy miles north of Manhattan, so in the summer Donald Trump was back in Queens and once more part of the family. But it would be a long way back into the good graces of his father.

There was not much question that Fred Trump Jr., Donald's elder brother, would one day be the heir to the family business. He was the third Fred Trump, beginning with the president's grandfather, who had emigrated from Germany. But fresh from the discipline of the New York Military Academy, Donald was a focused apprentice, an apt pupil, able to learn the harsh lessons his father was ready to teach. Freddy Jr., chafing under their father's relentless criticism and domination, was happy to have little brother Donald step in during the summers and absorb some of the attention.

It was during this time, home on summer vacation, that Donald Trump established his routine of following his father around to his various properties. He watched Fred Trump study each and every cost associated with his construction projects relentlessly, so that a contractor would never be able to overbid his work during a tough negotiation. His father was the first one to the job site and would demand perfection. Fred Trump not only knew every price, he also knew how to accomplish each and every task on a site, sometimes taking over a menial task to show his workers how to do it the right way. Workers could not show the slightest level of incompetence under the constant gaze of Fred Trump and his exacting standards.

Exiled from home, further hardened by the tough love of the military academy, Donald Trump thrived on his father's harsh regimen. His older brother Freddy did not. He had made an effort to take on family projects, but his father's constant criticism and interference wore him down. Freddy had other dreams and began to find solace in a drink with friends in the evening.

The oldest Trump child, Maryanne Trump Barry, was never considered in line to inherit the family business. In a rare interview, she told *New York* magazine that she never considered competing against Donald for the family business, or in any other venture. "I knew better even as a child than to ever attempt to compete with Donald. I wouldn't have been able to win."[5] Instead, she married and became a homemaker, eventually going to law school and working in the US attorney's office in Newark, New Jersey. Ultimately, she was appointed by the Reagan administration as a judge to the Federal District Court and then by the Clinton administration as a senior judge to the US Court of Appeals for the Third Circuit. It was no small feat to be advanced by both Republican and Democratic administrations but she remained modest about her accomplishments.

Maryanne Barry surfaced in the middle of the 2016 presidential campaign when she gave Donald advice after his on-air confrontation with the Fox News reporter Megyn Kelly. Donald quotes his sister as telling him, "Just be yourself."[6]

Donald's younger sister, Elizabeth Trump, stayed away from the family business and instead went to work at the New York office of Chase Manhattan Bank. She married James Grau in 1989 and eventually retired from banking to Florida. In *The Art of the Deal*, Elizabeth gets only a one-sentence mention, as Donald describes her as "bright but less ambitious."[7]

The youngest of the Trump siblings, Robert, joined the family business and worked for his brother for years. Trump fondly recounts a story in which, as a child, he borrowed some of Robert's building blocks and constructed a beautiful building. Not content to take it apart, Donald glued the pieces together to preserve his masterpiece and to establish his older-brother dominance.

It was Trump's dominance that eventually led Robert to resign from the Trump Organization and from public view. When the Taj Mahal casino in Atlantic City opened, issues with the slot machines caused an estimated loss between $3 million and $10 million in revenue. Trump exploded at his staff, including his brother Robert, prompting him to leave the Trump Organization for good.

Robert now lives quietly in Millbrook, New York, where he describes himself as "gainfully retired."[8] He is beloved by the community, where he spends his time supporting local businesses and charities.[9] Robert was one of his brother's biggest cheerleaders in his run for president.

Donald Trump's relationship with his elder brother, Freddy Trump, was more complicated. Freddy was free spirited, personable, and well loved. He was the antithesis of Donald, who was reserved and stubborn, with a laser-like focus on business.

The contrast caused great tension between Fred Sr. and his firstborn. Donald quoted his father as saying, "The most important thing in life is to love what you're doing, because that's the only way you'll ever be really good at it."[10]

Donald watched as his older brother floundered and ultimately crumbled under his father's stern leadership and exacting expectations. Freddy, while running a construction project, installed new windows instead of utilizing the existing ones to save money. Fred criticized and humiliated his son, and Freddy's drinking finally became an issue.

After graduating from the New York Military Academy in 1964, Donald Trump came home to try to claim a spot on his father's team. He commuted to Fordham University, a Jesuit school, and, then urged on by his father, he transferred to the University of Pennsylvania's renowned Wharton School.

Donald was conflicted about Freddy. His older brother loved flying, and when he finally fulfilled a lifetime wish, earning his wings as a pilot for Trans World Airlines, Donny proudly displayed the picture of his brother, in uniform, on his dresser in his Wharton School dorm room.

But the drinking followed Freddy to TWA, and the family was worried. At one point, perhaps feeling guilty to see himself supplanting his brother in the family business, Donald cornered Freddy and lectured him about his role as a leader in the family. He told him to get his act together, to straighten up, to take his rightful place at the head of the family business, and to drop the booze.

Stunned by his brother's decline, Donald Trump vowed never to touch alcohol or cigarettes. He might have many problems in life, he decided, but alcohol and a nicotine addiction would not be among them.

Had pressure from both Donald and his father driven Freddy away from the family and contributed to the drinking problem that eventually took his life? Some of the friends who knew all four men suspected as much. The *New York Times* reporter Jason Horowitz raised this possibility in a 2016 interview with Donald Trump. The usually confident and tough businessman turned politician was circumspect and uncertain. "I hope not," he said. "I hope not."[11]

Freddy Trump died an alcoholic in 1981, at the age of forty-three. When Donald Trump stood before the nation as its new president elect he remembered, "And my late brother, Fred, great guy. Fantastic guy. Fantastic family. I was very lucky."[12]

A LESSON AT THE VERRAZANO-NARROWS BRIDGE

On November 21, 1964, the Verrazano-Narrows Bridge was dedicated, and a young Fordham University freshman, Donald Trump, was there to see it. In the pictures, the sun shines bright and the skies are clear, but apparently there were intermittent showers that day. When Donald Trump recounts the day, he remembers the rain. It was a special day because he was there with his father, Fred. The bridge, given its own unique American spelling, was named for the explorer Giovanni da Verrazzano. It was heralded as a structural marvel and an architectural masterpiece, the largest-spanning bridge in the world at the time.[13]

The bridge project, however, had its share of detractors. Neighborhoods in Brooklyn had been razed in order to accommodate the venture, and there were workers who felt slighted for not being invited to the opening ceremony. There was even a small group of protesters who were upset that the bridge did not allow for pedestrian traffic.

Yet on that day in 1964, when the crowds gathered and the music began to swell, all the past problems and issues melted away as the full pomp and ceremony of the festivities began. Cars lined up, jockeying to be the first to pay the toll and cross the bridge. It took fifty-two limousines to chauffeur the visiting dignitaries, politicians, well wishers, and teams of people who helped complete the bridge. Chief among the guests was the planner of the bridge itself, Robert Moses.

Moses was a master builder who oversaw construction of many of New York City's greatest landmarks. Lincoln Center, the UN building, sections of Central Park, and the Henry Hudson highway were a few of his achievements. However, he was also a controversial figure whose highways and bridges were criticized for compounding the already swelling traffic congestion and displacing entire neighborhoods, bringing the charge that he actually created more slums due to the evictions his roadways required.[14]

Robert Moses led the ceremony, and on that bright and sunny day, ribbons were cut, music was played, and a series of speeches were given.[15] It was during these speeches that an eighteen-year-old Donald J. Trump would learn one of the most defining lessons of his formative years, a lesson so powerful it would fuel his success in the real estate industry and ultimately play its part in his bid for the White House.

Sitting quietly in the second row of the grandstand was the actual designer of the Verrazano Bridge, the structural engineer Othmar Ammann. Mr. Ammann was a quiet and unassuming man. His designs and oversight were present in many of the bridges and tunnels of New York City as well as the Golden Gate Bridge in California. He was well respected, highly regarded, and, in Trump's recollection, completely overlooked that day. Although he had flown in from overseas, Mr. Ammann was not prominent at the festivities, was not invited to cut the ribbon, and was not invited to speak. When Robert Moses did mention Mr. Ammann in his speech that day, he forgot to actually say his name. The young Trump was astounded.

Years later he told the *New York Times* reporter Howard Blum that, "all [I was] thinking about [was] that all these politicians who opposed the bridge [were] being applauded." It was Mr. Ammann, "who poured his heart into [the bridge], and nobody even mentioned his name. I realized then and there that if you let people treat you how they want, you'll be made a fool. I realized then and there something I would never forget: I don't want to be made anybody's sucker."[16]

As the speeches ended, cars patiently waiting finally got their chance to be among the very first to pay the toll and cross the bridge while the after parties began on either side of the bridge. Donald J. Trump walked away that day learning his first lesson in the importance of embracing the power of brand identity, which would require him to be the greatest salesman for his most important commodity: himself. Young Donald recognized that day that building an impressive structure would never be enough to gain the level of success he truly desired. He could learn to create the world's greatest towers and plazas, but what would it matter if no one ever remembered that he was the one who actually built them?

Tim Calkins, a marketing professor at the Kellogg School of Management at Northwestern University, explains Trump's brand identity this way: "Trump capitalized on the power of the Trump brand, which people associate with and aspire to luxury, wealth and celebrity."[17]

Never satisfied with being forgotten or overlooked, Trump transformed himself from being the son of a successful builder of moderate-income housing in Queens to one of the premier real estate developers in New York City and beyond. Now he has been transformed from a world-famous brand name and television personality to the face of a new and emerging political dynasty. A part of that process started that day in November 1964, where a brilliant but overlooked architectural designer sat quietly onstage, unmentioned by name, sheepishly avoiding the spotlight, while a young college student watched in utter disbelief and amazement at this perceived slight.

CHAPTER 11

SAVING NEW YORK CITY

*Each problem that I solved became a rule, which
served afterwards to solve other problems.*
——RENÉ DESCARTES

Befored Donald Trump ever thought of making America great again, he set his eyes on Manhattan, the island jewel of New York City. Beginning in the late 1960s, when Trump was launching his own real estate and building career, New York City had descended into hell. Fueled by an epidemic of crack cocaine, a crime wave made parts of the city practically uninhabitable.

The outer boroughs were the worst. With the crime wave came rampant urban decay. In his twenties, working in Queens and Brooklyn, Donald Trump soon learned the kind of dangers that came with real estate in a decaying city. When collecting rent from tenants who refused to pay, he would knock on the door and then stand to the side, lest the unruly tenant choose to open fire. This was not the kind of risk he envisioned when he followed his father into the family business. So Donald soon began to cast an eye across the East River to the gleaming skyscrapers on the other side.

At the time, Manhattan was not that much safer than the outer boroughs, and financially it posed even greater risks. One false business move could sink a person for life.

Crime had seeped into the streets and alleys around the great buildings of Manhattan. At night, New Yorkers were prisoners in their own towers. No part of the island was safe. Central Park was so dangerous that police seldom entered it after sunset.

Commercial business suffered. Corporations once proudly proclaiming a New York City address relocated quickly across the country. At first they moved to the other coast. Some to California and some to Seattle. But eventually they found new homes in the flyover states. Corporations moved to Dallas, Oklahoma City, Atlanta, and Denver. News of life in the suburbs of these cities and news of the welcome tax rates spread to other New York City corporations, which soon followed. Within time, buildings were abandoned and entire sections of the city fell into disrepair. But while others were leaving Gotham, Donald Trump, working with his father from their base across the East River in Queens and Brooklyn, saw Manhattan as an opportunity.

In spite of the urban blight, land on Manhattan island was not only expensive, the complications of doing business were legion. One had to navigate through courts, committees, and public hearings. The competition was savage, with the assassination of a reputation in a boardroom just as common in the business world as a mugging was on the street. Even so, the payoff was heady, far greater than anything Donald could hope to earn with his father. Finding success in Manhattan would force Donald to draw from the lesson he learned at the opening of the Verrazano-Narrows Bridge, because to find success in the real estate jungle of Manhattan, Donald would need to learn to sell his name.

According to Donald Trump's own story—a story that is disputed by critics—before he took on projects in Manhattan, he cemented his status as a real estate mogul with a successful deal in Cincinnati, Ohio. While his father's first foray into real estate development was a two-car garage, Donald's first step was a 1,200-unit apartment complex. Fred Trump put up his money to see what the son could do.

While other college students had been pursuing sports, drinking, and girls, Donald had been scanning the newspapers in search of federal foreclosures. According to his recollection of events, Donald convinced his father to go with him and check out one such place, Swifton Village, a failing apartment development that the government was desperate to offload. Using deft negotiating and the government's eagerness to drop the property, the Trumps were able to purchase the site for $6 million. They also were able to secure financing, which allowed them to avoid using any of their own money in the transaction. After the Trumps renovated Swifton Village and launched an advertising campaign, the apartments filled up nicely and the Trumps saw a substantial return.

Years later, a friend informed Donald that the neighborhood around the apartments was in decline. Trump immediately made his own inspection. He visited Cincinnati and drove the streets for hours, circling the neighborhoods. His friend's warning was confirmed and Trump immediately put the apartment complex up for sale.

Donald learned another valuable lesson that would serve him greatly in his 2016 presidential campaign. Read the numbers, listen to the experts, but get out on your own and take a look. Nothing beats getting on the ground yourself and seeing a situation up close. Sometimes your own eyes and ears offer the best marketing information available.

Trump ended up successfully selling Swifton Village to Prudential Estate Investment Trust after their appraiser failed, in Donald's estimation, to do his homework on the area. Donald recounts that the appraiser was more interested in having lunch at an exclusive restaurant as opposed to doing the same onsite evaluation Donald had done.

As Trump recalls it, Prudential was not very prudent, and because of their negligence, the firm ended up overpaying for an apartment complex that was emptying out in a declining neighborhood.[1]

Trump gained a $6 million profit and protected himself from the deal falling apart in the last minute by inserting a penalty clause. The tough negotiation, the lifetime of experience at his father's side, and the commitment to do the first-person, ground-level research gave Trump the confidence to take his first steps toward developing real estate in Manhattan. His father, Fred, was worried. "Don't go into Manhattan. That's the big leagues. We don't know anything about that. Don't do it."

But Trump could not be dissuaded. "Dad, I gotta go into Manhattan. I gotta build those big buildings. I gotta do it, dad, I gotta do it."[2]

Before buying anything, Donald Trump first moved onto the island. He rented a modest studio apartment on the Upper East Side and immediately began walking the streets, talking to anyone and everyone, and keeping his eyes and ears open for the promise of an opportunity.

In an early human-interest piece, Aristotle Onassis, at the time one of the world's richest men, had laid out his own formula for success. Get in the presence of great men, he had advised. Even the crumbs from their table are better than the best others have to offer.

One of Donald Trump's first successes involved hustling and talking his way into membership at Le Club. It allowed him access to the movers and shakers, the Manhattan elite whom he knew he needed to build his empire. John and Caroline Kennedy once hosted a joint birthday party there, and people like Al Pacino sometimes showed up unexpectedly. In fact, the very same people Donald rubbed shoulders with at Le Club would eventually become his tenants in the exclusive high-rises he would build across town. But for now, he was a no-name trying to prove himself in the cutthroat world of Manhattan real estate and a young man trying to come out from his father's shadow. Being part of the ambiance at Le Club was a big deal.

MAKING NEW YORK CITY GREAT AGAIN

When it was opened in 1919, the Commodore Hotel was hailed as a crowning achievement in architecture and design. It was owned by a division of the New York Central Railroad and was built as part of the Grand Central Terminal, the teeming center of railroad traffic coming into and out of the city.

At the time, the Commodore Hotel boasted the largest ball-room in the country.[3] Its lobby, with its own waterfall, seemed to stretch on forever. It was stunning to visitors. At one time it hosted an entire circus, including performing elephants.

The hotel was named after "Commodore" Cornelius Vanderbilt, the railroad magnate who established one of the nation's first inter-regional railroad systems, and shepherded the Manhattan Grand Central Depot, which later evolved into Grand Central Terminal.[4] A statue of Cornelius Vanderbilt was erected just outside its doors.

The Commodore Hotel was poised to cater to the growing busi-ness class streaming in from Grand Central Terminal. The March 1919 edition of *The Architectural Review* said that the hotel tran-scended "in scale any similar effort that has been made in this field anywhere in the world."[5] According to New Yorkers, it was a shin-ing example of everything that was right with the city. It was beauti-ful but by their standards not overdone, efficient but still luxurious, enormous but not impersonal. The Commodore Hotel truly lived up to the grandeur and splendor that its Vanderbilt namesake evoked.

Within time, the Commodore Hotel declined with the city. The faltering New York Central Railroad merged with the Pennsylvania

Railroad, and the company's many properties, including the hotel, began to suffer under new leadership and bad times. Soon the new Penn Central Transportation Company was forced to declare bankruptcy and offload its assets. Its railway operations were broken apart and morphed into the new Amtrak and Conrail.

Meanwhile, the city of New York, left with abandoned properties, was in desperate straits. It faced a rising crime rate, rising debt, and rising taxes, which only drove more businesses and residents further away. There was a general feeling of concern and even panic, with no way to stop the cycle.

In the late 1970s, the young Donald Trump sensed an opportunity. While scanning the newspaper he read that the Penn Central property disbursement was the responsibility of a man named Victor Palmieri. Donald had his eye on an abandoned railroad property along the Hudson River on Sixtieth Street. Talking his way into a meeting with Palmeri, Donald Trump sold the only thing he had: big dreams and high energy.[6]

It worked. Through another series of negotiations, meetings, and self-promotions, Trump convinced Palmeri and Penn Central that he was the right man to develop not only the property on Sixtieth Street but also on the Thirtieth Street yards. His newly formed Trump Organization, named so because the word "organization" made it sound large and important, announced that it had secured the rights to purchase vast tracts of the important land right outside the terminal. The story made the front page of the *New York Times*."[7]

Once these deals were announced, other competitors placed bids for the properties, and the city government, with its layers of corruption, began a long process of delay, holding back the approvals Trump needed to move ahead. The property on Thirty-Fourth Street was eventually developed as a convention center, but despite Trump's best efforts, it was built by another company. The property on Sixtieth Street stalled for twenty years before Trump was finally able to build something on it.

While progress was slow on his newly acquired properties, Trump pursued Palmeri for other intriguing opportunities. In addition to owning large tracts of land, Penn Central also owned a group of hotels and offices built around Grand Central Terminal, known in the past as Terminal City. One hotel in particular caught Trump's attention, the failing Commodore.

He immediately went out to see the state of the hotel for himself and was astounded. The Commodore had once catered to clients visiting on business or wanting a taste of luxury. Its neighborhood had been a successful, elegant, thriving center of art and commerce. It was now a slum. The hotel itself was barely occupied, with empty storefronts, a haven for the homeless, and a place to solicit a prostitute. The once famous lobby now hosted an X-rated massage parlor. But as Trump took in the squalor and the filth, he noticed a shift in the environment.

During the daylight business hours, streaming out of Grand Central Terminal were a flood of businessmen and women flowing in and around the hotel, making their way toward the opportunities and risks afforded by the great city. It was then that a twenty-eight-year-old Donald Trump saw what would become the benchmark of his presidential campaign. Despite the economic downturn, the quagmire of government red tape, and the constant buzzing of detractors, Donald saw an opportunity to take something that was decaying and rotting and restore it to its former grandeur. Here was an opportunity to bring life and vibrancy back to the once magnificent Commodore Hotel.

The ensuing transformation of the Commodore Hotel into the Grand Hyatt New York was polarizing and fraught with controversy.

Critics said that Trump was a cheap showman and an egomaniac who should not be given free rein on such a traditional property. Supporters laughed at the idea that a hotel that once hosted a circus in its lobby and whose founder had a statue of himself built outside should complain about Donald Trump. The young man's vision of the Grand Hyatt, they said, was in the grand tradition of New York City. They declared it a resounding success and its construction to be at the forefront of an economic revival for the city.

However, one thing was certain: with the Grand Hyatt under his belt, Trump had announced himself as the new face of real estate development and had ushered in the Trump empire that still lasts today. Eventually in 1996, the Trump Organization and Hyatt Corporation parted ways, not amicably, with Trump pocketing $142 million and the Hyatt renovating the hotel yet again in 2011 to purportedly remove all traces of Donald Trump.[8]

LOSING BATTLES, BUT WINNING THE WAR

In 1970, Trump tried to develop land on the old New York Central Railroad yard. Eventually, six other organizations were involved, from the Municipal Art Society to the Riverside Park Fund. For years, money, politics, and territorial disputes raged. Trump sold parts of the project to others. The plans saw many different variations, and work continues to this day. But there are now bike paths, jogging trails, apartments, and restaurants.

The whole project on the Upper West Side of Manhattan cost $3 billion, developing fifty-seven acres and leaving behind hundreds of apartments and shops. In 2016, after Donald Trump was elected president, local residents removed Trump's name from three of the prominent buildings.

While the Riverside South project stagnated, Donald Trump jumped to a new venture. It would be called Trump Tower, and it would be built on Fifth Avenue.

Once called "millionaires' row," Fifth Avenue had evolved into one of the most famous shopping streets in the world. The Empire State Building, Rockefeller Center, and Saint Patrick's Cathedral were all built on Fifth Avenue. There was Bergdorf Goodman, the Saint Regis Hotel, and, of course, Saks Fifth Avenue. When Donald Trump cast his gaze on the street, New York was in its epic decline. The street was home to abandoned buildings and secondhand shops with pretentious antique dealers promoting their treasures.

Donald Trump conceived of a building that was itself an all-inclusive community, with apartments, offices, and shopping. Trump Tower was opened in 1983. It was immediately popular and was the catalyst for the great return of a glorious street. If he had yet to make a dent in New York City, his presence was surely felt, and he had sparked the revival of one of the city's most famous avenues.

In her biography *Donald Trump: The Candidate*, Gwenda Blair gives a detailed account of Trump's rise in the world of real estate development and beyond. She looks to Trump Tower as a reflection of Donald himself, bold, brash, gaudy, and controversial, and to half the nation, this is an accurate reflection. To the other half, it still represents Trump, but more as a landmark of his success, the story of how he came back from the brink of bankruptcy, and overcoming the odds, won the presidency. Trump Tower is an eyesore to some and a must-see stop for others.

In 1984, he built a stunning thirty-nine-story apartment tower on East Sixty-First Street. The apartments had classic views of the city and added much-needed value to the neighborhood. As often happened when Trump built something, other developers came right behind, and the whole area recovered.

While some projects took years to bear fruit, others could be done at light speed. Wollman Rink in Central Park was done in record time and helped establish the Trump legend. In 1986, after six years and $12 million, New York mayor Ed Koch reluctantly turned over the ice-skating rink project to Donald Trump. He finished the job in four months for $2 million. Families immediately returned, and at least the southern end of the dark, crime-infested Central Park was liberated.

In 1994, Donald Trump joined a project to rebuild the old Gulf and Western Building on Columbus Circle. It had originally been constructed in 1969. The building had a problem of swaying with the strong winds that whipped through Manhattan. Trump took the building apart, reducing it to its skeletal foundation, and rebuilt it from the outside, creating condominiums, offices, and hotel rooms. The Trump International Hotel and Tower now rises above Columbus Circle and bears the prestigious address of 1 Central Park West. Today the building hosts one of the world's greatest restaurants. The circle became so prestigious that the massive Time Warner Center was built nearby, as was the Museum of Arts and Design.

In 1995, with Wall Street in decline, he bought the original Bank of Manhattan Trust building. It was an old art deco structure that had briefly held the title as the tallest building in the world. At the time of Trump's purchase, it was described as "a vacant, ruined hulk."[9] Various sources claim that Trump paid as little as $1 million or as much as $10 million for the place and that it may now be worth as much as $400 million. With the prestigious address of 40 Wall Street, it is now called the Trump Building.

The Trump World Tower, at the United Nations Plaza, began construction in 1999 to a chorus of complaints from city dwellers whose views were interrupted or who opposed the architectural design or who predicted increased air pollution. Walter Conkite, the retired anchor of the *CBS Evening News*, opposed the project. Several hundred thousand dollars was raised to block the building, but in the end its critics were like yapping dogs who could not stop the moving caravan.

Trump World Tower was opened in 2001 and for a time reigned as the tallest residential building in the world. Its grandeur was soon applauded and all the fuss was forgotten. Bill Gates, Harrison Ford, Derek Jeter, and Sophia Loren were said to be tenants.[10] Far from complaining, United Nations diplomatic celebrities soon loved the place. Trump sold the forty-fifth floor to the kingdom of Saudi Arabia for $4.5 million.[11]

DID DONALD SAVE THE CITY?

It is easy today to accept that New York City would have made a comeback at some point anyway. Just as revisionist historians now discount the accepted wisdom that the crime rate evaporated under New York mayor Rudolph Giuliani, numbers be damned. But it is not likely that either would have happened without both men. The future was far from certain when a young, dynamic Donald Trump jumped into the fray.

Writing for the *New York Post*, Steve Cuozzo made a compelling case for how Trump's love of the city, his extraordinary imagination, and his visionary investments helped spark a transformation.[12] What Trump dreamed of and what he did, even as a young man, makes today's New York City a fun, even magical place to work and live.

In the presidential election of 2016, the people of the city of New York voted overwhelmingly for Hillary Clinton. In Manhattan, 515,481 people voted for Clinton, and only 58,935 voted for Trump. If Donald Trump had taken the Javits Center for his own election night celebration, instead of the Clinton campaign, he would have had room for every single Trump voter in all of Manhattan.

The city's inhabitants clearly scorn the Trump buildings that tower around them, while competing eagerly to own one of the apartments for themselves, but thanks to Donald Trump, their city is again, today, one of the world's greatest urban jewels.

Although beset with controversy and financial setbacks, Donald Trump's buildings have inspired a renaissance of new neighborhoods. There are parks and bicycle paths where old abandoned railroad yards once spread their rusty iron webs. There are restaurants overlooking the rivers and the bays that surround Manhattan. In the summertime lazy sailboats glide by. Young women walk their dogs at sunset without fear of attack. Scenes that would never have happened in the urban blight that faced the cocky, ambitious businessman of the 1980s are now the postcard lifestyle of hundreds of thousands of city dwellers.

While half the nation watched the 2016 election night unfold with their jaws agape, countless others nodded their heads in knowing approval. Throughout his life, Trump was told repeatedly he could not build this, could not buy that, could not succeed here, and had no business trying that. Sometimes the correction came from his own father, but usually from his many detractors. Time and time again, while the process was polarizing, the results were always the same. Trump wins, regardless of whether you agreed with his definition of victory.

When he was told the Commodore Hotel restoration project would never succeed, he built it anyway. When he faced bankruptcy and financial ruin in the 1990s, Trump climbed back on top. When they scoffed at his announcement to run for president, he won anyway. Yes, the process in each success was muddy, and yes the results will always be contested, but in the end it is always the same. Trump wins.

The path he climbed from that day on the Verrazano-Narrows Bridge to the swearing-in on the steps of the Capitol followed the same route, selling himself to those who did not believe he could do it. History will most likely look back polarized over his presidency, as it does with nearly every aspect of his life. But for Trump that too is the win. History will look back. History will remember. And regardless of how he is remembered, he will be remembered. Trump wins.

THE MAKING OF *THE APPRENTICE*

Donald Trump's ventures in Atlantic City were not as successful. This seaside city boasted the original street map for the game Monopoly. In the 1920s it was the summer resort go-to place for New Yorkers—and New Jerseyites—a chance to walk the boardwalk, dine in restaurants overlooking the Atlantic Ocean, and taste the saltwater taffy. It was a gambling mecca, but became a city ruined by entrenched organized crime. Gambling was banned, but illegal drugs drove the city into urban decay.

In a desperate effort to reclaim some of its remembered, sentimental glory, gambling was restored in 1974, and new hotels and casinos began to pop up. In the 1980s Donald Trump decided to get in on the action. He would eventually buy into numerous hotels and casinos in the city. His first wife Ivana would help manage Trump Castle. In 1988 he would make his biggest commitment, buying the Taj Mahal casino from the television personality and businessman Merv Griffin and Resorts International. Opened in April 1990, it was then the most expensive casino ever built.

His daughter Ivanka would later appear in the documentary *Born Rich*, in which she would recount a story from that troubled time. She was nine or ten years old as she remembered, and she and her father were walking down Fifth Avenue. They spotted a homeless person sitting right outside Trump Tower. Donald Trump pointed to the man and told Ivanka, "That guy has $8 billion more than me."[13]

In the 2016 presidential election, Trump insisted on pointing out that he had never, personally, declared bankruptcy. But he did indeed use the bankruptcy laws when it helped in business. "They're very good for me." His hotel and casino businesses declared bankruptcy six times.

In March 2004, the *New York Times* published the story "Is Trump Headed for a Fall?"[14] The bond debt for his Trump Taj Mahal was at $2 billion. Revenue and profits were flagging. "This has nothing to do with me," he pointed out. "This has to do with a company in which I'm a major shareholder."[15]

Even while the Atlantic City enterprises struggled, Donald Trump was tapped to appear as a successful business mogul on his own reality television show. It was the creation of producer Mark Burnett, who had given viewers the megahit *Survivor*. Donald Trump would be his new celebrity star.

The Apprentice, premiered on January 8, 2004, on NBC. It was an instant hit, drawing twenty million viewers. The show included competing bands of entrepreneurs who vied for profits. The climactic conclusion involved Trump himself, whose corporate team would judge the results, eventually culminating with Donald Trump's stern rebuke to the losers, "You're fired."

The show's signature opening featured a flight over Manhattan, with Donald Trump's baritone voice as the narrator. "New York, my city. Where the wheels of the global economy never stop turning, a concrete metropolis of unparalleled strength and purpose that drives the business world. If you're not careful, it can chew you up and spit you out. But if you work hard you can really hit it big. And I mean really big . . .

"I've mastered the art of the deal and I've turned the name Trump into the highest-quality brand. And as the master I want to pass my knowledge along to somebody else. I'm looking for . . . the apprentice."[16]

Donald Trump was not the only star. His daughter Ivanka, Donald Trump Jr., and Eric Trump each became household names, and later, partly because of their celebrity, powerful surrogates on the presidential campaign trail. The Trumps were Presbyterians. Ivanka had converted to Judaism. This family had glamor. This family had diversity. They were the Kennedys and the Kardashians combined.

CONSIDERING THE WHITE HOUSE

Donald Trump had flirted with the idea of running for president since the 1988 election cycle. But he had no elective or appointed government experience, and no one had ever won the presidency without it. Not all had been politicians. Twelve times a general in the military had been elected president, but many of these men had also served in the Senate or as ambassadors or in an administration.

In 1992, when the businessman Ross Perot ran as an independent, earning 18.9 percent of the popular vote, it became conceivable that a nonpolitician and a nonmember of the military could be elected. In March 2011, an NBC/*Wall Street Journal* poll listed Trump as the favorite among possible GOP contenders. He was one point ahead of former Massachusetts governor Mitt Romney.[17]

There were many other hurdles for a potential president. The big one—money—Trump seemed to have in hand, at least sufficiently to make a run. But he was without a strong ground game. He had employees. He had fans. But not an army of activists who knew their jobs and who had rehearsed them, electing him to Congress or as a governor.

Also, not insignificantly, he was from New York. That could be a problem. The road to the GOP nomination started in the Iowa, where the Republican caucus would select the first delegates on February 1, 2016. It was a farm belt state populated by Catholics and Lutherans, and mostly evangelicals. It was not a friendly place for a New Yorker who had been married three times.

Former New York mayor Rudolph Giuliani had faced that reality in 2008 and had tried to enter the race in Florida, later in the delegate selection process. It just couldn't be done. There was too much power in sequential wins. A candidate who won in Iowa saw his fund-raising and media exposure and credibility skyrocket. And if he placed high or won the next week in New Hampshire, he was even closer to victory. If he won in South Carolina after New Hampshire, the momentum was too great and he was unstoppable. It was almost always over before it got to Florida.

Mitt Romney, a Mormon, or a member of the Church of Jesus Christ of Latter-Day Saints, was even more controversial. Many evangelicals had pronounced the Mormon church a cult, and it had cut to the bone. The bitterness between Mormons and evangelicals was great, yet many leaders in the GOP wanted him as their candidate. He was urban, wealthy, a talented executive who had saved the Winter Olympics from financial ruin. He had won election as governor in the liberal state of Massachusetts. He knew how to get things done. And the Mormons, although only 2 percent of the US population, knew how to organize. They were thrifty and hardworking; they were a fit for the GOP theme of family values; and they stuck together, making them a prolific fund-raising network. Most of all, they could help the Republican National Committee (RNC) fill positions in many states from the precinct levels up. And they brought some balance to a party that was overrun by evangelicals, who showed up only when there was a presidential contest and sometimes not even then.

As the 2012 cycle approached, the RNC, working with some key states, had reorganized its whole delegate-selection process to smooth the way for Romney. Mormons were strong in the Western and mountain states but estranged from evangelicals in Southern states. The Western state of Nevada moved its primary forward. Romney would do well there. Other Midwestern states that did not participate early were moved up as well. And the South? Dominated by Southern Baptist evangelicals? It was made proportional, not winner take all. So an evangelical-friendly candidate would not be able to knock out Romney on a Super Tuesday by sweeping multiple states. Romney would at least get some delegates there, and they would add to his aggregate total.

It was widely accepted in the GOP that Romney would make a great president. He would do what he had already done in Massachusetts and for the Olympics. He would govern well. But Romney, for whatever reasons that he alone knew, refused to meet with more than a handful of evangelical leaders. At the time, the born-again movement claimed almost 40 percent of the American population. Barack Obama had a full-fledged campaign, the Joshua Project, targeted to win their votes. Only one month before the election, Mitt Romney finally met with the noncontroversial Billy Graham for the first time.[18] If he would win the presidency, and there was a widespread feeling among Republicans that he would, it would happen without owing the evangelicals a dime.

And then he lost.

There was widespread discussion among GOP political activists. Some said the role of the evangelicals was diminished. Others recognized that they had not been involved and had stayed home in large numbers, and that should not happen again. Others said that the demographic changes in America had made the difference and had to be acknowledged or the Republican Party would go the way of the dinosaurs. One could not ignore the rise of the Hispanic vote, and the increasing dominance of the African American influence in art, culture, and media. The GOP had better get with it.

Republican Florida senator Marco Rubio was seen as a demographic dream. He was Hispanic, a Catholic who regularly attended an evangelical church, who came from one of the most important so-called battleground states on the electoral map. If a national candidate could carry Florida, he or she had a good chance of winning. Some said that Marco Rubio was the face of the future for the GOP. Others said he was needed now. He should be the nominee in 2016.

In 2014, Senator Rand Paul of Kentucky appeared on the cover of *Time* magazine as "the most interesting man in politics." Paul, a graduate of Duke University School of Medicine, was frighteningly bright. He was more than a born-again Christian, he was a thoughtful one; he said he had come to his faith like Dostoevsky, through a fiery furnace of doubt. He was the champion of criminal justice reform, finding that blacks and Hispanics were receiving longer sentences than whites for the same crimes. In fact, his leadership on this issue was an embarrassment to Democrats and won kudos from unlikely sources such as President Barack Obama.

Rand Paul also had a path to the nomination. His father, Congressman Ron Paul, had run for president in 2012 and had tapped into a dormant libertarian streak in the GOP that it hadn't even known existed. An army of young people had rushed into the political process and had taken over some of the state party offices. In 2012, Ron Paul had virtually tied with Rick Santorum and Mitt Romney in the Iowa Caucus and had come in second in New Hampshire the next week. There seemed to be a built-in army ready to go for Rand Paul. The media had dismissed the father, Ron Paul, who had railed against the inside corruption in Washington, including the Federal Reserve, but it was taking the son, Rand Paul, very seriously.

Then there was Mike Huckabee, the former governor of Arkansas. He had been a Baptist pastor before entering the political fray. He could play the evangelicals of Iowa like a violin. In 2008, Mitt Romney had dumped a fortune into the state, winning the all-important Ames, Iowa, straw vote in August 2011, and had been expected to win the 2008 Iowa Caucus. But Mike Huckabee had come out of nowhere to steal it away. Busses of churchgoing Christians descended on the polling places, and overnight, Huckabee was the front-runner for the presidential nomination.

Huckabee had lost to John McCain in New Hampshire, where evangelicals were much harder to find, and came within a whisker in South Carolina, where McCain beat him again, just barely. The national media dismissed Huckabee at that point, which was a false reality that they, themselves, created. As it happened, in addition to Iowa, Huckabee went onto win Georgia, Alabama, Tennessee, West Virginia, Arkansas, Kansas, and Louisiana. It had been a real race, voided by an all-powerful media.

Then there was Rick Santorum, the former Pennsylvania senator. He had just barely won the popular vote at the Iowa Caucuses in 2012. Like Huckabee, he was cheated out of his victory by a myopic and incompetent national media. A local Republican leader had sat on a few ballot boxes that had come from Santorum-rich counties. So the national media declared Mitt Romney the winner of a narrow three-way virtual tie. Later, when it was too late to help Santorum, they walked it back and admitted that he had won. There was still a lot of resentment, and Santorum had his loyal soldiers on the ground in the state, looking for a chance to avenge this wrong. But where would he get the money? Last time, the billionaire Foster Freiss had ponied up. There were donations to evangelical nonprofit companies, whose leaders gratefully fell into line. But would Santorum, a Catholic, have the money to do it again?

Senator Ted Cruz of Texas, was an evangelical Christian leader who would have no trouble finding money. And with money, anything was possible. Cruz had a clear path to the White House. Win Iowa, do respectfully against the establishment opponent in New Hampshire, and come back to nail it down in South Carolina.

South Carolina was everybody's coveted prize, the final victory to propel him or her to national prominence and clinch the race for the nomination. But the state was experiencing its own midlife crisis. Lindsey Graham, the senior senator from the state, was toying with the idea of running for president himself. Some of his friends said such a race would be run to stop Rand Paul, who Graham feared would win the nomination. Some believed that Graham's whole political career had been financed by the armaments industry, and Senator Paul was considered too cautious when it came to war and committing US troops on the ground.

It was assumed that if Graham got into the race, he would easily win his home state of South Carolina and thus take it off the board. But what if he did not go on to win the nomination? Would the South Carolina delegates lose their bargaining power at the Republican National Convention? Eventually, the state GOP would enact the "Graham rule." It said that if a candidate who won the South Carolina primary later withdrew from the presidential race, his or her delegates would go to the next runner-up. At the time, no one thought it would matter.

The governor of New Jersey, Chris Christie, would run and was a formidable campaigner. Christie had a plethora of pundits on Fox News who promoted him regularly.

Scott Walker, the governor of Wisconsin; Bobby Jindal, the governor of Louisiana; and John Kasich, the governor of Ohio; would all make the run. Ohio was a battleground state and Kasich had a proven record of governance. Jindal was a talented Indian American who represented the diversity that the Republican Party wanted to project. And Scott Walker was actually born in Iowa where his father was a Baptist minister. When the people of Iowa learned about Scott Walker, he would climb to the top of anyone's poll.

In fact, the first battle of words over the 2016 nomination pitted the crowded field of governors against legislators and nonpoliticians. The argument was that a governor had been an administrator. He had made appointments, enacted legislation, run a state. He or she was far better qualified than a congressman or a senator, whose job was to vote. Or a businessperson, who had no first-hand experience with politics at all.

The nonpoliticians considering a run wore their lack of experience on their sleeves. They were proud of it. They represented a change from the Washington process that had become corrupted by special interests.

Carly Fiorina, the former chief executive officer of Hewlett-Packard, would eventually enter the race, knowing that running as the only GOP female candidate, at a time when Hillary Clinton would be securing the Democratic nomination, she would be very much in the news. Being in the news translated into votes.

Ben Carson, a neurosurgeon whose speech in front of President Barack Obama at the National Prayer Breakfast in 2013 had gone viral, with millions of views, would be the only African American presidential candidate in either political party.

Finally, the unspoken specter that haunted the 2016 election was the former governor of Florida Jeb Bush. Both his father and brother had been American presidents. He inherited a massive network of some of the wealthiest political donors in the nation. His wife was Hispanic. He spoke fluent Spanish. He was Catholic.

An apocryphal story promoted by Maryland governor Martin O'Malley had circulated claiming that the chief executive officer of Goldman Sachs had said he would be "just fine with either Bush or Clinton."[19]

It was an eclectic field of candidates. No one could remember when there had been more viable choices. In 1988, the media had jokingly referred to the crowded Democratic field as "Snow White and the Seven Dwarfs." There was congresswoman Pat Schroeder and a list of less famous men. But this Republican list, of governors and famous legislators, many with stature in their own right, was like a field of giants.

DONALD TRUMP FINDS A LINK

Where did Donald Trump fit? What was his path to the White House? How could he, as a brash New Yorker with three marriages, compete in the farm belt, faith-based state of Iowa, where Rudolph Giuliani could not?

The fact was that the Trump family had been faithful Presbyterians in Queens. After moving to Manhattan, Donald Trump had surprised himself by becoming hooked on the powerful, positive preaching of an American icon—the Reverend Norman Vincent Peale. The great Marble Collegiate Church on Fifth Avenue became home for Trump. It was there, not at a nightclub, were he reportedly met his second wife, Marla Maples, the mother of his daughter Tiffany.[20] Rev. Peale knew how to punch the buttons of the struggling businessman, who at times was taking on the whole city of New York single-handedly.

Notwithstanding his profane and mischievous personality, Trump's latent spirituality was always near the surface. After the death of Peale in 1993, Trump missed the upbeat, affirmative message that God was not against him but for him.

Donald Trump was in his golden tower, high above Manhattan, flipping through the television channels one day when he saw a buoyant, attractive Florida televangelist named Paula White. "Faith causes changes," Paula White was famous for saying. "Anytime there is change, there is opportunity, including the opportunity to fail. But failing can be a step toward completion of a goal. You can fail your way to success."[21]

Trump was transfixed. He immediately called to tell her that she was fantastic. The two met on her next trip to New York City and became close friends thereafter.[22] Paula White, who had been married three times herself, was not quick to offer judgment about Donald Trump's personal life. But she would be his link to a religious world beyond the gray walls of the Marble Collegiate Church, a link to a world that he had never known.

"I can absolutely tell you that Mr. Trump has a relationship with God. He is a Christian, he accepts Jesus as his Lord and savior," said Paula White.[23] Nobody in New York paid attention or cared.

Meanwhile, an October 2014 Bloomberg–*Des Moines Register* poll showed that the contest for the GOP nomination was wide open. Likely caucus goers favored Mitt Romney 17 percent; Ben Carson 11 percent; Rand Paul 10 percent; Mick Huckabee 9 percent; House Speaker Paul Ryan 8 percent; Ted Cruz and Rick Perry 7 percent; Chris Christie 6 percent; Rubio, Bush, and Walker 4 percent; Rick Santorum 3 percent.[24] But Mitt Romney had declared unequivocally that he was not going to run.

From the sidelines, anxious, planning daily, Trump was watching closely.

CHAPTER 12

TRUMP AND THE CROWDED FIELD

The art of being wise is the ability to know what should be ignored.

—WILLIAM JAMES

On June 15, 2015, Lawrence O'Donnell of MSNBC, talked to his television audience about Donald Trump. "He is obviously never going to be president. He is obviously never going to be the Republican nominee for president and he is obviously never going to be a candidate for president."[1]

The next day, Donald Trump and his wife, Melania, descended the grand escalator at Trump Tower in New York City to speak to a crowd of supporters and journalists. "So, ladies and gentlemen, I am officially running for president of the United States," he said. "And we are going to make our country great again."[2]

Then he added, "I will be the greatest jobs president that God ever created."[3]

He had been toying with the idea of running for president for decades and had been an on-and-off-again rumored candidate since 1987. This was different.

In 2011, President Barack Obama ridiculed Donald Trump and openly mocked him at the White House Correspondents' Dinner. "Obviously we know about your credentials and breadth of experience," the President said. "For example, seriously, in an episode of *Celebrity Apprentice*, you, Mr. Trump, recognized that the real problem was a lack of leadership. You fired Gary Busey. And these are the kinds of decisions that would keep me up at night."[4] The whole ballroom roared with laughter.

The dinner's host, comedian Seth Meyers said, "Donald Trump has been saying that he'll run for president as a Republican, which is surprising, since I just assumed he was running as a joke."[5] More laughter.

In 2013, Donald Trump had begun to make serious plans and began positioning himself for this moment. His own publicly released financial statement put him at the head of a $9 billion fortune, yet he was going to run as an outsider, willing to challenge a corrupt Washington establishment and America's dominant economic competitors around the world.

"Politicians are all talk, no action," he said. "Nothing is going to get done."[6] He then went on to enumerate the reasons why America needed Trump. They were all new messages that day, but before the election was over, the master of commercial branding would have his audiences reciting them back to him and finishing the lines of his speeches.

He would take on the unfair trade practices of China. He would smash ISIS. He would build a wall on our border with Mexico, and Mexico would pay for it. He would repeal and replace Obamacare. These were themes that would be repeated over and over until they would be seared into the American consciousness. Donald Trump was the master of branding. It had worked in business. It had worked in television entertainment. And now it remained to be seen if it would work in the complicated and murky world of politics.

At first glance, the national media filed the obligatory stories about a Trump candidacy going nowhere. Eleven other candidates were now officially in the mix. Trump had a tough uphill climb. Early polls had him tied for tenth place at 4 percent, close to former Pennsylvania senator Rick Santorum, New Jersey governor Chris Christie, and former New York governor George Pataki.[7] He had already squeezed out Senator Lindsey Graham of South Carolina and Louisiana governor Bobby Jindal. And that was good news. The first national GOP debate would be hosted later in the summer by Fox News, and the network was limiting the stage to the top ten candidates in the most recent polls. Donald Trump had just barely made the cut.

But there was another story buried in his presidential announcement speech, and it was this story that began to show a longer shelf life. It was Trump's words on immigration. And they would forever scramble the presidential race and change the dynamics of the national conversation. Donald Trump suggested that "the US has become a dumping ground for everybody else's problems." There was scattered applause and cheers.

"Thank you. It's true, and these are the best and the finest. When Mexico sends its people, they're not sending their best. They're not sending you. They're not sending you. They're sending people that have lots of problems, and they're bringing those problems with us. They're bringing drugs. They're bringing crime. They're rapists. And some, I assume, are good people.

"But I speak to border guards and they tell us what we're getting. And it only makes common sense. It only makes common sense. They're sending us not the right people."[8]

While this story was panned in some of the first reports, when the video was edited and reworked for television, it was sensational. Depending on how much of the context was featured, it appeared that Trump was branding all Mexicans as rapists and criminals. And when partisan pundits rushed to make that judgment, the media fairly exploded with outrage. CNN ran a headline on a segment entitled, "Donald Trump Doubles Down on Calling Mexicans 'Rapists.'"[9]

Perception became reality. The media had no reason to explain it further; it tainted all Republicans. And Donald Trump's GOP rivals felt no need to defend him. It would only hasten his inevitable departure from the contest.

Nine days later, Univision canceled its telecast of the Miss USA pageant. Trump was a part owner of the event, and Univision was protesting his remarks about Mexicans.[10]

On June 29, 2015, NBC cut its ties with Trump, saying it would no longer televise the Miss Universe and Miss America pageants. "At NBC, respect and dignity for all people are cornerstones of our values," a statement read. "Due to the recent derogatory statements by Donald Trump regarding immigrants, NBCuniversal is ending its business relationship with Mr. Trump."[11] A few days later, on July 1, 2015, Macy's followed suit. The Trump menswear collection was no longer "a good fit" for their stores.[12] Trump was being portrayed as a racist and a xenophobe.

Trump's GOP opponents nodded knowingly. They knew what he meant. Most of them did not favor accepting convicted criminals as immigrants, legal or illegal, whether they were from Mexico or Sweden. And they knew very well how Castro had emptied his prisons in 1994, sending psychotic hardened criminals in the mix with innocent boat people.[13] It was called the Mariel Boatlift, taking its name from the port city in Cuba from which the immigrants sailed. They landed on our shores and we took them in, only to learn, too late, after months of mayhem, what Castro had done. But Trump's opponents now pointed out that his clumsy attempt to explain how immigration could be cynically used by Mexico and other Latin nations was exactly why he was not a viable, serious candidate. He didn't know how to articulate. He had no political sense. His timing was bad, his language was crude and blunt and open to misinterpretation. In a general election, any Democratic opponent would be able to take him out just as the media was doing right then before their eyes.

MURDER IN SAN FRANCISCO

And then a very startling thing happened. On July 1, 2015, Juan Francisco Lopez-Sanchez, an illegal immigrant from Mexico who had been deported five times, began firing a stolen .40-caliber handgun on a pier in a tourist spot in San Francisco. One of the bullets hit thirty-two-year-old Kathryn Steinle in the back.

The beautiful young lady lay dying on the sidewalk, bleeding out, begging for her father to save her. Jim Steinle, Kathryn's father, bent over her body and performed CPR before paramedics arrived. She died a short time later at San Francisco General Hospital.

The shooter, Juan Francisco Lopez-Sanchez, had last been deported in 2009. He had seven felony convictions. He was on probation in Texas at the time of the shooting. He had been convicted on a drug charge in Arizona. He had been convicted three times in Washington state for possession of heroin and for manufacturing narcotics. He had received a drug conviction and a jail term in Oregon before the US government deported him in 1994. He was back in the United States a few years later, where he was convicted once again of heroin possession. This process repeated again and again. He had been deported from the United States back to Mexico five times.

Finally, just before the murder, in the hands of policemen once again in San Francisco, Lopez-Sanchez was turned loose by authorities. San Francisco had a "sanctuary city" policy that prevented authorities from making inquiries about an individual's immigration status. And the federal immigration authorities, urged by the Obama administration to look the other way in such cases, refused to pick him up.

Those three events—the clumsy, ill-defined words on immigration by Donald Trump, followed by what some would perceive as the media's mischaracterization of his views, followed by the murder of Kathryn Steinle—catapulted his candidacy to the front of the national debate. It was the awkwardness of Trump's sentence structure that allowed the media to do its mischief. And when only days later a beautiful young lady was murdered at the hands of an illegal Mexican criminal who had been deported five times, it drove tens of thousands of Americans to research the story for themselves, cobbling together the different pieces.

All the controversy surrounding Donald Trump was not without its advantages. A new CNN/ORC poll showed him climbing to the top. Former governor Jeb Bush was first at 19 percent, then Trump at 12 percent, followed by former governor Mike Huckabee at 8 percent, neurosurgeon Ben Carson and Kentucky senator Rand Paul at 7 percent, with Florida senator Marco Rubio and Wisconsin governor Scott Walker just behind.[14] There were now fully seventeen Republican candidates for president, and Trump was certainly in the hunt.

There was growing concern inside the Bush family at this time. But they got some reassurance from an unlikely source. The Clintons. I had worked for many years inside the Bush family orbit and experienced the earlier estrangement between the two competitive, politically dynastic families. I had spoken with both Bush presidents about the Clinton scandals. The Clinton lifestyle had been appalling to the Bushes. But the Clinton Foundation was a major power in the world of philanthropy. And Bill Clinton was a charmer. And the members of the Bush family could be gentle souls.

The relationship grew strong when George H.W. Bush and Bill Clinton teamed up to help with the relief efforts after the 2005 tsunami in the South Pacific. And then again in response to Hurricane Katrina.[15]

By 2015, the Hillary Clinton campaign and the Jeb Bush campaign, boasted most of the same top donors. The major banks and corporations, which had grown fat off the Iraq War, led by President George W. Bush, all lined up for both candidates. A Clinton-Bush presidential race was a contest that the banks and companies could not lose.

The disturbing distraction of the Donald Trump campaign was unnerving. But word from my sources inside the Bush world, during this time, told of messages from Bill Clinton to President George H.W. Bush and President George W. Bush, which reassured the family that the Trump bubble would soon burst. The Clintons promised it would all be ended soon.

Meanwhile, the national media continued to confidently promote its own politically correct version of the story. On July 5, 2015, NASCAR cut its ties with Donald Trump. But large segments of the population were rapidly unraveling events for themselves. The public was doing the work of the journalists and television producers. It was creating its own personal narrative.

When Donald Trump visited Arizona on July 11, he was greeted by a crowd of 10,000 cheering people at the Phoenix Convention Center. Fox News covered the visit. The enthusiasm fed on itself. Many had imagined that they were part of a very small community of online activists who had pieced these stories together. They had the passion that comes from self-discovery and pride of authorship, but now finding themselves surrounded by thousands of others who had come to the same conclusion, their confidence was reinforced. Where had all these people come from?

The *Arizona Republic*, once a conservative newspaper, which would ultimately endorse Hillary Clinton for president, tried to downplay the moment, pointing out to its readers that the crowd was well short of what the Trump campaign had predicted. For his part, Arizona senator John McCain, who had been the GOP presidential nominee in 2008, was not impressed. McCain complained that Trump had "fired up the crazies."[16]

Even so, it was the largest rally of any 2016 presidential candidate so far, and it put to shame Senator McCain's own crowds. He seldom had more than one hundred people attending one of his own Arizona town hall meetings.

What Donald Trump would later call a movement—and it was indeed a movement—had been born. It was surely about immigration, at least in Arizona. Trump would build a wall and Mexico would pay for it. But it was about much more. It was about all the other things that Trump had said in his announcement speech. It was about the economy. It was about the transfer of wealth to a tiny few at the expense of the many. And it was about the corruption that many suspected made that happen. The media told them that is was globalization. That, in fact, things were getting much better. But many now doubted that. They were beginning to get to the fine print of the stimulus bill that even lawmakers publicly admitted they had not read, and they were seeing how the big corporations were exempted from the regulations that crippled everybody else. All in the name of creating jobs. But what kind of jobs? Seven-dollar-an-hour jobs? Free enterprise, starting your own business, and the American dream were dead. And the whole country was suffocating under political correctness. The media kept saying things were better, it had to be better, it was racist to suggest otherwise, but if it was better, then why hadn't it come to them? Who was better?

On July 17, 2015, *Huffington Post* declared it would henceforth publish stories about Donald Trump in the entertainment section, next to stories on the Kardashians and the *Bachelorette*.[17] He was a pariah.

The next day, it had plenty to report in its entertainment section. Trump was appearing at the Family Leadership Summit in Ames, Iowa, where he was asked about Senator John McCain, who had just called his followers "crazies." McCain had been captured during the Vietnam War and had endured torture in a North Vietnamese prisoner-of-war camp.

"He's not a war hero," said Trump. And then he immediately amended his comments. "He was a war hero because he was captured. I like people who weren't captured."[18]

Former Texas governor Rick Perry described Trump's comments disgraceful and called for him to drop out of the presidential race. Wisconsin governor Scott Walker, the man many thought would ultimately win the nomination, said, "I unequivocally denounce him."[19]

As outrageous and provocative as Donald Trump was appearing to most national observers, he was, at least, communicating with a spontaneity and honesty that some members of the public were apparently craving. They didn't trust politicians. Any politicians. And it was very clear that Donald Trump was not a politician.

And there was something more. There was the beginning of a disconnect between his live audience, the people in the room, and the national audience, who was reading and hearing him through a filter. His rough New York sarcasm and playfulness didn't always read well on the page or in one of his famous tweets or in an edited video clip, but often roused a live audience.

While there were some scattering of boos in Iowa when he had attacked McCain's war record, he quickly turned them into laughter and cheers when he said he didn't like McCain because he had lost the election, and Trump didn't like losers.

He then mocked the whole idea of political correctness, saying, "Hillary Clinton got up, and she said, 'I didn't like Mr. Trump's tone.' We have people, Christians, being . . . having their heads cut off in the Middle East, we have people dying all over the border, where I was right, 100 percent right. We have all of this, like medieval times, and she said 'I didn't like his tone.' And you know who else said that? Jeb Bush, 'I didn't like his tone.' What does it have to do with tone? We want results, this group wants results. We don't want tone."[20] Trump received a thunderous ovation. And this was in Iowa, from an evangelical and Catholic audience at the Family Leadership Summit.

At a rally in South Carolina, Trump responded to attacks from Senator Lindsey Graham by giving out his cell phone number to the audience. They burst into laughter.[21] While the media and his detractors, both Republican and Democrat, dismissed this as sophomoric and petty, the growing mass of Trump supporters reveled in his increasing attacks on the whole political class.[22] The more his rivals railed against his outrageous behavior, the more it endeared him to his own.

On July 23, 2015, Trump made a highly visible visit to the US-Mexico border to view the situation firsthand. Former presidential candidate Texas governor Rick Perry was critical of Trump's stance on illegal immigration and stated, "I hope he will explain to the Hispanic Americans he meets why he thinks they are rapists and murderers."[23]

Buses of journalists accompanied Trump's visit. According to a report in the *New York Times,* only twenty protesters demonstrated, gathered under a tree. Two Latino women got into an argument, one protesting Trump's depiction of some Mexican immigrants as rapists and the other insisting that it was actually often true.[24] A shouting match ensued.

THE REPUBLICAN DEBATES

On August 6, 2015, the first Republican primary debate took place at Quicken Loans Arena in Cleveland, Ohio. It was telecast by Fox News. It drew the largest television audience of any nonsporting event in cable history. It was also the biggest audience for any presidential primary debate in history. There was no doubt: Donald Trump was the reason.

Now leading in the GOP polls, and the nonstop subject of cable television and talk radio, Donald Trump was positioned front and center. And he delivered.

The moderator, Chris Wallace of Fox News, opened the debate by asking for a show of hands. Was any one of the candidates unwilling to pledge support "for the eventual nominee of the Republican Party and pledge to not run an independent campaign against that person"?[25]

Only Donald Trump raised his hand. It was a moment of supreme irony. Later, many of the candidates on that stage would refuse to support Donald Trump when he won the nomination, but now, convinced that he was a shooting star streaking quickly across the sky, they cloaked themselves in self-righteous commitments. Of course they would support the nominee. To do otherwise should be a disqualifier now.

One of the more mysterious and striking events in presidential debate history then unfolded. The coanchor of the debate was the Fox News star Megyn Kelly. She was a beautiful and erudite news anchor, trained as a lawyer, and she had prepared the perfect question for Donald Trump. The day before the debate, her question had been leaked to Trump Tower, and Mr. Trump had called the network irate, claiming that he was being set up.

Kelly had awakened that morning feeling fine, but that soon changed. The driver who picked her up offered her a cup of coffee. She declined. He persisted. She finally relented and within fifteen minutes she was deathly ill, vomiting violently. During the debate, she kept a blanket around her legs and a trash pail beneath the anchor desk.[26]

Undeterred Kelly posed a blunt question. "Mr. Trump, one of the things people love about you is you speak your mind and you don't use a politician's filter. However, that is not without its downsides, in particular, when it comes to women. You've called women you don't like 'fat pigs, dogs, slobs, and disgusting animals."[27]

"Only Rosie O'Donnell," Trump quipped, referring to a past public feud with the celebrity.[28]

Kelly went on to ask how Trump expected to be effective against Hillary Clinton with such a temperament.

Trump's answer took the discussion back to his message but then quickly veered off course, turning confrontational. He accused Kelly of a personal attack on him.

To the annoyance of the other Republican contenders, the Trump-Kelly conflab dominated the discussion postdebate, and the nation followed the drama. Trump told CNN that "There was blood coming out of her eyes, blood coming out of her wherever."[29]

Was Donald Trump intimating that her menstrual cycle had ignited her ire against him? Trump went on CNN's *State of the Union* and denied these allegations, telling the anchor, Jake Tapper, "Do you think I'd make a stupid statement like that? Who would make a statement like that? Only a sick person would even think about it."[30]

It dominated the news.

Trump's ongoing war with Megyn Kelly appeared to be political suicide. Fox News was the only major media outlet that gave Republicans their due. How could Trump hope to win without it? What was he doing?

Meanwhile, offended Trump supporters began to demand Kelly's resignation from Fox News. "On social media, I'm the one that's beloved," Trump bragged. "OK, because if you look at social media and what's happening, they are really coming out strongly in favor of Donald Trump. They agree."[31]

Trump's base saw him as a fearless independent, willing to combat opponents on any side of the political aisle and on any side of the media. Trump eventually cuts ties with Fox News in September, telling his audience on Twitter that "@FoxNews has been treating me very unfairly & I have therefore decided that I won't be doing any more Fox shows for the foreseeable future."[32] In the end, after Trump went on other networks and spoke ill against Fox News and Megyn Kelly, he met with the head of Fox, Roger Ailes, and was shortly back on the network.

While the media was picking him apart, Trump was continuing his game on the ground. On August 21, 2015, he was scheduled to hold a rally at the Civic Center in Mobile, Alabama but due to the overwhelming crowd that gathered, the rally was moved to the Ladd-Peebles Stadium. The major networks mostly panned the event, and when they mentioned it, they used terms to diminish its importance. It was described as a high school pep rally. In fact, it attracted a massive audience of thirty thousand devoted supporters.

The first person to get in line for this rally, at six a.m., was a retired marine, Keith Quackenbush. What he told the CNN reporter interviewing him was the foundation of the Trump supporter's belief system. "This isn't about Republicans, it isn't about Democrats," Keith began. "This is a movement of citizens across America tired of the BS."[33] Trump's plan to remove himself from the political establishment was working, and working very well. America was fed up, America wanted a change, and Trump was the only clear choice for any real change. Polls continued to show Donald Trump as the front-runner, with Jeb Bush his most consistent competitor. Trump began to target Bush. Day after day on the campaign trail and again in multiple media interviews, he referred to Bush as a nice person, without the energy to get the job done. He started calling him "a low-energy person."[34]

If the news coverage of Trump seemed unfair to his ardent supporters, at least he was being mentioned. No other GOP candidate could even get coverage. Trump was sucking all the oxygen out of the air.

Leading into the second debate, Donald Trump mocked Carly Fiorina's appearance in a *Rolling Stones* interview. "Look at that face," Trump said. "Would anyone vote for that? Can you imagine that, the face of our next president?! I mean, she's a woman, and I'm not supposed to say bad things, but really, folks, come on. Are we serious?"[35]

While calling into the popular *Fox & Friends* morning television show, Trump insisted that he had been misunderstood. No, he asserted, he did not mean her appearance. "I'm talking about persona, I'm not talking about looks."[36] In the same interview on Fox, he also joked that Senator Rand Paul was a clown and should have been given an IQ test in order to participate in the debates. Many saw Rand Paul, an ophthalmologist, as the brightest presidential candidates in either party.

Day after day, week after week, Trump dominated the news. In the days before the second Republican presidential debate, he finally agreed to sign a GOP loyalty pledge. It promised he would not run as a third-party candidate. The Republican national chairman, Reince Priebus, journeyed to Trump Tower in New York City to get the desired signature.

The second debate was held at the Reagan Library on September 16, 2015, and was a prime-time telecast on CNN. Reagan's Air Force One stretched out in the background. The frustrated Republican candidates, who had been counseled to hold their fire in the first debate, to let Trump flame out, who thought he wouldn't last, and that to engage him would cause one only to become his punching bag, now opened fire.

Only Barack Obama got more negative mentions than Donald Trump. Even Hillary Clinton was targeted less.[37] There was one exception. Texas senator Ted Cruz, no doubt hoping to inherit Trump's support after his inevitable collapse, lauded the New York businessman. "I'm very glad that Donald Trump's being in this race has forced the mainstream media finally to talk about illegal immigration."[38]

Many believed that Carly Fiorina stole the show at the debate. But when former governor Jeb Bush, tired of being Donald Trump's punching bag, took into his opponent with a sustained attack, it was easily parried by Trump, who labeled Bush as the puppet of special interests. In contrast, Trump said he had turned down millions of dollars from special interests. Nobody owned him. When Bush tried to interrupt, Trump quipped, "More energy tonight, I like that."[39] The audience laughed.

Coming out of the second debate, Carly Fiorina's support rose twelve points. Some said there may indeed by a woman president, and her name may not be Hillary.

The field began to lessen dramatically on September 21, 2015, when Wisconsin governor Scott Walker dropped out of the race. At the beginning of the year, he had soared to the top of the Iowa state polls, where the first GOP caucus in the nation would be held, but that was before the summer of Donald Trump. The billionaire businessman had wiped everybody else off the television screens. Walker, out of the limelight, could not raise the funds needed for his campaign.[40] At one time, seventeen candidates had crowded the field of GOP contenders. Now the number was down to ten.

THE IOWA CAUCUSES

Toward the end of 2015, the contest became more intense. Earlier voter preferences had mattered for fund-raising purposes. No one wanted to see his or her donation go to a loser. But now, as the February 1, 2016, Iowa Caucus loomed, it was time for the Republicans to start the delegate-selection process. These were the delegates who would attend the Republican National Convention in Cleveland in the summer of 2016. They would choose the Republican nominee. Those caucuses, state conventions, and primary contests were going to take place in rapid succession, and that process would start soon. The polls now were a very serious indicator of who would win those delegates and the nomination. There was no reason to hold back.

Just before the third GOP debate on October 28, 2015, a *New York Times*/CBS News national poll showed Ben Carson in the national lead over Trump. The poll also revealed that only 28 percent of Republicans had decided on their choice for a nominee.[41] Now the voters were finally shifting. Perhaps put off by the internecine battles among the GOP candidates, including Trump, a sizable number of likely voters showed support for the one candidate who had avoided antagonizing anybody: The African American neurosurgeon Ben Carson.

The third debate generated more criticism of the CNBC moderators and the questions than any criticism of the candidates themselves, including Donald Trump. Senator Ted Cruz won plaudits for nailing the moderators on it. Comedian Stephen Colbert roasted the moderators on his *Late Show*. A Matt Drudge poll had Trump winning the debate.

Coming out of the third debate, the numbers were even stronger for Ben Carson. An NBC/*Wall Street Journal* poll had Carson leading the race with the highest percentage that any candidate in the crowded field had yet achieved. It was Ben Carson 29 percent, Donald Trump 23 percent, Marco Rubio 11 percent, Ted Cruz 10 percent, and Jeb Bush 8 percent.[42]

On December 1, 2015, Sally Quinn wrote an article for the *Washington Post* entitled "Why Ben Carson Doesn't Believe in Hell."[43] When it comes to understanding Southern culture, including the arcane world of Southern Baptists and Pentecostals and other groups that Georgetown sophisticates take pride in not comprehending, Sally Quinn was, in fact, fully knowledgeable. Her late husband was the legendary Ben Bradlee, the executive editor of the *Washington Post*. And Bradlee knew just about all the intricate pieces of the American political puzzle.

So Sally Quinn knew exactly what she was doing when she sat down with Ben Carson and asked if he believed in hell. Carson was a conservative Christian and thus had strong support from evangelicals, who dominated the Iowa Caucus and the South Carolina primary that followed soon after. As long as evangelicals remained divided among Carson, Cruz, Huckabee, Santorum, and others, a nonevangelical like Trump had a chance.

Now, with Carson pulling away from the pack, it was time to get serious. As far as evangelicals were concerned, Ben Carson had a doctrinal flaw. He was a Seventh-Day Adventist, and, as such, he did not believe in a literal hell. Most evangelicals were unaware of this particular Adventist belief. Amazingly, fully 61 percent of Americans believed in a literal hell. For evangelical Christians, make that

87 percent.[44] And if we were to narrow it down to evangelicals participating in the Iowa Caucus, who knows how high the number would climb?

Had the Ted Cruz team inspired the Sally Quinn interview? Had it suggested the question? Regardless, it began to promote the story. Ben Carson, who was emerging as the long-awaited answer to Donald Trump, began to see his numbers in Iowa erode. Likely voters were moving to the evangelical Christian backup plan: Senator Ted Cruz.

This spelled serious problems for Donald Trump. Most Republican operatives saw the powerful Iowa evangelical vote split among Mike Huckabee, the 2008 winner, Rand Paul, Ted Cruz, and Rick Santorum, who had won in 2012. The strong Iowa Catholic vote would be split among Jeb Bush, Marco Rubio, Chris Christie, and once again, Rick Santorum, who was considered a "switch hitter."[45] It was the split vote among the serious Christians that allowed a tough-talking, crude, profane New Yorker a chance.

Cruz had money behind him. His unabashed appeal to evangelicals could win the day in the Iowa Caucuses and allow him to lose to Trump in New Hampshire the next week, only to come back for the knockout blow in evangelical-friendly South Carolina.

In the days after the Sally Quinn story, the Cruz team lined up evangelical leaders at an alarming rate. Before the month was out, Bob Vander Plaats, the most prominent voice of Iowa evangelicals and the CEO of the Family Leader, endorsed Cruz. Other leaders who had been waiting on the sidelines for two years now finally committed. As in the case of African American voters, the masses of conservative Christians tended to follow their leaders. There would be a delayed reaction as word spread, but the numbers would soon start showing in the national polls.

Cruz was perfectly happy to keep the peace with Donald, while Trump ravaged the competition. On December 11, 2015, he tweeted, "The Establishment's only hope. Trump & me in a cage match. Sorry to disappoint - @realDonaldTrump is terrific. #DealWithIt."[46]

On Monday, February 1, 2016, the GOP Caucus was held in the state of Iowa. The candidates had been working for this moment for years. All the private meetings and dinners, all the fund-raisers, all the debates, all the headlines, all the countless hours of television chatter, had finally culminated in this, the first-in-the-nation contest for delegates to the Republican National Convention. In all, 186,932 Republican voters gathered at caucus locations to vote for their choice. In the end, they would select a modest delegation of thirty to attend the convention.

Senator Ted Cruz of Texas was the winner. The final tally was Cruz 27.64 percent, Trump 24.3 percent, and Marco Rubio 23.12 percent. Carson's brief surge to the top had been deflated. He carried only 9.3 percent of the vote.

Reaction came on two tracks. First, it was clearly an antiestablishment vote. The two top vote getters were both considered troublemakers by the political and corporate leaders in New York and Washington, and both men carried the designation with pride. Trump was not even a politician. Cruz, although a sitting US Senator, was despised by his colleagues in Congress. The voters seemed to love him for it.

The second track clung to the hope that the establishment, the saner, more reasonable faction in the GOP, had finally emerged with its man. He was Marco Rubio, the senator from Florida. He would finally be the candidate that a divided establishment could rally behind. Now the rebels were divided by Cruz and Trump, and the establishment was united. Or so the argument went.

Still, there were lingering signals that this was not an ordinary election cycle. Senator Rand Paul of Kentucky had almost twice as many votes in Iowa as the man who two years ago was the first front-runner, Jeb Bush.

Ted Cruz was jubilant. He was the new front-runner. He led in the only count that mattered, delegates to the Republican National Convention. Cruz announced to the nation, "Iowa has sent notice that the Republican nominee and the next president of the United States will not be chosen by the media, will not be chosen by the Washington establishment."[47]

It was a shot at Donald Trump, whose antics had dominated the media's attention to the dismay of the rest of the field. And it was a shot at the Republican establishment that didn't want either man and was struggling to find a way to stop them.

Donald Trump, who was not used to losing, was uncharacteristically humble. "We finished second," he said. "And I have to say I am just honored."[48]

As often happened in politics and life, another story emerged too late to affect the results in Iowa but it would impact events later in other places. Caucus attendees in Iowa arrived at their meetings to be told that Ben Carson had withdrawn as a candidate. In some cases the message was carried by Cruz supporters, and it was in writing. Carson caucusgoers were told that their votes would have to go to someone else. Most of them, conservative Christians, would move to Ted Cruz. Some were suspicious.

The next day, the Ted Cruz campaign apologized to Ben Carson, and a statement was released from the senator. "Last night when our political team saw the CNN post saying that Dr. Carson was not carrying on to New Hampshire and South Carolina, our campaign updated grassroots leaders just as we would with any breaking news story," the Cruz statement read. "That's fair game. What the team then should have done was send around the follow-up statement from the Carson campaign clarifying that he was indeed staying in the race when that came out. This was a mistake from our end, and for that I apologize to Dr. Carson."[49]

It was too little, too late. Ted Cruz had won. Ben Carson, who had led the field for two months, had collapsed. And Donald Trump, the master of branding, had just been given the card he would later play to defeat his most serious challenger for the nomination. "Lyin Ted" had been born.

CHAPTER 13

AN UNLIKELY NOMINEE

One should use common words
to say uncommon things.
— ARTHUR SCHOPENHAUER

Donald Trump had not been idle in the weeks and months leading up to his loss in Iowa. If he was flagging in the polls, he was still very much the center of discussion. His November appearance on NBC's *Saturday Night Live* drew the highest ratings of the season, surpassing Miley Cyrus.[1] More telling, observers compared the numbers with those of the Democratic presidential contender Hillary Clinton. As a host, Trump's audience numbers beat Clinton's by 47 percent.[2] If his campaign was in question, it was still very clear that the nation was still watching Trump.

The fourth debate, which took place on November 10, 2015, did not go well for Trump. He was booed numerous times at the Fox Business and *Wall Street Journal* forum. When he went after John Kasich, the audience booed him; when he spoke out against the Trans-Pacific Partnership, he was lectured by Rand Paul, who had to instruct him that China was not a participant. Trump and Fiorina traded barbs over Russian president Vladimir Putin, and he was again booed when he railed against Fiorina's attempt to speak over Rand Paul. The audience applauded Kasich and Jeb Bush when they attacked Trump's immigration plan.

The general feeling among pundits was that Trump's repetitive rhetoric was tiring his voter base.[3] But Trump's team was not panicking. What did the pundits know or appreciate about branding?

On November 13, 2015, ISIS terrorists attacked six separate locations in and around Paris, France, killing 130 people and wounding hundreds of others.[4] There was a worldwide outpouring of sympathy, rage, and fear.

Donald Trump later told French journalists, "Do you really think that if there were people in the crowd who were armed and trained, things would have turned out the same way?

"I don't think so. They would have killed the terrorists. It makes sense.

"I always have a gun on me. I can tell you that if I had been in the Bataclan or in the cafés, I would have opened fire."[5]

Reports started to circulate that eight Syrian refugees had been caught in a border town in Texas. Trump posted via his Twitter account, "Eight Syrians were just caught on the southern border trying to get into the U.S. ISIS maybe? I told you so. WE NEED A BIG & BEAUTIFUL WALL!"[6]

The governor of Texas, Greg Abbott, also stated via Twitter, "THIS is why Texas is vigilant about Syrian refugees."[7]

As it turned out, the Department of Homeland Security confirmed that the Syrian refugees were two families made up of both two men and women, along with four children. They were seeking asylum. They had presented themselves to a boarder station in Laredo, Texas, as they attempted to cross the US-Mexico border.

The media focused on the flap, trying to show Trump was wrong, or even lying, about the eight Syrian refugees, but the sudden focus on the border provoked a rash of other embarrassing stories. It was learned that the previous day, Border Patrol agents had apprehended six illegal immigrants from Pakistan and Afghanistan who had surreptitiously stolen into Arizona. And this was followed by a report of five Syrian men who were being held in Honduras after attempting to illegally enter the United States.

The Homeland Security Committee chairman Mike McCaul said of the Syrian men in Honduras, "Some of these military-age males could present a threat to the United States. All we're asking for is a proper vetting."[8]

Officials reported that the border was under constant security threats. Events were happening daily; they were just not mentioned or covered by journalists. Finding the story turning to Trump's advantage, the mainstream media dropped the whole issue and shifted to other news. The events on the border, broiling every day, went dark again.

Meanwhile, in an interview with Yahoo News, Trump was asked about a database of Muslims and special ID cards noting their religion. At a campaign stop in Iowa, Trump confirmed to a reporter that "I would certainly implement that. Absolutely. It's all about management." And the registration would be mandatory. He went on to talk about monitoring activity in mosques and enhancing surveillance.[9]

Trump later attempted to clarify his position. It was the reporter who had suggested the database, he insisted.[10] But the damage was done. This would continue to be a rallying point for his opponents on both sides of the political aisle. He was now being compared to Hitler and was increasingly referred to as dangerous. And the controversies would get worse.

At a rally in Myrtle Beach, South Carolina, Trump was accused of mocking the disability of Serge Kovaleski, a *New York Times* reporter who has arthrogryposis, a disability affecting movement in his joints. Trump said he had never actually seen Mr. Kovaleski.

"I didn't know what he looked like. I didn't know he was disabled. [Kovaleski] was groveling, grovel, grovel, grovel. That was the end of it. All of a sudden, I get reports that I was imitating a reporter who was handicapped. I would never do that."[11] However, the damage had been done, and even though a video surfaced showing Trump made similar gestures when describing other people without disabilities, many were offended and incensed by his remarks.

As the fifth GOP presidential debate approached, Trump intimated that he would skip the debate altogether unless CNN paid him $5 million to attend. Trump promised to donate all that money to a charity, such as Wounded Warriors, an organization that benefited veterans. CNN refused to pay. Trump relented.

In the first week of December 2015, after the Sally Quinn interview with Ben Carson, the Trump team saw the numbers moving to Ted Cruz. Carson, who had been leading in the national polls, was collapsing. The evangelical vote in Iowa was not going to be split. It was coalescing behind the Texas senator. Donald Trump had to do something. It was one thing to be running against the kindly Dr. Ben Carson, but something altogether different taking on Ted Cruz, who was backed by millions of dollars.

BANNING MUSLIMS

On December 7, 2015, Trump posted a statement on his website titled "Donald J. Trump Statement on Preventing Muslim Immigration." The New York businessman cited research from the Pew Group and the Center for Security Policy that showed 25 percent of Muslims outside of the US "agree that violence against Americans here in the United States is justified as a part of global jihad" and that "51 percent of those polled agreed that Muslims in America should have the choice of being governed according to Sharia

[law]."[12] Trump called for a ban of Muslim immigration, "until we can find out what the hell is going on."[13]

There was a firestorm. Once again, the entire attention of the nation, and now the world, was focused on Donald Trump, but it was widely accepted that most of the attention was negative.

Polls showed Ted Cruz taking the lead in Iowa. On the same day, twenty Republican leaders gathered to speak with RNC chairman, Reince Priebus, about how a contested convention would work. If Trump were to somehow split the field and actually win the nomination, how could they use procedure to stop him? Their plan was to begin preparations to gather as many of the GOPs leadership and base around an alternative candidate as possible. The meeting began as a hypothetical conversation. It ended with ideas and plans to make it a reality.[14]

In January, the Republican Party's self-appointed boss, Karl Rove, declared in the *Wall Street Journal* that "if Mr. Trump is its standard-bearer, the GOP will lose the White House and the Senate, and its majority in the House will fall dramatically."[15]

That same month, just before the Iowa Caucus, a startling new poll showed that the evangelicals, the religious right, was rallying around the embattled Donald Trump. Jerry Falwell Jr., the president of Liberty University, endorsed him, which was followed by a Pew Research Center poll that showed GOP voters were not necessarily convinced Trump was "Christian" or even "religious" but supported him anyway.[16]

The study showed a major shift in attitude among Christian voters. It had long been assumed that morals, religious affiliation, and a Judeo-Christian perspective were of primary importance to this voter bloc. But the numbers now showed that national security, the economy, and a dislike for establishment politicians was foremost on their minds. Hillary Clinton would learn this when her team began its attack on Trump's morals. While many in the evangelical church were shocked by Trump's lifestyle, it was not enough to cause them to vote for Hillary or a third-party nominee. Hillary Clinton had her own set of problems. For the first time, evangelicals were looking beyond their religious beliefs and focusing on national issues.

EVEN THE POPE CAN'T STOP HIM NOW

In the immediate aftermath of the Iowa Caucus, the once crowded GOP field thinned substantially. Former governor Mike Huckabee withdrew. Rand Paul, who finished with twice as many votes as Jeb Bush, also pulled out. The national division over Trump was threatening his political base in Kentucky. He couldn't afford to toy with a presidential run and lose his seat in the Senate.

An eighth debate was held on February 6, 2016, at Saint Anselm College, Manchester, New Hampshire. ABC television and the *Independent Journal Review* provided the moderators. The debate featured a prosecutorial takedown of Marco Rubio by Chris Christie. And Trump and Cruz finally tore into each other. But the failed choreography of the introduction of the candidates became the most telling moment.

While the audience at Saint Anselm and on television heard the booming, exciting introductions of each of the candidates, apparently the candidates themselves waiting backstage could not. Or at least not easily.

Ben Carson stood waiting in the wings, not knowing that he had already been introduced. A network television camera showed the other candidates walking by him with a "what's your problem buddy" jaunt in their step. "I figured this out, why couldn't you?"

After being introduced, Donald Trump, the star of the show, paused backstage, between the curtains, talking with Ben Carson, helping him figure out what had happened. It was a tender moment. As events would show, it helped Carson eventually decide to endorse Donald Trump over Ted Cruz, the man who had sunk his boat in Iowa.

New Hampshire was a primary, not a caucus, which meant that Republicans would actually go to polling places to vote. It was held on February 9, 2016, one week after the Iowa Caucuses, and Donald Trump was the winner. He won big. Trump garnered 100,735 votes, almost three times the votes for Ted Cruz.

The full ramifications of this victory were almost immediately realized. The GOP establishment was clearly divided. While Marco Rubio had claimed the mantle for a week, having come in third place in Iowa, Jeb Bush squeezed ahead of him in New Hampshire and was now making the claim for himself. It got worse. Ohio governor John Kasich won 44,932 votes, coming in second, ahead of Cruz, Bush, and Rubio. Kasich was now, rightly, making the claim that the anti-Trump forces should coalesce behind him. The GOP establishment was now split three ways as the primary headed to South Carolina where Ted Cruz, a Southern Baptist, had an advantage in a Southern Baptist state.

Carly Fiorina and Chris Christie dropped out of the race. Carly had run out of money, and New Hampshire was the one place where Christie had to win. It didn't happen. He would go back to his home state of New Jersey where he could "take a deep breath" and consider his next move.[17]

On February 16, 2016, President Barack Obama openly criticized the Republican primary contest and stated flatly, in a news conference, "I continue to believe Mr. Trump will not be president."[18]

But once again, Donald Trump dominated the headlines. Only a few days before the South Carolina and Nevada primaries, the Pope criticized Trump on his immigration policies. His Holiness had just returned from a visit to Mexico and had the American election on his mind. It was the first time in history that a pope had openly attacked an America presidential candidate. "A person who only thinks about building walls, wherever they may be, and not building bridges, is not a Christian," the Pope said.

A rebuke from the Pope in ordinary times would be a killing political blow, but if it was going to happen, it could not have happened at a better time for the billionaire businessman. South Carolina was a state chocked full of evangelical Christians. They were Protestants and they were not impressed with a Catholic Pope telling them how to vote.

In his signature fashion, Trump retorted, "For a religious leader to question a person's faith is disgraceful. If and when the Vatican is attacked by ISIS, which, as everyone knows, is ISIS' ultimate trophy, I can promise you that the Pope would have only wished and prayed that Donald Trump would have been president."[19] Images began to be circulated by Trump supporters showing the massive wall around the Vatican, hinting at the hypocrisy of the Pope's attack on Trump.

The South Carolina primary took place February 20, 2016. In the days before the vote, South Carolina's governor, Nikki Haley, rebuked Trump, and threw her support behind Marco Rubio. It couldn't stop the flood. Donald Trump won 33 percent to Rubio's 22 percent, with Ted Cruz behind by only a razor-thin margin. Jeb Bush, who started the race as the front-runner, and may have been the third Bush family president in American history, suspended his campaign.

Three days later, Trump won the Nevada caucuses with 46 percent of the vote, beating Rubio and Cruz, who won 24 and 21 percent, respectively.

March 1, 2016, was known as Super Tuesday, or the SEC Primary, named after the Southeastern Conference of college football.

Eleven states would make their choice for the Republican presidential nominee.

The primary had once been a Southern event that rewarded that region for its long support of the Republican nominee in a general election. Most states had been winner take all, but that had been refashioned to suit the Mitt Romney candidacy, and states outside the South had been added, including Massachusetts, the state where Romney had once served as governor.

Ironically, the rules that had been changed to help advance the nomination of the Mormon Mitt Romney for the 2012 cycle now worked as a sand trap for Senator Ted Cruz, the evangelical answer to Donald Trump. Before the long day was over, Cruz carried Texas, Oklahoma, and Alaska. Marco Rubio carried Minnesota. But Donald Trump carried seven states. In the all-important delegate count, it was Trump 256, Cruz 219, and Marco Rubio 101.

NEVER TRUMP

Shortly after Donald Trump's win in South Carolina, the author was invited onto numerous television shows and declared that Donald Trump was unstoppable. My experience as a student of history and a participant in ten presidential campaigns informed me. No one could reach this point and not win the Republican nomination.

In February, I likened him to a modern-day Andrew Jackson, a profane, impolite outsider who challenged the Brahmin political class of his day. Afterward, several newspapers picked up on this comparison.

Curiously, I was almost alone in the conclusion that Trump would win the nomination, and do so on the first ballot. To be sure, some of the political commentators were making money off the candidates and weren't about to concede. Others were taking in large donations from concerned Republican donors who were looking for an alternative to the divisive Trump. They believed he could never win the general election and would bring the whole GOP down in disaster. A political operative could garner 15 percent of a television buy. Convincing Republican billionaire donors to place several million dollars in television advertising to stop Donald Trump could result in a personal fortune.

So they had good reasons to tell a television audience that Trump could still be defeated. And then, the television networks themselves, the news industry, had a vested interest in keeping a good story going. It brought ratings, which translated into advertising. Ironically, the "Never Trump" forces, who had reviled the media for its disproportionate coverage of Donald Trump, were now getting publicity that they didn't deserve.

On February 19, 2016, at a luncheon of Republican governors and donors in Washington, DC, Karl Rove urged drastic action to block Trump. The next day, "seated at a long boardroom table at the Willard Hotel,"[20] the colorful governor of Maine, Paul LePage, called for the group to make a public statement.

Later in the month, Marco Rubio took his own crude potshot at Donald Trump. For days, Trump had been referring to him as "Little Rubio," and the nickname was apparently getting to the senator. And then there were the national polls. Rubio had to do something to stay above water. Florida and round two of Super Tuesday was only days away. It was now or never for Rubio. If he couldn't beat Trump in Florida, then where could he win? He decided to hit back.

"He is taller than me," Rubio told an audience. "He's like six-two, which is why I don't understand why his hands are the size of someone who is five-two," Rubio said, laughing. "Have you seen his hands? And you know what they say about men with small hands?"[21]

Rubio was referring to Trump's penis size. It was the sort of thing that Trump himself might say, but Trump hadn't said it, Marco Rubio had said it. In an instant, the moral high ground that the establishment Republicans had claimed against Trump vaporized. Rubio had apparently been more hurt by Trump's attacks than he publicly acknowledged. It was a remarkably crude moment in presidential politics, one that didn't work well for Rubio.

The Republican establishment, the losers in this political power struggle, were working their way through the successive stages of grief, and they were very much behind in the process, still stuck in the enchantment of self-denial. Even before Super Tuesday, the Republican House Speaker, Paul Ryan, had spent the weekend in Utah and visited with the former presidential candidate Mitt Romney.

What Romney now could see plainly was that Donald Trump had no ground game. That is, he and his campaign had not recruited their own people to run for the delegate slots that they had won.

The Republican Party, like the Democratic Party, is a private club with its own rules. It is not governed by the US Constitution and each state Republican Party convention makes its own rules on how to select its delegates to the national convention. And all of these delegates are people, human beings, and they are elected at the precinct level and up. They know each other and help each other get elected.

When a candidate wins a primary, the state Republican Party rules dictate what those delegates should do, but there is great leeway. In 2016, the delegates in some states were required to vote for the winner of the primary only on the first ballot and were free thereafter to vote for whomever they wished. The delegates also controlled the Credentials Committee, which meant they could decide whom to accept as a delegate at the national convention and whom to turn away. Then there was the Rules Committee, which could change the rules of the convention altogether.

Mitt Romney understood this very well. He had faced down a delegate insurgency at the 2012 Republican National Convention. Security personnel had actually bodily removed unwanted delegates from the convention hall. These were arguably proper delegates who had been elected at their state Republican conventions, who were planning to vote for another candidate.

The exquisite Romney operation of 2012 had personally recruited most of the delegates to the Republican National Convention. They were a small family of less than three thousand people. Romney knew many of them and he knew their families. He could name some of their dogs. They had been carefully recruited, and they stacked the various RNC committees.

Romney had planned on winning the 2012 election, and his people, rightly, wanted a smooth renomination experience for an incumbent President Mitt Romney in 2016. With the help of Ben Ginsberg and others on his team, the rules of the Republican National Convention were written to smooth Romney's way in 2016. Yes, Donald Trump had won many of the caucuses and primaries, but the delegates, Romney noticed, who were selected at state conventions were many of the same people who, at one time, anyway, owed their allegiance to him.

Many of those same delegates were now urging Romney to do what Ron Paul had done to him: lead an insurgency at the national convention. But he had to speak up. He had to signal his intentions.

This Romney did on March 3, 2016, at the University of Utah. "Here's what I know," Romney intoned. "Donald Trump is a phony, a fraud. His promises are as worthless as a degree from Trump University. He's playing members of the American public for suckers: He gets a free ride to the White House, and all we get is a lousy hat."[22]

Romney was attempting to unify the Republican base and offer the suggestion that an alternative to Trump was possible. Feelers sent out to get cooperation from John Kasich were rejected. Attempts to get Cruz and Rubio to combine were also dismissed out of hand.

Romney's speech backfired stupendously. Whatever power he had with the delegates and soon-to-be delegates to the RNC evaporated. This was seen as power politics, the work of unelected power brokers wanting to keep their corrupt system in place at the expense of the people. What about all the people who had voted for Trump? Did their votes matter? Was the system rigged?

There is a disturbing postscript to this story. After winning the election, Donald Trump publicly invited Mitt Romney to Trump Tower in Manhattan, where the president elect was said to be considering the 2012 GOP nominee for secretary of state. Romney dutifully showed up before cameras to extol the virtues of the man he had once called "a fraud." Meanwhile, Romney surrogates were dispatched to television to talk up the idea. It was like Lincoln's "team of rivals," when he appointed former political enemies to cabinet posts to help unite a divided country.

Trump supporters were aghast. Was this a betrayal? What about the promise to "drain the swamp," that is, to move away from the established, professional politicians? One of the author's sources now says that the whole drama was Trump theater, designed to humiliate the man who had tried to derail his campaign. The same source said that Trump was unexpectedly surprised by Romney's good ideas.

"LITTLE MARCO"

Meanwhile, the Donald Trump personality parade went right on rolling. On the very night of the Mitt Romney speech, the remaining candidates met for a Fox News GOP presidential debate.

"Well, look, he was a failed candidate," Trump said, defending himself from Romney's attack. "He should have beaten President Obama. Easy. He failed miserably, and it was an embarrassment to everybody, including the Republican Party. He went away. It looked like he went away on vacation the last month."[23]

Cruz and Trump duked it out in this last debate before Super Tuesday II but, as usual, Trump won the sound-bite war. "And he referred to my hands," Trump said, holding his hands up to the camera. "If they are small, something else must be small. I guarantee you there is no problem. I guarantee."[24] The audience roared with shocked laughter.

Not every Republican leader was lined up against Donald Trump. Newt Gingrich, a former House Speaker and once a front-runner for the presidency himself, was one of the earliest and most public supporters of Trump. He took to Fox News to defend him. In February, while governors were meeting behind closed doors trying to stop Trump, Governor Chris Christie endorsed him.

On March 4, Dr. Ben Carson dropped out of the presidential race. "I did the math. I looked at the delegate counts, I looked at the states, I looked at the requirements, and I realized it simply wasn't going to happen, and if that's the case, I didn't want to interfere with the process."[25]

Dr. Carson likely remembered Trump's kindnesses earlier in the campaign, and he had been wounded by what he believed to be dirty tricks by the Ted Cruz campaign. Carson would soon be an active supporter for the Trump team. He would later help Trump find his vice presidential running mate.

On March 5, the so-called Super Saturday, Trump won Kentucky and Louisiana. Ted Cruz won Kansas and Maine. Cruz was calling it a two-man race and urging the Republican establishment to fall into line behind him.

Then came Super Tuesday II. It took place on March 15, 2016, and it was a blowout. Trump won 229 delegates, including Florida, Illinois, North Carolina, and Missouri. Governor John Kasich, who carried his own state of Ohio, had 81 delegates. Ted Cruz had 51.

Senator Marco Rubio lost his home state. For the whole day, he had won just 6 delegates. The defeat was so absolute that some speculated Rubio's career was over, that he would likely lose his Senate seat in November as well.

Trump's new style of campaigning, absorbing all the media attention, even if it took negative words and events to achieve that, and his branding talents, including his ability to fashion negative branding, was devastating.

The race was now down to two men. Donald Trump and Ted Cruz.

LYIN' TED

Donald Trump, the master of the brand, now focused on Ted Cruz, the last man standing between him and the Republican nomination. "In the case of Lyin' Ted Cruz," Trump said. "Lyin' Ted. Lies. Ooh, he lies. You know Ted? He brings the Bible, holds it high, puts it down, lies," Trump said. "And, you know, the evangelicals, they've been supporting Donald Trump. It's been great."[26]

Trump first used the moniker Lyin' Ted at a Super Tuesday rally on March 1, 2016, in Columbus, Ohio. By the time of the March 3 GOP debate in Detroit, Michigan, the phrase was so well known that Trump fans broke into delighted howls of laughter when he used it, and Cruz supporters booed.

"Excuse me. Excuse me," Trump said, defending himself from a Ted Cruz verbal cross, "I've given my answer, Lyin' Ted. I've given my answer."[27]

Some observers believed there were good reasons why Trump's nickname for Cruz worked so well. Early on, Cruz had been supportive of the New Yorker. "I've sung his praises. He's bold, he's brash, and I think the support he's gaining right now in the polls is because people are looking for someone willing to stand up to Washington."[28]

Was Cruz insincere? Only waiting for Trump to implode, as the experts all predicted, and then go in to pick up all the pieces? Those scattered, broken voters looking for a friend? In any case, he had been for him, now he was against him.

Trump hit Cruz on his big-money supporters, on his wife's job at Goldman Sachs, on his alleged dirty tricks against Ben Carson. And always, using that infuriating brand name, Lyin' Ted.

Ted Cruz was a wounded and enraged bear. And that was dangerous. On March 8, one of his surrogates appeared on the Neil Cavuto show on Fox News and made some mean-spirited comments about Melania Trump, his opponent's wife. "If she becomes the first lady," the guest told Cavuto, "she will be the first one to have posed in the nude, the first one to have been her husband's third wife, and the first one to have been born outside of the United States in one hundred years."[29]

Cavuto seemed uncomfortable and quickly changed the subject. Surely Melania Trump was not responsible for her husband's prior marriages.

A week later the allegedly pro-Cruz super PAC Make America Awesome began attacking Melania Trump with an ad targeted to people of faith. It promoted sexy pictures of Melania on Facebook. The pictures were taken from her earlier modeling career. The attack was specifically targeted to Mormon voters in Utah.

Liz Mair, a Ted Cruz advocate from the super PAC, appeared on CNN on April 2 to proudly claim the credit. Mair called Trump "a loudmouthed dick" on live TV.[30] CNN ran the story straight.

For the moment, Trump remained calm.

Some members of the Republican establishment realized that Ted Cruz was the only chance they had to stop Donald Trump. This was the year of the outsider. The choice was either to take Ted Cruz, the outsider in the Senate who played to the gallery and shunned the club, or to take Donald Trump and see the whole Republican Party collapse in November. On March 17, Senator Lindsey Graham endorsed Ted Cruz for president.[31] Mitt Romney announced that he would be voting for Ted Cruz in the Utah GOP primary.

The Never Trump movement, led by conservatives, was still not satisfied. While some GOP leaders were falling into line behind Ted Cruz, others were meeting in Washington, DC, to try to find an alternative candidate to run on a third-party ticket. Bob Fischer, a South Dakota businessman, Erick Erickson, the founder of RedState. com, and Bill Wichterman, who had worked for George W. Bush, had called the meeting. It got much unwarranted media hype. It was obviously too late. But if Fischer didn't think so, there were always political operatives ready to line up and take some of his money.[32]

On March 22, Donald Trump won all fifty-eight delegates in Arizona, while Ted Cruz won Utah. The next day former governor Jeb Bush endorsed Ted Cruz. Governor Scott Walker did the same a few days later, just before the Wisconsin primary.[33] On April 5, Cruz won the Wisconsin Primary statewide vote, 48 to 35 percent.

Donald Trump, meanwhile, finally responded to the attacks on his wife. He had let the attacks on Melania go unanswered in Utah and he had lost the state. In a Twitter message, Trump warned that if the Cruz campaign didn't leave his wife, Melania, alone, then he, Donald Trump, would "spill the beans on Heidi Cruz."[34] Whatever that meant.

Ignoring the earlier taunts and targeted attacks against Melania, the national media came down hard on Donald Trump. As far as it was concerned, he was attacking Heidi Cruz. This was the misogynist at work. When a tabloid story broke claiming that Ted Cruz himself was involved in extramarital relationships, the Texas senator hotly denied the allegations and accused the Trump campaign of planting the story.[35] The relationship could not have been more venomous.

Ironically, the New York primary loomed next. What seemed like long ago, in January, 2016, on a radio show in Boston, Ted Cruz had first referred disparagingly, to "New York values."[36] It was a backhanded way to appeal to evangelicals and conservative Catholics by knocking Donald Trump. New York was viewed by many as a city dominated by liberals and home to the despised, insufferable, mainstream media. It was also a way to counter the dubious Ted Cruz connection to Goldman Sachs.

Speaking to ten thousand people at a rally on Long Island, Trump reminded his audience, "Do you remember during the debate when he started lecturing me on New York values, like we're no good?" Trump said. He had answered the accusation by reminding the nation of the heroism during the terrorist attacks on the World Trade Center. "We all know people that died. And I've got this guy standing over there, looking at me, talking about New York values with scorn, distaste, with hatred, with hatred. So, folks, I think you can forget about him."[37]

Trump won New York with 59 percent of the vote.

When movie star Tom Hanks was asked about the Trump phenomenon, he told the press, "Donald Trump will be president when spaceships come down filled with dinosaurs in red capes."[38]

The next day, April 26, Trump won five more states in the so-called Acela primary, named after the Acela Express, an Amtrak train line that runs through Rhode Island, Connecticut, Delaware, Maryland, and Pennsylvania.

The whole Republican nomination had come down to the Indiana primary on May 3, 2016. An embittered Republican establishment poured in millions of dollars to bolster Ted Cruz. It would outspend Trump four to one. Cruz announced that if nominated, Carly Fiorina would be his running mate. On April 29, Indiana governor Mike Pence announced that he would be voting for Ted Cruz.

Donald Trump called into the *Fox & Friends*, the popular morning television show, raising the issue of a tabloid story about the father of Ted Cruz. "His father was with Lee Harvey Oswald prior to Oswald's being, you know, shot. I mean, this whole thing is ridiculous. What is that? Right prior to his being shot, and nobody even brings it up! They don't even talk about it. That was reported, and nobody talks about it. I mean, what was he doing? What was he doing with Lee Harvey Oswald shortly before the death? Before the shooting. It's horrible."[39]

Ted Cruz was angry. "I'm going to tell you what I really think of Donald Trump. This man is a pathological liar. He doesn't know the difference between truth and lies. He lies practically every word that comes out of his mouth and in a pattern that I think is straight out of a psychology textbook, his response is to accuse everybody else of lying."[40] Cruz went on to call him a "bully," a "narcissist," and a "serial philanderer."[41]

Donald Trump cruised to victory anyway, winning 53.3 percent of the vote and carrying every congressional district, taking all fifty-seven delegates in Indiana.

Within a few days, Ted Cruz dropped out of the race and John Kasich suspended his campaign.

At the Cannes Film Festival, on May 12, 2016, American movie star George Clooney educated a gaggle of clamoring international journalists. "There's not going to be a President Donald Trump," he explained. "That's not going to happen."[42]

On May 16, U.S. Rep. and House Minority Leader, Nancy Pelosi spoke on a podcast, "Donald Trump is not going to be President of the United States. Take it to the bank. I guarantee it."[43]

On May 26, the Associated Press reported that Donald Trump had secured enough delegates to put him over the top.[44] He was going to win the Republican Nomination.

Donald Trump and his wife, Melania, had come down the escalator at Trump Tower on June 16, 2015. Less than a year later, it was finally done. His father, Fred Trump, had taught him as a young man to embrace competition. Now he had triumphed over sixteen extraordinary political candidates in the most grueling contest of all. They were nine governors, five senators, a businesswoman, and a brain surgeon. Donald Trump had won the Republican nomination for president of the United States. Now the hard part.

CHAPTER 14

IT'S A TRUMP WORLD

If one tells the truth one is sure, sooner or later, to be found out.
—OSCAR WILDE

D onald Trump had done the impossible. Against all odds and against the sage pronouncements of the political experts, he had won the nomination. Now there was almost universal consensus: he was going to take the party down to defeat in November. It would be a disaster. The Republican Party would not recover for a generation.

Many compared the time to 1964, when Barry Goldwater had won the Republican nomination only to see his general-election campaign die a slow, agonizing death throughout the summer. Those measured months allowed the nation's biggest corporations, once considered Republican corporations, to abandon ship and cut their deals with the new administration. They found ways to make money by co-opting the special interest groups. They would use well-intended, newly enacted regulations to redress past wrongs and help the disadvantaged but also as weapons to stifle small businesses and speed up the achievement of their monopolies.

It would forever change politics. From then on, big companies gave to both Republican and Democratic causes, assured that there was a way to win with either one. That is, except in years like 2016, in which the outcome was certain. And in 1964, when the outspoken crank Barry Goldwater lost to the worldly, wise, experienced President Lyndon B. Johnson. Then, they need only give to the winner.

At that time, the Republican establishment had run for the hills, putting as much distance between itself and Goldwater as possible. But Richard Nixon was one member of the GOP establishment who had not. He was kindly toward the new Goldwater conservatives who had taken over the party, and he campaigned for Senate and House candidates in the fall. Four years later, in 1968, Richard Nixon won the White House for himself. It paid to be loyal. Especially when no one else was.

This time, only Newt Gingrich seemed to understand this dynamic. While other political figures rushed to speak out on television and distance themselves from the coming disaster, Gingrich defended Trump and pointed out the obvious: something out there was working.

The author was invited onto the Neil Cavuto show on Fox News and offered the same assessment. Why stereotype Trump? How did we know that he wouldn't pivot and be able to promote new general-election themes, using the same primary tactics of branding his opponent and dominating the news, and thus win in the general election as well?

In rapid succession, Governor Chris Christie, Ben Carson, and Rudolph Giuliani did the same thing. One by one they joined the Gingrich chorus and took what was then the bold step of jumping on board the Trump train.

FINDING MIKE PENCE

By mid-summer, Donald Trump was deep into his hunt for a vice presidential running mate. Senator Joni Ernst of Iowa was mentioned. A woman on the ticket against Hillary made sense.

Gingrich, Christie, Oklahoma governor Mary Fallin, former senator Scott Brown of Massachusetts, and Senators Jeff Sessions and Bob Corker, were all in the running.[1] Rumors had Trump's son-in-law Jared Kushner as favoring Newt Gingrich.

On the July 4th weekend, Trump and Indiana governor Mike Pence played a round of golf at the billionaire's club in Bedminster, New Jersey. At some point, near the seventeenth hole, Trump asked Pence what was going to happen in the upcoming campaign. "You're going to be president of the United States," Pence said declaratively.[2]

The next morning, Donald and Melania Trump had breakfast with Mike and Karen Pence. Trump made sure that their twenty-three-year-old daughter, Charlotte, was not left out of the conversation. The Pence family was moved by the gesture.

Trump tweeted, "Spent time with Indiana Governor Mike Pence and family yesterday. Very impressed, great people!"[3]

Mike Pence vetted well. It wasn't something that could be said of others on the Trump VP list. It wasn't that they were badly tainted, but rather that they had lived long, successful political lives and had the baggage that comes with the process. Trump was running against the Clintons and all of their baggage. There was no need to unnecessarily complicate that process. Others on the list needed more seasoning. It was the old Goldilocks story. Some porridge was too cold, some was too hot—Mike Pence was just right.

Raised as a Catholic, Pence was a born-again Christian, an evangelical, who was so respected and beloved in those circles that he would almost overnight wipe out much of the reluctance such individuals had for Donald Trump.

A few weeks later, Trump's plane had a mechanical failure and the team was stuck in Indianapolis. Pence invited the Trump campaign over to the Indiana governor's mansion. Trump flew in his kids to join the conversation. Over breakfast, Pence laid out his reasons why Trump had to prevail over Hillary and Bill Clinton. Jared Kushner was sold.

On Tuesday of that week, the two men had a dinner at the Capital Grille. Trump asked Pence if he would say yes to an offer for vice president.

"In a heartbeat," Pence replied.[4]

On July 13, 2016, Donald Trump called Mike Pence in the evening. "You're my guy," he said.[5] Trump would later tell *Time* magazine, "One of my great decisions in life was choosing Mike Pence to be my running mate. . . . He loves people and wants to help them every step of the way."[6]

The Pence choice caught some of the GOP establishment off guard. Almost all of its members voiced their approval, and some were surprised. But it was not enough to heal past wounds, and no one with any respectable political experience felt that Trump had a chance in the general election, regardless of who his running mate might be.

Heading into the summer, House Speaker Paul Ryan still refused to endorse Trump. Former president George H. W. Bush would not endorse him either, nor would former first lady Barbara Bush. Neither one would be coming to the Republican National Convention in Cleveland. Trump had humiliated their son. He had to pay the consequences.

Likewise, the forty-first president, George W. Bush, and the former first lady Laura Bush would not endorse the nominee. Nor would they be coming to the convention. Then there was the former governor of Florida, and one-time presidential candidate Jeb Bush himself. He also refused to endorse Donald Trump. And he, too, would stay home. How did the billionaire businessman like that energy?

The 2012 Republican nominee, Mitt Romney, still in disbelief, was also a holdout. And he would be a no-show for the national convention. Nor would John McCain, the 2008 Republican nominee, be coming to Cleveland. Had there ever been such a moment? Were the Trumps alone in the world? They had won the prize, but the prize they had won seemed to be melting in their hands.

THE REPUBLICAN NATIONAL CONVENTION

The mainstream media, playing to a history-deprived general public, was quick to portray the 2016 Republican National Convention as an anomaly. The Trumps were alone, isolated. The Republican rank and file had made their choice, and now they had to live with it. When had we seen that before? They had dared to pick Trump; now they were going to suffer the social rebuke that came with the decision.

But what the narrative that the national media was telling its viewers was not altogether accurate. In fact, at the last Republican National Convention, in 2012, when Mitt Romney had been nominated in Tampa, neither of the Bush presidents had been on hand to celebrate. Nor was either president present in 2008 for John McCain, although George W. Bush, the incumbent president, addressed the delegates via a live video. The reports were that his popularity was so deeply tarnished that the McCain team didn't want him there.

Former presidents often missed their party's national convention, and sometimes they went uninvited. In 1960, former president Harry S. Truman had held a press conference attacking the likely Democratic nominee, John F. Kennedy. Truman said he would not be attending the national convention in Los Angeles. Kennedy, a Catholic whose father was a billionaire, had allegedly relied on Mafia-influenced union officials in West Virginia to beat out his challenger Hubert Humphrey. The Democratic Party was split asunder.

Conventions were not about celebrating past presidents, especially when they were unpopular, as the Bushes were in 2016 and Truman was in 1960. It didn't mean these presidents would not later be rehabilitated by history, and even be considered great someday, as eventually happened to Truman and seems to be happening now with George H. W. Bush. But a convention was about the future. The people wanted to see their new nominee. What was he or she all about, and where would he or she take the country? It wasn't about massaging the egos of great people. National conventions no longer belonged to the bosses. They belonged to the voters. And they were a carefully choreographed infomercial for the nominee.

And so, in 1960, without Harry Truman, the Kennedys held their convention in Los Angeles and the American people celebrated what the Kennedy family was bringing to the country. And in 2016, without the Bushes or the McCains or the Romneys, the Trump family held their party's convention in Cleveland, Ohio, and showed to the nation what they would bring if given the chance.

Even so, the media drew great pleasure in reporting the divisions that appeared to be rending the Republican Party, now led by Donald Trump. Journalists made a point of reminding their audiences that the House Republican Conference chairwoman, Cathy McMorris Rodgers, wasn't coming. Senator Jeff Flake said he was going to be mowing his lawn. He lived in Arizona, where mowing a lawn was not known to be an arduous task. John Kasich, the very governor of the state of Ohio, would not be attending, even though the event would be taking place in Cleveland, Ohio, his home state.

Reince Priebus, the chairman of the Republican National Committee, who had won kudos for trying to hold the party together with rubber bands and scotch tape, seemed to have Donald Trump's blessing to reach out, offering plumb speaking opportunities to heal the party, but many were taking a pass. JPMorgan Chase, Motorola,

General Electric, Ford Motor Company, Wells Fargo, UPS, Apple, and many others that had given hundreds of thousands of dollars to pay for Mitt Romney's convention in 2012 now backed out altogether.

On Monday, July 18, 2016, Rudolph Giuliani, the former mayor of New York City, gave the true believers red meat. The theme of the night was "Make American Safe Again." Relatives of family members killed in Benghazi spoke. Parents of a son killed by an illegal alien spoke.

Giuliani praised police officers, some of whom had recently been targets of assassination in American cities. "When they come to save your life, they don't ask if you're black or white. They just come to save you."[7]

Using a quote from Barack Obama, he said, "What happened to 'There is no black America, no white America, there is just America'?"

The next day, Governor Chris Christie gave a prosecutor's tour de force of how he would pursue Hillary Clinton. The theme was "Make American Work Again," but Christie's speech stole the show. Somewhere in the California delegation a chant began, and it would not stop until the election four months later. "Lock her up! Lock her up!"[8]

On Wednesday, July 20, Senator Ted Cruz of Texas gave his speech. The audience hung on every word, expecting him to endorse Donald Trump for president. There was no way that Trump would have allowed him to speak if they hadn't cut a deal. But as he neared the end of his speech, the audience could see that he was not going to do it, and he was booed off the stage. Trump had called him "Lyin' Ted," and it had hurt. In fact, it had stuck and would very possibly follow him for life. As might this moment, when he accepted the nominee's generous offer to speak in prime time but petulantly declined to endorse him.

Later Cruz would explain that he was not in the habit of endorsing men who attacked his wife, attempting to turn his actions that night into an act of gallantry.

Chris Christie called the moment selfish. Tennessee congresswoman Marsha Blackburn said that she would tell Cruz the same thing she would tell her kids when they were growing up. "Get over yourself. Or as Taylor Swift would say, 'shake it off!'"[9] Later, on September 23, Ted Cruz would endorse Donald Trump. But by then no one cared. As far as the national media was concerned, this was ample proof that the Republican Party was split beyond repair and headed to defeat in November.

A speech by Peter Thiel, the cofounder of PayPal, electrified the convention. "Instead of going to Mars," he said, "we invaded the Middle East. . . . It's time to end the era of stupid wars and rebuild our country."[10] Journalists immediately claimed that the speech was anti-Republican. They were having a hard time comprehending the changing face of the GOP and where all of the new voters were taking the party. This was no longer the party of George W. Bush and Mitt Romney.

THE TRUMP FAMILY AFFAIR

For most television viewers, Donald Trump's family dominated the Republican National Convention. This was surely one of the reasons for Trump's popularity. Hillary Clinton would later reveal as much in a national debate. When each of the candidates would be asked to say something nice about the other, Hillary would say that she was impressed with Donald Trump's children. So was the nation. And while the national media kept reassuring the electorate that the Trumps would not actually win the presidency, television viewers couldn't help but fantasize what it would be like to have such a remarkable family living in the White House.

On Monday night at the Republican National Convention, the same night that Rudolph Giuliani gave his rousing partisan speech, the nation met Melania Trump, the nominee's Slovenian-born wife. Melania Knauss Trump, a former professional model, was beautiful and poised, and spoke with a charming Eastern European accent. The nation learned that she was fluent in six languages. She would be an elegant and exotic first lady, like nothing before in American history. She could conceivably give an address to audiences in Berlin, Paris, Rome, Zagreb, and Ljubljana, speaking to each one of them in their own language.

Melania Knauss and Donald Trump had been married in 2005, at the Episcopal Church of Bethesda-by-the-Sea in Palm Beach, Florida. A reception was held at Donald Trump's Mar-a-Largo estate, and a long list of celebrities attended, including Senator Hillary Rodham Clinton.

The Trumps' baby, Barron William Trump, was born the following year.

Melania impressed the convention of staid Republicans and the television audience of millions with an eloquent, kindhearted speech. But the national media was furious. Here was an accomplished woman, the wife of a billionaire, happily devoted to the upbringing of her son. She clearly did not need to be first lady.

The media response was not long in coming. She was accused of plagiarism. And hour by hour, journalists began to pile on. She had said, "From a young age, my parents impressed on me the values that you work hard for what you want in life, that your word is your bond, and you do what you say and keep your promises, that you treat people with respect."[11]

In 2008, at the Democratic National Convention in Denver, Michelle Obama had said that she and Barack were raised with many of the same values, "that you work hard for what you want in life: that your word is your bond, and you do what you say you're going to do."[12]

In fact, she had not copied entire paragraphs of speeches as in the case of President Obama, who on two different occasions had borrowed from Governor Deval Patrick's speeches, or as in the famous case of Joe Biden's speech borrowed from a British politician, Neil Kinnock.

These instances involved almost verbatim quotes. For example, on June 3, 2006, Patrick had said, "I am not asking anybody to take a chance on me. I am asking you to take a chance on your own aspirations." [13]

On November 2, 2007, Barack Obama had changed only one word. "I am not asking *anyone* to take a chance on me. I am asking you to take a chance on your own aspirations." (Author's italics.)[14]

On Tuesday, Tiffany Trump spoke to the convention. Named after the famous jewelry store next door to Trump Tower, Tiffany is the beautiful daughter of Donald Trump and his second wife, Marla Maples. She was raised in California with her mom, away from the limelight of New York City, but she always stayed in touch with the other siblings, and they were together on holidays. Tiffany was sometimes taken under the wing by Ivanka Trump, her half-sister. In 2016, she graduated from the University of Pennsylvania with a degree in sociology and urban studies.

"He motivates me to work my hardest," Tiffany told the Republican convention. "And to always stay true to who I am and what I believe."[15]

That same night, Donald Trump Jr., spoke to the convention. "I've seen it time and time again," he said in a deep baritone voice. "That look in his eyes when someone says it can't be done. I saw that look a little over a year ago when he was told he couldn't possibly succeed in politics. Yes, he did."

Don Jr., along with Ivanka and Eric Trump, were the three children of Donald's first wife, Ivana Trump. Like his father, a Wharton graduate, Don Jr. had taken some risky turns in life before finding himself. Don had set out on his own after college, moving to Colorado and, for a time, actually living in a truck.

His father had laid down the law to all of his children: no alcohol or cigarettes. It was the family lesson that Freddy's life had taught. Why should any of the rest of them have to experience it for themselves? But Donald Jr. had his own lessons to learn and his own conclusions to make. For a time, he was a bartender.

Somehow, the prodigal son woke up, if that was indeed the story, and came home. Donald Trump Jr. was soon a critical member of the triumvirate, running the family business, an integral part of the Trump Organization, and a fixture in many American homes as a regular on NBC's show *The Apprentice*.

It was his father who introduced him to the model named Vanessa Kay Haydon. She had once dated Leonardo DiCaprio. Don and Vanessa fell in love, married, and had five children. Their popular family tweets helped create the Trump family personality following.

On Wednesday night, the same night that Ted Cruz, Newt Gingrich, and Mike Pence addressed the convention, Eric Trump, the nominee's third child and second son, stole the show.

Wearing a gray suit with a pink tie, which was color-coded to the backdrop behind him, Eric spoke to the delegates. He described how his father had sat the family down to prepare them for the presidential campaign that was coming.

"None of us could predict what lay ahead," Eric said. "The records he would break, the stadiums he would fill, the movement he would start. Today, my father stands before you with the most primary votes of any Republican candidate in the history of our nation."[16]

Toward the end of his speech, he urged the viewers to "vote for the candidate who can't be bought, sold, purchased, bribed, coerced, intimidated, or steered from the path that is right and just and true."[17]

Supporters of Donald Trump would later counter their critics by touting his children. Didn't the remarkable Trump family reflect well on the father?

At the convention, each of the adult Trump children gave a speech. And each speech contained balanced content and was expertly delivered. They spoke with sincerity, with humanity, and they all came in on time, delivering their speeches in crisp, fifteen-minute time slots, while the politicians before and after tended to drone on too long. The Trumps, who had often performed on their father's television show, understood the medium. They didn't speak to the few thousand in the room, they spoke to the millions in living rooms, hospital beds, and sports bars across the country.

The nation had smiled with the Bush twins, whose 2004 convention performance was supposed to inform the public on what was trendy.[18] There was an awkward Cheech and Chong sense to the moment. It was dated before the year was out. And the nation had accepted that Patti Davis, Ronald Reagan's daughter, would pose nude for *Playboy*. Americans understood when her brother, Ron Reagan Jr., who rejected his father's politics, would actually give a speech at the 2004 Democratic National Convention. That was fine. Each had a right to his or her own views. They accepted that Malia and Sasha Obama were children and had a right to privacy. But not since the Kennedys had the nation seen a political family circle the wagons as the Trumps did, defending their father and each other, and do so with such power and eloquence.

On the last day of the convention, Ivanka Trump introduced her father, just as she had done in June 2015 when he had announced his run for president. They had a special bond, Donald and his daughter. Ivanka had never craved Barbie dolls for birthdays and Christmas; she preferred Legos and erector sets. She looked out the window of Trump Tower and imagined what building she would be adding to the skyline someday. What would fit in that patch of sky, or over there?[19]

Ivanka was the second child of Donald and his first wife, Ivana, the Czech-born model. She had been away at boarding school when he and her mother had been divorced, and she had learned about it from the front page of a newspaper. But whatever hurt existed between daughter and father seemed to be transcended by their shared sense of ambition. As with Don Jr. and Eric, she was also a graduate of the Wharton business school.

Long before her father became a politician, she was known as a beauty, a businesswoman, and a social celebrity. As a teenager, she appeared on the cover of *Seventeen*. She would walk the runways for Versace and be featured in ads by Tommy Hilfiger and Sassoon. But her business success would also land her on the cover of *Forbes*.

Ivanka was herself a living brand. Like Madonna or Cher, she was universally known by that one name. In fact, she was known by the first letter of that name: "I." It was stamped on her clothing, which even now competes with Ralph Lauren in stores across the world, appealing to upscale, chic shoppers.

In 2009, Ivanka married Jared Kushner, a real estate developer, in a Jewish ceremony at the Trump National Golf Club in Bedminster, New Jersey. "Everything is simply perfect!" she tweeted. "I'm getting married today!" Kushner would play a critical role in Donald Trump's presidential campaign. Ivanka would give birth to their third child in March 2016, and only four months later, she would walk out onstage in Cleveland to introduce her father to the Republican National Convention.

"For more than a year, Donald Trump has been the people's champion," she told the delegates. "And tonight he is the people's nominee! . . . This is the moment, and Donald Trump is the person to make America great again!"[20]

Ivanka expanded the Republican base by talking about his outreach to the poor and about his practice of equal pay. "Politicians talk about wage equality, but my father has made it a practice at his company throughout his entire career," she told the delegates. "He will work for equal pay for equal work, and I will fight for it too. Right alongside of him."[21]

As in the case of the other family members' speeches, Ivanka's speech came through right on time, and then, there he was onstage, the unlikely nominee. Donald Trump.

Not many had seen it coming.

THE MAN WHO WON ANYWAY

On the day of Donald Trump's announcement for president, Harry Enten, writing for the widely respected *FiveThirtyEight*, predicted that Trump had a better chance of playing in the NBA Finals than winning the Republican nomination.[22]

Stuart Stevens, a former senior adviser to Mitt Romney, had predicted that Trump would drop out of the race before a single vote was cast in a primary or caucus.

Even when Trump took the lead in some polls, his chances earned no respect. "Everything we know about how presidential nominations work says Trump isn't going to be the nominee," wrote Jonathan Bernstein, a columnist for *Bloomberg View*, "or ever come close."[23]

The *New York Times* columnist Ross Douthat tweeted, "The entire commentariat is going to feel a little silly when Marco Rubio wins every Republican primary."[24]

When the contest reached December 2015, and the first-in-the-nation Iowa Caucuses were only days away, Nate Cohn offered the widely accepted opinion that Trump still wouldn't make it. "His high numbers may be driven by unsustainable factors—like voters who are less likely to turn out."[25] The *New York Times* ran the Cohn commentary with the headline "How Donald Trump Could Win and Why He Probably Won't." [26]

That same month Bill Kristol on ABC television talked about a third party and then said, "I was semiserious. I don't think Trump will be the nominee."[27]

In January, former governor Jeb Bush, the son and brother of American presidents, would tell an audience what he had been saying for months: "Donald Trump will not win the nomination and he will not be president."[28] He had good reasons to believe it. He would outspend Donald Trump eight to one.

In March, after losing every state except Minnesota to Donald Trump, Senator Marco Rubio insisted that the billionaire still could not win. Rubio, who had outspent his opponent five to one, said Republicans would not nominate Trump because "they know the nomination of Donald Trump means the end of the modern conservative movement and the end of the modern Republican Party in a very devastating way."[29]

Even into April, when Donald Trump had the nomination well in hand, Ted Cruz pulled an upset in Wisconsin and Trump's detractors rose up out of their graves to pronounce his defeat. Jacob Weisberg, the editor in chief of *Slate*, pronounced Wisconsin as the end for Donald Trump. "Pundits who underestimated Trump's potential last autumn have been hesitant to come out and state what has now become apparent: He is probably not going to be the Republican nominee after all."[30]

Yet, there he was, on a spotlit stage, with a golden TRUMP glowing above him, the man who they said couldn't win the nomination. "Friends, delegates, and fellow Americans: I humbly and gratefully accept your nomination for the presidency of the United States."

Trump hit the themes of a rigged system that resonated so effectively on his road tours. "Big business, elite media, and major donors are lining up behind the campaign of my opponent because they know she will keep our rigged system in place."[31]

And then he hit the themes that would feed into his remarkable upset in the general election. "I have visited the laid-off factory workers, and the communities crushed by our horrible and unfair trade deals.

"These are the forgotten men and women of our country. People who work hard but no longer have a voice.

"I am your voice."[32]

At the end of the Republican National Convention, a CNN/ORC poll showed Donald Trump leading Hillary Clinton, 44 to 38 percent.[33] But nobody outside the RNC, except maybe the filmmaker Michael Moore, believed it would happen.

"The American presidential election is over," wrote Hussein Ibish in *The National*. "Republican candidate Donald Trump has virtually no hope of winning."[34]

PART IV

CLASH OF
THE TITANS

CHAPTER 15

THE COMEBACK OF HILLARY CLINTON

The art of living is more like
wrestling than dancing.
—*MARCUS AURELIUS*

A s the election of 2016 narrowed to its two opponents, a large portion of the American people appeared to be in a state of shock. How had it come to this? How had they ended up with two very flawed candidates? The negative qualities of both Donald Trump and Hillary Clinton were more pronounced than those of any other contenders in recent memory, and one of them would be president.

The nation, including the corporate media, seemed to take a perverse pride in being superior not only to the choices but also to the process itself. There was talk about a third party emerging, but that hardly survived the first national interviews with the third-party candidates. The Libertarian presidential contender, Gary Johnson, was asked to talk about Aleppo, the city in Syria that was at the apex of that nation's civil war, and whose inhabitants were an example of refugees caught in the middle of world events. He drew a blank.

In fact, an argument could have been made that Trump and Clinton were highly evolved creatures, designed for this time in history, to battle to the death in the arena. Each in its own unique way had crushed all other opposition. Trump with bully and bluff. Clinton with cunning and guile. Nobody was saying that this was a clash of pygmies, that the flaws of the candidates made them small. No, this was a clash of titans.

HILLARY'S RETURN TO THE NATIONAL SPOTLIGHT

In November 2000, former first lady Hillary Rodham Clinton was elected to the United States Senate by the state of New York. She was the first woman senator to represent the state, and the only first lady to ever be elected to office.

The campaign itself was a massive showdown of partisan warfare. Both Democrats and Republicans poured money into the state. In the end, Hillary and her opponent, Congressman Rick Lazio, spent more than $90 million. It was a record amount, driven by those who alternatively hoped for or feared a Clinton return to national power.

Hillary Clinton ran a stellar campaign. She made a point to visit every county in the state and not only rallied her base but made a special effort to reach out to New York Republicans living in the northern counties. Borrowing from the playbook of her husband, Hillary Clinton played to the political middle, promising tax cuts to companies for job creation, tax credits to high-tech investment firms, and individual personal tax credits for long-term health care and college tuition. She won the election with 55 percent of the vote. Hillary Clinton was back.

From the very beginning, she was no ordinary senator. She returned to Washington, DC, as the most famous and accomplished first lady in American history. A celebrity. A fundraising behemoth. Many believed she was on her way to the White House.

As a senator, Hillary voted for the war in Afghanistan and for the Iraq Resolution, which took the United States to a war with the dictator Saddam Hussein. She would come to regret the latter. The war would be seen by many as a mistake of history, plunging the region into unending chaos.

Even so, Hillary's critics applauded her work ethic as a US senator. She would serve on five different Senate committees and was easily amenable to bipartisan ideas and projects. In New York, she won praise for an office that efficiently handled a staggering volume of constituent problems.

Even so, while establishing a reputation as an effective and hard-working senator, in 2003, Hillary Clinton began laying the groundwork for a presidential run in 2008, when George W. Bush would end his second term. Hillary knew well that getting to the White House took more money than anyone might ever dream of, and it took more time, too. In 2006, even while she was placing the building blocks for her presidential run, she was easily reelected to the U.S. Senate. She won 67 percent of the vote.

On January 20, 2007, Hillary Clinton announced in a short video on her website that she was forming an exploratory committee to run for president of the United States in the 2008 election. "I'm in, and I'm in to win," she announced.[1] She would focus on three things: affordable health care, deficit reduction, and bringing the right kind of an end to the Iraq War.

An Associated Press story referred to her controversial time as first lady, mentioning that she was a polarizing figure for many voters.[2] Several leading Democrats were leery, warning about her vulnerability in a general election. Even so, throughout the first half of 2007, in polls of likely Democratic primary voters, Hillary Clinton led a crowded field of candidates. She was widely considered to be the front-runner. In September, she was leading in all the first six states of the Democratic primary and caucus contests. Only an Illinois junior senator, Barack Obama, and the North Carolina senator John Edwards even polled into the double digits.

By the end of the year, after a calm, brilliant performance in a primary debate, the newcomer Barack Obama was showing strength. It was a remarkable time in American history. While supporters of Hillary Clinton reminded voters that she would be the first woman president, supporters of Senator Barack Obama were pointing to the fact that he would be an African American president in a country where many of its founding fathers owned slaves.

The first national contest for the Democratic Party presidential nomination, the Iowa Caucuses, took place on January 3, 2008. Senator Barack Obama was the upset winner. Hillary Clinton came in a disappointing third place, behind John Edwards.

The next week she was at a coffee meeting with some undecided female voters in the freezing coastal town of Portsmouth, New Hampshire. Someone asked how she kept going. Clinton hesitated, and her voice teared up as she gave her answer. It was a rare feminine moment for the woman who was often viewed by the public as having ice in her veins. Women responded and turned up at the polls the next day, giving her a narrow upset win over Barack Obama. The race was on.

It would not have been a Clinton campaign without some controversy. Both Hillary and Bill came under fire, fair or not, for playing the race card against Barack Obama. Hillary's chief strategist wrote that "his roots to basic American values and culture are at best limited."[3]

The Clinton cochairman in New Hampshire talked about Obama's drug use as a young man. Online rumors started picking up that Obama was a Muslim and that he had not been born in the United States. Donald Trump would later point out that the Clinton campaign of 2008 had started the whole "birther movement"; that is, the widespread online discussion claiming that Barack Obama was not born in the United States. In February, a picture of Obama in traditional Somali clothes appeared in the *Drudge Report*. It fed the idea that Obama was a secret Muslim. Drudge said the picture had been sent around by the Clinton campaign.[4]

As the race got hot, the *New York Times* wrote, "Mrs. Clinton will be making a terrible mistake—for herself, her party and for the nation—if she continues to press her candidacy through negative campaigning with disturbing racial undertones."[5]

Yet another Clinton scandal broke. Hillary Clinton claimed that while visiting the Tuzla Air Base in Bosnia in 1996, she landed "under sniper fire" and had to run "with our heads down to get into the vehicles" that took them to the base.[6] News footage and eye-witness accounts proved that statement to be false.[7] She was seen walking slowly, shaking hands as she went, greeting children and even accepting flowers from one Muslim child.[8] She later said that she misspoke and clarified her statement. She was not "under sniper fire," she said, but rather "under the threat of sniper fire."[9]

The big showdown was set for Super Tuesday, February 5, 2008. There had never been anything like it. Twenty-four states held primaries or caucuses. Barack Obama won the most states and delegates. Hillary Clinton carried the all-important states of New York, New Jersey, California, and Massachusetts. She would later win Pennsylvania, as well. The argument was that Obama won states that would vote Republican in a general election. His victories were meaningless. Hillary had won the states that a Democrat had to win against a Republican opponent.

By the final primaries in June 2008, Barack Obama had won 1,763 delegates to Hillary Clinton's 1,640. He had won the nomination and he would win the presidency in the fall.

Hillary Clinton ended the race millions of dollars in debt. It had been a grueling contest. It had been close. Clinton supporters pointed with pride to the fact that during the 2008 primary contest, she had won the total popular vote of all participants, more than Obama. It was a pyrrhic victory—one that she and her followers would sadly celebrate again in 2016.

SECRETARY OF STATE

On January 21, 2009, Hillary Rodham Clinton was sworn in as secretary of state in the Obama administration. Her confirmation hearings were dominated by discussions about the fledgling Clinton Foundation. How would Hillary be able to avoid the obvious conflicts of interest?

Hillary Clinton assured the Senate that she would keep the two worlds compartmentalized. "Steps already being taken," she said, "are sufficient to avoid even the appearance of a conflict of interest."[10]

In a letter to the State Department, Clinton made sweeping promises of how scrupulously clean she would be. "I will not participate personally and substantially in any particular matter that has a direct and predictable effect on my financial interests or those of any person whose interests are imputed to me," she wrote.[11]

The letter was airtight: "To avoid even the appearance of a conflict, my husband and I are also voluntarily taking steps that go above and beyond the requirements of the law and ethics regulations with respect to his personal income earned from speeches and consulting as well as with respect to the William J. Clinton Foundation and its initiatives."[12]

The Senate, the State Department, and the Obama White House were relieved.

The most dramatic moments during Hillary Clinton's tenure as secretary of state happened during the crisis in Benghazi, Libya.

On February 15, 2011, Libyans joined the uprisings across Africa and the Middle East called the Arab Spring. The Arab masses were uniting to throw off the yoke of long-standing dictatorships, many that had made accommodations with the United States, and some, such as that of the Egyptian dictator Hosni Mubarak, that had been subsidized by US money for many years. Egypt had played a part in stabilizing the region, and with American assistance had helped broker peace with Israel. Upsetting that delicate balance without a plan to replace it seemed foolhardy.

One of the more controversial figures in North Africa was the Libyan dictator Muammar Gaddafi. His country had been a base for terrorist operations for years. But with the American invasion of Iraq, Gaddafi had grown openly compliant, abandoning any pretense of building a nuclear program and sending signals to the West that he was reformed and cooperative.

Nevertheless, Secretary of State Clinton saw the Arab Spring uprising as an opportunity to oust Gaddafi. And many agreed with her. The idea was pressed via a United Nations Security Council resolution.

The Gaddafi regime was ultimately toppled; however, the State Department and the Obama administration had no plan for a post-Gaddafi Libyan government. President Obama called this failure to plan the biggest mistake of his presidency.[13]

Secretary Clinton's famous response concerning Gaddafi's death was, "We came, we saw, he died."[14]

Secretary Clinton then assigned Ambassador John Christopher "Chris" Stevens to travel to Benghazi, the birthplace of the uprisings, to interact with the National Transitional Council, a group that had opposed Gaddafi and hoped to assume governmental control of Libya. Stevens set up an unofficial compound as a base of operations while the US embassy in Libya was waiting to reopen. It was the unofficial nature of this compound that led to a lack of security support and personnel from the State Department, despite repeated requests from from Steven's staff.

The number of violent terrorist attacks was on the rise worldwide. Nevertheless, during 2012, the State Department reduced the amount of security agents in Libya from thirty-four individuals to only six.[15] On September 11, 2012, a series of attacks was made on the Benghazi compound and a CIA annex. As a result, four Americans were killed, including Ambassador Stevens.

Critics said that the response during the attack from the White House, the Department of Defense, and the State Department was disingenuous and concerned itself more with public relations than with the lives of those involved. Discussion in meetings and in statements to the media focused on a YouTube video, produced in America, which had been offensive to Muslims, suggesting that this was the provocative reason behind the attack. Internal discussions considered whether any soldiers sent to the region to help should be dressed in civilian clothes, and whether Congress should be notified of any military action.

The public tended to believe that this was a planned terrorist attack on the anniversary of 9/11, directed against an American embassy. In fact, similar riots and attacks took place across the Islamic world, even beyond the Arab nations.

The Obama administration was sensitive to the idea that was circulated online suggesting that, for all his mistakes, President George W. Bush had never allowed another terrorist attack on American soil during his administration. He had kept us safe. It was apparently important to the Obama administration to make sure that these events were not seen as a terrorist attack on an American embassy compound, but rather as a spontaneous mob of Muslims reacting to a bigoted, disrespectful, anti-Islamic video produced in the United States. The blame for the deaths of Americans in Benghazi could be laid at the feet of intolerant Americans in the United States. The fact that the uprisings happened worldwide on the anniversary of 9/11, the Obama White House insisted, was purely coincidental.

Even a week later, the US ambassador to the United Nations, Susan Rice, continued to promote what is now recognized as a deliberately misleading narrative. "It was spontaneous—not pre-meditated," she told ABC News.[16] She was suggesting that the world-wide demonstrations against America on the anniversary of 9/11 were the result of the privately published video that most Americans had never seen. This was the fault of American, anti-Islamic bigotry.

Even while Obama officials were promoting this story to the public, and Hillary Clinton was sorrowfully telling this story to the families of the dead Americans, including the family of Ambassador Christopher Stevens, she privately emailed her daughter, Chelsea, with the simple message that Americans, including an ambassador, had been killed by terrorists in Benghazi.[17]

Later, after this email and others were made public without her permission, she admitted that the attack in Benghazi was indeed a terrorist attack and blamed her confusion on the "fog of war."[18] When questioned by the Senate Foreign Relations Committee on the false narrative, Secretary Clinton raised eyebrows by responding, "What difference, at this point, does it make?"[19]

Frustrated over an inability to get accurate information about Benghazi, the chairman of the House Oversight Committee wrote Mrs. Clinton in December 2012 asking if she had perhaps used a private email account. There were public pictures of Mrs. Clinton using her BlackBerry device. She did not reply. The State Department refused to answer the question.[20]

Angry over the attacks against her and the State Department, insisting that they were completely partisan, Secretary Clinton convened an independent panel to look into the Benghazi incident. The panel was "scathing in its criticism of the State Department and singled out four officials for serious management and leadership failures."[21] But the panel stopped short of saying that the American lives could have been saved by the presence of additional personnel.

Said Clinton, "My job is to admit that we have to make improvements and we're going to."[22]

Republican Senator Lindsey Graham of South Carolina said that Mrs. Clinton was getting "away with murder."[23]

In February 2013, Hillary Clinton resigned as secretary of state. Asked if her Benghazi experience would rule out a possible run for president, Clinton said, "You have to have a thick skin because [politics] is just going to be a contact sport as far as we can look into the future."[24]

The next few months saw a series of significant events drop one by one. At the time, some were momentous and others were not seen for their full import. In March 2015, the State Department's inspector general announced that Hillary Clinton had been using a non-governmental, privately maintained server for her personal email use. The private server had been kept in the basement of her home in New York. The Congressional Oversight Committee finally had its answer. Yes, Hillary Clinton had been using private emails. So what?

In April 2015, Hillary resigned from the Clinton Foundation's board of directors.

And then the big one. On April 12, 2015, Hillary Clinton announced once again that she was running for president of the

United States. Many believed that this time, she was going to succeed.

One month later, on May 5, 2015, the author Peter Schweizer released his book *Clinton Cash*. It was an exposé of the Clinton Foundation, including allegations of pay-to-play and quid-pro-quo deals in return for substantial donations. It was largely panned by the mainstream media. The political season had begun, and it was hot. And once more, Bill and Hillary Clinton were smack dab in the middle of it.

WHO CARES ABOUT YOUR DAMN EMAILS?

It was universally believed that Clinton's main competition for the Democratic nomination would be Massachusetts senator Elizabeth Warren and Vice President Joe Biden. Warren was a favorite of progressives, the new politically correct name for liberals. A dynamic personality, Warren would have been a popular new figure for the Democrats and could have easily replaced Clinton as the first woman elected president of the United States.

Joe Biden, some believed, was the natural heir to the Obama administration. No vice president in modern time, except for Dick Cheney, had refused to run for president during an open term. And Cheney had been experiencing severe health problems, which made him an exception. Joseph "Beau" Biden III, the vice president's accomplished son, had died of brain cancer in May 2015, and before his passing had reportedly encouraged his dad to run for president.[25]

Hillary Clinton had amassed a formidable war chest. After a lifetime in politics, Hillary knew full well how much money it would take to win, and she stayed focused on that process while her competition dithered and consulted supporters. The more that the

Clintons raised money, the more that others with money jumped on board the rolling bandwagon.

In previous years, most of the major American corporations had donated to the Clinton Foundation. Since they already had an investment in the Clintons, why not stick with the team? Warren was encouraged to stay out of the race. Her time would come, she was told. Hillary was too well connected and too well financed, the Democratic Party was on board with her candidacy. Elizabeth Warren did not want to become the target of the Clinton machine. Better to wait and in the meantime be part of the history making team.

There was one opponent who would not scare easily. He was Vermont senator Bernard "Bernie" Sanders. A Jew from Brooklyn who was dismissed as a socialist, Bernie was not expected to pose any kind of a challenge to Hillary Clinton. But he was tapping into a political crosscurrent of youth that stretched oddly across the entire American partisan landscape. In 2012, a hard right conservative movement in the Republican Party had coalesced behind the libertarian candidate Ron Paul. Paul's supporters believed that the economic system was rigged and that big corporate monopolies were gaming that system, using the Federal Reserve and destroying free enterprise. Although the two politicians had opposite solutions, Bernie's anti–Wall Street message sounded similar themes, and some of these young people, finding no home in the GOP, began to "feel the Bern."

Sanders made his announcement for president on May 26, 2015. He refused to organize a super PAC, relying instead on small donations. The Clinton team looked on derisively and smiled. It would be good for the process to actually have an opponent—although they were given pause when Bernie raised a cool $1.5 million on his first day. And this from actual people. In June, Sanders and Clinton both visited Iowa, where Sanders drew the bigger crowds.

The Democratic candidates for president squared away in a nationally televised debate on Tuesday, October 13, 2015, in Las Vegas. Anderson Cooper of CNN asked Hillary Clinton about her use of a private email server and the controversy that had been raging.

When it was Bernie Sander's turn, he snapped, "I think the Secretary of State is right, the American people are sick and tired of hearing about your damn emails."[26] The audience erupted in cheers and Hillary Clinton beamed.

But Sanders could not have enjoyed his treatment by the Democratic Party's leadership. As leaked emails would later show, the party was working behind the scenes for Hillary Clinton. Nor could he have enjoyed the work of the national media, which openly favored Clinton and Donald Trump, the latter a ratings magnet and a likely foil for Hillary's historic general election run. A year-end report found that the news programs on the three traditional networks, NBC, CBS, and ABC, spent 234 minutes on Donald Trump stories and a combined 10 minutes on Bernie Sanders.[27] Leaked emails would later show that the Clinton camp had been given a debate question in advance from network personnel who favored her.

In May, the chief financial officer of the Democratic National Committee wrote a derogatory email about Bernie Sanders titled "No shit."

"It might [make] no difference, but for KY and WVA can we get someone to ask his belief [?] Does he believe in a God [?] He had skated on saying he has a Jewish heritage. I think I read he is an atheist. This could make several points difference with my peeps. My southern Baptist peeps would draw a big difference between a Jew and an atheist."[28]

On July 24, the eve of the Democratic National Convention, the chairwoman, Debbie Wasserman Schultz, resigned. Leaked emails had shown what many had long suspected. She had been favoring Hillary Clinton throughout the primary system, stacking the cards against Bernie Sanders.[29] A *New York Times* headline declared, "Released Emails Suggest the D.N.C. Derided the Sanders Campaign."[30]

The Democratic National Convention was held in Philadelphia July from July 25 to 28. Former secretary of state Hillary Clinton defeated Senator Bernie Sanders, winning 59.67 percent of the delegates to Sanders' 39.16 percent, making Clinton the first woman ever nominated for president by a major party, in American history.

Hillary Clinton named as her running mate Virginia senator Tim Kaine, a favorite of Wall Street, and a disappointment to the Sanders crowd.

The opening days of the convention saw thousands of the Bernie delegates and friends in the audience booing some of the speakers, but as the convention wore on a spirit of unity of purpose began to take hold.

Minnesota senator Al Franken ignored the hecklers in the audience and deadpanned about earning a "doctorate in megalomaniac studies at Trump University."[31]

Bill Clinton, in what may have been his last great speech to the nation, talked about Hillary Clinton as the love of his life and the one who should have been president all along and still could be.

By the time Hillary Clinton took the stage, the negative had been purged from the convention floor, and she zeroed in with laser-like focus on her upcoming contest with Donald Trump. "A man you can bait with a tweet," she said, "is not a man we should trust with nuclear weapons."[32]

First Lady Michelle Obama gave perhaps the best speech of the whole event. And at the end of the convention, President Barack Obama said, "I can say with confidence there has never been a man or a woman—not me, not Bill, nobody—more qualified than Hillary Clinton to serve as president of the United States of America."[33]

The race was on, and few doubted that Hillary Clinton would now defeat the Republican nominee, Donald J. Trump. It had been a long, lifetime journey through a gantlet of political attacks and controversies, but Hillary Clinton had endured. Now fate, which could sometimes be so cruel, had given her a straw man opponent for the final lap of her path to the White House. A man who had called women "fat pigs, dogs, slobs, and disgusting animals."[34] This was a contest she relished. She would not only beat him, she would enjoy beating him. It would be all downhill. She waved to the delegates and delighted in her moment of triumph. She had a smile on her face.

CHAPTER 16

CROOKED HILLARY

The greatest minds are capable of the greatest vices as well as the greatest virtues.
—RENÉ DESCARTES

I n April 2016, even before he had been officially named the Republican nominee, Donald Trump announced to a cheering crowd his new nickname for his likely Democratic opponent. She would be "Crooked Hillary."

At the time, some polls and surveys suggested that Clinton had a 94 percent chance of winning the Democratic nomination and Trump a 66 percent chance of winning the Republican nomination.[1] But the master of branding, the businessman Donald Trump, had no time to waste.

Most Americans had only a vague understanding of the early Clinton scandals. The sheer volume of issues prohibited understanding. Political advisers for the Clintons believed that she had survived the old scandals, and in the new terminology of the political season, those issues were "baked in" to the polling numbers. The people who didn't like her would never change and need not be won over anyway, and the people who supported her already knew that there were negative issues but had decided that if they were too serious she wouldn't be running for president. Her stand on the issues was the important thing. She would win with the voters who had elected Barack Obama twice, she would win with more money and newer technology than Obama ever had. She would run a state-of-the-art political campaign.

Still, there was that dark, nagging shroud that ghosted the candidate. In February, when Gallup had asked voters for the first word that came to mind when they heard "Hillary Clinton," the answer was "dishonest/liar/don't trust her/poor character."[2]

Negative Clinton books had become a cottage industry and were almost guaranteed to land on the bestseller lists.

The most serious scandals were the latest—the email controversy and the Clinton Foundation. If Bernie Sanders was tired of hearing about her damn emails, Donald Trump couldn't get enough of them and constantly referred to her use of a private server as criminal activity being investigated by the FBI, which was, in fact, uncomfortable but true.

THE EMAIL SCANDAL

The evolution of the email scandal was confusing to most voters. For those who didn't like Mrs. Clinton, it was more proof that she was dishonest. For those who wanted her to win and felt that she was constantly attacked by political foes who opposed her policies, it was an exaggerated crisis. She had made a mistake, she had admitted it, and it was time to move on. Even the FBI had done so.

The question was, what about the three million voters in seven battleground states who hadn't yet made up their minds? What did they think? And when the FBI reopened its investigation, it killed the argument that the issue was over. Some argued that because of the volume of emails involved, it would never be over. The investigation would follow her into the White House.

How had it come to this? What was the way out for Secretary Clinton, or at least a way to an electoral majority? What explanation would be enough?

In January 2009, when Hillary Clinton had been sworn in as secretary of state, she had used her own personal email account on a private server kept on her own property. This contravened government policy, which called for her operations to be conducted on an authorized system. A few months later, governmental guidelines were strengthened, requiring all government records to be kept on federal systems.

After the Benghazi debacle, the House Oversight Committee wrote Mrs. Clinton asking if she had used a private email account. She ignored the letter. Two months later, she resigned as secretary of state.

In the following months, pressured by the committee, but acting slowly, the State Department finally revealed that it had, indeed, found emails between Mrs. Clinton and her staff that were written by the secretary on a private email server that was set up in the basement of her home in Chappaqua, New York.

The committee had suspected that this might have been the case all along. It wanted those emails to do its work. It was investigating the loss of life in the Benghazi crisis. What had happened, and why?

In August 2014, after a delay of twenty months, the State Department turned over 15,000 pages of documents, which included a few emails from Mrs. Clinton that were on her private, unauthorized account.

The House Oversight Committee asked for all the emails.

In December 2014, two years after the committee investigating Benghazi had asked for Hillary Clinton's emails, and only after receiving a formal request for the documents from her own former staff at the State Department, Hillary turned over 55,000 printed pages representing 30,000 emails.

It was soon realized that the released emails referred to other messages and emails that had not been turned over. Realizing that they were being misled, the committee demanded those messages too. To mollify the committee, the State Department handed over another batch of emails, but it was now clear that thousands of them were missing.

With a news story about to break in the *New York Times*, the State Department informed the House committee that Mrs. Clinton had been using her personal email server exclusively while serving as secretary of state. Mrs. Clinton said she had asked the State Department to release emails from the 30,000 she had given them. She also mentioned that she had deleted another 32,000 emails that were personal messages.

This announcement caused a firestorm. What was Secretary Clinton hiding? What was in the deleted emails?

The next month she announced her candidacy for president of the United States.

In July 2015, the FBI began its investigation into Secretary Clinton's misuse of classified documents. The *New York Times* published a story asserting that contrary to her claims, her emails had, indeed, included classified documents.[3] "The inspectors general of the State Department and the nation's intelligence agencies said the information they found was classified when it was sent and remains so now."[4]

Public arguments raged over Mrs. Clinton's actions. Had she violated multiple laws? Had she mishandled classified materials? Had she obstructed justice by destroying emails relevant to the House committee's investigation? Even beyond violating department protocol, why had Mrs. Clinton not turned over her emails to the State Department when leaving office? Laws prohibited federal employees from taking documents, including top-secret documents, with them when they left office.

In May 2016, the State Department's inspector general released a report criticizing Mrs. Clinton's use of a private server and her failure to turn over State Department documents upon leaving office.

On July 5, 2016, only days after the US attorney general, Loretta Lynch, met privately with Bill Clinton on an airport tarmac in Phoenix, Arizona, James Comey, the director of the FBI, testified before Congress. "Although there is evidence of potential violations of the statutes regarding the handling of classified information," Comey said, "our judgment is that no reasonable prosecutor would bring such a case."[5]

It was now clear that Hillary Clinton's repeated claims that she had never sent out classified information on her server were not truthful. It was also clear that she had not spoken truthfully when she claimed that she used a private server only because it would simplify her life to have one device. She had not been truthful when she claimed that the State Department had allowed her to set up her own server. She had not been truthful when she said her emails were never breached. She had spoken falsely when she claimed that the only emails she had deleted were personal. It was now apparent that emails had been deleted for political purposes. Investigators were able to retrieve many of the deleted emails that contained classified and politically embarrassing information.[6] She had been untruthful when she had said in a national debate that documents had been retroactively classified as top secret after she had already sent them.

On September 3, 2016, the FBI released its report on its interview with Hillary Clinton.[7]

On October 28, 2016, the FBI announced the discovery of new Hillary Clinton emails on Anthony Weiner's computer. It reopened its case.[8] Now there were reportedly 650,000 documents to review. The FBI promised a computerized system that would weed out previously cleared documents and allow the agency to zero in on only the messages pertinent to the case.

On November 6, 2016, the Sunday before the election, FBI Director James Comey delivered a letter to Congress saying that the agency's investigation was complete and that the FBI had not changed its conclusions on Hillary Clinton. She should not be prosecuted. Clinton's team said that the issue had now been officially put to rest. She was innocent. It was over.

Donald Trump told an audience in Grand Rapids, Michigan, that the FBI couldn't possibly have reviewed 650,000 emails. The people, he said, would decide on Tuesday.

November 8, 2016: the American people headed to the polls—and they decided.

QUID PRO QUO

The one FBI investigation into Hillary Clinton that is still ongoing, even after the election, is the inquiry into the Clinton Foundation. This is the most serious issue of all.

The Clintons created the William J. Clinton Foundation, later renamed the Clinton Foundation, even before they left the White House. It would be a way for the former president to raise money for his presidential library and to do some good in the world. It was something that all presidents did in one form or another. The foundation provided a legal shell to be able to travel, promote peace, and continue the legacy of the president during his retirement years.

Eventually, for the Clintons the foundation would provide another amazing utility. It would solve a problem that had puzzled them for years, since the days at the Fu Lin Chinese restaurant in Little Rock, Arkansas: how to legally receive and spend foreign money. Money from China and other places had flowed like water running downhill to the Clintons. It snaked its way around every barrier, seeking the lowest ground. Now the Clintons could carve out some canals of their own and help it get to the right place.

As the Clinton Foundation grew, there were concerns. For example, a nonprofit could not just be a bank. It could not just let streams of money flow into its ocean and wait to spend it later to help Hillary run for president. There had to be ongoing projects, activities, expenditures, and the projects had to fit the stated purpose of the charter of the organization as approved by the IRS.

In the 1970s, the IRS had pursued the venerable Billy Graham Association for "illegally retained income." A nonprofit had to use its money. The Clintons could not just store it up to one day pay salaries to Chelsea's great-grandchildren. By the 2016 election year, the Clinton Foundation had raised $2 billion.

Its board of directors also had to be independent and not stacked with employees or directors who could be controlled. In this case, Chelsea Clinton herself was on the board. So was Cheryl Mills, who had served as the president's deputy White House counsel during the impeachment trial and was the first lady's chief of staff when she was secretary of state. Mills would presumably serve her again in the White House. Could she be considered an independent board member? People who knew her said definitely so.

Critics observing this process would say that Barack Obama's IRS, which carefully monitored Christian religious nonprofits, would not be picky about the powerful Clinton Foundation, especially given that Hillary Clinton would soon be its boss. Before she became secretary of state, Obama had asked for assurances from Hillary Clinton that the foundation would be kept separate from official duties, and she had given strongly worded promises.

Another, more serious issue in the original plan for the foundation was determining its mission statement. It was absolutely necessary that the money coming into a nonprofit be spent according to its stated purpose. For example, if the Clinton Foundation was organized for the purpose of addressing hunger in Haiti, then its money had to go to that cause. Charity-monitoring organizations and the media would rate the validity and ethical underpinnings of a nonprofit based on the percentage of money that actually went to its program, as opposed to its salaries and administration.

The purpose of the Clinton Foundation was to "strengthen the capacity of people in the United States and throughout the world to meet the challenges of global interdependence."[9]

It was a perfectly crafted cause. Everything that the Clintons could do to build relationships and form a team for a second run for president could also be done through the legitimate work of the foundation. This was not illegal or even unethical, but it was a very convenient truth.

The foundation would need specialists in communications, speechwriters, media experts, social media gurus, website designers, travel coordinators, a de facto mini–State Department, legislative-affairs experts, government-liaison officers, public relations talent, protocol advisers, security teams, lawyers, and, not to mention, its own private email servers. Most of all, it would need mailing lists and teams of fund-raisers. And all these people, occasionally outsourced, or sometimes permanent staff, could be financed by that foreign money that had been seeking to find its way to the Clintons for half their lifetime.

The conflicts of interest were immediate. In 2009, Secretary Clinton traveled to Russia to secure a multibillion-dollar deal for aircraft built by Boeing. In return, Boeing donated $2 million toward the World's Fair, despite a State Department decision to not solicit funds from the aircraft manufacturer and to cap donations from any company to the US involvement in the fair at $1 million.[10] The World's Fair was considered one of Secretary Clinton's first major successes at the State Department. A grateful Boeing then went on to donate nearly $1 million to the Clinton Foundation, as well as participate in a fund-raising effort for her presidential campaign. Boeing stated that the deal with Russia had no bearing on its decision to donate to the Clinton Foundation.[11]

Over the years, allegations of mismanaged funds, undelivered promises, and pay-to-play access to the State Department were mixed with successful initiatives in construction, health care, and economic development.[12]

Controversy began to mount when Hillary Clinton apparently violated her pledge to President Obama and Congress by allowing the foundation to receive significant donations from foreign governments. Even more troublesome was a lack of transparency. Journalists found numerous unreported donations coming from countries such as Algeria and Qatar.[13] At the time, agents within the FBI wanted to investigate the Clinton Foundation, but the Obama Justice Department did not feel there was enough evidence to warrant a further look.[14]

ABC News released a story concerning Rajiv K. Fernando, a top Clinton Foundation donor and Democratic Party fund-raiser. Mr. Fernando was given a position on the International Security Advisory Board (ISAB) despite having no qualifications or experience in the areas of nuclear weapons and arms control. Emails originating within Secretary Clinton's staff described efforts to "protect the secretary's and under secretary's name" and to avoid answering ABC News for twenty-four hours. Mr. Fernando resigned from the ISAB two days later.[15]

During the summer of 2016, the Associated Press reported an analysis of Clinton Foundation donors. Eighty-five out of the 154 private citizens who had met with Hillary Clinton had also given money to the Clinton Foundation. CNN rushed to defend Secretary Clinton, giving her a chance to explain,[16] but there was not much clearer evidence of pay-to-play than those damning numbers.

When it became clear that neither the Justice Department nor the mainstream media was willing to take on the Clinton Foundation, major companies gave major donations and then hired Clinton's friends and former colleagues to lobby her and the State Department for what they wanted. The State Department was basically for sale.

Microsoft, ExxonMobil, and Pfizer each gave between $1 to $5 million to the Clinton Foundation and then asked Hillary for help with problems over visas, securing infrastructure, licenses for software, intellectual property rights overseas, hydraulic fracturing, and "government procurement."[17] Several Clinton fund-raisers called "Hillblazers" followed their donors into the lobbying process to make sure the State Department delivered.

During the election, Hillary Clinton would accuse Donald Trump of getting cozy with Russian president Vladimir Putin. Although the two men had never met, they had exchanged nice words. But as secretary of state, Clinton encouraged American tech companies to help fund Skolkovo, the Russian version of Silicon Valley. In return, Skolkovo raised millions of dollars for the Clinton Foundation.

Clinton took the relationship with Russia a step further. Her State Department approved a deal that allowed the Russian government to control almost 20 percent of American's uranium production. The company involved, Uranium One, donated $2.6 million to the Clinton Foundation.[18]

The maze of corruption was so deep and so complex and involved so many government and international players that it has spawned many books without any end in sight. The critics said that dictators, terrorists, and corporate oligarchs had grown fat, while hundreds of thousands of people in Africa and Haiti had been abandoned.

A GIFT TO THE TERRORISTS

Throughout her tenure as secretary of state, Hillary Clinton was constantly nagged by questions surrounding the terrorist group Boko Haram. Why wouldn't she declare the organization a terrorist group and thus help isolate its power? It had threatened to assassinate the US ambassador in Nigeria. It had blown up the United Nations' headquarters in Abuja. It was killing more civilians annually than Al Qaeda or any other terrorist organization in the world.

The Pentagon asked Mrs. Clinton to make the move. The CIA and the FBI joined in. Finally, the Obama White House suggested that the secretary of state should make the call. But Hillary Clinton refused. It became a source of puzzlement for the television pundits. CNN interviewed Congressman Peter King, who said, "For the life of me I cannot understand why."[19]

For two years, the team at *Fox & Friends* was totally flummoxed, asking repeatedly, "What is the problem? Why won't she do this?"[20]

With a new story about donors to the Clinton Foundation, the possible reasons behind Hillary's Boko Haram policy came into clear focus. Gilbert Chagoury, a Lebanese-Nigerian billionaire, had allegedly donated money to the earlier Clinton presidential campaign, and he had donated $1.6 million to the Clinton Foundation. Chagoury owned the luxurious five-star Eko Hotel in downtown Lagos and the five-star Presidential Hotel in Port Harcourt, Nigeria. The latter complex sprawled out on spectacular tropical land, a maze of marble, brass, and glass with stunning views. Labeling

Boko Haram as a terrorist group would have been bad for tourism, the third-largest source of hard currency for Nigeria and the economic lifeblood for the hotel business.

A year after Hillary Clinton resigned as secretary of state, on the night of April 14, 2014, Boko Haram descended on a boarding school in Chibok, Nigeria, and kidnapped 276 girls. The girls were carted off in trucks. They were raped, and some were sold as sex slaves across Africa. Several managed to escape, jumping off the speeding trucks, even while guns were pointed at their heads. One broke her legs in the jump. Another rolled over and pretended to be dead, lying frozen in place, urinating where she lay, until nightfall allowed her to move off into the forest without being seen, beginning her long journey to freedom.

When the news broke, Hillary Clinton rushed to the front of the line and joined a chorus of public figures proclaiming worldwide, "Bring back our girls."

But it was only after Mrs. Clinton resigned that President Barack Obama and his new secretary of state, John Kerry, declared that Boko Haram was a terrorist organization.

The national news media ignored this story, but it did feel the need to report on a related issue. Clinton's billionaire buddy Gilbert Chagoury turned up on a no-fly list maintained by the Department of Homeland Security. The agency was asked to apologize for the mix-up, which it promptly did. ABC news covered the story.

"IF THIS STORY GETS OUT, WE ARE SCREWED."[21]

Getting money into a nonprofit can sometimes be a lot easier than getting it out. Especially if you want that money for yourself. Of course, the Clintons could always give themselves a million-dollar-a-year salary from their foundation, but that was nowhere near enough money, and there was the political cost of taking a salary. Much better to take a speaking fee.

After leaving the White House in 2001, both Bill and Hillary Clinton gave 729 speeches right up through her announcement to run for the White House.[22] The couple earned over $153 million in speaking fees. Concern was raised when it was revealed that the couple earned over $7 million speaking to the big banks that Hillary was publicly condemning.[23]

When Hillary Clinton became secretary of state, Bill Clinton's lecture fee went from $150,000 to $600,000. It was obvious that people were not paying that kind of money for a speech they could watch free of charge on YouTube. They were paying for something more, and they had to have "proof of life" so to speak. That is, they must see a picture of the kidnapped baby or a finger or something to prove they were not handing over millions of dollars for nothing. The Clintons needed a salesman, someone who would assume the risks and negotiate the deals. One of those men, at least for some critical donors, turned out to be a trusted former personal counselor and assistant to Bill Clinton named Doug Band. He was the creator and driving force behind the Clinton Global Initiative.

We now know the story in glorious detail thanks to Chelsea Clinton. In 2011, well-intentioned Chelsea was troubled by Doug Band's firm Teneo, whose tentacles were everywhere in Clintonland. This forced Band to write a series of memos outlining how the whole process worked. Yes, he and Teneo were in the middle of it, but he had personally brought millions of dollars in donations from Coca-Cola, Dow Chemical, Ericson, UBS, Barclays, and many other banks and corporations. If Teneo had made money as well, there was a very good reason. It was his work that was bringing in these millions not only to the Clinton Foundation but also personally to Bill Clinton, himself.[24] If his work was laden with conflicts of interest, then the former president's work would be seen the same. The two were joined at the hip.

Doug Band wrote to Hillary Clinton's campaign chairman, John Podesta, "John, I would appreciate your feedback and any suggestions. I'm also starting to worry that if this story gets out, we are screwed."[25]

The emails were outed by WikiLeaks, but the public, already numb with Clinton scandals, didn't have the patience to grasp a story that could not be distilled into 140 characters.

It was Russia's fault, campaign staffers told the media. Russia had hacked the emails. Were the American people going to allow Russia to decide its elections?

CHAPTER 17

AN OCTOBER SURPRISE FOR TRUMP

No one is so brave that he is not disturbed by something unexpected.
—*JULIUS CAESAR*

On October 7, 2016, one month before the presidential election, a videotape was sent out to news agencies and then posted online. There was the Republican candidate, Donald Trump, back in September 2005, newly married to his wife, Melania, making lewd and sexually explicit comments about women. It was devastating. None of the corruption scandals of the Clintons could compare to the shock value of this news. Carnality trumps corruption every time. The American public was shocked.

In the tape, Trump was in a conversation with Billy Bush, then a host of the show *Access Hollywood* and they were on a bus driving to the set of another television show. Trump was going to appear as a guest on the popular soap opera *Days of Our Lives.*

Talking about a married woman that Trump wanted he said, "You know, and I moved on her actually. You know she was down in Palm Beach. I moved on her and I failed. I'll admit it. I did try and fuck her. She was married."[1]

"That's huge news," says Billy Bush.

"No, no, Nancy. No, this was. And I moved on her very heavily, in fact I took her out furniture shopping. She wanted to get some furniture. I said, 'I'll show you where they have some nice furniture.' I took her out furniture [shopping.] I moved on her like a bitch, but I couldn't get there, and she was married.

"Then all of a sudden I see her, she's now got the big phony tits and everything. She's totally changed her look."

Then the man talk on the bus explodes with recognition as the bus approaches Arianne Zucker, who was going to be with Trump on the show.

"I better use some Tic Tacs," Trump said, "just in case I start kissing her. You know I'm automatically attracted to beautiful—I just start kissing them. It's like a magnet. Just kiss. I don't even wait.

"And when you're a star they let you do it. You can do anything."

"Anything you want," agrees Billy Bush.

"Grab them by the pussy," says Trump. "You can do anything."

The tape had been made without Trump's knowledge, and it was eleven years old. But it was new to the American public, and it was shocking.

Only hours after the story broke early on a Saturday morning did Donald Trump disavow the comment. "Everyone who knows me know these words don't reflect who I am," he said. "I've never said I'm a perfect person, nor pretended to be someone I'm not. I've said and done things I regret, and the words released today on this more-than-a-decade-old video are one of them. I said it was wrong. And I apologized.

"I've traveled the country talking about change for America. But my travels have also changed me. I pledge to be a better man tomorrow, and will never, ever, let you down."[2]

After viewing the tape online, Hillary Clinton wrote on Twitter, "This is horrific. We cannot allow this man to become president."[3]

Hillary Clinton's running mate, Senator Tim Kaine of Virginia, was in Las Vegas. "It makes me sick to my stomach,"[4] he said.

The executive vice president of the Planned Parenthood Action Fund said that what Trump was describing on the tape was "sexual assault."[5]

Outrage was universal. Not only among Democrats but among Republicans as well. Congressman Paul Ryan, the Speaker of the House of Representatives, canceled a planned appearance with Donald Trump in Wisconsin set for the next day. "Women are to be championed and revered, not objectified. I hope Mr. Trump treats this situation with the seriousness it deserves and works to demonstrate to the country that he has greater respect for women than this clip suggests."

Senate Majority Leader Mitch McConnell of Kentucky called Trump's comments "repugnant and unacceptable in any circumstance."

Former presidential candidate Mitt Romney said, "Hitting on married women? Condoning assault? Such vile degradations demean our wives and daughters and corrupt America's face to the world."[6]

Republican National Chairman Reince Priebus said, "No woman should ever be described in these terms or talked about in this manner. Ever."

In the afternoon, South Dakota senator John Thune, a Republican, said that "Donald Trump should withdraw and Mike Pence should be our nominee effective immediately."[7]

Only minutes after the comments from Republican leaders, Donald Trump's wife, Melania, issued a statement of her own. "The words my husband used are unacceptable and offensive to me. This does not represent the man that I know. He has the heart and mind of a leader. I hope people will accept his apology, as I have, and focus on the important issues facing our nation and the world."[8]

Ivanka Kushner, the candidate's daughter, immediately stood up for her father. She was quoted as saying to him privately, "It's eleven years old, you have to fight back. You have to say you're sorry. But you have to fight back."[9]

Trump's adviser Steve Bannon urged Trump to bring Bill Clinton's victims to the next presidential debate. They should just be there to shake Hillary's confidence.

On Monday, October 10, 2015, an NBC/*Wall Street Journal* poll showed Hillary Clinton with a fourteen-point lead over Donald Trump.[10] The poll had Clinton at 52 percent of the vote and Trump at only 38 percent.

Meanwhile, Republican House Speaker Paul Ryan told fellow GOP members of congress that he would not defend Trump, nor would he campaign with him for the remainder of the election contest. He was done. In a phone call to fellow House members, Ryan said, "Do what's best for you in your district."[11] In the fractured GOP, it was now every man for himself.

Trump shot back on Twitter. "Paul Ryan should spend more time on balancing the budget, jobs and illegal immigration and not waste his time on fighting the Republican nominee."[12]

The media went into high gear to track down the time line on the release of the video and the source. No, it was not planted by the Clinton campaign, but NBC had apparently held it for maximum effect. According to one source, during the network's coverage of the summer Olympics in Rio de Janeiro, Billy Bush, an anchor at the event, mentioned that he had a "tape of Trump being a real dog."[13] Tipped off by the comment, staff members at NBC began an exhaustive search and eventually found the tape. After the network had its lawyers review it for days, a frustrated employee at NBC leaked it to the *Washington Post* and the story broke.

Meanwhile, if the Clinton campaign had not released the tape, they were apparently tipped off that it was coming. As soon as the *Washington Post* story hit, a top national journalist was told that Melania Trump was talking divorce. The journalist was offered alleged details and quotes that showed substantial preparation behind the story but higher ups in the Clinton campaign refused to confirm some of the key facts that held it together. The journalist concluded that it was a false story being promoted by the campaign and refused to take the bait.[14]

My sources inside the Trump camp later confirmed that the Melania-divorce story was "fake news" promoted by political enemies

Finally trying to recover from what appeared to be a fatal, knockout blow, Donald Trump sought to counterpunch. It had worked in the past. "Bill Clinton has actually abused women and Hillary has bullied, attacked, shamed and intimidated his victims," Trump said. "We will discuss this more in the coming days. See you at the debate on Sunday."[15]

Trump supporters were already moving through the five stages of grief over a lost election. They were in denial, angry, bargaining. Some had already moved into depression. Clinton supporters were still stunned, rereading the numbers on their winning lottery tickets. The rest of the nation was just appalled.

THE BASKET OF DEPLORABLES

The Clinton-Trump debates had none of the dignity and moral clarity of the historic Lincoln-Douglas debates of 1858. They had none of the serious black-and-white gravitas of the Nixon-Kennedy televised debates of 1960. But for pure entertainment value, in an age where ratings were king and accuracy an occasional accident, the Clinton-Trump debates were the show of the century.

Hillary Clinton was a fierce, experienced, hardworking debater who was ready for any question or topic and whose only challenge was to appear spontaneous when she clearly was not.

Trump was the master of branding, of one-liners, of show business. He knew how to attract viewers.

They both knew that the attention span of the audience was short, and that its memory was also short. They both owed their success to the latter. Clinton would rely on preparation, Trump on his personality.

The first debate was held at Hofstra University in Hempstead, New York, on September 26, 2016. Lester Holt of NBC was the moderator.

The Clinton campaign had experienced a couple of setbacks that had made the race suddenly razor thin. Hillary had told an audience at a fund-raiser that "you could put half of Trump's supporters into what I call the basket of deplorables. Right? The racist, sexist, homophobic, xenophobic, Islamophobic—you name it."[16]

A few days later she had stumbled and momentarily collapsed while getting into her car after a 9/11 remembrance ceremony. For years, the Internet had been alive with conspiracy theories about lingering issues from a 2013 blood clot she had experienced in her head.[17] Her fall now seemed to confirm what the mainstream media had been ridiculing and ignoring.

No, her staff explained, she had stumbled because she was weak from a lingering bout of highly contagious pneumonia. Hillary probably should have gone to bed but instead she had tried to brave it out.

Well then, when she stumbled and almost fainted, why hadn't she been taken immediately to the hospital? Why had her staff taken her to see her daughter, Chelsea, and her granddaughter? Why had they announced she had spent the afternoon playing with her granddaughter? And when she finally exited the building, why had a little girl been escorted through the barriers to offer her flowers for all the photographers to see? Was that the plan? For a person with highly contagious pneumonia?

Well, scratch that. It wasn't contagious after all. Sorry about that. It was a noncontagious form of pneumonia.

And then it was later learned that members of her own staff had contracted pneumonia as well. They were home in bed. If it was not contagious, how had they contracted it?

David Alexrod, a political adviser to Barack Obama, quipped, "Antibiotics can take care of pneumonia. What's the cure for an unhealthy penchant for privacy that repeatedly creates unnecessary problems?"[18]

This was the burden that Hillary Clinton carried into the debate at Hofstra. But as difficult as the days had been leading up to the first debate, and as close as the polls had narrowed, there was still a very clear Electoral College advantage for Clinton that seemed insurmountable. The consensus was that Donald Trump needed to win the debate to win the election.

Both candidates came to the battle prepared.

Making a play on words, Hillary Clinton referred to Trump's economic program as "trumped-up, trickle-down economics."[19]

Trump hit the issue of jobs. "We have to stop our jobs from being stolen from us."

When Hillary interrupted to promote her ideas, Trump countered, "You haven't done it in thirty years—or twenty-six years. You haven't done it. You haven't done it."[20]

At one point, after taking a pounding, seeking to find some good humor out of the situation, Hillary Clinton said, "I have a feeling that before the evening is over I will be blamed for everything that has happened."

Trump deadpanned sarcastically. "Why not? Why not?"[21]

The audience couldn't help but laugh, and Hillary Clinton too. "Why not?" she said in feigned exasperation.

Eventually, Hillary Clinton took charge, zeroing in on the fact that Trump had not released his tax records, while she had done so, and finally baiting him with stories about how he had acquired his wealth. This sent Trump down blind allies trying to prove his business acumen and correct the details of a proud record that no one but he himself seemed to care about.

"I will release my tax returns, against my lawyers' wishes," Trump finally said, "when she releases her thirty-three thousand emails that have been deleted."[22]

Almost every pundit and writer declared Hillary Clinton the winner of the debate. The author of this book was an exception. Appearing the next morning on the Fox Business Network, I surprised the host by saying that Donald Trump had won. He won the early part of the debate, I explained, when the three million undecided voters in seven battleground states were still watching. That was the part of the debate that addressed economic issues, and that was the audience he would need on Election Day.[23]

A WOUNDED ANIMAL

The second presidential debate took place on October 9, 2016, only forty-eight hours after the damaging tape from *Access Hollywood* had been released. It was held at Washington University in Saint Louis. Anderson Cooper of CNN and Martha Raddatz of ABC were the moderators. Both were respected professionals. And yet both were viewed by many Republicans as clearly partisan, in Hillary Clinton's camp. After the election, critics would say that Martha Raddatz appeared to be crying on national television over what Hillary Clinton's loss would mean to members of American armed forces.

This moment in time illustrated why the Republican National Committee had long been negligent in negotiating a fair debate format for its nominees. Almost all debates took place at universities that were entrenched bastions of liberal views and opinions, some quite separate from the views of the American populous as a whole. And such debates were almost always moderated by liberal Democrats. My own early count of presidential debate moderators over the years had found 146 Democrats, 5 Independents and 5 Republicans. The town hall format being used in this second debate had been formulated in 1992, with Bill Clinton in mind. The man behind it was on Hillary Clinton's debate-prep team.

Donald Trump was like a bull between two matadors. He turned to one, only to be stabbed by the sword of the other. Bleeding and snorting, carrying the swords stuck all over his body, he kept trying to establish some sense of perspective. He tried to talk about jobs, about the inner city, about immigration.

Anderson Cooper's first six questions were directly or indirectly about the lewd tape and about character. There was a feeling that Trump deserved it. It was appropriate. Anderson Cooper was a journalist. The tape couldn't be passed over lightly.

"I'm not proud of it," Trump said, "I apologize to my family. I apologize to the American people. Certainly I'm not proud of it."[24] But he had not assaulted anyone, he protested. These were just words, he kept explaining. He had not done anything.

Anderson Cooper wanted more, so Trump continued his apology, "I'm very embarrassed by it," he reiterated, "I hate it."[25] He tried to talk about ISIS, but Anderson Cooper would have none of it. With prosecutorial precession he kept repeating the same question, over and over, in a different way, to his witness. "Just for the record, though," Cooper added, "are you saying that what you said on that bus eleven years ago that you did not actually kiss women without consent or grope women without consent?"[26]

And when Trump's answer was insufficient, Cooper asked it again, "So, for the record, you're saying you never did that?"

Then again, after Trump's answer, Cooper asked it all over again, "Have you ever done those things?"

Finally Cooper had had enough. "Thank you, Mr. Trump," he said sternly, cutting off the candidate in midsentence. "Thank you, Mr. Trump."

And then, satisfied that he had been sufficiently pummeled, Trump was finally turned over to his political opponent.

"Secretary Clinton," Anderson Cooper intoned very seriously, "do you want to respond?"

It was as if he were passing the ball to a teammate. Having been worked over by the principal and the assistant principal, it was now the parent's turn to speak to the young, recalcitrant, misbehaving Donald Trump. He would just have to take his medicine.

"Well, like everyone else," Hillary said solemnly, "I've spent a lot of time thinking over the last forty-eight hours about what we heard and saw. You know, with prior Republican nominees for president, I disagreed with them on politics, policies, principles, but I never questioned their fitness to serve.

"Donald Trump is different. I said starting back in June that he was not fit to be president."

For those who supported Hillary and saw Trump as the classic misogynist boor, who liked to call him a racist, it was all entirely fitting. A justifiable *Götterdämmerung*. Never let it be said that you had him on the ropes and didn't finish him off. Go for the knockout.

Even so, considering the improbable events that would follow, it is very likely that the moment was overdone. There was some expiation in the process. Trump was alone in the arena. Bleeding. No one in the world defending him. Surely nobody was going to vote for him anyway. He wasn't going to be president. That had been decided. So again, exactly what did he do wrong? What was this public purge of Trump all about?

And then, who was meting out the justice? Hillary Clinton? *Access Hollywood*? Moderators from CNN and ABC? This was the team that would lecture America on the evils of objectifying women? No one was struck by the irony that *Access Hollywood* would offer America such advice. Or that such advice would come from a moderator from ABC, the network that had once promoted a sitcom called *Good Christian Bitches*.[27] And Hillary Clinton? Who had revictimized the women whose only crime had been to try to correct false stories that had been made public by others? Trump, even then, suffering from his self-inflicted wounds, recognized that irony and pointed out the hypocrisy.

Later in the debate Donald Trump hit back. "If you look at Bill Clinton, far worse," he said. "Mine are words, and his was action. His was what he's done to women. There's never been anybody in the history of politics in this nation that's been so abusive to women. So you can say any way you want to say it, but Bill Clinton was abusive to women.

"Hillary Clinton attacked those same women and attacked them viciously. Four of them here tonight. One of the women who is a wonderful woman, at twelve years old, was raped at twelve. Her client she represented got him off and she's seen laughing on two separate occasions, laughing at the girl who was raped. Kathy Shelton, that young woman is here with us tonight.

"So don't tell me about words. I am absolutely—I apologize for those words. . . .

"And I tell you that when Hillary brings up a point like that and she talks about words that I said eleven years ago, I think it's disgraceful, and I think she should be ashamed of herself, if you want to know the truth."

There was applause. This was happening forty-eight hours after the *Access Hollywood* tape. It wasn't enough, no one had illusions about what would happen on November 8, but it was surely a remarkable moment. Trump had been bled for thirty minutes onstage and there was still an hour to go and he was already counterpunching.

Clearly irritated, Martha Raddatz ordered the audience to stop their applause.

If the story from *Access Hollywood* was a bombshell that was expected to settle the election in Hillary's favor, the story of Kathy Shelton that Donald Trump raised in the debate, was certainly a grenade that provided some unexpected punch. Avid Clinton watchers, pro and con, knew it well. But the public had never heard of it. And that was part of its seduction.

There, indeed, was Hillary Clinton being interviewed by a friendly academic, apparently laughing about how she, as a lawyer, had helped her client, an alleged rapist of a twelve-year-old girl, walk free. According to a story in the *Washington Post*, "Once appointed, she aggressively defended the alleged rapist; at one point, she attacked the 12-year-old's credibility, writing in an affidavit that she had been informed 'the complainant is emotionally unstable with a tendency to seek out older men and to engage in fantasizing.'"[28]

No one would compare its political impact to the *Access Hollywood* tape that was played and replayed for hours on national television. The Kathy Shelton story had been ignored. But it was insidious, and because Donald Trump talked about it in the debate, it drove many to the Internet that night. Could this be true? How could this possibly be true? Why wasn't I told? Why did Donald Trump have to tell me? What else is not being said?

It was worse online, the story had no explanation, and Hillary Clinton's interview and laughter were played without her defense and without a respectful, intelligent, well-groomed media personality ready to explain it away.[29] My own daughters, outraged by Trump's comments to Billy Bush, googled the Hillary Clinton interview that night and were stunned.

Midway through the debate, Donald Trump was landing some blows. No one felt it would make any difference in the long run, but after what had happened over the last two days, it was breathtaking machismo. It was a miracle that Trump was still standing. Barely.

Toward the end of the debate, a question was raised about a speech that Clinton had made for Goldman Sachs in 2013. It had been leaked to the public against her will. She had reportedly said that politicians needed both public and private positions. Was she signaling that she might have to say some things truthfully but privately to Goldman Sachs, and something else to the public, just to win the election?

Clinton explained that she was referring to the Stephen Spielberg film *Lincoln,* in which the president is depicted as having used different arguments in front of different groups of people.

Donald Trump, in a sophisticated channeling of Senator Lloyd Bentsen, who in 1988 had rebuked vice presidential candidate Dan Quayle for invoking John F. Kennedy, now commented on Hillary Clinton's mention of Lincoln. "She lied," Trump said of Hillary. "Now she's blaming the lie on the late, great Abraham Lincoln.

"Honest Abe never lied."[30]

The *Washington Post* made an effort to defend Hillary Clinton, running a story headlined "Being Truthful Isn't What Made Abraham Lincoln a Great Politician."[31] If the media couldn't raise Hillary to the level of honest, it felt it might make things better by lowering Lincoln a little bit. Still, no one could have imagined that a debate that had started with Donald Trump going in as misogynist, with the Republican Party splitting at the seams all around him, would come out with Hillary Clinton being portrayed as a liar.

Once again, the consensus was that Hillary Clinton had won the debate. And Donald Trump had taken a big hit with the *Access Hollywood* tape. There was a universal consensus that it had been a fatal hit. He was unrecoverable. He could never be president. But there was a grudging acceptance that he had very possibly recovered the base of his support. He had bottomed out. He had stanched the bleeding. He would lose badly, even historically, but it would not be a complete wipeout.

"It's just words, folks," Trump said about Hillary Clinton. "It's just words."[32]

Then, soon after the second debate, a story broke. Jessica Leeds, a seventy-four-year-old from New York said that Donald Trump had grabbed her breasts and attempted to put his hand up her skirt without consent. Allegedly, it had happened thirty years earlier on a flight to New York. Another claim came from Rachel Crooks, a real estate developer, who said that Trump kissed her on the mouth in 2005 without consent.[33] Within days, similar stories appeared. A reporter for *People* magazine said that she had been pinned against the wall by Donald Trump and his butler had walked in on them and saw it.

The Trump campaign denied the stories. "For the *New York Times* to launch a completely false, coordinated character assassination against Mr. Trump on a topic like this is dangerous," said his campaign's spokesman, Jason Miller.[34]

When television reporters found Anthony Senecal, the Trump butler, there was a brief sensation. But when the butler denied the story of the *People* magazine reporter, he was quickly moved off the public stage. Senecal said flatly that he had never seen anything inappropriate, and that the incident alleged by the reporter, with him present, "never happened."[35] Mr. Senecal said that his employer, Donald Trump, had always been a generous and kindly boss.

TRUMP'S NEW TELEVISION NETWORK

The final debate took place in Las Vegas at the Thomas and Mack Center at the University of Nevada on October 19, 2016. Chris Wallace of Fox News was the moderator. I had known his father, Mike Wallace, and knew him to be a complete professional, a man who was intimidated by nobody and whose dedication to getting the story and getting it right trumped any political agenda. The public didn't really know that Mike Wallace was a Democrat, because that was irrelevant to a story. But times had changed.

Like his father before him, Chris Wallace seemed committed to the dying tradition of journalism that called for getting to the facts and letting the chips fall where they may. No matter who was elected president, Chris Wallace would not be mourning the loss of an invitation to the White House Christmas party. The Fox News channel, where he worked, had a reputation for covering both sides of a story, and its nighttime lineup, driven by audience preference, was noticeably more conservative than liberal.

From the very beginning, it was apparent that Wallace was going to target the most important issues that faced the nation. He started talking about Supreme Court nominees, and then he went right to the issue of abortion and choice. It was remarkable that until this moment, these two important subjects had never been raised in the hours of debating.

Midway through the debate Trump stole the show, and many believed doomed whatever long chances he still had left to make a comeback in the remaining days of the election, by refusing to say if he would accept the results of the balloting. Insisting that the process was "rigged" he said, "I will look at it at the time. I will keep you in suspense."[36]

"That's horrifying," Hillary Clinton said, and she later expanded on the thought. "He's talking down our democracy, and I, for one, am appalled."[37]

A story in *Politico* called it "the biggest mistake of his life."[38]

One of Donald Trump's best moments came when he demanded an explanation for a damning email that had come to light. "In a speech you gave to a Brazilian bank for which you were paid $225,000, we've learned from WikiLeaks, that you said this: 'My dream is a hemispheric common market with open trade and open borders.'"[39]

It was the nightmare of conspiracy theorists come true. A nation of millions of poverty-stricken factory workers, with a tiny few oligarchs and their bankers at the top making billions of dollars off their government-protected monopolies, the masses voting in Socialist solutions and keeping the entrepreneurs at bay.

Toward the very end of the debate, there was another encounter about abortion, and it was graphic. Chris Wallace asked for Hillary's position on late-term abortions. "You have been quoted as saying that the fetus has no constitutional rights."[40]

Hillary gave her reasoned response, knowing that this was one of the rare women's issues that worked against her, although attitudes were changing, especially because of the Zika virus. Still, according to a poll conducted by STAT and Harvard, "only 23 percent said they favored allowing a woman to obtain an abortion after 24 weeks—

when the question did not raise the possibility of microcephaly."[41] According to the study, "generally, the vast majority of Americans oppose late-term abortions."[42] The United States was one of only seven nations that allowed elective abortions after twenty weeks.[43]

Trump was quiet, even respectful, but he spoke solemnly, "Well, I think it's terrible if you go with what Hillary is saying in the ninth month you can take the baby and rip the baby out of the womb of the mother, just prior to the birth of the baby. Now, you can say that that's okay and Hillary can say that that's okay, but it's not okay with me. . . . In the ninth month. On the final day. And that's not acceptable."[44]

Ben Ginsberg, the man who had helped run campaigns from George W. Bush to Mitt Romney, one of the GOPs most respected éminences grises, concluded of Trump, "He had his best debate, by far. But it doesn't matter."[45]

The public seemed to agree. CNN declared Hillary Clinton the winner of the debate by 52 to 39 percent. A few days later, on October 23, 2016, an ABC News poll had Clinton leading Trump by twelve points. It was considered an insurmountable lead, with the real problem for Trump being the unfair tilt toward Clinton in the Electoral College.

Rumors spreading among staff and employees at Fox News said that Trump was planning to write a book called *Rigged*. He would use the book and an accompanying website to put in motion plans for his own television network that would compete with Fox. He would use his massive mailing list. He would take Sean Hannity with him, who would be the star. And behind the scenes, the television genius Roger Ailes would be guiding the ship. It was all about ready to sail. The election was over. Even Fox News could see it. Even Trump could see it. Or so the rumors had it. One could hear the buzz of detail discussed in the green room at Fox News.

In fact, the Trump campaign already had its own nightly news-cast on Facebook called Trump Tower Live. But the idea of Trump TV was only talk. Since the campaign was collapsing, some were scrambling aboard this phantom idea. Sean Hannity totally denied any involvement to the talk radio host Mark Levin. And he told Gabriel Sherman of *New York* magazine, "I've never even discussed Trump TV with anyone."[46]

An insider who knew all the players on the Trump team and had a pipeline into the Trump Tower said it was just nerves. It was about finding a place to land. It happens at the end of all losing campaigns. People scatter, they have to find work. But then, this one was not quite over.

There were still the three million undecided voters in seven toss-up states. They had to vote one way or the other. They had to sift through all that had been said. They had to discern what was true and what was false. They would stand alone in the ballot box, with-out Anderson Cooper or Martha Raddatz or Chris Wallace, and would have to pull the lever or punch the card. They would have to figure out all of the competing claims and counterclaims and decide what was best for the country. What was best for them?

CHAPTER 18

HILLARY THE ENABLER

Sometimes even to live is an act of courage.
—Seneca

At the time of this writing it is hard to determine who shot first in the bloody political month of October 2016. It is likely that both sides were planning an October surprise and so stumbled into each other in the dark.

According to sources inside the Trump campaign, Clinton operatives were circulating the story of the *Access Hollywood* tape in late September 2016. According to the same sources, NBC was trying to find a way to get someone else to actually out the tape so NBC would not be blamed for throwing the election. When it was finally leaked to the *Washington Post*, NBCNews.com followed with a complete story seven minutes later, giving evidence to the idea of a coordinated effort.[1]

In a story for TheWrap.com, a source claims that "somebody at NBC News or the Today Show leaked the tape."[2]

Whatever the details may have been, the Trump team was not idle. Anticipating a hit, and hearing some of the details, it rushed forward with its story of Hillary Clinton as the enabler of Bill Clinton's sexual assaults on women and her victimization of those women when they dared to speak up about it.

News agencies sneered that the stories were old news, and most ignored them. The Trump campaign said that the stories were now corroborated with detail that hadn't existed in the 1990s and that the role of Hillary, not considered relevant or tasteful at the time, was now vividly clear, with evidence to back it up. In any case, the fact that television network executives deemed the stories unacceptable only drove people to the Internet. Fox News covered them straight, and their brief segments were enough to provoke the stampede.

Few believed that these were stories that would sway Clinton supporters, but they might just swing back a few of the Trump supporters who had moved to Hillary over the *Access Hollywood* tape. And they might remind Republican politicians who had abandoned Trump just what they would be getting in a return to power for the Clintons.

On October 2, 2016, only days before the *Access Hollywood* tape was released to the *Washington Post*, Kathleen Willey, a former White House aide, went public with new details about her story of assault at the hands of Bill Clinton. "This is no longer about Bill Clinton's transgressions or his infidelities or girlfriends or sex . . .it's not about that anymore," Willey said in an interview with the *Washington Examiner*. "What it's about is the actions that his wife has taken against the women that he has raped and assaulted."[3]

THE NIGHTMARE FOR KATHLEEN WILLEY

The story of Kathleen Willey is a story of a remarkable emotional survivor. It is an example of how much shock and pain a person can endure and still come out reasonably intact.

On November 29, 1993, two months before the Paula Jones lawsuit broke into the news, Kathleen Willey, a volunteer in the White House social office, met with the president in the Oval Office.

Willey told the president that she and her husband, Ed, were in trouble. Financial trouble. But it was worse than that. According to the carefully researched book *Their Lives* by Candice Jackson, "her husband, Ed Willey, was facing disgrace and financial ruin as a lawyer who had bilked clients out of substantial sums of money to cover his personal tax liens."[4]

From all appearances, Ed and Kathleen Willey had led a charmed life. He was the son of a Virginia state legislator. They had two children. A February 1998, *Time* magazine article described them as a couple that skied in Vail for winter vacations, drove luxury cars, and made hefty donations to the Democratic Party.[5] Bill and Hillary Clinton apparently knew them both. After reading Linda Tripp's grand jury testimony, one can get the impression that Kathleen Willey knew that Bill Clinton was a "player"—that is, he was prone to sexual activity outside his marriage—and that she, Kathleen Willey, strongly suspected that he was attracted to her.

According to a deposition Willey gave to the Paula Jones' attorneys, the president welcomed Willey into the Oval Office when the meeting began and gave her a hug. He returned to his chair behind the desk, and she was seated right across from it. She told the president that her situation was desperate. She and her husband were under great pressure. She told the president that she needed a paid job.

According to Willey's deposition, at some point during the meeting, they moved to a small passageway that led off from the Oval Office into a small kitchen galley, where the president prepared them both a cup of coffee, and they continued to talk about her situation.

But when the conversation ended and she started walking for the door back into the Oval Office, he stopped her and hugged her again, as if comforting her, promising to help. But the hug lingered. Then, according to Willey, he attempted to kiss her. And he "put my hands on his genitals." She says she rebuffed this and removed her hands immediately. Her interrogator asked if the president was aroused, and she said, "Yes."[6]

She later told the investigative journalist Michael Isikoff that she believed Paula Jones was telling the truth because Clinton's face was beet red during this encounter.[7]

At her interrogator's further persistence, she said that he had touched her breast, and at some time during this encounter, the president said, "I've wanted to do that for a long time."[8]

When free from the president's embrace, Kathleen Willey says she fled the Oval Office.

Immediately after, Kathleen Willey encountered Linda Tripp. According to Tripp, Kathleen seemed excited, even exhilarated by what had happened. Later, Kathleen would surmise that she had been in such utter shock that she couldn't have known what impressions she portrayed.

Clinton supporters would use this post–Oval Office reaction to make the point that her story was probably false and if something had happened, she was clearly not traumatized by it. According to later testimony from Monica Lewinsky, the president told her the allegations were ludicrous because Willey was not well endowed and he, the president, would not pursue a woman with small breasts.

Later in the day Kathleen Willey became anxious. She was unable to reach her husband and when she finally went home, hoping to find him, he was not there.

Early the next morning she would learn that on that same day, November 29, 1993, the same day that she said that the president had sexually assaulted her in the passageway near the Oval Office, her husband, Ed Willey, had walked off into the woods and shot himself. His body was found on a path in the woods in rural King and Queen County, Virginia. It was ruled a suicide.

Twenty-two years later, Kathleen, still reeling from that day, wrote her husband a letter. "We can't seem to find our way back to any semblance of a family we once shared. The holidays are nothing but god-awful. The magic of Christmas is gone forever. And to this day, for the life of me, I can't remember my last words to you."[9]

JUANITA BROADDRICK AND AN ACCUSATION OF RAPE

A week after Kathleen Willey's 2016 reemergence and shortly after the political crisis erupted over Trump's comments on the *Access Hollywood* tape, Juanita Broaddrick, seventy-three years old and in retirement from a career as a nursing home administrator, appeared again in the public eye. "Bill Clinton raped me," she said. "And Hillary Clinton threatened me. I don't think there's any comparison."[10]

Juanita Broaddrick first met Bill Clinton in April 1978. He was the attorney general of Arkansas visiting a nursing home in the small town of Van Buren. She was an attractive thirty-five-year-old employee at the place. When Clinton spotted her, he invited her to call his campaign office in Little Rock. As it turned out, she was in the city the next week anyway, attending a symposium for nursing home administrators, so she gave him a call.

He suggested that they have coffee together and rushed right over to her hotel, the Camelot Inn. Complaining about reporters in the hotel lobby, Clinton insisted that they have their coffee in her room. And that's when Juanita says it happened.

As in the case of every other woman accuser of Bill Clinton, Juanita Broaddrick was apparently willing to live with her own private pain. For many years she kept silent. Her story was the stuff of gossip around Arkansas. Eventually, as stories of Clinton women began to spread, reporters and investigators from all over the world came to her door. But the trauma of those memories was too great. "I wouldn't relive it for anything,"[11] she said.

Just like the other women, someone else outed her story, and she was soon sitting before lawyers and investigators representing Paula Jones, the independent counselor's office, and the House Judiciary Committee. Although the records of those interviews were supposed to remain sealed forever, the news of what had happened soon spread to Clinton enemies and friends.

"All these stories are floating around," Broaddrick said. "Different stories of what really happened, of what people think happened and I was tired of everybody putting their own spin on it."[12] It was especially galling when tabloids began suggesting that her husband had cut a deal with the Clintons to remain quiet. Then there were the relentless attacks from the Clinton White House and friends in the media.

"It's important to me to tell what happened," Juanita finally said. "I don't know how people are going to take this. I don't know what they're going to think after all these years and months why I've come forward."[13]

In January 1999, only a month after Bill Clinton's impeachment in the US House of Representatives, Juanita Broaddrick sat down with NBC's most experienced investigative journalist, Lisa Myers, and told her remarkable story.

Myers asked Broaddrick if she had ever given Bill Clinton reason to believe that she might be "receptive."[14]

Broaddrick said, "No. None. None whatsoever."[15]

Broaddrick said that Bill Clinton tried to kiss her, and she resisted. When he tried a second time, he started biting her lip. The top part of her lip.

She said that she tried to pull away from him, and he forced her down on the bed.

Juanita Broaddrick began crying as she told her story. She said that she was very frightened. That she tried to get away from him. That she told him "No, [I] didn't want this to happen. But he wouldn't listen to me."[16]

Lisa Myers insisted again, "Did you resist, did you tell him to stop?"

Broaddrick said, "Yes, I told him, 'Please don't.' He was such a different person at that moment, he was just a vicious, awful person."[17]

"You said there was a point at which you stopped resisting?" Myers asked.

And Broaddrick described the moment as "a real panicky, panicky situation. I was even to the point where I was getting very noisy, you know, yelling to 'Please stop.' And that's when he pressed down on my right shoulder and he would bite my lip."

The waist of her skirt and her pantyhose were torn.

"When everything was over with," Broaddrick said, "he got up and straightened himself, and I was crying at the moment and he walks to the door, and calmly puts on his sunglasses. And before he goes out the door he says, 'You better get some ice on that.' And he turned and went out the door."

At the time, the Clinton White House ridiculed Broaddrick's story. If it were true, why had she waited so long to tell it? "It was a horrible, horrible experience," she told the journalist Lois Romano, "and I just wanted it to go away."[18]

"Any allegation that the president assaulted Ms. Broaddrick more than 20 years ago is absolutely false," said a statement from the Clinton White House. "Beyond that we are not going to comment."[19]

Juanita had attended the symposium in Little Rock with a close friend, Norma Rogers. According to a journalist who spoke with Rogers, "she returned to the hotel room that day to find Broaddrick badly shaken and her lip swollen. They quickly packed and left, stopping to get ice for Broaddrick's lip on the way back to Van Buren."[20]

There was not much they could do. They didn't even consider telling the police. At the time, Attorney General Bill Clinton was the chief law enforcement officer in the state of Arkansas.

The Juanita Broaddrick story, as horrific as the charges were, went nowhere. President Bill Clinton was not going to be prosecuted on a twenty-year-old rape charge. And since the president had not tried to influence Broaddrick's testimony, it was a story that did not fit the specific charges of impeachment for perjury or obstruction of justice.

The full NBC version of Lisa Myer's interview with Juanita Broaddrick never aired. There were parts of the story in which Ms. Broaddrick talked about Hillary's role in the controversy, and NBC decided to leave those parts on the cutting room floor.

In 2016, when the network went after Donald Trump and his relationships with women, its former talented investigative reporter Michael Isikoff told Sidewire.com, "Broaddrick told her story to NBC and the *Washington Post* in '99. Both organizations closely vetted her story and chose to run it. Also NBC has the full tape of the original Lisa Meyers interview. Folks have made much of the fact that her claim about the conversation she had with Hillary wasn't in the interview that ran. Broaddrick said it was cut out; Lisa Myers has since agreed. Broaddrick said this then—and NBC chose to cut it out."[21]

Reflecting on the irony and hypocrisy of politics and news organizations, Isikoff wryly observed how amazing it was to watch Democrats, who once attacked Bill Clinton's accusers, now embrace Donald Trump's accusers, while Republicans who believed the Clinton accusers were now attacking the women who were accusing Trump.[22]

If the television networks had too much invested in a Hillary Clinton presidency to risk running her full story, Juanita Broaddrick was nonetheless relieved to finally begin the process of telling her story transparently. "I feel like I have gotten the biggest weight off my shoulders," she said. "I did it because of my twin granddaughters—they're 12. When they ask me about this in a few years, I want them to say, 'That was a neat thing you did.' I didn't want them asking me, 'Why didn't you come forward?'"[23]

In 2016, with Hillary Clinton on the verge of being elected president of the United States, Juanita Broaddrick was now telling the world what the American news media had left on the cutting room floor.

VICTIMS AGAIN

There was a feeling among supporters of Bill and Hillary Clinton that they, not the women who accused them of sexual harassment and character assassination, were the true victims. Hillary herself promoted this idea to her inner circle. Her close Arkansas friend Jim Blair once described her as asserting, "These people are not going to run over us."[24]

Toward the end of January 1998, after the Monica Lewinsky story broke, Hillary Clinton conducted four days of strategy sessions within the White House in which she advocated a strong, sustained counterattack against the independent counsel Kenneth Starr. The Clintons' communications director, Ann Lewis, met with special consultants and key staff to address this prevailing question: "How do we finally turn the corner where we can get people raising legitimate questions about Starr?"[25]

Hillary decided that she, herself, would take the fight public. She flew up to New York City on January 26, with plans to appear on the NBC *Today* show the following morning. She spent the night in a suite reserved for her at the Waldorf-Astoria and awoke at five a.m. to prepare for the interview.

Matt Lauer of *NBC* began his interview, but the first lady quickly took charge. She expressed great concern "about the tactics that are being used and the kind of intense political agenda at work here."[26]

At one point Lauer told Mrs. Clinton, "You have said, I understand, to some close friends, that this is the last great battle, and that one side or the other is going down here."

Hillary said, "Well, I don't know if I've been that dramatic. That would sound like a good line from a movie. But I do believe that this is a battle. I mean, look at the very people who are involved in this. They have popped up in other settings. This is—the great story here for anybody willing to find it and write about it and explain it is this vast right-wing conspiracy that has been conspiring against my husband since the day he announced for president."[27]

In 2016, Hillary Clinton was asked if she still believed in a "vast right-wing conspiracy" and she insisted it was still very much in existence and better funded than it had been eighteen years before.[28] The CNN anchor Anderson Cooper listened politely without questioning the statement. No one seemed to mind that Hillary had also told Matt Lauer eighteen years before, in that same famous interview, that she believed her husband's "denial of allegations that he had entered into a sexual relationship with a White House intern."[29] Seven months later, Clinton admitted to the nation that he had lied.

If there was a right-wing conspiracy, who were its members? When did they meet? What was their plan and purpose for America? Every major corporation and nation in the world had invested millions of dollars into the Clinton Foundation. By Election Day, Hillary Clinton had amassed 240 newspaper endorsements, including almost every major newspaper in the country. Donald Trump had 19.[30] She had outraised and outspent him financially five to three. Her super PAC was the largest in American history. If it was a conspiracy, it certainly wasn't vast.

Who were these people that Hillary said were trying to run them over?

She described Gennifer Flowers in an ABC News interview as "some failed cabaret singer who doesn't even have much of a résumé to fall back on." And she insisted to *Esquire* magazine that if she had the opportunity to ever cross-examine Flowers, "I mean, I would crucify her."[31]

George Stephanopoulos remembers a crisis over a woman making allegations in *Penthouse* magazine. According to Stephanopoulos, Hillary insisted, "We have to destroy her story."[32]

While no one can prove that Hillary herself hired the detectives or coordinated with them about what to actually do or say to the women, the detective in question was a fellow classmate of Hillary's in law school who was paid $100,000 for his work, and that work, the reader will remember, included destroying Gennifer Flowers' reputation beyond all recognition.

Hillary Clinton opposed the early settlement to Monica Lewinsky, which she came to regret. Hillary described Lewinsky as a "narcissistic loony toon."[33] She told friends that Monica had seduced her husband.[34]

Juanita Broaddrick would meet Hillary Clinton three weeks after her traumatic experience with her husband. This was years before the Lewinsky scandal, when Bill was running for governor of Arkansas. On this occasion, Broaddrick strongly suspects that Mrs. Clinton signaled that she should remain silent about what happened.

Broaddrick was at a private Clinton fund-raiser taking place in a home. A friend of hers had driven the Clintons in from the airport and pulled her aside to say that "the whole conversation was about you coming from the airport. Mostly from Mrs. Clinton."[35]

And then Broaddrick saw "them coming through the kitchen area. And some people there are pointing to me. He goes one direction and she comes directly to me. Then panic is sort of starting to set in with me. And I thought, 'Oh my God, what do I do now?'"[36]

Hillary exchanged some small talk and then pointedly said, "I just want you to know how much Bill and I appreciate the things you do for him."

Broaddrick was dumbfounded.

And Hillary said, "Do you understand? Everything you do."[37]

Juanita Broaddrick said that during the encounter she had tried to pull away and that Hillary had gripped her arm with force, almost to the point of pain, to make sure she got the point. Juanita Broaddrick left immediately.

Clinton defenders point out that there are many possible explanations to that encounter. Clinton detractors say that it has the awkward sound of truth to it; that is, such a story, if invented, would not be conclusive anyway. If one were malicious, one could make up a moment less mysterious.

Since Broaddrick is the primary witness, her own impression is instructive. "What really went through my mind at that time," she said, was the feeling that "she knows. She knew. She's covering it up and she expects me to do the very same thing."[38]

Kathleen Willey described a lunch with Sidney Blumenthal and Christopher Hitchens. According to Willey, Blumenthal said, "Well, she looks good today. She's not going to look good by Friday," meaning that the Clintons and their allies in the media were going to destroy her.

Willey sensed that she was being watched and followed, and her suspicions were soon confirmed when friends tipped her off that strangers were asking about her. She had to replace three tires on her car. The mechanic said, "It looks like someone has shot out all your tires with a nail gun. Is there someone out there who doesn't like you?"[39] Chills went down her spine.

Two days before her deposition, she was approached by a man while she was jogging. "He passed and then he stopped and said, 'Hey Kathleen, did you ever find your cat? Yeah, that Bull's-eye was a pretty nice cat.' Then, he stood back and he said, 'You're just not getting the message are you?'"[40] They even knew the name of her cat.

It was a few days later that the skull of a cat was left on her front porch.

Now alone, with her husband dead, Willey was terrified. A post-man alerted her to the fact that a rather creepy-looking person had stopped by the post office to ask for directions to her house.

Clinton allies, including major publishers and journalists, mocked such stories and even when they were run to ground and proven real, no one could prove a direct Clinton connection.

Jared Stern, a former marine, was hired to obtain Kathleen Willey's phone records. A story in the *Washington Post* reported that "Stern was so uneasy about unspecified work he was asked to do on Willey that he called her and, using an alias, warned her someone was out to do her harm."[41]

The Jared Stern trail was tracked back to Nathan Landow, a Democratic fund-raiser. According to Landow, his longtime personal lawyer had hired Stern and had done so without his, Landow's, knowledge and neither the first lady nor the president were anywhere near the matter.[42]

All this pressure mounted as Willey's testimony in the Paula Jones case approached. At one point, White House spokesperson Mike McCurry "warned reporters to think twice about covering the Willey subpoena at all."[43]

As it turned out, Kathleen Willey, terrified and alone, was remarkably courageous for standing up for herself. She hadn't wanted to see her story go public. Another anonymous woman called Michael Isikoff, then a writer at *Newsweek*, and said that she too had been invited into the White House by Bill Clinton. That like Willey, she was a major Democratic donor. That like Willey, she was taken down the narrow passageway just off the Oval Office. And that like Willey, she had been sexually assaulted by the president. She claimed that she had resisted the president and pushed him away and he had "finished the job himself."[44] A reporter, hearing a similar story from two unconnected sources, had to take them seriously.

Before Kathleen Willey, Hillary Clinton's tactics against women accusers was to label them nuts, sluts, gold diggers, or political tools. But in fact, some of the accusers were Democratic Party stalwarts. Kathleen Willey and Monica Lewinsky worked in the White House and were part of the Clinton team. Ed and Kathleen Willey had started the Virginians for Clinton organization in their own office. They were certainly not tools of a right-wing conspiracy. Paula Jones admitted to a television reporter that she had no idea what was meant by a conservative or a liberal. She was not into politics.

While some sold their story to tabloids or later posed for *Penthouse* out of financial desperation, long after they had been left penniless, many never took a dime for their stories, and haven't to this day.

Here is the rub: Not one of them purposely went public with their story on her own. In every case, some other person or circumstances forced the story into the public eye. And yet, as the Trump campaign pointed out, these women were viciously attacked by the Clinton machine. Hillary's mind-set was, "These people are not going to run over us."[45]

Paula Jones filed her lawsuit because she was defamed in a story that had falsely claimed she had been Bill Clinton's girlfriend and had serviced him in a Little Rock hotel room. The irony is that the Clintons could have immediately resolved this issue by agreeing with her that it was not true and urged the Arkansas State Troopers to apologize to her for their false story.

Once the Paula Jones lawsuit was filed, it was too late. Her lawyers deposed other rumored girlfriends such as Gennifer Flowers and Sally Perdue, trying to establish that Clinton had a serial problem. It was this legal strategy that forced Juanita Broaddrick, Kathleen Willey, and a list of other women to come forward with their stories. They were outed against their will.

In many cases, these women lied for the Clintons and denied their relationships even after they were outed. Some of them lied under oath, committing perjury for the Clintons and only recanted when they were trapped by conflicting evidence and when they were thus offered immunity from further prosecution, immunity that required future cooperation and honesty.

Several of the women fought the subpoenas and resisted talking in the first place. The Clintons and their professional machine did not care. They used the women's denials to show that they were unstable. During the 2016 campaign, a Clinton insider talked about how they overwhelmed Wikipedia to showcase the conflicting testimonies and destroy the credibility of the women.

Most of the Clinton victims were suddenly audited by the IRS. All of them were attacked no matter what they did. If they took money, or if they didn't. If they supported Bill Clinton and lied for him and tried to avoid the public eye it didn't matter. And their friends were targeted as well. When Gennifer Flowers' roommate, Lauren Kirk, spoke to a reporter from the *New York Post*, she was promptly fired from her job as a Dallas real estate agent.

Thus, the women were victimized twice. First by Bill Clinton and second by Hillary Clinton and her cooperative network of journalists and television producers. As a young lady, in her commencement speech at Wellesley College, Hillary Clinton had said, "Part of the problem with just empathy with professed goals is that empathy doesn't do us anything."[46]

In an interview in October 2016, Kathleen Willey repeated her argument, "I want to say this to the mainstream media . . . these are not infidelities. A rape is not an infidelity. These are crimes. Any other person would be in jail for a very long time.

"She will annihilate any enemy, anybody who has spoken against her, across the board. . . . She will spend her entire administration ruining these people. That's what she will do." [47]

This was a voice of a liberal Democrat who had given money to the Clintons and who had worked in their White House and who had remained silent for years to protect them.

At the time, no one expected that the reemergence of the former Clinton victims would greatly change the trajectory of the 2016 presidential race. They believed that Donald Trump had been hurt fatally by the *Access Hollywood* tape. So too, as it turned out, was the other voice on the tape hurt. Billy Bush was cut from the NBC *Today* show lineup on October 17, 2016.

Nevertheless, the public stories of the Clinton women gave some pause. That same month, the liberal website *Slate* ran a story by Michelle Goldberg with the headline "Juanita Broaddrick's Rape Allegations Are Credible. Her Attacks on Hillary Clinton Are Not."[48] The election was only days away.

CHAPTER 19

THE NEXT WHITE HOUSE?

It is not only for what we do that we will be held responsible,
but also for what we don't do.
—*Molière*

The expected election of Hillary Clinton as president of the United States was to be a moment of historic proportions. Back to back, two great events would have occurred in our nation's history, each one adding weight to the other. The 2008 election of President Barack Obama represented the rise to power of a black man, this in a nation whose founding fathers simultaneously gave birth to unprecedented liberty to millions, while many of them personally owned black slaves. And the 2016 election of Hillary Clinton would represent the rise to power of a woman. But there was another nagging, inconvenient footnote that troubled a small minority of leaders in business, media, and academia. Some wondered if it was keeping the election unnecessarily close. At the moment when Hillary Rodham Clinton was sworn in as the nation's chief executive, she would also become, at once, the most corrupt president in American history. And her first man, who would follow her into the White House, would come as a walking time bomb of scandals, many of them unresolved, still ticking.

On November 4, 2016, only days before the election, ABC News ran a report titled "A Hint of Momentum for Clinton, with Issues a Defining Factor."[1] The story, based on an ABC/*Washington Post* poll showed that Hillary Clinton had a 47 to 44 percent lead over Trump; the good news for Clinton, according to ABC, was that she led on the issues dealing with terrorism, health care, and immigration. Trump tied her on the economy and beat her badly on only one topic. He beat her on the issue of corruption.[2] But did that matter?

The marriage of politics and corruption is not new. Ronald Reagan once observed, "It has been said that politics is the second-oldest profession. I have learned that it bears a close resemblance to the first."[3]

Reagan himself saw sixteen people from his administration indicted over the Iran-Contra scandal, including a secretary of state and officials at the CIA and from the military. And Barack Obama saw his own appointees at the IRS arguably use their positions to frustrate his political enemies while they pleaded the Fifth Amendment before a congressional inquiry. His Veteran's Administration saw unresolved scandals that persisted throughout his entire time in office. And it was his attorney general who met privately with Bill Clinton, even while the Justice Department was supposedly investigating Clinton's wife.

The 2016 election struck observers as unprecedented in its political violence. But in fact, partisan politics had always been mean spirited. And it had always fed on scandal. George Washington despaired over the bitterness that was emerging, even within his own cabinet, over the dueling philosophies of how the government should be run.

Pamphleteers working for Washington's secretary of state, Thomas Jefferson, smeared Treasury Secretary Alexander Hamilton, accusing the later of having an affair with a Mrs. Maria Reynolds and being blackmailed by her husband. Pro-Hamilton pamphleteers accused Jefferson of sexual relations with his slave Sally

Hemings.[4] Mean-spirited politics had been with us from the beginning of our nation and happened wherever people worked together,
in government, the military, religion, the arts, and academia.

In the presidential election of 1884, the American electorate had
to choose between a corrupt politician who took bribes in return for
favors, and an outrageous, New York misogynist.[5] The American
public was stunned. How had it come to this? Were there no better
choices?

The New York misogynist was counsel in a prestigious law firm
in Buffalo. He and his partners shared the sexual favors of a young
lady, and when she became pregnant, he assumed paternity of the
child. His partners were all married. He was single. It seemed to be
the right thing to do.

There's more. When one of the law partners died, the future
presidential candidate agreed to be the guardian of his daughter. He
had literally known her since birth. Everyone expected the law partner to marry the mother, the widow, but he had other plans.

When the daughter, his ward, turned twenty-one, they were
married. In the White House. He was Grover Cleveland, forty-six,
the president of the United States, and she was Frances Folsom, the
youngest first lady in American history.[6] Cleveland, sensitive to public opinion, was careful not to kiss the bride or show any public affec-
tion during the wedding, but the controversial marriage was con-
summated anyway. They left the White House with two children.

Republican James Blaine was the corrupt politician who lost
the election to Grover Cleveland. Blaine had long been seen as a
president-in-waiting. As early as 1876, then Speaker of the House,
he was touted as the front-runner, but a scandal soon interrupted
the process. It centered on an alleged bribe from the Union Pacific
Railroad. According to the charges, the Union Pacific paid Blaine
$65,000 for worthless bonds of the Little Rock and Fort Smith Rail-

road. Blaine insisted that he lost money on the transaction. Directors at the Union Pacific denied the whole affair. Democrats in Congress demanded an investigation, which appeared to exonerate Blaine until the famous Mulligan letters surfaced.

James Mulligan, a Boston clerk, said that the accusations were accurate, he had helped arrange the deal, and that furthermore he had letters to prove it. At the bottom of one of the letters was the damning request, in the hand of James Blaine, "Kindly burn this letter."

Blaine and Mulligan met privately in a hotel room, and Blaine left with the letters in his hands. No one knows what was said between the two men, and Blaine would never release the letters. The Republicans declared that the whole affair was a partisan witch hunt, and by 1884, James Blaine, then a former secretary of state, was running for president again.

It was an election that left the country depressed by its choices. Grover Cleveland was the admitted father of a child out of wedlock, this at a time when men sat in prison for committing adultery. James Blaine was refusing to release the old Mulligan letters that might incriminate him in a pay-to-play scheme of outright bribery.

There were two partisan chants. Democrats jeered and shouted at Blaine supporters, "Burn, burn, burn this letter." And Republicans jeered and shouted back to Cleveland supporters, "Ma, ma, where's my pa? Off to the White House, ha, ha, ha." In spite of the controversy, Grover Cleveland is often rated highly by historians and seemed to have acquitted himself well as president.

In recent history, no scandals reached the level of corruption of the Nixon administration.

His vice president, Spiro Agnew, was forced to resign in a tax-evasion scheme. News was released in 1973 that Agnew had taken $100,000 in bribes during his time as the Baltimore county executive, the governor of Maryland, and as vice president.

The major scandal of the Nixon administration began with a break-in of the Democratic Party Headquarters in the Watergate apartment complex in Washington, DC. But it was the attempt to cover up the story that led to the crisis. Nixon would use the CIA, the FBI, and the IRS to pursue journalists who were trying to uncover the truth. Eventually, forty government officials were indicted or jailed. This included the president's White House chief of staff and White House counsel, and the attorney general of the United States. Facing almost-certain impeachment, Richard Nixon resigned the presidency on August 9, 1974.

There is a long list of corruption in American political life. It would be unfair to hold the Clintons up as the only exemplars of this behavior. But there were some very troubling characteristics that applied more strongly to the Clintons than to the others. For one thing, many scandals happened on the president's watch but did not involve the president or the first lady themselves.

President Andrew Jackson's spoils system led to widespread embezzlement, including $1.2 million from the New York City customs house. But Jackson touched none of the money nor knew how it had happened.

President Ulysses S. Grant was president during the breakup of the Whiskey Ring. Three of his cabinet members were charged with bribery, but not Grant. The Credit Mobilier scandal involved overpaying the Union Pacific and included millions of dollars in bribes to the vice president and several US senators. Again, Grant himself, was not involved.

President Warren G. Harding served in the White House for only two years before his death in 1923, but his administration became notorious for its corruption. Ironically, in his own time, Harding was considered one of the most popular presidents in history. He was also considered quite godly. Through relatives and close friends, Harding built an alliance with leaders of the Seventh-Day Adventist Church, which was unaware of his double life. When he died, the mainstream media mourned him as a giant but then, slowly, relentlessly, the scandals began to unravel.

The Teapot Dome scandal, which involved Harding's close friend, Secretary of the Interior Albert Fall, is the most notorious. It involved leasing oil drilling rights on land in exchange for "loans" and other complicated kickbacks. But the list of scandals, once started, kept coming.

Historians still argue over how much the president himself was involved, but he certainly was aware of some of the more salacious pieces. He knew of attempts to keep the lid on the crisis; for example, a timely suicide and a key witness who was rushed off to Europe to get beyond the reach of the press.

After Harding's death, when the extent of the damage began to unfold, even his close Seventh-Day Adventist supporters finally threw in the towel. It turned out that Harding had been leading a double life. While serving as president in the middle of Prohibition, the president privately drank whiskey, serving it to his guests. He kept his White House adequately stocked at all times, whereas ordinary people were locked up in prison for doing the same thing.

There are many differences between the long list of historical accounts of corruption in the White House and the story of Bill and Hillary Clinton. In some cases, such as Andrew Jackson, the president himself never touched the scandals and was only part of attempting to reform a bad system. In other cases, the obloquy involved other actors, with the president becoming corrupted by trying to cover things up, either selfishly to protect his own legacy or generously to protect his own people.

The difference for the Clintons was that they themselves

benefited from the actions that led to scandal. Either they banked money that they controlled personally or through friends they appointed; or they won power; or, in the case of Bill Clinton's sexual appetite, his emotional and physical needs, were met at the expense of the reputations and emotional well-being of his victims.

This is not to say that the Clintons did not do good things, even great things. Nor is it to say that their foundation did not do good things. That their White House did not achieve success. One could also say that Nixon accomplished many good things. That his opening with China changed the world. This is only to say that the nature of the Clintons' scandals, when compared with those of past presidents, seems to be more often born out of self-interest.

One of the most pronounced features of the Clintons' scandals in American history is the scale of the corruption. While the scandal of James Blaine ruined his chances for winning the presidential election in 1884, the total amount of money involved in the alleged Union Pacific bribes was close to $1 million in today's inflation-adjusted dollars. And remember, Blaine denied the charges, claiming, much as the Clintons would, that there was really no scandal at all, that he was the victim of a partisan witch hunt.

Richard Nixon's famous slush fund had prompted a televised explanation. It was called the "Checkers speech," named after the dog his children had received from a donor. The fund required a Price Waterhouse audit to track the donors and their possible motives. The speech was watched by the largest television audience in history at that time. The famous fund in question amounted to $18,000.

According to CNN, the Clintons earned $153 million in speaking fees from major corporations in the months and years leading up to Hillary's announcement to seek the Democratic presidential nomination.[7] Their average pay for a single speech is $210,795, much greater than the entire scandalous Nixon slush fund. "An investigation from the Associated Press ties those fees to government influence."[8] Meanwhile, the Clintons had amassed $2 billion in their foundation, having accepted money from governments, banks, and major corporations all around the world.

The idea that the Clintons' scandals would somehow be dismissed by history upon the election of Hillary Clinton as president was always a fool's wish. There was no way that the plea from James Blaine in the Mulligan letters—"Kindly burn this letter"—would remain a pronounced moment in history while Hillary Clinton's erasure of 33,000 emails, even after being served a congressional subpoena, or her order to have her aides smash their cell phones with hammers, while they themselves were granted immunity from the friendly Obama Justice Department, would be panned.[9]

The monumental scale, the sheer weight of the events, is something that history would simply not ignore. When all the people who needed to make money made their money, and future presidents came and went, and future generations could look at these events without partisan censorship from corporations who were invested, the work of history would ultimately have its say.

And finally, what distinguished Bill and Hillary Clinton's controversies from the other, more onerous political scandals in American history was the fact that the issues had been ongoing, uninterrupted throughout a lifetime. The ethical questions surrounding the Clintons preceded them into office, continued unabated during their time in the White House, resulted in impeachment, reoccurred during Bill's period of retirement, took no respite during a second presidential campaign, and would now be carried back into the White House with them again.

Ulysses S. Grant's own personal scandals occurred during retirement. Harding's scandals flared into the open after he died.

Nixon retired and diligently worked his way back as a respected statesman, with never another taint of misdeed in anything he wrote or did. And the sexual scandals of Franklin D. Roosevelt, who died with his mistress in Warm Springs, Georgia, or of John F. Kennedy and Lyndon B. Jonson were never known by the public. We read about them only later. But the Clinton scandals were known and they persisted, with hundreds of loose ends and unanswered questions. And yet many very responsible persons in American society, including responsible figures in the national corporate media, were prepared to put the Clintons back into power, expecting them to behave, believing that they would certainly now respect this amazing opportunity they had been given a second time.

THE FIRST HUNDRED DAYS OF THE CLINTON WHITE HOUSE

With the election of Hillary Clinton all but assured, journalists on the Clinton plane and on the campaign trail began to pepper her with questions. What would the Clinton White House look like? What role would Bill Clinton play? Would Chelsea Clinton be the first lady? What would be the legislative agenda?

"We'll begin to get to work right away," she told members of the press, "and reach out to everybody that we can possibly touch to start talking about what we can do together."[10]

Early in the summer the Clinton team had rolled out a detailed policy agenda, but some things could change. There were variables that the Clintons just could not control. What if the Republicans held on to the Senate? The Democrats were doing everything they could to make sure that didn't happen, but the Clinton machine prided itself on being prepared for every contingency, and the polls had narrowed, making the Senate a tougher challenge.

"I think there's a big agenda where we can find common ground," she said.[11] And she emphasized her two major legislative initiatives: immigration reform and an infrastructure rebuilding program, which would stimulate the economy.

Immigration reform called for "full and equal citizenship" to millions of immigrants, even those without legal residency.[12]

Some of this depended on how badly Clinton would beat Trump in the coming election, and how the Republican Party would react to the thrashing. Carmel Martin, the executive vice president for policy at the Center for American Progress, expressed the hope that Trump's loss to Hillary would empower the more moderate wing of the Republican Party.[13] This would open endless possibilities for Hillary's White House.

Then there was the Supreme Court. If the Democrats could take control of the Senate, Hillary Clinton could fast-track her nominee.

Much was at stake. Hillary's victory would be a historic milestone, but if she won big, even more could be done for the country. So the challenge now was not just winning, but rather winning big. The danger was that she was so far ahead, some people might stay home, thinking she had it in the bag.

Reporters were curious about what would happen to Clinton friends and enemies. What would Hillary Clinton do, for example, about James Comey? Could the FBI director be fired? Journalists ran stories saying yes. In fact, Bill Clinton had fired FBI Director William Sessions, who was caught up in an ethics crisis and had refused to resign.[14]

On November 3, 2016, five days before the election, Hillary was asked point-blank if she would call for James Comey's resignation after winning the presidency. "I'm not going to, you know . . . get ahead of myself by assuming I'll be fortunate enough to be elected," Clinton said in a Sirius XM interview. "That's really up to you and your listeners. People have to turn out or nothing I'm going to be proposing will come into reality. But I also would never comment on any kind of, you know, personnel issue."[15]

James Comey would have to wait to find out.

WHAT TO DO ABOUT BILL CLINTON?

What role would Bill Clinton play in Hillary's White House? Reporters were full of questions and had been discussing this among themselves. They had raised the issue on the campaign plane during the summer, and Hillary had said that she had been thinking it through. She had jokingly said that she might call him "First Dude" or "First Laddie."[16]

Later on, as the election neared and her lead widened, the talk became more serious. "I think part of what we'll have to figure out is what do you call the male spouse of a female president?" she asked. "Now, it's a little bit more complicated with him because people still call former presidents 'Mr. President.' So I have to really work on this."

Then, only days before the election, Hillary seemed to have decided, "I've already told my husband that if I'm so fortunate enough to be president," she said to an audience on the campaign trail, "and he will be the first gentleman, I expect him to go to work to make sure we get those jobs growing and incomes rising."[17] This raised more questions. Would Bill Clinton sit in on cabinet meetings? First Lady Rosalynn Carter had done so.

There was no precedent for a first gentleman. What laws would bind him? What ethical limits would restrain him? First ladies gave speeches and accepted donations to favorite charities in return. Would that apply to Bill Clinton? Would he be able to continue his lucrative speaking career? He said that he wanted to do so, although he also promised he would be very careful to avoid any conflict of interest. But the Clintons had made similar promises to the Obama White House when Hillary had become secretary of state.

Would he speak for a company that donated heavily to his Presidential Library or to the Clinton Foundation? Could he write a book? Other first ladies had done so, why not him? And how much of a cash advance could a friendly publishing company, owned by a friendly Wall Street conglomerate, wanting and needing government contracts, legitimately offer him?

Journalists on the Clinton plane were much too well behaved, too loyal to Hillary and the sisterhood, to ask such questions, and they couldn't trust a colleague to get the information, lest they be betrayed and lose favor, but their editors and their producers sometimes asked such questions. And it was all imminent now anyway, Hillary was going to be president and they would all learn about those things with the public.

During the last days of the *Late Show with David Letterman*, in the summer of 2015, Bill Clinton had been invited on to talk about Hillary Clinton's campaign. Letterman wanted to know what the odds would be of him moving back into the White House. Clinton was careful to answer. "If [Hillary] wins the election," Clinton had said, "the chances are 100% I'll move back." Clinton then added, "If I'm asked."[18] It may have been tongue in cheek, but on another level it was revealing.

There were many awkward questions about the Clintons' personal life. There was the Letterman question of geography. Where would Bill Clinton live? Would he live in the White House? Which room? First Lady Eleanor Roosevelt, who was often estranged from her husband, had had her own rooms. Her close friend and sometime companion Lorena Hickok had her own room in the White

House living quarters as well. Would any of Bill's friends be allowed sleepovers? Would he meet friends and business associates at the White House?

Even given a media sympathetic to the Clintons, and the assurances that relationships would be kept private, what problems would such an arrangement pose for national security? How would the intelligence community be able to parse the needs of the nation with the necessity of their own political survival with Hillary Clinton as their boss? This was a woman whose own Secret Service agent in the 1990s referred to her as the "first bitch" behind her back.[19]

Would Bill Clinton be able to take a prospective donor to dinner at the White House Mess, for example? Or let him or her catch a ride with him back to Washington or New York on Air Force One?

Would he have an entire suite of offices in the East Wing, just as a first lady would? Or would he be tucked away in the Old Executive Office Building? If he lived separately from his wife, it would confirm what critics had long maintained, that theirs was a marriage of convenience. But if he ran his business from the White House, when would it cease to be his business and become blatant corruption of power?

There was some indication that Chelsea Clinton, the daughter, would assume the more traditional role of first lady.[20] This was not a wholly unreasonable idea. Many daughters and daughters-in-law had assumed such a role for a president, especially in the early years of American history. But this too created its own set of questions. Where would her "first man" live? He was a banker for Goldman Sachs; would he operate out of the White House as well, or take a leave of absence from the bank that runs America? Friends of Chelsea insisted that she and her husband would live in a place of their own and not in the White House.

Finally, Bill Clinton was seventy years old. And while he had the best of medical care, it was possible that he might die during eight years of Hillary Clinton in office. If so, it would be a massive funeral, a truly unique moment in world history. But what if the reverse happened? Many questions were raised about Hillary's 2012 fall, concussion, and hospitalization. What if she should become incapacitated? It happened to Woodrow Wilson, and his new wife, the first lady, became his doorkeeper and nurse. When critics complained that she was running the country, she protested that she was doing no such thing, she was only determining whom he would see and what he would read and sign. What would the vice president's staff do if Bill Clinton moved to become the doorkeeper to an incapacitated Hillary Clinton?

It was a credit to the Clinton camp that it had delayed such questions until this moment, with victory upon them. These were not questions that were helpful. They reminded the electorate of how messy and complicated things were. Better to keep it simple.

There had been a general feeling, for many years, that Bill Clinton would do well to disappear. For Hillary's sake.

Poll after poll showed that the principal characteristic the American people wanted in a president was leadership. Sometimes that would change, but not often and not for long. For example, after the Reagan recession in 1982 the electorate insisted it wanted someone who could handle the economy, as it did again in 1992. After the Clinton-Lewinsky scandals, the public's focus shifted to the character of the candidate. But always near the top and usually the sole deciding factor in a voter's choice was that a candidate demonstrated that he or she had leadership qualities.

This was clearly the central question in deciding the 2004 presidential contest between President George W. Bush and Massachusetts senator John Kerry. It came down to who was the best leader. The candidates evenly exchanged points on almost every other characteristic, but when Gallup asked which candidate "is a strong and decisive leader," George W. Bush soared off the charts. It appeared that this was the point of delineation.[21]

One of Michael Deaver's right-hand men once told me that projecting a sense of leadership was the sole driving force behind Ronald Reagan's political success. There was not even a close second. In my own personal interviews with President Reagan, he often spoke of leadership in the lives of his heroes, including Douglas MacArthur, George Patton, and others.

And there's more. It was not just leadership, but a particular kind of leadership that was apparently the attraction. One could call it the second law of political leadership. Namely, leadership can't be shared. It must be borne alone.

A leader who stands in the shadow of his or her mentor is not a leader at all. He has to cast his own shadow. And so, all throughout American history, presidents have had to break with their predecessors, no matter how popular they once were.

Benjamin Harrison was elected president in 1888. He had been the grandson of President William Henry Harrison, but he spent his whole life trying to distance himself, to establish his own credibility and reputation. He knew that the American people would not elect him because of his grandfather. "I want to avoid anything that is personal," he wrote to his staff. "And I want it understood I am grandson of nobody."[22]

Meanwhile, Benjamin Harrison appointed Robert Todd Lincoln, the son of Abraham Lincoln, as the ambassador to the Court of Saint James. It was an inspired choice, and Lincoln, who had already served as secretary of war under James Garfield, was soon being touted as a future president himself.

The media and many in the rival Democratic Party were scandalized. Joseph Pulitzer himself led the outrage. His paper, the *New*

York World, wrote that "rotten Republicanism has learned to revere things that savor of monarchy and aristocracy. It would transmit the Presidency as their fathers' successors to crowns."[23]

The message was clear. Leadership was not passed on. It had to be earned by one's own sweat and guile. To do otherwise was immoral, anti-American, and invoked the specter of a class system.

In modern times, separation from a mentor or previous president was almost a rite of passage. President Dwight David Eisenhower, a war hero and a beloved leader, was one of the most popular figures in America. But in 1960, his vice president, Richard Nixon, had to break away to prove his own abilities. The process became almost painful to watch. When Eisenhower was asked in a news conference to name one major idea he had picked up from his vice president, Ike said, "If you give me a week I might think of one. I don't remember."[24]

Only days before the 1960 presidential election, Nixon broke with Eisenhower on the issue of rural electrification, promising to maintain the subsidized 2 percent loan rate and abandoning Ike's plan to return the process to the free market.[25]

George H. W. Bush was vice president to one of the most popular and greatest leaders in American history, Ronald Reagan, but he had to make a clear break to be his own man.

When Vice President Al Gore announced his candidacy for president in 1999, he made a very clear statement of separation from Bill Clinton, the president he had served. Gore said that Clinton had not only lied to the nation, he had personally, privately, lied to him. "What he did was inexcusable," Gore said in a television interview, referring to the Monica Lewinsky scandal, "and particularly as a father, I think it was terribly wrong."[26]

In the year 2000, George W. Bush had to make a clear break from his father. My conversations and memos to him, beginning in

1997, were carefully hidden because I had been on his father's White House staff. Privately, the two men talked right up to the son's election, but publicly, Governor Bush wanted no connection to his dad. When the father, George H. W. Bush, was brought in to campaign in New Hampshire and sentimentally referred to "this boy of mine, this George," the campaign team never called on him again.

So it was: successful presidents stood on their own two feet. They could not be seen as someone's son or the next man in, like a replacement for an injured football lineman.

President Hillary Clinton had to stand alone. And that meant Bill Clinton had to disappear from the stage. And that had happened. Hillary Clinton knew this great historical argument well. As did her husband. Indeed, in 1993 she was on the receiving end when her husband became president, and it was publicly proclaimed that she would solve the nation's health care crisis. Senators and policy makers, even some Democrats, objected. Who had elected her? Well, it was explained, Bill and Hillary are a team. You get two for the price of one. But the nation wouldn't have it, and Bill Clinton was forced to end any idea of a copresidency with his wife. Hillary was consigned to the more traditional role of first lady.

Now the nation's new chief executive, its leader, would be Hillary Clinton, and hers could not be seen as a second Bill Clinton presidency. She needed to be seen running the nation and reaching out to unite the people.

Alone.

That great transference of power and intellect, from Bill to Hillary, had been achieved, and it was one of the great unrecognized political successes of the Clintons. It was something that they could not brag about openly without diminishing themselves. But they could take private pride in what had happened. It had looked easy, like a Willie Mays' circus catch in center field. But it was not easily done. And it had taken both of them to make it work. Now, with victory upon them, Bill Clinton was needed again. He was let out of the closet to help finish this political race and secure the White House.

EXPANDING THE BASE

While polls showed the coming success, the Clintons and the Democrats faced a problem in the remaining days and weeks of the 2016 presidential campaign. On November 1, 2016, only a week before the vote, several large insurance companies were dropping out of the Affordable Care Act exchanges, with the result that premiums on policies would jump.

President Barack Obama did not want to see his signature achievement, ObamaCare, crash and burn. His legacy depended on the election of Hillary Clinton. Obama called Hillary to suggest that she talk about how the program needed to be fixed. It was sure to come up in the next debate, and she should not hold back out of a sense of loyalty to him; she should go right to it. Obama not only understood the political necessity, he also agreed that there needed to be some adjustments in the program.

Within the Clinton campaign, Bill Clinton seemed to be the perfect messenger. The former president had been chaffing on the sidelines, he had been in the deep freeze long enough. He was eager to get back into the game.

In fact, Bill Clinton had been a source of irritation to the campaign at times. He regularly called his wife's campaign manager, Robby Mook, to talk strategy. He regaled Mook with reminders of how he, Bill Clinton, had won so many political races by moving to the middle. He replayed how Hillary had finished so strong in her

run for the Senate from New York, by moving to the middle. It was
no big secret. There were votes they were leaving on the table. Votes
that were easy to pick up.

Hillary had the African American vote. She had the Hispanic
vote. The effort they were putting in to drive up those numbers to
perfection was extravagant. It isn't clear at what point Bill Clinton
heard about the last-minute decision by Donna Brazile to siphon
millions of dollars from the campaign to dump into voter turnout in
California and Louisiana. If so, he would have been dumbfounded.
Yes, it was important to win the popular vote, but not at the expense
of losing the presidency.

The point he made to Mook was that the campaign couldn't
completely duplicate the Barack Obama vote. Hillary Clinton was
not Barack Obama. She had different strengths and weaknesses
with the electorate, and she had to play to her own strengths, not
just Obama's.

Bill Clinton argued that they were forgetting the white union
voters in Wisconsin, Michigan, Ohio, and Pennsylvania. Yes, Wisconsin. They were making no appeal to Catholics, nothing to evangelicals. And then there was the "Bubba" vote. Call it racism if you
want, but the fact was that there were too many boxes left unchecked.
White, broke, former union workers, so-called Reagan Democrats.
There were voters out there who were not even being asked for their
vote.

To keep him happy and let him do his thing, Bill Clinton was
dispatched in the first week of October to all the so-called Rust Belt
states. And then he was briefed on the ObamaCare mission and
given the task to make the calibrated changes. This would be a delicate dance, it had to be done right, but he knew he was operating
with the knowledge and blessing of both Hillary and Barack Obama.

On October 5, 2016, in Flint, Michigan, Bill Clinton was speaking at a campaign rally when he was asked to comment on the Affordable Care Act.

"So you've got this crazy system," said Clinton to the crowd, "where all of a sudden 25 million more people have health care and then the people who are out there busting it, sometimes 60 hours a week, wind up with their premiums doubled and their coverage cut in half. It's the craziest thing in the world."[27] He was calling ObamaCare crazy.

Bill Clinton was not only moving to the middle, he was doing even better—he was expanding the base. Barbara Bush had been prochoice while her husband was prolife. That's what first ladies did, they expanded the political base, and who could complain about what the wife said? A presidential husband could not be faulted for defending his wife. That was loyalty. So this was the gender reversal of the same thing. Clinton, as first gentleman, was expanding the base, picking up voters that Hillary couldn't touch. Reassuring those white, so-called Reagan Democrats that he felt their pain and if they elected Hillary, well, he would be around to advocate for them. So here he was, offering the antidote to the coming raise in health care premiums, calling the whole thing crazy.

The national media was shocked by Bill Clinton's choice of words. Barack Obama was amused. "You never know what that guy is going to say," he laughed.[28] Clinton had pulled a Trump. He chose words that guaranteed a story that might have otherwise been missed. "It's the craziest thing in the world," Clinton had said.

Donald Trump pounced, saying that he bet Clinton "went through hell last night" with his wife.[29] John Podesta, the Clinton campaign chairman, told Jeff Zeleny of CNN that "[he] would have chosen different words for that."[30]

Bill Clinton was in eastern Ohio the next day as part of his continuing Rust Belt tour that he felt was so important. He was contrite, backstepping from the language he had used while saving face by insisting he was right, saying, "There are still problems with it."[31]

THE CELEBRITY CRUSADE

With the election now only days away, the Clinton campaign decided to not hold anything back. To throw out all the stops. Use everything it had. That meant both presidents, Bill Clinton and Barack Obama. And both first ladies too. There was a long list of Hollywood and Nashville celebrities ready to go. And they were all turned loose to do their thing.

Hollywood had been especially helpful. In September, the old cast of the NBC television show *Will & Grace* had reunited to attack Donald Trump, who was called a "dick" in the special video.[32] NBC was apparently so impressed that it went into discussion to bring the show back.

October 24, 2016, Miley Cyrus, an American singer and actress, was sent by the Clinton campaign to George Mason University in Virginia. In an Instagram post to her fans, the star posted a contorted picture of her abundant rear end. She was bent over with her face between her legs. The caption read, "Good morning!!!! Kiss my ashtanga ass if you aren't voting for @hillaryClinton#imwithher."

October 29, with the race well in hand, the Clintons dispatched Lena Dunham, a fixture on the campaign, to help out in North Carolina. Lena, the creator of the HBO series *Girls*, had generated some controversy when she wrote about sexually abusing her younger sister during their years growing up together.[33] But Dunham was such a hopped-up Clinton fan, her very enthusiasm seemed to win converts.

On November 4, 2016, a gaggle of celebrities gathered to create a video urging America to get out and vote. Referring to Trump as "garbage" and comparing him to Hitler, they sang, "Jesus fucking Christ / Holy fucking shit / you've got to vote."[34]

"If this video motivates one person," the actress Rachel Bloom said, "especially in a swing state, to just get out there, then it will have been worth it. I just personally didn't want to say I did nothing. I wanted to say I tried."[35]

In Cleveland, Ohio, Hillary Clinton laughed and hugged Jay-Z and the blockbuster star Beyoncé. "I want my daughter to grow up seeing a woman lead our country and know that her possibilities are limitless," Beyoncé told the crowd.[36]

Jay-Z performed for the families and young people who came out to support Hillary. Continuously using the F-bomb and the N-word, which is considered disrespectful to African Americans, he rapped off his famous hits like "FuckWithMeYouKnowIGotIt." A crowd of thousands cheered.

"If you feelin' like a pimp n——, go brush your shoulders off," Jay Z rapped.[37] "Ladies is pimps too, go and brush your shoulders off. N—— is crazy baby, don't forget that boy told you. Get that dirt off your shoulders."[38]

On November 7, 2016, a Monmouth University poll had Hillary Clinton beating Donald Trump 50 to 44 percent. Fox News had her winning 48 to 44 percent. The *New York Times*/CBS News poll said it would be 47 to 43 percent.[39]

On the last day of campaigning, the Clintons flew across the country. Her personal aide, Huma Abedin, was now back in her good graces after the flap about Clinton emails found on her husband's computer.

In Philadelphia, Bruce Springsteen, who had previously called Donald Trump "a moron,"[40] described him as a man "whose vision is limited to little beyond himself." Said Springsteen, "Tomorrow those ideas and that campaign is going down."[41]

When Bill Clinton introduced First Lady Michelle Obama, he called her "the finest surrogate supporter any candidate for president ever had."[42]

"We deserve a leader who will ensure that our daughters are safe and respected," Michelle Obama said. "And that our sons understand that truly strong men are compassionate and kind."[43]

President Barack Obama was at the rally in Philadelphia, praising Hillary, "She will work, she will deliver, she won't just tweet."[44] It would be his last campaign speech as president.

In Philadelphia, the Hillary Clinton campaign picked up entertainer Jon Bon Jovi, who performed at the great rally in Pennsylvania, and then flew on with the campaign to North Carolina, where he was joined onstage by Lady Gaga. A teenage Ivanka Trump once hung a full-length poster of Jon Bon Jovi on the door of her bedroom closet. Bon Jovi read a letter from a Hillary Clinton supporter: "I'm a Republican. I'm a gun owner. I'm a Catholic. And I'm with her."[45]

Lady Gaga, wearing what some thought looked like a Nazi SS black shirt, complete with a red armband, told the audience, "I'm with her. So ladies and gentlemen. Put your voting shades on, practice your walk to the polls and go out and vote for Hillary Clinton. I think it's time to come to mama."[46] Her shirt, it was later revealed, had belonged to Michael Jackson.

The good news back on the campaign jet home was that Hillary Clinton was now predicted to win in all of the toss-up states with the exception of Ohio, and that state was neck and neck. She was up in Florida, North Carolina, Michigan, Wisconsin, Pennsylvania, and Nevada,[47] and she seemed to have an insurmountable lead in all of those states. It meant that she had a lock on the Electoral College.

Donald Trump now had no path to victory. Hillary Clinton was the next president of the United States. The exhausted staff popped open bottles of champagne.

At 3:30 a.m. on November 8, 2016, the Clinton campaign jet, a Boeing 737, *Stronger Together*, arrived home at Westchester County airport in White Plains, New York. Hundreds of volunteers waited anxiously behind a fence on the cold tarmac. When the jet pulled into a parking position before the crowd, a flag-draped stairway was driven out to the front door. Meanwhile, the back door dropped down and journalists and some of Clinton's exhausted team exited the plane and headed for the motorcade lined up to take them away.

And then the front door opened and the crowd cheered as senior staff emerged one by one and then gasped as Jon Bon Jovi descended the stairs. More delay. Then someone spotted Bill Clinton near the front door, his unmistakable crop of gray hair. And the cheers picked up again.

Above the noise of the crowd one could hear the voices of young girls, brought out in the middle of the night by their mothers to witness this moment. To catch a glimpse of the person who would be the first woman president. Their little voices screeching at a higher decibel than those of their mothers and sisters.

Then finally, after the long, cold delay, with crowds of photographers gathered at the bottom of the stairway poised to capture the moment, there was Hillary Rodham Clinton. She was wearing a red pantsuit. Bill Clinton was gripping her shoulders to help guide her to the railing, and then she walked down the jet stairway on her own, to the cheering crowd, her husband a step or two behind, where he would be walking for the next eight years.

For a few minutes, the Clintons waved to the crowd, and then, exhausted from a long day, disappeared into their cars and sped off into the night.

In the coming hours, all across the United States, the people would be voting. The happy crowd at the Westchester County airport began to disperse, happy that they had waited until almost four a.m., for that moment. It was frigid and it was late, but they took great comfort in knowing that they had all just seen, in person, the next president of the United States.

CHAPTER 20

LANDING THE PLANE

Every man takes the limits of his own
field of vision for the limits of the world.

—SCHOPENHAUER

There is an old aviation cliché that goes, no matter what else happens, keep flying the airplane.

Pilots have walked away from almost-impossible situations. They've been out of fuel, lost their engines, suffered torn fuselages, but they lived to walk away only because they kept flying the airplane, all the way down, looking for a place to land, avoiding the power lines and trees, finding the right pasture or highway where they could make their emergency landing. There was no guarantee of success, but if they panicked or gave up, they would be sure of death.

There was no question about who had given the campaign lift. That would be Donald Trump, a political novice, an outsider. He had defied all odds and all expectations and had taken his long-shot campaign into the stratosphere. Donald Trump had redefined modern politics.

For months, political pundits and professionals had laughed at his lack of a ground game, at his deficient fundraising, at his divisive and outlandish comments. This was a campaign and a candidate in serious need of discipline. But all was not what it had seemed.

Donald Trump had defied the normal rules of political aviation. He had used his public relations and branding skills to energize an enthusiastic base. His success was not random. It was calculated.

Trump knew how to get media attention. And he was proving the old adage that bad news could be just as helpful as good news. It was something that normally worked best in show business and entertainment, but because of the crowded GOP field it was working, at least this time, in politics as well.

While political opponents would outspend Trump by vast amounts, no one could compete with him for so-called earned media; that is, free coverage of his campaign in newspapers, on television, and on radio talk shows. Throughout the 2016 election cycle, Jeb Bush would outspend him eight to one in paid advertising during the GOP primary season. Hillary Clinton would outspend him three to one. In almost any other circumstance, those facts alone would end a political campaign. But in the competition for earned media, for free coverage, Trump would beat Bush by nine to one and Clinton by almost three to one during the general election campaign. According to one calculation, Donald Trump had earned close to $2 billion in free media coverage.[1] Trump was showing politicians how a good businessman could run a campaign.

There were many faces around Trump at the early stage, and one that must be mentioned was Roger Stone. The Trump Organization used Stone as a lobbyist for its casino business. And there was no doubt that he and Donald Trump had many early conversations about politics.

Stone was controversial, he was dark, he was alledgedly a master of dirty tricks. He once worked with Black, Manafort, Stone, and Atwater. It was for a brief time the most feared and powerful political consulting firm in the world. But Atwater was dead, Black had lost some of his shine, and Manafort was making money in Eastern Europe.

The problem was that Stone was up against the Clinton machine. It could call a television network and get the talent disciplined, maybe even fired. What could he do? Stone set out early to investigate Bill Clinton's women victims to see what he could find.

Six months before the launch of his campaign, Donald Trump brought in a veteran political consultant to help plan his presidential run. He was Corey Lewandowski, and for a time he would be the most important force in the Trump world outside of his own children. Lewandowski's motto was "Let Trump Be Trump."

It was exactly what was needed at the time. The billionaire businessman was defying all political logic in his public pronouncements, and Lewandowski, as campaign manager, was flexible enough to understand that something unprecedented was at work and it shouldn't be interrupted.

Lewandowski ran everything else, and Trump was turned loose to grab the headlines which, in a crowded field of seventeen candidates, almost assured he would be among the leaders. The exposure alone guaranteed it.

Trump came in second in Iowa and won the New Hampshire primary. Given the sequential power of these early victories, Lewandowski had helped pilot the plane a substantial part of the way to the Republican nomination.

Corey Lewandowski was reportedly not without his flaws. He was acerbic and could be volatile. In March 2016, at a press conference in Jupiter, Florida, a female reporter claimed she had been physically and forcefully manhandled by Lewandowski. The story got wide coverage, with Trump defending the honor of his campaign manager.

There were stories of shouting and misunderstanding inside the Trump team. It may have been part of the Lewandowski relationship with Trump. He may have admired Trump's spontaneity because he shared the same instincts. And Trump may have tolerated his campaign manager and even been impressed by his choleric outbursts because he had used them to advantage himself. They shared similar strengths and weaknesses.

But it was one thing to "let Trump be Trump." It was something altogether different to "let Lewandowski to be Lewandowski." After a closed-door meeting in Trump Tower between Donald Trump and his two sons, Donald Jr. and Eric, the decision was made to make a change.[2]

The new campaign manager was Paul Manafort. With Trump headed for the nomination and the national convention, it was widely accepted that Manafort was a good choice. It was likely that he had been brought to the attention of Trump by Roger Stone, Manafort's old partner, which led some journalists to conclude that Stone was still hanging around.

Trump's weakness had been a ground game. He had won delegates in primaries and caucuses and state conventions, but he had not actually recruited the men and women to serve as those delegates. In many cases, old Romney-recruited delegates were going to the national convention to represent states that Trump had won. Each state GOP delegation operated under different rules. Some of the delegates could be released to vote their conscience after the first ballot. Given the divided nature of the Republican Party, these people could wreak havoc in the Rules Committee and the Credentials Committee. Trump needed an experienced hand at running a convention.

Paul Manafort knew things about operating a convention that had taken many years to learn. He quickly shut down any potential problems. Only weeks before, experienced hands were proclaiming that it would be a contested nomination. Manafort ended such speculation almost immediately. But Manafort failed to have a system in place to vet Melania Trump's speech, a glaring mistake that may have been unfairly laid at his feet. He did not have a reputation for bringing the party together, which Trump needed next. Manafort had helped Senator Robert Dole win the presidential nomination and run his convention in 1996 but had failed to rally his competitors for a general-election victory. It, too, may have been an unfair criticism, but there were also other, more serious issues.

Paul Manafort, like many seasoned political consultants, suffered from success. He had worked too many political campaigns and some in Eastern Europe, where the rules were less confining. There were growing concerns that the Clinton machine was hot on his trail and negative stories about his political work in Eastern Europe would surface. There was a *Politico* story claiming that Manafort's name "appeared on a handwritten ledger in Ukraine for secret cash payments."[3]

The Trump family team moved quickly. Donald Jr., Eric, and, this time, Trump's son-in-law Jared Kushner called for a change. Kushner had been Manafort's promoter within the campaign, but there was now a feeling that the new campaign boss had not been entirely transparent about his past work.

What was clear was that Donald Trump the politician had all the same strengths of Donald Trump the businessman. He moved quickly to make changes, without sentimentality. Too much was at stake. Manafort had played his part. Now something different was needed.

In August 2016, approaching the last sprint to the finish line, the Trump campaign looked to two new, seasoned political hands to guide it the rest of the way. Kellyanne Conway, a feisty conservative political operative who had worked to promote Ted Cruz, and Steve Bannon, a conservative filmmaker and the high-energy genius behind *Breitbart News*.

Lively, brilliant, combative, Kellyanne Conway had an immediate, visible impact as Trump's new campaign manager. Conway had launched her own polling firm in 1995 and was a veteran of multiple political campaigns. With Steve and Kellyanne on board, Donald Trump's rhetoric took on a more effective political tone. There was more discipline. He began to use the teleprompter. He was even more apologetic about past mistakes and misstatements. If Bill Clinton was unable to convince Hillary and John Podesta to speak to white workers in Rust Belt states, Kellyanne Conway appeared to have more success at convincing Donald Trump to reach out to women, blacks, Hispanics, and the poor.

Was this the result of such advice reaching critical mass? She, being one more voice saying the same thing, lining up behind Manafort, the former Fox News boss Roger Ailes, and others, with Trump finally listening? Or had Kellyanne Conway been able to bring new logic to the reasons why Trump needed rhetorical tweaks to his tweets? Whatever the answer, it worked. Trump was on track.[4]

Conway immediately began to chip away at Hillary Clinton's massive lead among women voters. Hillary Clinton kept reminding women that she would be the first woman president, but she could not close the deal with many of them. Women would say, "You share my gender, that's really fascinating, that's kind of cool, but do you share my vision, do you share my values?"[5]

At the same time he announced Kellyanne Conway as campaign manager, Trump announced Steve Bannon as chief executive officer of the Trump presidential campaign. The American news media was flabbergasted. The Associated Press published a story with the headline "Trump Puts Flame-Throwing Outsider on the Inside."[6]

Tactically, Bannon helped keep the campaign from collapse after the *Access Hollywood* tape. He arranged a press conference just before the second debate in which suddenly, without warning, Bill Clinton's female accusers were produced. The media could not pivot away quickly enough and had to give the ladies some minimum coverage.[7]

Strategically, Steve Bannon made a career out of bashing the political elites who ran Washington and their moneymaking corporate allies in the Boston–New York–Washington corridor. Billions of dollars had been drained from middle-class America to the big banks and big companies under the last two presidents, George W. Bush and Barack Obama. Thousands had lost their jobs and the value of their homes.

The media labeled Breitbart and Bannon as "right wing," but it was not really easy to define the growing political movement he represented. Its following was much wider, involving libertarians and even liberal Democrats, angry at a corrupt insider establishment.

A Republican president, George W. Bush, had waged a war, paying for it off the books by big international banks, and driving the country into its greatest economic crisis since the Great Depression. And he had been followed by a Democratic president who had watched over the greatest transfer of wealth from the poor to the rich in American history, a process that had been carefully chronicled by liberal studies at the University of California, Berkeley.[8]

When the Tea Party emerged, Steve Bannon was right in the middle of it. "In the last 20 years," he told a meeting, "our financial elites and the political class have taken care of themselves and led our country to the brink of ruin."[9]

Bannon had helped feed this discontent into the Trump campaign, where it could quickly be heard and seen in the candidate's rhetoric. In the last weeks of the presidential election, Trump's call to "drain the swamp" targeted this sentiment and this sense of outrage. Pat Caddell, a Democratic pollster and former aide to President Carter, described Bannon as the intellectual forerunner of a movement, saying, "His ideology is that of the outsider and the insurgent."[10]

Of course, all throughout the campaign, the Trump family kept coming back, an army of angels, stepping in and out of personnel and policy issues, having a larger-than-life influence on unfolding events, keeping a watchful eye on who was loyal and who was not. Sniffing around to see who was lining their own pockets with hefty commissions and outside deals. There were parts of the political game that were eerily reminiscent of the business world. They could smell a rat even before they could see him.

In the final few months, Jared Kushner, the Trump son-in-law, stepped up and made a difference. Kushner, an orthodox Jew from a family of registered Democrats, believed that his father-in-law was sincere in his desire to help turn the country around and resented the unfair barbs and accusations that were being flung at him. He began seeking out the best return on investment for the campaign, and that involved tapping the wisdom of friends in Silicon Valley. "Some of the best digital marketers in the world."[11]

Jared Kushner began running tests. "We played Moneyball, asking ourselves which states will get the best ROI for the electoral vote," he said. "I asked, 'How can we get Trump's message to the consumer for the least amount of cost?'"[12]

Sitting in Trump Tower, eating McDonald's Filet-O-Fish sandwiches, Donald Trump and Kushner worked on how to put this information to work. Ultimately, they would use Twitter and Facebook to find likely Trump voters. The resulting data soon became the road map for the campaign. The numbers told them where to advertise and what ads to run. Anti-ObamaCare ads worked well for viewers of *NCIS* and immigration ads worked well for viewers of *The Walking Dead*.[13] It was a science.

Especially critical, the data told them where to have rallies. Where to have the candidate visit. And ultimately, what states were winnable and what communities in those states would be the most supportive.

THE REPUBLICAN PRINCE

Still, there was one nagging issue that had no solution. Donald Trump still had no ground game. Trump's message, his earned media, his money, and strategic voter targeting could not remedy this serious problem. This was how President Barack Obama had defeated Mitt Romney in 2012. Hillary Clinton had built on this model. And she had built substantially. It was the key to turning out the vote. People did not respond to emails and phone calls like they did to a human being. She was fielding an army of paid staffers that outnumbered Trump five to one and on top of that a volunteer militia of 960,000, most of whom were women, who the political pros knew from experience could outwork men at least two to one.

It was the most impressive ground game in all of American political history. She was far ahead, with no chance of the GOP catching up. Barring a plane crash, Hillary Clinton would not only win the 2016 election, she would likely outperform all the polls.

Trump by contrast had no ground game at all. It had been his Achilles's heel from the beginning. He didn't seem to understand its importance. He had defied gravity in a crowded field where the competition divided the vote. It turned out that he hadn't needed a ground game. The experts had been wrong. But there were limits to his luck. Most observers, including the national media and the Clinton campaign, knew that it would not work in a general election.

There was only one man inside the Trump campaign who fully

appreciated the danger and could do anything about it, and that was the chairman of the Republican National Committee, Reince Priebus. For many months, Priebus had been at the center of the storm. As chairman, he had to remain scrupulously neutral, with seventeen candidates vying for the nomination and some of them—Jeb Bush, for example—money-raising behemoths, representing political dynasties that were networked deep and wide throughout the party. Two of the Republican Party's living presidents were Bushes.

Priebus had cut his political chops in Wisconsin politics and was well connected to Paul Ryan, the House Speaker and congressman from Wisconsin, as well as Scott Walker, the governor of the state and one of the early front-runners for the nomination.

Reince had been pushed by all the candidates and almost all of the RNC's major donors to do something about Donald Trump. It was said that his language and his aberrant behavior was destroying the Republican brand and would cost the party the presidency, the House, the Senate, and the Supreme Court. It had reached a crisis point where some were no longer blaming Trump, they were blaming Priebus. Why wasn't he doing something to protect the Republican Party?

When it became clear that Donald Trump had actually won the Republican nomination, Reince Priebus quickly came on board. He insisted that donors and senior party leaders had to fall into line. Like it or not, the billionaire had won and he had won fair and square. The Republican Party was going to cooperate. Reince rejected pressure to focus on down-ballot races and let the nominee drift out on his own. He knew that the top of the ticket would drive the vote, and he had to stay with the nominee.

After the Republican National Convention, Priebus picked up an important ally, Trump's vice presidential pick, Governor Mike Pence of Indiana. Pence was a source of stability and an example to the GOP faithful that Trump had good instincts and made good personnel choices. Pence was a known quantity. And he insisted that he knew the nominee's heart and that all was good. Still, it was not going to be easy. State by state, leader by leader, Reince Priebus listened and nodded and cajoled, pulling the Republican leaders kicking and screaming back into the fold.

In August 2016, Priebus made a conscious strategic decision. He would build the ground game needed to win the general election. While all the pundits and pollsters said it was too late, that the party was going down to a historic defeat, he would direct the money and the effort as if the contest were winnable. He would keep flying the plane.

There were many critics. They recommended a comprehensive television advertising blitz. Priebus may have been tempted. Almost all the professionals recommended it. Ironically, they would go on the television talk shows to complain about his decision. At this late date, it was the quickest way to the voters' heads and hearts, they said. Advertising practically dictated what kind of toothpaste consumers bought, and, in the past, it had defined elections. In 1964, Lyndon Johnson's television ad depicting a little girl picking daises before a nuclear bomb detonated in the distance helped sink Republican senator Barry Goldwater's campaign. Goldwater was considered too risky to be president.

In 1988, a television ad showing prisoners, including murderers, being furloughed in and out of prison's revolving door reminded voters that Democratic presidential candidate Governor Michael Dukakis had made such a decision in Massachusetts and it had resulted in the torture and murder of a family.

What was unsaid was that professionals almost always recommended television and radio advertising because they earned a 15 percent commission on the time purchased. It was a lot of money.

And an RNC chairman, if he was smart, could expect some nice quid pro quo for throwing that business out to the right companies or persons.

And was there time to build an army on the ground? No one outside Trump Tower believed it would make a difference. They were too far behind. The election was lost.

In September 2016, in Florida, a must-win state for Donald Trump, the RNC had one field office. One. Clinton had fifty-one, and its staffers were well on their way to completing assignments that their Republican counterparts hadn't even begun.

But by Election Day 2016, Reince Priebus had built the largest field operation in Republican Party history. There were 315 field offices, with 7,600 paid employees. They had knocked on twenty-four million doors and had made twenty-six million phone calls. Florida had grown from that single field office to sixty-two, with 1,173 paid staff. Donald Trump would narrowly carry the state on Election Day.[14]

In October, when the famous *Access Hollywood* tape hit, some said that Donald Trump had a few very brief moments when he seriously questioned the advisability of resigning as the Republican nominee. Mike Pence would finish the campaign. There were too many important issues at stake. He owed it to all those people he had met at the rallies. They needed jobs, they needed a change. He voiced these feelings to some family members and people he loved, including Reince Priebus.

A source close to the campaign and Trump family members told this author that Reince Priebus weighed in heavily in this dark hour. Trump had to stay the course, Priebus insisted. There was no one else. A move to Mike Pence would signal collapse and leave the GOP hopelessly shattered. But Trump could still make it. He should not give up. Millions of Americans loved him for standing up to the Clinton machine. He, alone, had built this movement of followers.

They looked to him for leadership. But he was more than a leader, he was their friend. They had no one else. He could not walk away. He was irreplaceable. Reince Priebus, Mike Pence, the campaign staff, the family, they would all support him and help carry the load, but he had to get up off the mat and keep fighting, no matter how hopeless it seemed right now.

Reince Priebus remembered hearing about the closing weeks of the George McGovern campaign. The Democrats had marveled at the crowds who had begun to flood to his rallies in 1972. McGovern could not believe the polls that had him losing badly. The McGovern crowds generated a lot of energy. But McGovern had indeed lost, as the polls had said. The massive rallies, with their thousands of cheering supporters, had been a mirage. And so, Reince Priebus may have had his moments of self-doubt. If so, he never expressed them. As the most experienced voice in Trump Tower, he continued to speak victory. There was still time. Just barely. Clinton was a flawed candidate, representing a corrupt system. They were taping into something at those Trump rallies. They had to keep doing the right things and not throw in the towel.

On October 23, 2016, a *New York Times* headline read "Hillary Clinton Has the Biggest October Lead of Any Presidential Candidate Since 1984."[15] That year was the reelection of Ronald Reagan. She was doing as well as Reagan had done in his reelection landslide. He had carried every state in the union except Minnesota, his opponent's home state. And the battle over Minnesota had been close, running late into the night.

Reince Priebus was the calm in the middle of the storm. "It's okay." He was in the middle of building the massive ground game; there was no time to worry about what might happen when there were still so many things left undone. Everyone else was working too. They couldn't start worrying until they had finished their work.

THE WORLD AGAINST TRUMP

During the summer, with Clinton and Trump each appearing at their respective national conventions, public figures and entertainment celebrities began to pile on for Clinton. Some wanted to help the first woman president get elected. Others wanted to get their stories on the record so that the Clinton East Wing would add them to the annual White House Christmas party.

On May 16, 2016, *Entertainment Tonight* ran the headline, "Jennifer Lawrence and Angelina Jolie Really Hate Donald Trump." [16]

On July 7, Charlie Sheen was interviewed in *Extra* in a piece entitled "Charlie Sheen's Unfiltered New Attack on Donald Trump."[17]

"It is amazing," Sheen said, "to see how far he's gotten . . . [it's] baffling. What he's done is impossible . . . but it also speaks to people's desperate need or want for something different, but it doesn't need to be that different."[18]

The story explained that Sheen was now focusing on health, after recently revealing that he was HIV positive. He was now the spokesperson for a new condom line LELO HEX.[19]

On July 30, Chrissy Teigen tweeted about Trump, "I fucking hate him." [20]

Kristen Bell, the star of *Veronica Mars*, sent a personal tweet to Trump, "get ur head outta ur ass."[21]

Meanwhile, Mac Miller, the rapper who had topped the charts a few years back with his single "Donald Trump," stopped by *The Nightly Show with Larry Wilmore*. "I only have one thing to say," Mac said. "I fucking hate you, Donald Trump."[22]

In August, celebrities scattered all over the world spoke up. Robert De Niro was at a film festival in Sarajevo. "It's crazy," he said, "that people like Donald Trump . . . he shouldn't even be where he is, so God help us," he said. "What he's been saying is really totally crazy, ridiculous. . . . He is totally nuts."[23]

Promoting the movie *Suicide Squad* to an Australian news out-let, the actor Will Smith was upset with Trump's language. He said his grandmother would be outraged if he said such things. "For a man to be able to publicly refer to a woman as a fat pig, that makes me teary," he said. "And for people to applaud, that is absolutely fucking insanity to me."[24]

The entertainer Cher compared Trump to Joseph Stalin and Adolf Hitler.[25] She was such a hit with the crowd that the Clinton campaign used her as a surrogate speaker, sending her to a fund-raiser where she called Trump a "consummate liar" and an "insane and sociopathic narcissist."[26]

When Neil Young learned that Donald Trump liked his music, he demanded that the billionaire businessman stop using it and then produced a video in which he appeared onstage, shouting, "Fuck you, Donald Trump!"[27]

The indie rock band Wavves banned all proponents of "All Lives Matter," as well as all "Donald Trump supporters" from their shows.[28]

By July, even Donald Trump's celebrity friends were turning their backs on him. Khloé Kardashian told people, "I didn't care to do *Celebrity Apprentice*. My mom made me do it. . . . I hated every minute of it. I was put in situations I would never be in in real life . . . stressing myself out, and then dealing with [Trump] and about to be fired, I'm like, 'Fuck you. I don't want to do this.'"[29]

In September, Barbra Streisand launched a verbal attack on Trump from on stage and told her audience that she hoped in a few months she'd be singing for the next president Clinton.[30]

Comedian Chelsea Handler told the *Daily Beast* that a Trump win would be the end of civilization.[31]

J. K. Rowling, the author of the *Harry Potter* series, said that Trump was worse than Voldemort, the fictional villain she created in her *Harry Potter* books.[32]

Win Butler, a musician in the band Arcade Fire, bashed Trump in an October interview with Red Bull Music Academy. He called the businessman a "complete fucking nightmare and a clown and a joke," adding, "It really is an extremely important election. You don't have to hang out with Hillary. But, Jesus Christ, vote for Hillary Clinton. Everyone register because it could not be heavier. The consequences could not be more dire."[33]

The celebrity talking points all seemed to reflect the same refrain. Trump was hateful, they said. He used foul language. He was racist. But communicating that message with hateful, foul, racist language was more effective to audiences in California and New York City than to audiences in Iowa, Florida, Wisconsin, Michigan, Ohio, Pennsylvania, and North Carolina, where the election would be decided. It was not clear how the Clinton campaign expected the entertainers to move voters. It is doubtful that the celebrities had enough moral influence to shift any of the vast numbers of undecided Catholic or evangelical votes, for example, to Hillary Clinton. It is much more likely that those votes were being driven back into the Republican column by the well-intentioned, but politically challenged celebrities.

Even so, the celebrity full-court press was certainly driving up the numbers in California and New York. In those states, it seemed like the whole world hated Donald Trump because he was hateful. And they feared Donald Trump because he was appealing to the fears of voters. It was an oxymoronic argument that brought smiles to the faces of unemployed, union Democrat workers in Youngstown, Ohio.

Earlier in the year, actor Richard Gere had compared Trump to the Italian dictator Benito Mussolini. Gere then made the extraordinary claim that electing Trump as president would be a "slippery slope" to deporting Jews and black people.[34] Gere added, without any irony, that "intelligent people aren't seeing this."[35]

This was getting to Jared Kushner, the Jewish son-in-law of Donald Trump. His wife, the candidate's daughter, Ivanka Trump Kushner, was also Jewish. He would be deporting his daughter? Where did this nonsense come from? "You can't not be a racist for 69 years, then all of a sudden become a racist, right?" Kushner asked in bewilderment. "You can't not be an anti-Semite for 69 years and all of a sudden become an anti-Semite because you're running."[36]

On October 7, 2016, David Letterman gave a devastating rebuke to Trump in the *New York Times*.[37] "I kept telling people he will absolutely not get elected. And then David Brooks said he'll get the nomination and he will be crushed in the general election. And I thought: Yeah, that's exactly what's going to happen. I stand by that."[38]

Parallel to the celebrity crusade, a Clinton surrogate effort was taking place on other fronts as well as, academic, media, and political.

Stephen Hawking, touted as the smartest man in the world, called the Republican nominee a demagogue and said he "couldn't explain Donald Trump's political rise."[39] He could explain black holes but he could not explain Trump. The Harvard Republican Club announced it would not support Trump, who was a "threat to the survival of the Republic."[40]

The popular horror writer Stephen King said he was afraid of Trump.[41]

The Hillary Clinton campaign boasted that "there are five living U.S. presidents. None of them support Donald Trump."[42]

In an article in *Politico*, President Barack Obama characterized Trump's support as "paper thin." He mocked him for taking on the global elite "only after failing to be accepted as a member of the global elite himself."[43]

Obama then added, "He seems to be in the middle of the game making excuses all the time for why he might be losing." Obama observed with bemusement, "It's always interesting to me to see people who talk tough but don't act tough. Because if you're tough, you don't make excuses."[44]

The media was relentless. National Public Radio, paid for by taxpayers, was criticized by some for offering a steady drumbeat of pro–Hillary Clinton public-relations commentary. In one segment, Donald Trump was compared to the segregationist George Wallace.[45]

When Trump said that the elections might be rigged and he didn't know if he would accept the results, media personalities reacted with anger.

Renowned presidential historian Michael Bechloss said, "Fifty years from now historians will remember this debate for exactly one thing and that is Trump refusing to say that he'll accept the results of the election. I think it is radical. I think it is revolutionary."

And then he added with emphasis, "Absolutely horrifying."[46]

Nicolle Wallace of NBC, a former White House assistant in the Republican administration of George W. Bush, said that "by refusing to say that he would accept the results of the election on November 8th, he may as well have laid down in his own coffin with a hammer and nail and pounded it in himself." [47]

Jake Tapper of CNN called Trump's refusal "one of the most stunning things I've ever heard in a presidential debate, ever."[48]

Bob Schieffer of CBS said, "It's dangerous to be talking that way because it threatens and raises questions about the very foundations of what this nation is about."[49]

Meanwhile, simultaneously, the flow of WikiLeaks memos showing the corporate media coordination with the Hillary Clinton campaign was being ignored. Potential major stories sat idle. From the beginning, top mainstream media reporters had accepted invites to private dinners and meetings with John Podesta and other Clinton staffers, meetings at which campaign coverage was discussed.

It was learned that Donna Brazile, formerly featured on ABC, then CNN, later the Democratic National Committee chairperson, had leaked a town hall question to Hillary Clinton's staff in advance of the debate.[50] All the blame was heaped on Brazile. No one questioned why Clinton had accepted the gift and not objected.

Glen Thrush, *Politico*'s senior writer, sent an article to John Podesta for advance approval, adding the note, "Please don't share or tell anyone I did this. Tell me if I fucked up anything."[51]

John Podesta was allegedly receiving drafts of *New York Times* articles prior to publication. Memos revealed by WikiLeaks seemed to show coordination between the Clinton staff and release times of Associated Press articles. [52]

The list of media personnel and organizations synchronizing with the Clinton political machine went on and on, day after day, and was disheartening to any objective reader who took the time to read them. Journalists who were trusted and respected, whose intellect and on-camera charm were admired, were accused of selling themselves to power. "Please let me know if I can be of any service to you," wrote a *Huffington Post* contributor, Frank Islam, to John Podesta.[53] Journalism had died long ago. But now some believed that the very pretense of journalism was disappearing before our eyes. The immediate impact was the evisceration of the Donald Trump presidential campaign.

Intoxicated with its power and apparently with plenty of time to spare, the Clinton campaign began to muscle even some of its own cast of on-air supporting journalists. The slightest misstep could end a career. Matt Lauer of NBC, listed as a past member of the Clinton Global Initiative, was vilified for asking too many of the wrong questions of Hillary Clinton in a televised commander-in-chief forum.[54] When liberal Democratic anchor Mika Brzezinski of MSNBC offered an on-air critique, the Clinton campaign called NBC and tried to have her taken of the air.[55]

As Election Day neared, even the bravest Republicans now started hedging their bets.

Former California governor Arnold Schwarzenegger, the man who would take over the Donald Trump role in *The Apprentice*, issued a statement stating that "as proud as I am to label myself a Republican, there is one label I hold above all else—American. So I want to take a moment today to remind my fellow Republicans that it is not only acceptable to choose your country over your party—it is your duty."

The *Daily Beast* claimed that Brent Scowcroft, a foreign policy adviser to four Republican presidents, was supporting Clinton. Henry Paulson Jr., the former treasury secretary for George W. Bush, announced he was joining the "Never Trump" movement.[56]

On October 23, 2016, Republican strategist Karl Rove declared flatly that "Trump can't win."[57] Appearing on the *Fox News Sunday*, Rove said, "I don't see it happening. If he plays an inside straight, he could get it, but I doubt he's going to be able to play it."[58]

Rove said that Trump was leading comfortably in states to receive 168 electoral votes. He would need 270. Rove gave him a very slight lead in Ohio but said he was behind in North Carolina and Arizona, states that Romney won. Clinton's lead in Florida was considered severe.

On October 28, in yet another blow to the Trump campaign, Julian Assange, the editor in chief of WikiLeaks, made a final prediction: Hillary Clinton would win the American presidency after all. "I don't think there's any chance of Donald Trump winning the election, even with the amazing material we are publishing." Then, drawing on his own source material, he explained why "Because most of the media organizations are strongly aligned with Hillary Clinton."[59]

Assange contended that the media had united behind the Clinton machine and its narrative that the Democratic emails had been hacked by the Russians and therefore should be ignored. "This is not the interference of electoral process," Assange argued. "This is the definition of electoral process—for media organizations and, in fact, everyone to publish the truth and their opinion about what is occurring. It cannot be a free and informed election unless people are free to inform."[60] But Assange was assuming that the American media was driven by a desire for information. That ship had sailed long ago.

On November 2, 2016, Rob Garver wrote what appeared to be a definitive postmortem on the Donald Trump campaign: "If This Poll Is Right, Trump Can't Win Florida—Or the Election."[61] Garver analyzed a Florida poll conducted by the College of William and Mary and TargetSmart, a popular Democratic polling company.

The report estimated that 3.6 million people had already voted in Florida, which represented a hefty portion of the 8.4 million votes that would eventually be cast. The numbers showed that Hillary Clinton was leading Donald Trump 55 to 38 percent. But even worse, they showed that Trump was experiencing substantial defections from the registered Republican ranks. Twenty-seven percent of early GOP voters were casting their ballots for Hillary Clinton.[62]

CHAPTER 21

I ALMOST NEVER LOSE

*The higher we soar, the smaller we
appear to those who cannot fly.*
—FRIEDRICH NIETZSCHE

Shortly after Donald Trump announced his presidential campaign, he talked to reporters about how relentlessly he would be pursuing his goal. He complained about Mitt Romney's last days on the campaign trail in 2012. "It was no different than a golfer who missed a putt on the 18th hole," he told them. "Something happened to him. And that's not going to happen to me."[1]

Trapped by his own words, Donald Trump had to finish his 2016 campaign strong. People tended to forget that he was a seventy-year-old man, older than Reagan had been when he ran for president. So no matter what the odds, no matter how heartbreaking the end would be, he had to run full blast. He had to lead the Republican race across the finish line. Everyone on his team was all go. He could not control what happened, but he could control what he did.

In the last two months of the campaign, Donald Trump made 106 campaign appearances. Hillary Clinton made 71.[2]

According to *USA Today*, it all came down to Florida. Clinton could win without it, but Trump could not. Hillary Clinton simply had to keep Florida in her column, as it was now, and it would all be over.

The same newspaper had polls showing Clinton winning the

eighteen states and the District of Columbia that had all gone blue, or Democratic, since 1992. That gave her 242 electoral votes, only twenty-eight shy of what she needed.

"If we win Florida, we will win this election," President Obama told a cheering crowd in Miami.[3]

"The Republican path to the White House is always narrow, at least in the modern era," said Larry Sabato, a professor at the University of Virginia. The professor was also saying that Trump had to win Florida.

"If Trump wins Pennsylvania, Ohio, Michigan and Wisconsin, in addition to all the states GOP nominee Mitt Romney won in 2012, he wouldn't need Florida," Sabato clarified. He then he added, "But tell me how he's going to do that?"[4]

On the Sunday afternoon before the Tuesday election, the FBI closed its investigation of Hillary Clinton. She was finally cleared. Again.

In the final hours, *Time* magazine described "a difficult climb for Trump. . . . If Clinton wins Florida or Ohio, Trump's campaign is almost certainly over."[5]

Appearing on Fox News the day before the election, Reince Priebus admitted that the Electoral College was stacked against them. "We've got to be good. Donald Trump has always said that on the map, they start with an advantage, but if you look at what's happening around the country and you look at how this thing is closing, you want to be the candidate who has a little bit of wind at their back and right now, Donald Trump's got some wind at his back. That's where you want to be."[6]

Just to be sure, Donald Trump went back to Pensacola, Florida. No, no, it's good, he was told. You've got it. That's one city you will win. "Well, just as a show of gratitude," he said. And in Pensacola, he told his supporters, "In six days, we are going to win the state of Florida and we are going to win the White House."[7]

On Monday morning, in Sarasota, Florida, Trump spotted a mask of himself in the crowd and held it up, for a side-by-side comparison. "Look at this mask. Look at this mask. Oh wow, wow that's beautiful. Look at that. Looks just like me!" he exclaimed. "Nice head of hair, I'll say that."[8]

And then he shouted, "Election Day will be Brexit plus, plus, plus."[9] "Brexit" referred to the surprise vote of the British people to leave the European Union. The pollsters had not seen it coming. The establishment bankers, corporations, and politicians of the United Kingdom had been aghast. The people had risen up in their wrath and overthrown the established insiders.

"I think we've beaten them," Reince Priebus said.[10]

"I'm asking you to dream big," Donald Trump told an audience in Scranton, Pennsylvania, late the night before the election. "It will be the greatest vote you ever cast in your lifetimes. We're going to have a great victory tomorrow, folks. They have no idea."[11]

MELANIA'S WARNING

There were some, a very few, who had long ago decided that Donald Trump would win.

There was Michael Moore, on the left, the provocative, iconoclastic filmmaker who was too honest for his own good. "Not a team player," the Clinton folks might have said, which he would have pinned on his lapel as a compliment. He wanted Hillary Clinton to win but was not fooled by the echo chamber of the New York media, Hollywood celebrities, and inside-the-beltway intellectual consonance. He, especially, understood how people felt and thought around his hometown of Flint, Michigan. Like Donald Trump buying a property, he had walked the neighborhoods of the Rust Belt, on the ground, and seen things that the proud pollsters, on their cell phones in the Acela corridor or in Silicon Valley, had missed.

Then there was Ann Coulter, the conservative scribe and provocateur of the left. She had predicted a Trump presidency only three days after the billionaire had announced he was running. She had made an appearance on the HBO show *Real Time with Bill Maher* on June 19, 2015. Bill Maher had asked Coulter which candidate had the best chance of winning the presidency.

"Of the declared ones? Right now?" Coulter had asked. And then she answered the question: "Donald Trump."[12]

The audience howled with laughter. The other guests on the show were almost gleeful to see the author and the sharp tongued television pundit willingly self-immolate before millions of viewers. If anyone deserved the humiliating, scornful moment in the stocks, they seemed to be saying, it was Ann Coulter.

When the laughter didn't stop, the director in the control booth ordered the camera back to Ann Coulter, the lens focused, watching, waiting, looking for the trembling bottom lip, the blinking eyes. Ann Coulter held firm, shaky, but firm, a kindly smile frozen on her face, as wave after wave of laughter washed over her.

Donald Trump? Elected president?

But the first true believer, the first one to really declare that he would win, was one of the first to know what he was planning to do. On April 2, 2016, there had been a very revealing Donald Trump interview with the journalists Bob Woodward and Robert Costa. It was held at the Trump International Hotel in Washington, DC.[13] Corey Lewandowski, Donald Trump Jr., and Hope Hicks, a media aide, were there. Woodward and Costa were trying to nail down the exact moment that Trump had decided to run for president, and that was proving difficult. It was obviously a decision that had come from somewhere very deep and subconscious. Trump himself probably didn't know.

"I'm the Lone Ranger," Trump had finally said, giving up. And then he started talking about his wife, Melania, and a conversation that had taken place a year before he had announced his candidacy. "I think my wife would much have preferred that I didn't do it. She's a very private person." He then said flatly that Melania had told him, "I hope you don't do it."

Melania had said, "We have such a great life, why do you want to do this?"[14]

He had answered her gently, but the conversation had unfolded very much like the one that had taken place with his father, Fred Trump, many years before, when Fred had tried to stop him from building in Manhattan. "Don't go into Manhattan. That's the big leagues. We don't know anything about that. Don't do it," Fred had told him. He had wanted him to stay in Queens and Brooklyn. They had a good life there. They knew the rules and they knew the players. It was dangerous in Manhattan.

But Donald Trump could not be dissuaded. "Dad, I gotta go into Manhattan. I gotta build those big buildings. I gotta do it, Dad, I gotta do it."[15]

It was something quite similar to what he told his wife, Melania, about the run for president. "I sort of have to do it, I think," he told her. "I really have to do it. Because it's something I'd be—I could do such a great job." And then he spoke in the past tense, as if Melania had taken it away. "I really wanted to give something back . . . I really wanted to give something back."[16]

Melania Trump, perhaps understanding him better than his own father did, gave him a different reply. "If you want to do it," she said emphatically, "then you should do it."

But then she added this prophetic warning. "I hope you don't do it, but if you run," she told him, "you'll win."[17]

On November 8, 2016, Donald and Melania Trump, with Trump's daughter Ivanka, son-in-law Jared Kushner, and one of the grandchildren, traveled by Secret Service escort to their polling place at Public School 59 in Midtown Manhattan.

Hours earlier, two women had ripped off their shirts and paraded around bare breasted in protest. They had anti-Trump slogans painted across their bodies. Photos online showed the word "hate" written on one and "balls" written on the other, along with other slogans that were not legible.[18]

According to a news report, Donald and Melania Trump were greeted by a crowd of booing Clinton supporters, and a group that shouted, "New York hates you."[19]

Melania, stately and elegant, in a long beige cloth coat and sunglasses, had walked toward the door of the school and waited a moment, until Donald emerged and caught up with her. He stopped to purchase a cupcake from a young boy.

After they voted, a reporter shouted over the crowd inside the school, "So, who did you vote for?"

"Tough decision!" Trump deadpanned to laughter.

And then, with Trump smiling and waving at the crowd as if they were his friends, he and his family disappeared into a motorcade of black cars and sped off for Trump Tower. The crowd booed after him, but it didn't matter. He was gone and couldn't hear them. Besides, prophets never had honor in their own towns. And New York would not decide this election. Voters in Pensacola and Kenosha and Saginaw and Toledo and Scranton would be making that decision. And they would not likely be steamrolled by the drumbeat of Hollywood, and bare-breasted New York women and hyperventilating, self-important news anchors who imagined that their misrepresentations were passing unnoticed over the heads of unemployed Rust Belt workers like the jets they flew from coast to coast.

In the dark, early-morning hours of Wednesday, November 9, 2016, the day after the voting had been completed across America, Donald Trump was declared the president elect of the United States. Professor Larry Sabato had said that the only way he could win without Florida would be to win Wisconsin, Michigan, Ohio, and Pennsylvania. "But tell me how he's going to do that?"[20]

It had happened. He had done just that. He had won them all, and Florida too. Donald Trump had won 306 electoral votes to 232 for Hillary Clinton. The celebrity-powered social campaign and the slavish corporate media had worked to drive up the vote for Hillary Clinton in California and New York. As a result, she had won the popular vote, 48.2 to 46.1 percent. But it was small consolation to the opinion makers, who had seen the voters scamper away from them like unruly children.

They had been wrong. Almost all of them had been wrong. Entertainers betting on winning the Presidential Medal of Freedom in the East Room. Pundits and journalists who had sacrificed their independence and integrity for a little power. Major corporations and banks that had found ways to give millions to the Clintons over the years, with the Clintons telegraphing back that they would find a way to pay their debts. The Lannisters always pay their debts.

"I hope you don't do it," Melania Trump had told him two years earlier, "but if you run, you'll win."[21]

He had won. Donald Trump had been elected president of the United States. And he had warned anyone who would listen. "I don't lose often," he told them. "I almost never lose."[22]

ENDNOTES

INTRODUCTION

1 http://theweek.com/speedreads/659039/megyn-kelly-asks-karl-rove-larry-sabato-about-that-poll-showing-donald-trump-ahead.

2 Ibid.

3 http://www.richmond.com/news/virginia/article_c9fa6ec8-d1b8-51e9-b5f5-8b8994531068.html

4 http://www.businessinsider.com/hillary-clinton-endorsements-newspaper-editorial-board-president-2016-2016-9/#akron-beacon-journal-hillary-clinton-is-the-change--she-knows-her-way-around-the-partisan-battles-the-country-doesnt-need-a-revolution-it-isnt-a-wreck-it-requires-the-right-brand-of-change-15

5 http://fortune.com/2016/12/09/hillary-clinton-donald-trump-campaign-spending/

6 http://thehill.com/blogs/ballot-box/presidential-races/299779-dems-outnumber-gop-in-paid-staff-5-1

7 http://www.thedailybeast.com/articles/2016/11/14/seven-reasons-why-hillary-clinton-lost-and-donald-trump-won.html.

8 http://www.newyorker.com/news/benjamin-wallace-wells/hillary-clintons-powerful-concession

9 http://www.nytimes.com/2016/11/13/us/politics/hillary-clinton-james-comey.html

10 http://www.cnn.com/2016/11/09/politics/hillary-clinton-concession-speech/

11 Ibid.

12 https://www.brainyquote.com/quotes/quotes/j/johnfkenn130001.html

CHAPTER 1: THE LOST VOTERS OF ELECTIONS PAST

1 http://www.washingtontimes.com/news/2016/oct/21/cardinal-timothy-dolan-shares-touching-moment-betw/

2 Ibid.

3 http://www.reuters.com/article/us-usa-election-poll-electoral-idUSKCN12M0JR

4 http://www.washingtontimes.com/news/2016/oct/28/james-comey-fbi-director-reopens-clinton-email-inv/

5 https://www.youtube.com/watch?v=45djGBWdgIw

6 http://www.cnn.com/2016/10/28/politics/fbi-reviewing-new-emails-in-clinton-probe-director-tells-senate-judiciary-committee/

7 https://www.youtube.com/watch?v=hHSS824pHbU

8 http://www.nytimes.com/2016/10/29/us/politics/fbi-hillary-clinton-email.html

9 http://pagesix.com/2015/07/08/if-hilary-makes-it-to-the-white-house-so-will-huma-abedin/

10 http://www.cnn.com/2016/10/28/politics/fbi-reviewing-new-emails-in-clinton-probe-director-tells-senate-judiciary-committee/

11 http://www.politico.com/story/2016/06/bill-clinton-loretta-lynch-224972

12 http://www.cnn.com/2016/10/28/politics/fbi-reviewing-new-emails-in-clinton-probe-director-tells-senate-judiciary-committee/

13 https://www.youtube.com/watch?v=hHSS824pHbU

14 http://www.wsj.com/articles/clinton-ally-aids-campaign-of-fbi-officials-wife-1477266114

15 https://www.washingtonpost.com/world/national-security/hes-got-to-get-control-of-the-ship-again-how-tensions-at-the-fbi-will-persist-after-the-election/2016/11/03/d28fc6c6-a050-11e6-8832-23a007c77bb4_story.html?utm_term=.49ea6376e3a1

16 http://articles.latimes.com/1993-12-21/news/mn-4179_1_white-house

17 http://www.breitbart.com/2016-presidential-race/2016/06/20/exclusive-secret-service-agent-book-raging-hillary-clinton-threw-bible-at-agents-colleague/

18 Author's interview with a White House service personnel member, 1 December 2016.

19 Ibid.

20 Ibid.

21 Hillary Clinton, *Living History* (New York: Simon & Schuster, 2003), 371–72.

22 http://content.time.com/time/nation/article/0,8599,6836,00.html

23 http://www.nytimes.com/2016/10/03/us/politics/hillary-bill-clinton-women.html.

24 Ibid.

25 http://www.wnd.com/2016/01/death-list-and-irs-ravaged-women-of-clinton/

26 https://www.gop.com/reliving-hillarys-history-dnc-fundraising-scandals-during-the-clinton-presidency/

27 Ibid.

28 http://freebeacon.com/politics/audio-bill-clinton-privately-mocked-paula-jones-as-an-attention-seeking-floozy/

29 http://www.nytimes.com/1994/03/30/business/washington-at-work-a-tax-lawyer-now-atop-the-irs.html

30 http://www.wnd.com/1999/03/1332/

31 http://www.nytimes.com/1997/01/09/us/head-of-irs-plans-to-leave-but-denies-political-pressure.html

32 http://www.nytimes.com/1999/09/14/opinion/public-interests-bill-s-little-gift.html

33 http://www.wsj.com/articles/SB120277819085260827

34 Ibid.

35 http://www.realclearpolitics.com/articles/2008/05/bill_hillary_and_the_faln.html

36 Ibid.

37 http://www.cnn.com/US/9909/22/fbi.faln.01/

38 http://nypost.com/2016/01/17/after-pardoning-criminal-marc-rich-clintons-made-millions-off-friends/

39 Ibid.

40 http://www.nytimes.com/2001/01/24/opinion/an-indefensible-pardon.html

41 http://www.bloomberg.com/politics/articles/2016-11-01/fbi-surprises-with-files-on-bill-clinton-01-pardon-of-marc-rich

42 http://nypost.com/2016/01/17/after-pardoning-criminal-marc-rich-clintons-made-millions-off-friends/

43 Ibid.

44 http://www.realclearpolitics.com/video/2016/11/04/giuliani_theres_a_revolution_going_on_inside_the_fbi_and_its_now_at_a_boiling_point.html

45 http://www.wsj.com/articles/clinton-ally-aids-campaign-of-fbi-officials-wife-1477266114

46 http://www.wsj.com/articles/laptop-may-include-thousands-of-emails-linked-to-hillary-clintons-private-server-1477854957

47 Read more at https://www.brainyquote.com/quotes/authors/j/james_comey_2.html

CHAPTER 2: THE LOST VOTERS OF ELECTIONS PAST

1   http://www.newsmax.com/Newsfront/ed-klein-bill-clinton-hillary-clinton-james-comey/2016/11/15/id/759037/

2   http://www.catholicworldreport.com/Item/5125/fake_catholic_groups_and_the_catholic_spring_emails.aspx

3   http://www.breitbart.com/big-government/2016/10/18/wikileaks-podestas-phony-catholic-group-pushed-church-support-iran-deal/

4   http://www.catholicworldreport.com/Item/5125/fake_catholic_groups_and_the_catholic_spring_emails.aspx

5   https://wikileaks.org/podesta-emails/emailid/4364

6   https://www.washingtonpost.com/news/acts-of-faith/wp/2016/10/12/wikileaks-emails-show-clinton-spokeswoman-joking-about-catholics-and-evangelicals/

7   https://www.washingtonpost.com/posteverything/wp/2016/11/22/why-did-obama-win-more-white-evangelical-votes-than-clinton-he-asked-for-them/

8   http://wordunplugged.com/forty-five-percent-born-again/

9   https://www.washingtonpost.com/news/the-intersect/wp/2016/11/04/no-john-podesta-didnt-drink-bodily-fluids-at-a-secret-satanist-dinner/

10 Ibid.

11 Ibid.

12 https://victorialsanders.wordpress.com/2016/11/12/hate-didnt-elect-donald-trump-people-did/

13 http://www.nbcnews.com/politics/first-read/first-read-how-rural-america-fueled-trump-s-win-n681316

14 http://www.ers.usda.gov/topics/rural-economy-population/rural-poverty-well-being/poverty-overview.aspx

15 http://hechingerreport.org/students-rural-areas-less-likely-go-four-year-colleges-top-universities/

16 http://www.nytimes.com/2015/03/16/us/evangelicals-aim-to-mobilize-an-army-for-republicans-in-2016.html

17 https://cruxnow.com/church-in-the-usa/2016/09/23/struggling-catholics-trump-taps-conservative-catholic-advisers/

18 http://dailycaller.com/2016/12/14/dnc-poured-millions-into-chicago-fearing-hillary-might-win-election-but-lose-popular-vote/

19 http://www.cnn.com/2016/11/08/politics/hillary-clinton-final-day-diary/

20 http://www.whatthefolly.com/2016/11/07/transcript-hillary-clintons-speech-in-grand-rapids-michigan-part-7/

21 http://www.nytimes.com/2016/11/13/us/politics/hillary-clinton-james-comey.html

22 http://time.com/4559784/hillary-clinton-donald-trump-final-days/

23 Ibid.

24 Ibid.

25 Ibid.

26 http://www.cnn.com/2016/11/07/politics/2016-election-last-day/

27 Ibid.

28 http://www.chicagotribune.com/news/nationworld/politics/ct-donald-trump-hillary-clinton-presidential-election-20161107-story.html

29 Ibid.

30 http://www.foxnews.com/politics/2016/11/02/trump-clinton-make-final-push-for-florida-in-last-days-campaign.html

CHAPTER 3: FORGOTTEN NO LONGER

1 https://www.youtube.com/watch?v=o9sLEVOn43I

2 http://gawker.com/the-best-of-new-york-times-columnist-ross-douthat-s-inc-1774768281

3 http://observer.com/2016/11/war-room-exit-polling-from-source-in-trump-world/

4 http://www.vanityfair.com/news/2016/11/election-night-2016-live-clinton-trump

5 http://nypost.com/2016/11/07/clintons-election-after-party-will-be-a-block-from-trump-tower/

6 Author's interview with Anatoly Lazarev, November 2016.

7 http://www.infowars.com/report-hillary-became-physically-violent-after-she-realized-she-had-lost-the-election/

8 http://www.snopes.com/hillary-clinton-had-drunken-meltdown-after-losing-the-election/

9 https://spectator.org/goodbye-gwen/

10 Author's interview with staffer.

11 From conversations with a Secret Service agent.

12 http://video.foxnews.com/v/5201610541001/?#sp=show-clips

13 http://abcnews.go.com/Politics/donald-trump-spending-election-night/story?id=43396332

14 http://www.slate.com/blogs/the_slatest/2016/11/09/john_podesta_says_clinton_campaign_is_calling_it_a_night.html

15 https://grabien.com/file.php?id=127805

16 http://www.dailymail.co.uk/news/article-3919238/Twitter-mocks-desperate-Wolf-Blitzer-stunned-reaction-Trump-s-success.html

17 http://abcnews.go.com/Politics/donald-trump-spending-election-night/story?id=43396332

18 http://www.washingtonexaminer.com/article/130902

19 http://www.politico.com/magazine/story/2016/10/john-podesta-emails-wikileaks-press-214367

20 http://ijr.com/2016/11/732345-15-of-the-most-priceless-reactions-to-trump-win-from-a-media-who-said-he-didnt-stand-a-chance/

21 Ibid.

22 Ibid.

23 http://townhall.com/tipsheet/cortneyobrien/2016/10/31/more-evidence-cnn-was-colluding-with-clinton-n2239498

24 http://ijr.com/2016/11/732345-15-of-the-most-priceless-reactions-to-trump-win-from-a-media-who-said-he-didnt-stand-a-chance/

25 http://www.cnn.com/2016/11/11/us/obama-trump-white-backlash/

26 http://www.lifenews.com/2016/11/09/comedian-jena-friedman-tells-activists-get-your-abortions-now-were-f/

27 http://www.thewrap.com/donald-trump-martha-raddatz-crying-election-night/

28 http://www.newsbusters.org/blogs/nb/scott-whitlock/2016/11/09/stunned-chris-matthews-loser-hillary-won-debates-had-best-ad

29 Ibid.

30 http://www.foxnews.com/politics/2016/11/14/tucker-carlson-theres-this-massive-and-terrible-disconnect-between-governed-and-governing.html

31 http://www.newsbusters.org/blogs/nb/curtis-houck/2016/11/09/msnbcs-odonnell-claims-us-crying-fear-trump-williams-reminds-crew

32 http://www.newsbusters.org/blogs/nb/scott-whitlock/2016/11/09/journalist-jonathan-alter-sneers-decency-lost-last-night

33 http://nypost.com/2016/11/09/trump-victory-is-a-win-for-the-little-guy-over-the-elite/

34 https://www.brainyquote.com/quotes/quotes/d/donaldtrum733773.html

35 http://www.npr.org/2016/11/09/500715254/transcript-donald-trump-speaks-at-victory-rally

36 http://www.nytimes.com/2000/01/02/magazine/the-lives-they-lived-fred-c-trump-b-1905-the-fred.html

37 Ibid.

38 http://www.cnn.com/2016/11/11/us/obama-trump-white-backlash/

39 http://www.npr.org/2016/11/09/500715254/transcript-donald-trump-speaks-at-victory-rally

40 http://www.businessinsider.com/these-10-corporations-control-almost-everything-you-buy-2012-4

41 http://www.cbsnews.com/news/inequality-1-percent-99-percent-income-growth/

42 https://www.washingtonpost.com/politics/i-will-never-leave-this-race/2015/12/08/af1b1d46-9ad2-11e5-8917-653b65c809eb_story.html

CHAPTER 4: WHY ANOTHER CLINTON PRESIDENCY?

1 http://nypost.com/2015/07/23/bill-told-hillary-to-run-for-office-instead-of-marrying-him/

2 http://www.psychiatrictimes.com/sexual-addiction/sexual-addiction-diagnosis-and-treatment

3 http://www.nytimes.com/2016/10/03/us/politics/hillary-bill-clinton-women.html.

4 Gennifer Flowers, *Passion and Betrayal* (Del Mar, CA: Emory Dalton Books, 1995), 7.

5 Candice Jackson, *Their Lives* (Los Angeles: World Ahead Publishing, 2005), 110.

6 Clinton, *Living History*, 98.

7 Victor Lasky, *It Didn't Start With Watergate* (New York: E. P. Dutton, 1977).

8 Author's interview with Rosalynn Carter.

9 http://www.nytimes.com/1992/05/08/us/after-riots-riots-60-s-riots-90-s-frustrating-search-heal-nation.html

CHAPTER 5: AN EARLY CLINTON SCANDAL PRIMER

1 https://www.washingtonpost.com/news/the-fix/wp/2016/07/25/4-brutal-poll-numbers-that-greet-hillary-clinton-at-the-democratic-national-convention/

2 http://www.nytimes.com/1994/04/23/us/the-whitewater-affair-the-overview-hillary-clinton-takes-questions-on-whitewater.html

3 Ibid.

4 http://link.springer.com/article/10.1007%2FBF02920493?wt_mc=Affiliate.CommissionJunction.3.EPR1089.DeepLink

5 http://www.nytimes.com/1996/01/08/opinion/essay-blizzard-of-lies.html

6 Ibid.

7 http://www.rushlimbaugh.com/daily/2015/04/23/whitewater_explainer_for_millennials

8 http://www.nytimes.com/1992/03/08/us/1992-campaign-personal-finances-clintons-joined-s-l-operator-ozark-real-estate.html.

9   https://www.youtube.com/watch?v=crFFSFUffbA

10 http://www.wsj.com/articles/clinton-ally-aids-campaign-of-fbi-officials-wife-1477266114

11 https://www.youtube.com/watch?v=IxuwzBOY1Q4

12 http://www.wsj.com/articles/travel-back-to-an-early-clinton-scandal-1473982077

13 http://www.nytimes.com/1996/01/05/us/memo-places-hillary-clinton-at-core-of-travel-office-case.html.

14 Ibid.

15 Ibid.

16 http://www.nytimes.com/1996/01/08/opinion/essay-blizzard-of-lies.html

17 http://www.dailywire.com/news/5998/trump-suspicious-vince-fosters-death-here-are-7-aaron-bandler

18 http://articles.latimes.com/1996-08-02/news/mn-30561_1_legal-fees

19 http://www.breitbart.com/big-government/2016/09/29/linda-tripp-reopens-vince-foster-filegate-travelgate-scandals/

20 Ibid.

21 http://www.dailymail.co.uk/news/article-508210/The-man-knew-The-truth-death-Hillary-Clintons-close-friend-Vince-Foster.html

22 http://www.dailywire.com/news/5998/trump-suspicious-vince-fosters-death-here-are-7-aaron-bandler

23 http://deadline.com/2016/10/donald-trump-hillary-clinton-forced-to-say-something-positive-about-other-presidential-debate-1201833833/

24 https://www.congress.gov/congressional-report/104th-congress/house-report/862/1

25 Clinton, *Living History*, 371–72.

26 http://www.nytimes.com/1996/01/06/us/elusive-papers-of-law-firm-are-found-at-white-house.html

27 http://www.washingtonpost.com/wp-srv/politics/special/whitewater/stories/wwtr960825.htm

28 http://www.washingtonpost.com/wp-dyn/content/article/2005/09/18/AR2005091801019.html

29 Clinton, *Living History*, 371–72.

30 http://www.nytimes.com/1996/06/10/us/clinton-apologizes-over-use-of-fbi-to-get-gop-files.html

31 http://content.time.com/time/nation/article/0,8599,6836,00.html

CHAPTER 6: THE FU LIN CHINESE RESTAURANT

1   http://moneynation.com/hillary-clinton-net-worth/

2   https://www.washingtonpost.com/politics/clintons-raised-nearly-2-billion-for-foundation-since-2001/2015/02/18/b8425d88-a7cd-11e4-a7c2-03d37af98440_story.html

3   http://www.politifact.com/truth-o-meter/statements/2014/jun/10/hillary-clinton/hillary-clinton-says-she-and-bill-were-dead-broke/

4   http://www.nytimes.com/1987/08/06/obituaries/jesse-unruh-a-california-political-power-dies.html

5   http://articles.latimes.com/1994-06-29/news/mn-9956_1_defense-funds

6   http://www.washingtonpost.com/wp-srv/politics/special/clinton/stories/legal022599.htm

7   Patrick Healy, "Clinton Sees Fear Realized in Trouble with Donor," *New York Times*, 12 September 2007.

8   R. Tyrrell Jr., *The Clinton Crack-Up* (Nashville: Thomas Nelson, 2007), 110.

9   http://www.washingtonpost.com/wp-srv/politics/special/campfin/stories/trie052299.htm

10 R. Tyrrell Jr., *Clinton Crack-Up* (Nashville: Thomas Nelson, 2007), 110.

11 http://pqasb.pqarchiver.com/latimes/doc/293383626.html?FMT=ABS&FMTS=ABS:FT& type= current&date=Sep%2021,%201996&author=ALAN%20C.% 20 MILLER &pub=Los% 20Angeles%20Times%20(pre-1997%20Fulltext)&edition=&startpage= 16 & desc= Democrats%20Return%20Illegal%20Contribution

12 http://www.washingtonpost.com/wp-srv/politics/special/campfin/stories/china1.htm

13 http://www.dailymail.co.uk/news/article-3713478/ANOTHER-90s-scandal-returns-haunt-Clintons-Chinese-billionaire-illegal-donations-Bill-s-election-campaign-faces-Congress-quiz-arrested-FBI-bribery.html

14 http://www.washingtonpost.com/wp-srv/politics/special/campfin/players/chung.htm

15 http://articles.chicagotribune.com/1997-07-30/news/9707300004_1_dnc-officials-white-house-christmas-johnny-chien-chuen-chung

16 https://www.gop.com/reliving-hillarys-history-dnc-fundraising-scandals-during-the-clinton-presidency/

17 http://www.nytimes.com/2000/03/03/us/2000-campaign-campaign-finance-longtime-fund-raiser-for-gore-convicted-donation.html

18 http://townhall.com/columnists/michellemalkin/2002/02/13/maria_hsias_revenge

19 Ibid.

20 http://www.wnd.com/2004/09/26786/

21 http://www.cnn.com/ALLPOLITICS/1998/05/20/poll/

CHAPTER 7: THE OTHER WOMEN

1   https://www.washingtonpost.com/local/enabler-or-family-defender-how-hillary-clinton-responded-to-husbands-accusers/2016/09/28/58dad5d4-6fb1-11e6-8533-6b0b0ded0253_story.html

2   http://www.dailymail.co.uk/news/article-3709157/How-Bill-Clinton-s-tawdry-affair-White-House-intern-Monica-Lewinsky-outraged-staff-devastated-Hillary-end-LOSING-presidency.html

3   http://www.theblaze.com/stories/2013/08/13/america-is-1-at-something-unfortunately-its-porn-web-sites/

4   https://www.washingtonpost.com/local/enabler-or-family-defender-how-hillary-clinton-responded-to-husbands-accusers/2016/09/28/58dad5d4-6fb1-11e6-8533-6b0b0ded0253_story.html

5   Gary J. Byrne, *Crisis of Character* (New York: Center Street, 2016), 166-167.

6   http://www.weeklystandard.com/hillary-and-the-rodeo-queens/article/2004640

7   Ibid.

8   Ibid.

9   http://www.timecoverstore.com/product/bill-clinton-1992-01-27/

10 http://www.politico.com/magazine/story/2016/09/hillary-clinton-2016-60-minutes-1992-214275

11 https://www.washingtonpost.com/archive/lifestyle/1992/01/28/campaign-92-the-muck-starts-here/4bd59ef7-f9c3-4856-821f-e37bb0ec41f7/

12 Ibid.

13 https://spectator.org/49976_his-cheatin-heart/

14 Ibid.

15 Ibid.

16 Ibid.

17 http://www.nytimes.com/1998/03/14/us/testing-president-accuser-jones-lawyers-issue-files-alleging-clinton-pattern.html

18 https://www.washingtonpost.com/archive/lifestyle/2001/01/28/curtain-call/db3785a6-5837-4009-8382-1ac3f9860e7e/

19 http://contrariansview.org/onashisite/WebVAX/ET/ambr23Jan94.html

20 http://articles.latimes.com/1992-07-20/entertainment/ca-4109_1_sally-jessy

21 http://www.weeklystandard.com/hillary-and-the-rodeo-queens/article/2004640

22 http://ontology.buffalo.edu/smith/clinton/women1.html

23 http://www.weeklystandard.com/barnes-it-always-helps-to-have-the-right-enemies/article/2005431

24 https://en.wikipedia.org/wiki/FUBAR_(disambiguation)

25 http://www.weeklystandard.com/hillary-and-the-rodeo-queens/article/2004640

26 http://contrariansview.org/onashisite/WebVAX/ET/ambr23Jan94.html

27 Ibid.

28 Ibid.

29 Ibid.

30 http://www.dailymail.co.uk/news/article-3427366/He-frilly-nightie-danced-playing-sax-Former-Miss-Arkansas-says-Bill-Clinton-bed-confided-Hillary-sex-women-fears-Hillary-vendetta-sleeps-loaded-semi-automatic.html

31 https://www.youtube.com/watch?v=aY_Aur5Yj7U

32 Ibid.

33 https://www.youtube.com/watch?v=h9SQHFU8J_M

34 http://www.newsbusters.org/blogs/nb/pj-gladnick/2016/01/20/new-york-times-identifies-wrong-woman-carville-trailer-park-quote

35 Ibid.

36 http://articles.baltimoresun.com/1994-12-02/news/1994336011_1_paula-jones-lip-gloss-clinton

37 http://www.slate.com/articles/news_and_politics/dialogues/features/1996/did_clinton_harass_paula_jones/_2.html

38 http://www.thedailybeast.com/articles/2016/10/17/paula-jones-to-penthouse-the-right-used-me.html

39 http://www.washingtonpost.com/wp-srv/aponline/20001024/aponline231805_000.htm

40 http://freebeacon.com/politics/audio-bill-clinton-privately-mocked-paula-jones-as-an-attention-seeking-floozy/

CHAPTER 8: MONICA LEWINSKY AND IMPEACHMENT

1 http://www.cnn.com/ALLPOLITICS/time/1998/09/14/affair.state.html

2 http://nypost.com/2016/06/18/monica-lewinsky-ironically-freaked-out-that-bill-cheated-on-her/

3 http://www.cnn.com/ALLPOLITICS/1998/01/21/transcripts/lehrer/

4 Ibid.

5 Ibid.

6 Gary J. Byrne, *Crisis of Character* (New York: Center Street, 2016), 112–14.

7   http://www.washingtonpost.com/wp-srv/politics/special/clinton/icreport/srprintable.htm

8   https://www.youtube.com/watch?v=otBFsw3O8VA

9   http://law2.umkc.edu/faculty/projects/ftrials/clinton/lewinskydress.html

10 http://www.nytimes.com/2003/06/04/us/in-book-hillary-clinton-details-pain-from-lewinsky-affair.html

11 Ibid.

12 http://law2.umkc.edu/faculty/projects/ftrials/clinton/lewinskydress.html

13 http://www.washingtonpost.com/wp-srv/politics/special/clinton/stories/clinton081898.htm

14 Ibid.

15 http://politicalticker.blogs.cnn.com/2014/02/10/report-documents-reveal-hillary-clintons-private-reaction-to-her-husbands-cheating-scandal-with-monica-lewinsky/

16 Ibid.

17 http://www.dailymail.co.uk/news/article-3075274/Monica-Lewinsky-offered-1MILLION-Las-Vegas-sex-museum-DNA-stained-blue-dress-wore-Clinton-affair.html

18 http://fortune.com/2016/10/12/bill-clinton-affairs-millennial-voters/

CHAPTER 9: THE SELLING OF THE WHITE HOUSE

1   https://archives.nbclearn.com/portal/site/k-12/flatview?cuecard=2967

2   http://www.slate.com/articles/news_and_politics/politics/2015/10/lincoln_bedroom_guests_are_still_donating_to_hillary_clinton_many_of_bill.html

3   http://www.cnn.com/ALLPOLITICS/1997/02/26/clinton.lincoln/

4   Ibid.

5   http://www.politifact.com/virginia/statements/2013/aug/26/ken-cuccinelli/cuccinell-overstates-mcauliffes-role-lincoln-bedro/

6   http://www.nytimes.com/2001/02/23/us/clinton-pardons-democrats-this-time-clintons-find-their-support-buckling-weight.html

7   Ibid.

8   Ibid.

9   Ibid.

10 Ibid.

11 http://www.nytimes.com/2001/02/23/us/clinton-pardons-democrats-this-time-clintons-find-their-support-buckling-weight.html

12 http://www.cnsnews.com/news/article/pardoned-financier-marc-rich-dies-switzerland

13 http://nypost.com/2016/11/02/why-bills-pardons-are-a-real-problem-for-hillary/

14 http://www.bloomberg.com/politics/articles/2016-11-01/fbi-surprises-with-files-on-bill-clinton-01-pardon-of-marc-rich

15 http://www.wsj.com/articles/SB120277819085260827

16 http://www.dailywire.com/news/6396/exclusive-faln-victims-son-says-hillary-was-key-aaron-bandler#

17 http://www.realclearpolitics.com/articles/2008/05/bill_hillary_and_the_faln.html

18 Ibid.

19 Ibid.

20 Ibid.

21 Ibid.

22 http://www.nytimes.com/1999/09/14/opinion/public-interests-bill-s-little-gift.html

23 http://www.nytimes.com/2007/07/04/us/politics/04clintons.html

24 https://www.washingtonpost.com/archive/politics/2001/01/21/clintons-take-away-190000-in-gifts/36773cf2-8120-4d58-b903-d76d39a6cc3f/?utm_term=.e52fb79d247e

25 http://www.factcheck.org/2016/05/the-clinton-furniture-flap/

26 http://www.nytimes.com/2002/02/13/nyregion/clintons-accused-of-a-failure-to-disclose-gifts-true-value.html

CHAPTER 10: DONALD TRUMP, OUT OF THE SHADOWS

1   https://www.washingtonpost.com/lifestyle/style/young-donald-trump-military-school/2016/06/22/f0b3b164-317c-11e6-8758-d58e76e11b12_story.html

2   Ibid.

3   http://www.npr.org/2015/11/10/455331251/this-is-where-donald-trump-played-by-the-rules-and-learned-to-beat-the-game

4   Gwenda Blair, *Donald Trump: The Candidate* (New York: Simon & Schuster, 2007), 13.

5   http://www.cnn.com/videos/politics/2015/09/08/donald-trumps-siblings-foreman-dnt-erin.cnn

6   http://www.nytimes.com/2015/08/19/us/politics/familiar-talk-women-from-donald-trump-sister.html

7   Donald Trump, *The Art of the Deal* (New York: Random House, 1992), 70.

8   http://pagesix.com/2016/01/17/donald-trumps-brother-robert-emerges/

9   http://www.townandcountrymag.com/society/money-and-power/news/a8479/robert-trump/

10 Donald Trump, *The Art of the Deal* (New York: Random House, 1992), 67.

11 http://www.nytimes.com/2016/01/03/us/politics/for-donald-trump-lessons-from-a-brothers-suffering.html

12 http://www.vox.com/policy-and-politics/2016/11/9/13569124/donald-trump-wins-2016-presidential-election-victory-speech-transcript

13 http://www.smithsonianmag.com/history/history-verrazano-narrows-bridge-50-years-after-its-construction-180953032/

14 http://www.nytimes.com/2007/01/23/arts/design/28pogr.html

15 http://www.nytimes.com/learning/general/onthisday/big/1121.html

16 http://www.nytimes.com/2015/09/01/opinion/putting-donald-trump-on-the-couch.html

17 https://www.washingtonpost.com/graphics/politics/2016-election/trump-campaign-marketing/

CHAPTER 11: SAVING NEW YORK CITY

1   Donald Trump, *The Art of the Deal* (New York: Random House, 1992), 92.

2   https://www.youtube.com/watch?v=q_q61B-DyPk

3   *Architectural Review* 8, no. 3 (March 1919): 75.

4   http://www.history.com/topics/cornelius-vanderbilt

5   *Architectural Review* 8, no. 3 (March 1919): 55.

6   Donald Trump, *The Art of the Deal* (New York: Random House, 1992), 104.

7   Ibid., 106.

8   http://www.nytimes.com/2011/01/12/business/12hyatt.html

9   http://nypost.com/2016/02/07/how-donald-trump-helped-save-new-york-city/

10 http://www.nytimes.com/2002/10/27/style/boite-understated-in-trump-style.html

11 http://www.nydailynews.com/news/politics/exclusive-donald-trump-made-millions-saudi-government-article-1.2777211

12 http://nypost.com/2016/02/07/how-donald-trump-helped-save-new-york-city/

13 http://decider.com/2016/03/27/born-rich-documentary-ivanka-trump/

14 http://mobile.nytimes.com/2004/03/28/business/is-trump-headed-for-a-fall.html

15 Ibid.

16 https://washingtonspectator.org/trump-ratings-revisited/

17 http://www.politico.com/story/2011/03/poll-trump-tops-romney-pawlenty-050746

18 https://billygraham.org/story/billy-graham-mitt-romney-meet/

19 http://www.politifact.com/truth-o-meter/statements/2015/jun/02/martin-omalley/had-goldman-sachs-ceo-said-his-picks-are-hillary-c/

20 http://www.nytimes.com/2016/09/06/nyregion/donald-trump-marble-collegiate-church-norman-vincent-peale.html

21 http://www.inspiringquotes.us/author/1447-paula-white

22 http://www.politico.com/story/2016/07/donald-trump-pastor-paula-white-225315

23 Ibid.

24 https://www.bloomberg.com/politics/articles/2014-10-14/bloombergdes-moines-register-iowa-poll-without-romney-a-wideopen-2016-field-in-republican-caucuses

CHAPTER 12: TRUMP AND THE CROWDED FIELD

1   http://www.msnbc.com/transcripts/the-last-word/2015-06-15

2   http://www.cnn.com/2015/06/16/politics/donald-trump-2016-announcement-elections/

3   http://abcnews.go.com/Politics/donald-trump-announces-2016-presidential-campaign-make-country/story?id=31799741

4   http://www.insideedition.com/headlines/15264-was-trump-motivated-to-run-for-president-after-obama-ridiculed-him-at-2011-dinner

5   Ibid.

6   https://www.washingtonpost.com/news/post-politics/wp/2015/06/16/donald-trump-to-announce-his-presidential-plans-today/

7   http://www.cnn.com/2015/06/16/politics/donald-trump-2016-announcement-elections/

8   http://www.realclearpolitics.com/video/2015/06/16/trump_mexico_not_sending_us_their_best_criminals_drug_dealers_and_rapists_are_crossing_border.html

9   http://www.cnn.com/videos/tv/2015/06/25/exp-presidential-candidate-donald-trump-immigration-intv-erin.cnn

10 http://money.cnn.com/2015/06/25/media/univision-donald-trump-mexicans/

11 http://time.com/3940305/nbc-donald-trump-immigration/

12 http://www.usatoday.com/story/news/politics/2015/07/01/macys-donald-trump-menswear/29560123/

13 http://www.independent.co.uk/news/criminals-in-exodus-from-cuba-us-fears-castro-emptying-his-jails-into-florida-1386288.html

14 http://www.cnn.com/2015/07/01/politics/donald-trump-poll-hillary-clinton-jeb-bush/

15 http://nymag.com/daily/intelligencer/2015/06/history-clinton-bush-friendship.html

16 http://www.politico.com/story/2015/07/john-mccain-donald-trump-immigration-phoenix-120216

17 http://www.huffingtonpost.com/entry/a-note-about-our-coverage-of-donald-trumps-campaign_us_55a8fc9ce4b0896514d0fd66

18 http://www.politico.com/story/2015/07/trump-attacks-mccain-i-like-people-who-werent-captured-120317

19 Ibid.

20 https://www.c-span.org/video/?327045-5/presidential-candidate-donald-trump-family-leadership-summit

21 https://www.c-span.org/video/?327258-1/donald-trump-remarks-sun-city-south-carolina

22 http://www.politico.com/story/2015/07/donald-trump-gives-out-lindsey-grahams-cell-phone-number-120414

23 http://www.usatoday.com/story/news/politics/elections/2016/2015/07/23/donald-trump-legal-immigration-laredo-texas-rick-perry/30578537/

24 http://www.nytimes.com/politics/first-draft/2015/07/23/donald-trumps-border-visit-stirs-passions-in-laredo/

25 https://www.washingtonpost.com/news/post-politics/wp/2015/08/06/annotated-transcript-the-aug-6-gop-debate/?utm_term=.1a2d6ed6ec36

26 http://tvline.com/2016/11/10/megyn-kelly-donald-trump-poison-debate-memoir/

27 https://www.washingtonpost.com/news/post-politics/wp/2015/08/06/annotated-transcript-the-aug-6-gop-debate/

28 Ibid.

29 https://www.washingtonpost.com/news/post-politics/wp/2015/08/07/trump-says-foxs-megyn-kelly-had-blood-coming-out-of-her-wherever/?utm_term=.27b8fe73e247

30 http://cnnpressroom.blogs.cnn.com/2015/08/09/trump-defends-his-blood-remarks-who-would-make-a-statement-like-that-only-a-sick-person-would-even-think-about-that/

31 Ibid.

32 http://www.usatoday.com/story/news/politics/onpolitics/2015/12/14/donald-trump-campaign-timeline-six-months/76936436/

33 http://www.cnn.com/2015/08/21/politics/donald-trump-rally-mobile-alabama/

34 http://www.businessinsider.com/donald-trump-jeb-bush-insult-2015-8

35 http://www.rollingstone.com/politics/news/trump-seriously-20150909?page=13

36 http://video.foxnews.com/v/4475310939001/?playlist_id=930909787001#sp=show-clips

37 http://fivethirtyeight.com/live-blog/2016-election-second-republican-presidential-debate/

38 https://www.washingtonpost.com/news/the-fix/wp/2016/05/03/ted-cruz-is-mad-as-hell-at-donald-trump-he-should-be-angry-at-himself/

39 http://www.politico.com/story/2015/09/gop-debate-takeaways-trump-fiorina-213759

40 http://time.com/4075749/scott-walker-fundraising/

41 http://www.nytimes.com/politics/first-draft/2015/10/27/poll-watch-ben-carson-edges-ahead-nationally-in-timescbs-news-poll/

42 http://www.nbcnews.com/politics/2016-election/nbc-wsj-poll-carson-surges-lead-national-gop-race-n456006

43 https://www.washingtonpost.com/news/post-politics/wp/2015/12/01/why-ben-carson-doesnt-believe-in-hell/

44 http://www.newsmax.com/DougWead/carson-cruz-trump-2016/2015/12/16/id/705984/

45 Ibid.

46 https://www.washingtonpost.com/news/the-fix/wp/2016/05/03/ted-cruz-is-mad-as-hell-at-donald-trump-he-should-be-angry-at-himself/

47 http://www.cnn.com/2016/02/01/politics/iowa-caucuses-2016-highlights/

48 Ibid.

49 http://www.politico.com/story/2016/02/ben-carson-ted-cruz-cheating-iowa-218615

CHAPTER 13: AN UNLIKELY NOMINEE

1 https://www.washingtonpost.com/news/arts-and-entertainment/wp/2015/11/09/donald-trump-brought-big-ratings-to-saturday-night-live-but-how-does-that-compare-with-other-top-episodes/?utm_term=.f7e2f377356e

2 http://www.ew.com/article/2015/11/08/donald-trump-snl-ratings

3 http://www.chicagotribune.com/news/nationworld/ct-donald-trump-bad-debate-20151111-story.html

4 http://www.cnn.com/2015/12/08/europe/2015-paris-terror-attacks-fast-facts/

5 http://www.dailymail.co.uk/news/article-3444222/I-gun-Trump-tells-French-magazine-ISIS-attacked-Paris-opened-fire.html

6 https://twitter.com/realDonaldTrump/status/667329429912338432

7 http://www.star-telegram.com/news/state/texas/article45480042.html

8 Ibid.

9 http://www.foxnews.com/us/2015/11/19/donald-trump-says-would-absolutely-implement-muslim-database-if-elected.html

10 https://twitter.com/realDonaldTrump/status/667777348029292544?ref_src=twsrc%5Etfw

11 http://www.nbcnews.com/politics/2016-election/trump-s-worst-offense-mocking-disabled-reporter-poll-finds-n627736

12 https://www.donaldjtrump.com/press-releases/donald-j.-trump-statement-on-preventing-muslim-immigration

13 Ibid.

14 https://www.washingtonpost.com/politics/gop-preparing-for-contested-convention/2015/12/10/d72574bc-9f73-11e5-8728-1af6af208198_story.html

15 http://thehill.com/blogs/ballot-box/presidential-races/265223-karl-rove-trump-would-cost-gop-the-wh-senate

16 http://www.readingeagle.com/ap/article/republicans-prefer-a-religious-candidate-but-theyre-willing-to-give-donald-trump-a-pass

17 http://time.com/4215559/chris-christie-drops-out-new-hampshire-primary-results/

18 https://www.bloomberg.com/politics/articles/2016-02-16/obama-says-donald-trump-wont-be-elected-president-in-2016

19 http://www.latimes.com/world/la-fg-pope-on-trump-wall-20160218-story.html

20 http://www.nytimes.com/2016/02/28/us/politics/donald-trump-republican-party.html

21 http://abcnews.go.com/Politics/history-donald-trump-small-hands-insult/story?id=37395515

22 http://www.cnn.com/2016/03/03/politics/mitt-romney-presidential-race-speech/

23 http://www.slate.com/blogs/the_slatest/2016/03/03/best_gop_lines_and_quotes_of_the_mar_3_fox_news_debate.html

24 https://www.washingtonpost.com/news/the-fix/wp/2016/03/03/the-fox-news-gop-debate-transcript-annotated/

25 https://www.washingtonpost.com/news/post-politics/wp/2016/03/04/ben-carson-officially-drops-out-of-the-presidential-race/

26 http://www.politico.com/blogs/2016-gop-primary-live-updates-and-results/2016/04/trump-ted-cruz-lying-222226

27 https://www.washingtonpost.com/news/the-fix/wp/2016/03/03/the-fox-news-gop-debate-transcript-annotated/

28 https://www.washingtonpost.com/news/the-fix/wp/2016/05/03/ted-cruz-is-mad-as-hell-at-donald-trump-he-should-be-angry-at-himself/

29 https://dougwead.wordpress.com/2016/03/28/war-of-wives-inside-the-trump-cruz-fight/

30 http://www.mediaite.com/tv/liz-mair-calls-trump-a-loudmouthed-dick-live-on-cnn/

31 http://www.politico.com/blogs/2016-gop-primary-live-updates-and-results/2016/03/lindsey-graham-endorses-ted-cruz-220932

32 http://www.politico.com/story/2016/03/top-conservatives-gather-to-plot-third-party-run-against-trump-220786#ixzz430DyazyK

33 https://www.washingtonpost.com/news/post-politics/wp/2016/03/23/scott-walker-says-hell-make-an-endorsement-decision-next-week-for-maximum-impact/

34 https://dougwead.wordpress.com/2016/03/28/war-of-wives-inside-the-trump-cruz-fight/

35 http://thehill.com/blogs/ballot-box/presidential-races/274320-cruz-blames-trump-and-his-henchmen-for-tabloid-report

36 https://www.washingtonpost.com/politics/cruz-confronts-new-york-values-in-the-empire-state/2016/04/08/c4bbd528-fd9c-11e5-9140-e61d062438bb_story.html

37 Ibid.

38 http://time.com/4307323/tom-hands-donald-trump-spaceships-dinosaurs/

39 http://www.realclearpolitics.com/video/2016/05/03/trump_ties_ted_cruzs_father_to_lee_harvey_oswald_jfk_assassination.html

40 http://www.realclearpolitics.com/video/2016/05/03/cruz_explodes_pathological_liar_trump_a_narcissist_at_a_level_i_dont_think_this_country_has_ever_seen.html

41 Ibid.

42 http://www.telegraph.co.uk/news/2016/05/12/george-clooney-vows-donald-trump-wont-be-us-president/

43 http://www.recode.net/2016/5/16/11679242/nancy-pelosi-trump-guarantee-kara-swisher-podcast

44 http://www.nytimes.com/2016/05/27/us/politics/donald-trump-republican-nomination.html?_r=0

CHAPTER 14: IT'S A TRUMP WORLD

1 http://www.politico.com/story/2016/07/trump-joni-ernst-mike-pence-vice-president-225083

2 Philip Elliott, "Mike Pence Is No Ordinary Wingman," *Time*, December 26, 2016, 54.

3 http://www.politico.com/story/2016/07/trump-joni-ernst-mike-pence-vice-president-225083

4 http://www.nytimes.com/2016/07/17/us/politics/donald-trump-mike-pence.html

5 Ibid.

6 Elliott, "Mike Pence Is No Ordinary Wingman."

7 http://www.pennlive.com/news/2016/07/rudy_giuliani_fired_up_in_rnc.html

8 https://www.washingtonpost.com/news/the-fix/wp/2016/11/22/a-brief-history-of-the-lock-her-up-chant-as-it-looks-like-trump-might-not-even-try/

9 http://www.tennessean.com/story/news/politics/2016/07/21/marsha-blackburn-channels-taylor-swift-tells-ted-cruz-shake-off/87391954/

10 http://www.businessinsider.com/peter-thiel-slams-republicans-in-convention-speech-2016-7

11 http://www.politico.com/story/2016/07/melania-trump-michelle-obama-225793

12 Ibid.

13 http://www.dailywire.com/news/7589/7-democrats-who-were-caught-plagiarism-including-aaron-bandler

14 Ibid.

15 http://www.slate.com/blogs/xx_factor/2016/07/20/tiffany_trump_s_sad_vague_rnc_speech.html

16 https://www.bustle.com/articles/173963-transcript-of-eric-trumps-rnc-speech-proves-how-proud-he-is-to-be-a-member-of

17 Ibid.

18 http://www.washingtonpost.com/wp-dyn/articles/A51005-2004Aug31.html

19 *Born Rich*, directed by Jamie Johnson and Jamie and Dirk Wittenborn (Wise and Good Film, 2003).

20 https://www.youtube.com/watch?v=YAksO-_uibs

21 http://www.cosmopolitan.com/politics/news/a61613/ivanka-trump-speech-republican-national-convention/

22 http://www.politico.com/story/2016/05/trump-pundits-wrong-predictions-222789

23 https://www.bloomberg.com/view/articles/2015-10-19/trump-candidacy-will-fade-as-other-republicans-rise

24 https://twitter.com/douthatnyt/status/647401086056271872

25 http://www.nytimes.com/2015/12/15/upshot/how-trump-could-win-and-why-he-probably-wont.html

26 Ibid.

27 http://abcnews.go.com/Politics/bill-kristol-donald-trump-mystique-disappear-iowa-loss/story?id=35945758

28 https://rawconservative.com/2016/01/burningbush/

29 http://www.dailymail.co.uk/news/article-3473094/Marco-ultimate-optimist-losing-one-state-far-says-no-way-TRUMP-win.html

30 http://www.slate.com/articles/news_and_politics/politics/2016/04/trump_probably_won_t_be_the_nominee_how_will_the_gop_get_rid_of_him.html

31 http://www.cnn.com/2016/07/22/politics/donald-trump-rnc-speech-text/

32 Ibid.

33 http://www.cnn.com/2016/07/25/politics/donald-trump-hillary-clinton-poll/

34 http://www.thenational.ae/opinion/comment/why-donald-trump-wont-win-the-us-election

CHAPTER 15: THE COMEBACK OF HILLARY CLINTON

1 http://www.nbcnews.com/id/16720167/ns/politics/t/clinton-im-im-win/#.WELhx_krKUk

2 Ibid.

3 http://www.huffingtonpost.com/james-rucker/can-black-people-trust-hillary_b_9312004.html

4 Ibid.

5 http://www.nytimes.com/2008/05/09/opinion/09fri1.html

6 http://www.politifact.com/truth-o-meter/statements/2008/mar/25/hillary-clinton/video-shows-tarmac-welcome-no-snipers/

7 http://www.cnn.com/2008/POLITICS/03/25/campaign.wrap/index.html

8 https://www.washingtonpost.com/news/fact-checker/wp/2016/05/23/recalling-hillary-clintons-claim-of-landing-under-sniper-fire-in-bosnia/

9 http://www.businessinsider.com/hillary-clinton-bosnia-sniper-fire-2016-6

10 https://www.gpo.gov/fdsys/pkg/CHRG-111shrg54615/html/CHRG-111shrg54615.htm

11 https://www.judicialwatch.org/wp-content/uploads/2015/04/Hillary-R-Clinton-Termination-EA.pdf

12 Ibid.

13 http://www.bbc.com/news/world-us-canada-36013703

14 http://www.cbsnews.com/news/clinton-on-qaddafi-we-came-we-saw-he-died/

15 http://benghazi.house.gov/NewInfo

16 http://abcnews.go.com/blogs/politics/2012/09/ambassador-susan-rice-libya-attack-not-premeditated/

17 http://www.factcheck.org/2012/10/benghazi-timeline/

18 Ibid.

19 http://www.politifact.com/truth-o-meter/statements/2016/jul/19/ron-johnson/what-you-need-know-about-hillary-clintons-infamous/

20 http://www.nytimes.com/interactive/2016/05/27/us/politics/what-we-know-about-hillary-clintons-private-email-server.html

21 http://nypost.com/2013/02/01/clinton-formally-resigns-as-secretary-of-state/

22 Ibid.

23 Ibid.

24 Ibid.

25 http://www.nytimes.com/2015/08/02/opinion/sunday/maureen-dowd-joe-biden-in-2016-what-would-beau-do.html

26 https://www.theguardian.com/us-news/2015/oct/13/bernie-sanders-hillary-clinton-damn-email-server

27 https://www.democracynow.org/2015/12/15/headlines/report_top_news_shows_give_trump_234_minutes_sanders_10_minutes

28 http://mondoweiss.net/2016/07/believed-criticism-disturbing/

29 http://www.nytimes.com/2016/07/23/us/politics/dnc-emails-sanders-clinton.html

30 Ibid.

31 http://www.ajc.com/news/national-govt--politics/sen-franken-dnc-may-underestimating-trump/YEmtldGvKdnfNT7FqWykQL/

32 http://variety.com/gallery/quotes-2016-democratic-national-convention-hillary-clinton-michelle-obama-bernie-sanders/#!1/hillary-clinton-2-2/

33 http://www.hollywoodreporter.com/video/obama-at-democratic-convention-hillary-915198

34 https://www.washingtonpost.com/news/the-fix/wp/2015/08/08/so-which-women-has-donald-trump-called-dogs-and-fat-pigs/

CHAPTER 16: CROOKED HILLARY

1 http://www.nytimes.com/2016/04/24/opinion/sunday/is-hillary-clinton-dishonest.html

2   http://www.gallup.com/poll/189524/dishonest-socialist-lead-reactions-dems.aspx?g_source=Election%202016&g_medium=newsfeed&g_campaign=tiles

3   http://www.nytimes.com/2015/07/25/us/politics/hillary-clinton-email-classified-information-inspector-general-intelligence-community.html

4   Ibid.

5   http://www.dailywire.com/news/7177/fbi-yes-queen-hillary-broke-law-no-she-wont-be-ben-shapiro

6   Ibid.

7   https://static01.nyt.com/packages/pdf/politics/hillaryclintonfbi.pdf

8   http://www.nytimes.com/2016/10/29/us/politics/fbi-hillary-clinton-email.html

9   https://www.clintonfoundation.org/clinton-global-initiative/about-us/leadership-team

10 http://www.seattletimes.com/seattle-news/times-watchdog/as-hillary-clinton-bolstered-boeing-company-returned-the-favor/

11 https://www.washingtonpost.com/politics/for-hillary-clinton-and-boeing-a-beneficial-relationship/2014/04/13/21fe84ec-bc09-11e3-96ae-f2c36d2b1245_story.html

12 https://www.washingtonpost.com/politics/how-the-clintons-haiti-development-plans-succeed--and-disappoint/2015/03/20/0ebae25e-cbe9-11e4-a2a7-9517a3a70506_story.html

13 http://www.reuters.com/article/us-usa-election-foundation-idUSKBN12Z2SL

14 http://hosted.ap.org/dynamic/stories/U/US_CAMPAIGN_2016_CLINTON_FOUNDATION?SITE=AP

15 http://abcnews.go.com/Politics/clinton-donor-sensitive-intelligence-board/story?id=39710624

16 http://www.cnn.com/2016/08/29/opinions/ap-gets-it-wrong-on-clinton-reyes/

17 http://www.dailywire.com/news/10280/clinton-foundations-7-worst-scandals-aaron-bandler

18 Ibid.

19 https://www.youtube.com/watch?v=WDJLVgSckXI&feature=youtu.be

20 https://www.youtube.com/watch?v=tINSj-JxwfQ&feature=youtu.be

21 http://www.maxkeiser.com/2016/10/im-starting-to-worry-that-if-this-story-gets-out-we-are-screwed/

22 http://www.cnn.com/2016/02/05/politics/hillary-clinton-bill-clinton-paid-speeches/

23 http://www.usnews.com/news/articles/2016-04-22/heres-who-paid-hillary-clinton-22-million-in-speaking-fees

24 http://conservativetribune.com/wiki-story-gets-out-were-screwed/

25 http://www.maxkeiser.com/2016/10/im-starting-to-worry-that-if-this-story-gets-out-we-are-screwed/

CHAPTER 17: AN OCTOBER SURPRISE FOR TRUMP

1   https://www.washingtonpost.com/politics/trump-recorded-having-extremely-lewd-conversation-about-women-in-2005/2016/10/07/3b9ce776-8cb4-11e6-bf8a-3d26847eeed4_story.html

2   http://www.businessinsider.com/donald-trump-women-video-apology-billy-bush-clinton-2016-10

3   https://www.washingtonpost.com/politics/trump-recorded-having-extremely-lewd-conversation-about-women-in-2005/2016/10/07/3b9ce776-8cb4-11e6-bf8a-3d26847eeed4_story.html

4   Ibid.

5   Ibid.

6   http://www.politico.com/story/2016/10/mitt-romney-donald-trump-comments-women-229325

7   http://www.latimes.com/nation/politics/trailguide/la-na-trailguide-updates-south-dakotas-thune-joins-chorus-1475946585-htmlstory.html

8   http://heavy.com/news/2016/10/read-melania-trump-responds-to-donald-trumps-vulgar-2005-tape-what-did-reaction-billy-bush-statement-wife/

9   http://nymag.com/daily/intelligencer/2016/10/trump-campaign-final-days.html

10 http://www.scribd.com/document/327067170/161027-NBCWSJ-October-N-500-Poll?content=10079&ad_roup%20Online+Tracking+Link&campaign=Skimbit%2C+Ltd.&keyword=ft500noi&source=impactradius&medium=affiliate&irgwc=1

11 http://www.businessinsider.com/paul-ryan-defend-donald-trump-campaign-2016-10

12 Ibid.

13 http://www.businessinsider.com/how-the-donald-trump-tape-got-leaked-2016-10/#august-2016-the-new-york-post-reported-that-billy-bush-while-covering-the-rio-olympics-bragged-about-having-a-tape-of-trump-being-a-real-dog-nbc-staffers-overheard-and-thats-reportedly-how-the-search-for-the-tape-started-1

14 http://www.inquisitr.com/3574847/melania-trump-divorce-rumors-speculation-grows-after-donalds-wife-refuses-to-make-joint-appearance-following-trump-tapes-released/

15 http://www.cnn.com/2016/10/07/politics/donald-trump-campaign-crisis/

16 http://www.nytimes.com/2016/09/12/opinion/about-the-basket-of-deplorables.html

17 http://www.cnn.com/2012/12/31/politics/hillary-clinton-hospitalized/

18 http://www.cnn.com/2016/09/12/politics/david-axelrod-rips-clinton-privacy/index.html

19 https://www.washingtonpost.com/news/the-fix/wp/2016/09/26/the-first-trump-clinton-presidential-debate-transcript-annotated/

20 Ibid.

21 https://www.youtube.com/watch?v=45V4MIDpslQ

22 https://www.washingtonpost.com/news/the-fix/wp/2016/09/26/the-first-trump-clinton-presidential-debate-transcript-annotated/

23 https://www.youtube.com/watch?v=UyefV5P2sOw

24 http://www.nytimes.com/2016/10/10/us/politics/transcript-second-debate.html

25 Ibid.

26 Ibid.

27 https://en.wikipedia.org/wiki/GCB_(TV_series)

28 https://www.washingtonpost.com/news/fact-checker/wp/2016/05/19/did-clinton-laugh-about-a-rapists-light-sentence-and-attack-sexual-harassment-victims/?utm_term=.2861b4552c64

29 Ibid.

30 http://www.latimes.com/nation/politics/trailguide/la-na-second-presidential-debate-live-trump-and-clinton-fight-over-abraham-1476070443-htmlstory.html

31 https://www.washingtonpost.com/news/wonk/wp/2016/10/10/being-truthful-isnt-what-made-abraham-lincoln-a-great-politician/

32 http://www.nytimes.com/2016/10/10/us/politics/transcript-second-debate.html

33 http://www.foxnews.com/health/2016/10/13/trump-sexual-assault-allegations-why-some-victims-stay-silent.html

34 Ibid.

35 http://www.thegatewaypundit.com/2016/10/trumps-butler-debunks-another-accusers-story-never-happened/

36 http://www.latimes.com/nation/politics/trailguide/la-na-trailguide-third-presidential-will-trump-accept-election-results-1476929623-htmlstory.html

37 Ibid.

38 http://www.politico.com/story/2016/10/hillary-clinton-donald-trump-debate-230067

39 https://www.washingtonpost.com/news/the-fix/wp/2016/10/19/the-final-trump-clinton-debate-transcript-annotated/

40 Ibid.

41 https://www.statnews.com/2016/08/05/stat-harvard-poll-zika-abortion/

42 Ibid.

43 http://www.breitbart.com/big-government/2016/11/19/poll-64-voters-support-banning-abortions-5-months-pregnancy/

44 http://insider.foxnews.com/2016/10/19/watch-trump-clinton-spar-late-term-abortions

45 http://www.politico.com/story/2016/10/hillary-clinton-donald-trump-debate-230067

46 http://nymag.com/daily/intelligencer/2016/10/trump-campaign-final-days.html

CHAPTER 18: HILLARY THE ENABLER

1 http://www.thewrap.com/how-access-hollywood-found-the-trump-tape-and-why-nbc-news-probably-leaked-it-exclusive/

2 Ibid.

3 http://www.washingtonexaminer.com/bill-clinton-accuser-kathleen-willey-hillary-was-complicit-in-his-sexual-misconduct/article/2603352

4 Candice E. Jackson, *Their Lives*, (World Ahead Publishing, Inc., 2005) 141.

5 http://content.time.com/time/magazine/article/0%2C9171%2C987743%2C00.html

6 http://www.washingtonpost.com/wp-srv/politics/special/pjones/docs/willey031398.htm

7 Author's email exchange with Michael Isikoff.

8 http://www.washingtonpost.com/wp-srv/politics/special/pjones/docs/willey031398.htm

9 http://www.theamericanmirror.com/kathleen-willey-pens-heartbreaking-remembrance-of-her-husband/

10 http://www.npr.org/2016/10/09/497291071/a-brief-history-of-juanita-broaddrick-the-woman-accusing-bill-clinton-of-rape

11 http://www.washingtonpost.com/wp-srv/politics/special/clinton/stories/janedoe022099.htm

12 http://beforeitsnews.com/obama-birthplace-controversy/2016/08/juanita-broaddrick-transcript-nbc-dateline-report-conducted-january-20-1999-bill-clinton-rape-allegation-american-thinker-where-is-the-coverage-of-juanita-broaddrick-hillary-clintons-role-2507954.html

13 Ibid.

14 Ibid.

15 Ibid.

16 Ibid.

17 Ibid.

18 http://www.washingtonpost.com/wp-srv/politics/special/clinton/stories/janedoe022099.htm

19 Ibid.

20 Ibid.

21 https://sidewire.com/politics/2016/10/13/surf-turf-with-tim-burger-blain

22 Ibid.

23 http://www.washingtonpost.com/wp-srv/politics/special/clinton/stories/janedoe022099.htm

24 https://www.washingtonpost.com/local/enabler-or-family-defender-how-hillary-clinton-responded-to-husbands-accusers/2016/09/28/58dad5d4-6fb1-11e6-8533-6b0b0ded0253_story.html

25 http://www.washingtonpost.com/wp-srv/politics/special/clinton/stories/hillary012898.htm

26 Ibid.

27 https://en.wikipedia.org/wiki/Vast_right-wing_conspiracy

28 http://www.cbsnews.com/news/hillary-clinton-the-vast-right-wing-conspiracy-is-even-better-funded-now/

29 http://www.washingtonpost.com/wp-srv/politics/special/clinton/stories/hillary012898.htm

30 http://www.businessinsider.com/hillary-clinton-endorsements-newspaper-editorial-board-president-2016-2016-9/#the-new-york-times-our-endorsement-is-rooted-in-respect-for-her-intellect-experience-toughness-and-courage-over-a-career-of-almost-continuous-public-service-often-as-the-first-or-only-woman-in-the-arena-1

31 https://www.washingtonpost.com/local/enabler-or-family-defender-how-hillary-clinton-responded-to-husbands-accusers/2016/09/28/58dad5d4-6fb1-11e6-8533-6b0b0ded0253_story.html

32 Ibid.

33 Ibid.

34 http://www.cnn.com/2016/10/11/politics/hillary-clinton-donald-trump-bill-clinton-accusers/

35 http://www.breitbart.com/2016-presidential-race/2016/05/07/bills-sex-accusers-echo-trump-hillary-enabler/

36 Ibid.

37 Ibid.

38 Ibid.

39 Jackson, *Their Lives*, 153.

40 https://www.youtube.com/watch?v=KyjLH0mHBNI

41 http://www.washingtonpost.com/wp-srv/politics/special/clinton/stories/landow013199.htm

42 Ibid.

43 Jackson, *Their Lives*, 150.

44 Isikoff, Michael, *Uncovering Clinton*, (New York: Crown, 1999.) p. 152-153.

45 https://www.washingtonpost.com/local/enabler-or-family-defender-how-hillary-clinton-responded-to-husbands-accusers/2016/09/28/58dad5d4-6fb1-11e6-8533-6b0b0ded0253_story.html

46 http://www.wellesley.edu/events/commencement/archives/1969commencement/studentspeech#8Dc0zPXzdl4JpV63.97

47 https://www.youtube.com/watch?v=NvoRcPXURwg

48 http://www.slate.com/articles/double_x/politics/2016/10/juanita_broaddrick_s_rape_allegations_are_credible_her_attacks_on_hillary.html

CHAPTER 19: THE NEXT WHITE HOUSE?

1 http://abcnews.go.com/Politics/hint-momentum-clinton-issues-defining-factor-poll/story?id=43281152

2 Ibid.

3 http://www.worldalmanac.com/blog/2007/11/the_second_oldest_profession.html

4 http://www.nytimes.com/2016/10/17/opinion/our-feuding-founding-fathers.html

5 https://dougwead.wordpress.com/2016/04/25/trump-clinton-bad-choice/

6 http://www.history.com/this-day-in-history/grover-cleveland-gets-married-in-the-white-house

7 http://www.cnn.com/2016/02/05/politics/hillary-clinton-bill-clinton-paid-speeches/

8 http://www.usnews.com/news/articles/2016-04-22/heres-who-paid-hillary-clinton-22-million-in-speaking-fees

9 https://www.washingtonpost.com/politics/2016/live-updates/general-election/real-time-fact-checking-and-analysis-of-the-final-2016-presidential-debate/fact-check-trumps-claim-clinton-destroyed-emails-after-getting-a-subpoena-from-congress/

10 http://tribune.com.pk/story/1214946/100-days-clinton-white-house-look-like/

11 https://www.yahoo.com/news/100-days-clinton-white-house-look-020530725.html

12 Ibid.

13 Ibid.

14 http://articles.latimes.com/1993-07-20/news/mn-15006_1_law-enforcement-agencies

15 http://www.politico.com/story/2016/11/clinton-comey-resignation-if-elected-230680

16 http://www.wsj.com/articles/first-dude-bill-clinton-would-reshape-historic-role-1469490618

17 https://www.thesun.co.uk/news/2132414/bill-hillary-clinton-us-election-2016-name/

18 http://ca.complex.com/pop-culture/2015/05/bill-clinton-talks-moving-back-into-white-house-letterman#!

19 Author's interview with White House service administrator.

20 http://www.parentherald.com/articles/60108/20160810/chelsea-clinton-assume-first-lady-mom-hillary-wins-presidential-seat.htm

21 http://www.gallup.com/poll/12544/values-seen-most-important-characteristic-presidential-candidates.aspx

22 Doug Wead, *All the Presidents' Children* (New York: Atria Books, 2003), 300.

23 Ibid., 181.

24 http://www.cleveland.com/books/index.ssf/2013/02/eisenhower_and_nixon_two_terms.html

25 Ibid.

26 https://partners.nytimes.com/library/politics/camp/061699wh-dem-gore.html

27 http://www.cnn.com/2016/10/04/politics/bill-clinton-obamacare-craziest-thing/

28 http://nypost.com/2016/10/07/bill-clintons-obamacare-rant-was-scripted-and-approved-by-obama/

29 http://www.cnn.com/2016/10/04/politics/bill-clinton-obamacare-craziest-thing/

30 http://www.cnn.com/2016/10/07/politics/reality-check-bill-clinton-obamacare/

31 http://www.cnn.com/2016/10/04/politics/bill-clinton-obamacare-craziest-thing/

32 http://deadline.com/2016/10/will-and-grace-new-season-negotiations-1201843730/

33   https://www.theguardian.com/books/2014/nov/05/lena-dunham-statement-abuse-claims

34   http://www.breitbart.com/big-hollywood/2016/11/04/jesus-fcking-christ-please-vote-celebs-curse-storm-hillary-clinton/

35   http://ew.com/article/2016/11/04/rachel-bloom-funny-or-die-video-vote/

36   http://www.rollingstone.com/music/news/see-beyonces-powerful-speech-at-jay-zs-clinton-rally-w448773

37   http://www.mediaite.com/online/jay-z-delivers-uncensored-concert-for-hillary-complete-with-n-words-and-f-bombs/

38   http://www.infowars.com/jay-z-repeatedly-drops-n-word-f-bomb-during-concert-for-hillary-clinton/

39   http://www.nytimes.com/interactive/2016/us/elections/polls.html?_r=0

40   http://www.rollingstone.com/music/news/see-bruce-springsteen-perform-rip-trump-at-clinton-rally-w449082

41   http://www.billboard.com/articles/news/7565922/bruce-springsteen-jon-bon-jovi-hillary-clinton-philadelphia-rally

42   http://www.nytimes.com/2016/11/08/opinion/michelle-obamas-challenge-for-hillary-clinton.html

43   http://www.huffingtonpost.com/entry/michelle-obama-clinton-philadelphia_us_582107f8e4b0d9ce6fbe302d

44   http://www.motherjones.com/politics/2016/11/obama-speech-philadelphia

45   http://www.billboard.com/articles/news/7565922/bruce-springsteen-jon-bon-jovi-hillary-clinton-philadelphia-rally

46   http://www.billboard.com/articles/news/7572357/lady-gaga-michael-jackson-jacket-hillary-clinton-rally

47   http://www.nytimes.com/interactive/2016/us/elections/polls.html?_r=0

CHAPTER 20: LANDING THE PLANE

1   http://www.nytimes.com/2016/03/16/upshot/measuring-donald-trumps-mammoth-advantage-in-free-media.html

2   http://www.nytimes.com/2016/06/21/us/politics/corey-lewandowski-donald-trump.html

3   http://www.politico.com/story/2016/08/paul-manafort-resigns-from-trump-campaign-227197

4   http://time.com/4462283/donald-trump-kellyanne-conway-campaign-manager/

5   Ibid.

6   http://bigstory.ap.org/article/f476183e30664524a534f5c0b997f98c/trump-puts-flame-throwing-outsider-inside

7   http://www.breitbart.com/2016-presidential-race/2016/12/17/steve-bannon-strategy-helped-bring-donald-trump-victory-election-day/

8   http://www.cbsnews.com/news/inequality-1-percent-99-percent-income-growth/

9   http://www.nytimes.com/2016/11/27/us/politics/steve-bannon-white-house.html

10 Ibid.

11 http://www.news.com.au/world/north-america/jared-kushner-tells-how-he-helped-donald-trump-win-the-us-election/news-story/4db200bf9e71c32c9e4dc43d4105c760

12 Ibid.

13 http://www.dailymail.co.uk/news/article-3961098/Kushner-speaks-credit-Donald-s-win-ran-Trump-campaign-like-tiny-startup-used-Silicon-Valley-connection-target-voters-insisting-didn-t-push-Christie.html

14 http://www.politico.com/story/2016/11/reince-priebus-trump-victory-231159

15 http://www.politicususa.com/2016/10/23/hillary-clinton-biggest-october-lead-presidential-candidate-1984.html

16 http://www.etonline.com/news/188884_jennifer_lawrence_and_angelina_jolie_really_hate_donald_trump/

17 http://extratv.com/2016/07/07/charlie-sheens-unfiltered-new-attack-on-donald-trump/

18 Ibid.

19 Ibid.

20 https://www.bustle.com/articles/176465-chrissy-teigens-10-best-election-tweets-are-a-hilarious-reminder-she-can-do-no-wrong

21 http://ew.com/article/2016/07/08/donald-trump-kristen-bell-frozen/

22 http://ew.com/article/2016/03/10/mac-miller-hates-donald-trump/

23 http://www.huffingtonpost.com/entry/robert-de-niro-trump-totally-nuts_us_57af38cbe4b007c36e4ef734

24 http://www.news.com.au/entertainment/movies/new-movies/will-smith-really-cant-stand-donald-trump/news-story/1ab6831512b3031650e4223a485f68c3

25 http://www.rollingstone.com/music/news/watch-cher-compare-donald-trump-to-hitler-stalin-w435970

26 http://www.cnn.com/2016/08/24/politics/cher-hillary-clinton-fundraiser-donald-trump/

27 http://www.rollingstone.com/music/news/neil-young-onstage-f--ck-you-donald-trump-20160611

28 http://ew.com/article/2016/07/07/wavves-trump-all-lives-concerts/

29 http://ew.com/article/2016/07/26/khloe-kardashian-nene-leakes-more-apprentice-slam-trump-chelsea/

30 http://people.com/celebrity/barbra-streisand-disses-donald-trump-repeatedly-during-l-a-concert/

31 http://www.thedailybeast.com/articles/2016/09/30/chelsea-handler-i-would-never-have-donald-trump-on-my-show.html

32 http://www.telegraph.co.uk/news/worldnews/donald-trump/12039134/donald-trump-harry-potter-worse-voldemort-jk-rowling.html

33 http://ew.com/article/2016/10/03/donald-trump-arcade-fire-win-butler-nightmare/

34 http://www.dailymail.co.uk/news/article-3475780/Trump-version-Mussolini-blasts-Richard-Gere-Actor-says-electing-billionaire-slippery-slope-deporting-Jews-black-people.html

35 Ibid.

36 http://www.jta.org/2016/11/22/news-opinion/politics/jared-kushner-again-defends-trump-against-anti-semitism-claims

37 http://www.nytimes.com/2016/10/08/arts/television/letterman-has-no-love-for-damaged-trump.html

38 Ibid.

39 http://www.cnn.com/2016/05/31/politics/stephen-hawking-donald-trump-demagogue/

40 http://www.thecrimson.com/article/2016/8/5/republican-club-not-support-trump/

41 https://www.washingtonpost.com/news/the-fix/wp/2016/09/24/master-of-horror-fiction-stephen-king-says-trump-presidency-scares-me-to-death/

42 https://www.hillaryclinton.com/feed/there-are-five-living-u-s-presidents-none-of-them-support-donald-trump/

43 http://www.politico.com/story/2016/10/obama-attack-trump-ohio-229799

44 Ibid.

45 http://www.npr.org/2016/04/22/475172438/donald-trump-and-george-wallace-riding-the-rage

46 http://mediamatters.org/video/2016/10/20/msnbcs-presidential-historian-calls-trump-not-accepting-results-election-absolutely-horrifying/213976

47 http://mediamatters.org/video/2016/10/19/nbc-s-nicolle-wallace-trump-put-nail-his-own-coffin-refusing-say-he-d-accept-election-results/213954

48 http://mediamatters.org/video/2016/10/19/cnns-jake-tapper-trumps-suggestion-he-might-not-accept-results-election-was-staggering/213953

49 http://mediamatters.org/video/2016/10/19/cbs-bob-schieffer-excoriates-trump-refusing-accept-election-results-not-way-we-do-it-united-states/213961

50 https://www.sott.net/article/331637-MSM-scripted-controlled-WikiLeaks-10-most-damning-Clinton-emails

51 Ibid.

52 Ibid.

53 Ibid.

54 http://www.dailymail.co.uk/news/article-3780677/Clinton-s-campaign-attacks-Matt-Lauer-fundraiser-saying-failed-Commander-Chief-Forum-NBC-exec-calls-performance-disaster.html

55 http://townhall.com/tipsheet/mattvespa/2016/12/09/msnbcs-mika-brzezinski-the-clinton-campaign-tried-to-take-me-off-the-air-n2257624

56 http://www.thedailybeast.com/articles/2016/07/25/the-biggest-gop-names-backing-hillary-clinton-so-far.html

57 http://www.huffingtonpost.com/entry/karl-rove-donald-trump-cant-win_us_580cb4c1e4b000d0b15727dc

58 Ibid.

59 http://www.zerohedge.com/news/2016-10-27/assange-predicts-trump-will-lose-accuses-clinton-campaign-trying-hack-wikileaks

60 https://www.rt.com/usa/364461-assange-clinton-wikileaks-hack/

61 http://www.thefiscaltimes.com/2016/11/02/If-Poll-Right-Trump-Can-t-Win-Florida-or-Election

62 Ibid.

CHAPTER 21: I ALMOST NEVER LOSE

1 http://www.dailymail.co.uk/news/article-3204963/Trump-says-Mitt-Romney-choked-2012-s-not-going-happen-blasts-GOP-nominee-New-Hampshire.html

2 http://fivethirtyeight.com/features/the-last-10-weeks-of-2016-campaign-stops-in-one-handy-gif/

3 http://www.usatoday.com/story/news/politics/elections/2016/11/04/heres-why-donald-trump-almost-certainly-cant-win-without-florida/93259368/

4 Ibid.

5 http://time.com/4562091/election-results-2016-trump-clinton-final-hours/

6 http://townhall.com/tipsheet/katiepavlich/2016/11/07/priebus-on-election-eve-n2242489

7 http://www.usatoday.com/story/news/politics/elections/2016/11/04/heres-why-donald-trump-almost-certainly-cant-win-without-florida/93259368/

8   http://www.nbcnews.com/politics/2016-election/trump-s-last-day-campaigning-trumpisms-abound-n679186

9   Ibid.

10 http://townhall.com/tipsheet/katiepavlich/2016/11/07/priebus-on-election-eve-n2242489

11 http://time.com/4562091/election-results-2016-trump-clinton-final-hours/

12 http://townhall.com/tipsheet/leahbarkoukis/2016/11/10/ann-coulter-deserves-an-apology-n2243832

13 https://www.washingtonpost.com/politics/in-turmoil-or-triumph-donald-trump-stands-alone/2016/04/02/8c0619b6-f8d6-11e5-a3ce-f06b5ba21f33_story.html

14 https://www.washingtonpost.com/news/post-politics/wp/2016/04/02/transcript-donald-trump-interview-with-bob-woodward-and-robert-costa/

15 https://www.youtube.com/watch?v=q_q61B-DyPk

16 https://www.washingtonpost.com/politics/in-turmoil-or-triumph-donald-trump-stands-alone/2016/04/02/8c0619b6-f8d6-11e5-a3ce-f06b5ba21f33_story.html

17 Ibid.

18 http://www.latimes.com/nation/politics/trailguide/la-na-election-day-2016-topless-protesters-arrested-at-trump-s-1478619953-htmlstory.html

19 http://www.nbcnews.com/card/clinton-arrives-new-york-polling-place-vote-n679621

20 http://www.usatoday.com/story/news/politics/elections/2016/11/04/heres-why-donald-trump-almost-certainly-cant-win-without-florida/93259368/

21 https://www.washingtonpost.com/politics/in-turmoil-or-triumph-donald-trump-stands-alone/2016/04/02/8c0619b6-f8d6-11e5-a3ce-f06b5ba21f33_story.html

22 http://theinvestigatornews.com/2016/11/whole-life-winning-dont-lose-often-almost-never-lose-donald-trump/

ACKNOWLEDGMENTS

M y special thanks to Jess Regel of Foundry Literary and Media for giving me her guidance and help with this project. It would never have happened without you, Jess. Thanks to my publisher, Rolf Zettersten, for believing we could do the impossible and in record time. There are not many in this industry who could have pulled it off. Thanks to my executive editor, Kate Hartson, who made miracles happen. To Grace Tweedy, editorial assistant and the entire team at Hachette Books. Then there was the fun part, promoting an amazing story. Thanks to Patsy Jones, head of the marketing team at Hachette.

This project would have been impossible without my wife, Myriam, who ran our world, while I listened and wrote what my sources told me. Thanks to my daughters, Chloe and Camille, who helped research and edit. Thanks to David Dunbar for his help in tracking down the elusive story of Chinese money in an American political campaign. Thanks so Marc Romero who completed a study on debate moderators, to Roger Shaffer who provided endless material, and to Dennis Scardilli who researched polls and numbers.

Finally, thanks to the secret service agents, journalists, political operatives and public participants who treasured these events enough to risk careers and safe retirements to make sure that this remarkable story was not lost to American history.

This may contain confidential material. If you are not an intended recipient, please notify the sender, delete immediately, and understand that no disclosure or reliance on the information herein is permitted. Hachette Book Group may monitor email to and from our network.